The papers in this volume, a multidisciplinary collaboration of anthropologists, linguists, and psychologists, explore the way in which cultural knowledge is organized and used in everyday language and understanding. Employing a variety of methods, which rely heavily on linguistic data, the authors offer analyses of domains of knowledge ranging across the physical, social, and psychological worlds, and reveal the crucial importance of tacit, presupposed knowledge in the conduct of everyday life.

Many of the papers included examine American cultural knowledge; others, by anthropologists, provide accounts from very different cultures. Collectively, the authors argue that cultural knowledge is organized in "cultural models" – story-like chains of prototypical events that unfold in simplified worlds – and they explore the nature and role of these models. They demonstrate that cultural knowledge may take either proposition-schematic or image-schematic form, each enabling the performance of different kinds of cognitive tasks. Metaphor and metonymy are shown to have special roles in the construction of cultural models: the former allowing for knowledge to be mapped from known domains of the physical world onto conceptualizations in the social and psychological domains as well as in unknown physical-world domains; the latter providing different types of prototypical events out of which cultural models are constructed. The authors also reveal that some widely applicable cultural models recur nested within other, more special-purpose models, thereby lending cultures their thematicity. Finally, they show that shared models play a critical role in thinking, one that has gone largely unappreciated in recent cognitive science – that is, that of allowing humans to master, remember, and use the vast amount of knowledge required in everyday life.

This innovative collection will appeal widely to anthropologists, linguists, psychologists, philosophers, students of artificial intelligence, and other readers interested in the processes of everyday human understanding.

Cultural models in language and thought

Cultural models in language and thought

EDITED BY

Dorothy Holland
University of North Carolina, Chapel Hill

Naomi Quinn
Duke University

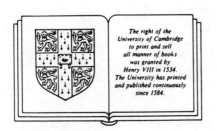

The right of the
University of Cambridge
to print and sell
all manner of books
was granted by
Henry VIII in 1534.
The University has printed
and published continuously
since 1584.

Cambridge University Press

CAMBRIDGE
NEW YORK   NEW ROCHELLE
MELBOURNE   SYDNEY

Published by the Press Syndicate of the University of Cambridge
The Pitt Building, Trumpington Street, Cambridge CB2 1RP
32 East 57th Street, New York, NY 10022, USA
10 Stamford Road, Oakleigh, Melbourne 3166, Australia

First published 1987
Reprinted 1987

Printed in the United States of America

Library of Congress Cataloging-in-Publication Data
Cultural models in language and thought.

Papers originally presented at a conference.

1. Language and culture.   2. Cognition and culture.
I. Holland, Dorothy C.   II. Quinn, Naomi.
P35.C8   1987   401'.9   86-17524

British Library Cataloguing in Publication Data
Holland, Dorothy

Cultural models in language and thought.

1. Ethnopsychology   2. Cognition
I. Title   II. Quinn, Naomi
390   GN502

ISBN 0 521 32346 0 hard covers
ISBN 0 521 31168 3 paperback

Contents

Preface

This volume represents an interdisciplinary effort that has brought together anthropologists, linguists, and psychologists who study human cognition. In recent years, cognitive scientists from these three fields and others have converged in the study of knowledge, its organization, and its role in language understanding and the performance of other cognitive tasks.

Here, we present a cultural view. We argue that cultural knowledge – shared presuppositions about the world – plays an enormous role in human understanding, a role that must be recognized and incorporated into any successful theory of the organization of human knowledge. As we summarize in the introductory chapter, cultural knowledge appears to be organized in sequences of prototypical events – schemas that we call *cultural models* and that are themselves hierarchically related to other cultural knowledge. This volume, then, is an interdisciplinary investigation of cultural models and the part they play in human language and thought.

Earlier versions of most of the chapters in this volume were assembled and presented at a conference held in May 1983 at the Institute for Advanced Study in Princeton, New Jersey. However, to think of the book as a conference volume would be to fail to appreciate its history, which goes back some time before the Princeton conference. As histories should, this one has a lesson. It tells how, under felicitous circumstances, institutional support can enable scientific collaboration even across disciplinary boundaries.

The developments described in this volume were underway in the late 1970s. One of us, Naomi Quinn, then a member of the Social Science Research Council Committee on Cognitive Research, organized an interdisciplinary workshop under the auspices of that committee to draw together some of the new ideas about culture and cognition. Held in August 1979 in La Jolla, California, under the rubric "The Representation of Cultural Knowledge," that workshop numbered among its participants four of the contributors to the present volume – Roy D'Andrade, Edwin Hutchins, Dorothy Holland, and Naomi Quinn. As a substantive statement about the role of cultural knowledge in the understanding process, the workshop could be fairly characterized as premature. Many of the talks and much of the discussion had a tentative quality. Several of the formal discussants, deliberately recruited from fields of cognitive science outside of anthropology, made clear their skepticism about that discipline's contribution to cognitive studies. The perspective represented in this volume was incipient at La Jolla, but undeveloped. Yet the workshop was a necessary first step toward defining a common enterprise and setting a theoretical agenda.

Naomi Quinn's involvement in the activities of the SSRC committee enabled her to identify other people outside of her own field who were working toward similar ideas about cultural knowledge. She became better acquainted with the thinking of committee members Eleanor Rosch, a psychologist, and Charles Fillmore, a linguist, whose ideas and observations were to figure importantly in the approach developed in this book. At La Jolla, she met for the first time psychologists Allan Collins and Dedre Gentner and heard a paper on folk models they were presenting at an overlapping conference. At another committee activity that summer in Boulder, Colorado, she met linguist George Lakoff (though not for the first time, he reminded her) and obtained from him a copy of the book in manuscript, *Metaphors We Live By,* which he and Mark Johnson had just completed. Lakoff later invited Quinn to be an observer at his Conference on Cognitive Science, Language, and Imagery funded by the Alfred P. Sloan Foundation and held in Berkeley in the spring of 1981; there, she met Charlotte Linde and other linguists with similar interests.

At neighboring universities, the two of us talked on about our common view of "folk knowledge," which was still crystallizing out of work in cognitive anthropology and related fields of cognitive science. We decided to organize a multidisciplinary symposium for the 80th Annual Meeting of the American Anthropological Association in Washington, D.C., in December 1981. We called it "Folk Theories in Everyday Cognition." The resulting group of participants, and the papers they presented, encouraged our vision.

Contributions by Lutz, Price, Sweetser, and White in this volume began as meeting papers delivered at that symposium; Holland, Hutchins, and Lakoff also participated, giving different papers than those they ultimately presented at the Folk Models conference that culminated in this book. The earlier La Jolla workshop had served as a beginning; the AAA symposium has a somewhat different but equally important role as a dry run for the conference to follow.

Among members of the American Anthropological Association, it is popular to question the intellectual defensibility of meetings sessions, with the limited time constraints they place on paper and discussion length and the peripatetic audiences they attract. These critics overlook the important role of sessions like the one we organized as preliminaries to more ambitious professional activities. Relatively untaxing of organizational and fund-raising effort, the AAA symposium was an opportunity to gauge whether the new ideas about "cultural knowledge," "folk theories," and

"folk models" (which eventually became "cultural models") were sufficiently developed to merit a larger conference. It was also an occasion
to experiment with the composition of the group, so that in the end we
might identify and include individuals, whatever their disciplines, whose
perspectives and enthusiasms matched our own in substantial ways. Finally, it served to orient individual efforts toward production of conference
papers. It was shortly after the well-attended AAA symposium, with its
high-quality papers, that we decided the time was ripe to seek funding
for a full-scale conference.

By then, unable to raise new operating funds, and having already spon-
sored a series of valuable conferences and workshops, the SSRC Committee on Cognitive Research was soon to be disbanded. The conference
proposal we submitted to the Anthropology Program of the National
Science Foundation was adapted from one Quinn had earlier drafted as
a section of the final, unsuccessful umbrella proposal intended to fund
the continuing activities of the SSRC Committee. NSF funded our proposal. Concerned that the grant might not cover all the expenses for this
large conference, we applied to the Wenner–Gren Foundation for Anthropological Research for supplementary support. Working in consultation
with NSF, Wenner–Gren contributed funds to fly our most distant participant, Roger Keesing, from Australia.

Quinn was a member of the Institute for Advanced Study during the
academic year 1982–83, as part of a group of researchers in cognition.
Learning that the Institute sometimes hosted conferences, she explored
the possibility of holding the conference there. The advantages, in terms
of facilities, supporting staff, and location, quickly became evident. We
formally proposed to Institute Director Harry Woolf and to Clifford
Geertz, the anthropologist on the faculty of the School of Social Science,
that they host the conference, and they graciously agreed. Subsequently,
the project was granted an additional small amount by the Institute out
of Exxon Educational Fund monies at its disposal; these funds allowed
us to invite interested "observers" from the Institute and from surrounding universities to conference meals, to interact further with conference
participants.

It was clear to us by its close that a promising framework for the investigation of cultural knowledge was emerging at this conference, and
that the research that had been reported in the delivered papers was sufficiently developed and interrelated to warrant publication. Scientists working independently along similar lines had been brought together to exchange ideas and to articulate a common approach. We are hopeful that
publication of their chapters, with the integrating volume introduction
we have provided, will convince other cognitive scientists of the heretofore
largely neglected role of cultural presuppositions in human cognition and
also demonstrate to other anthropologists the usefulness and promise of
a cognitive approach to culture.

We have detailed the history of the efforts that led to this publication to make the point that institutional support of scientific projects such as this one has a cumulative effect not easy to assess in the short term. The book is the product of a lengthy, tentative process of regrouping and exchange, a process realized in several formal gatherings organized according to several different professional formats and made possible by the funding and facilities of an array of different institutions operating with different institutional mandates and designs. They were all indispensable. We hope *Cultural Models in Language and Thought* will testify to the value of such repeated institutional support for organized meetings, large and small.

We are indebted to all these supporting organizations, and to all their individual staff members with whom we worked. We came to appreciate keenly the special competencies that some of these individuals have for making the scientific process work. Lonnie Sherrod, staff associate at the Social Science Research Council, shepherded the Committee on Cognitive Research during most of Quinn's tenure on it and did so with an acute sense of what was happening in that quarter of the social sciences and what could be helped along. Stephen Brush, then the staff associate in the Anthropology Program at NSF who was responsible for oversight of our grant, shared much good advice about how to make an intellectually satisfying conference happen. Mary Wisnovsky, assistant to the director, and Grace Rapp, her assistant in the Office of the Director at the Institute for Advanced Study, are two unforgettable people with a special talent for making a conference happen smoothly and painlessly, even making it fun to give one. The postconference editing task has been lightened enormously by the skilled assistance of Carole Cain and Anne Larme, two anthropology graduate students at the University of North Carolina, Chapel Hill. We thank them all.

D.H.
N.Q.

Contributors

Allan Collins
Bolt, Beranek and Newman, Inc.
10 Moulton Street
Cambridge, MA 02238

Roy D'Andrade
Department of Anthropology
University of California,
    San Diego
La Jolla, CA 92093

Dedre Gentner
Department of Psychology
University of Illinois,
    Urbana-Champaign
Champaign, IL 61801

Dorothy Holland
Department of Anthropology
University of North Carolina,
    Chapel Hill
Chapel Hill, NC 27514

Edwin Hutchins
Institute for Cognitive Science
University of California,
    San Diego
La Jolla, CA 92093

Paul Kay
Department of Linguistics
University of California,
    Berkeley
Berkeley, CA 94720

Roger M. Keesing
Department of Anthropology
Research School of Pacific Studies
Australian National University
P.O.B. 4
Canberra, A.C.T. 2601, Australia

Willett Kempton
Center for Energy and
    Environmental Studies
School of Engineering/Applied Science
Princeton University
Princeton, NJ 08544

Zoltán Kövecses
Department of English
ELTE, Pesti B.u. 1
Budapest, Hungary

George Lakoff
Department of Linguistics
University of California, Berkeley
Berkeley, CA 94720

Charlotte Linde
Structural Semantics
P.O. Box 707
Palo Alto, CA 94302

Catherine Lutz
Department of Anthropology
State University of New York,
    Binghamton
Binghamton, NY 13901

Laurie Price
Multipurpose Arthritis Center
Trailer 16, Building 272H
Medical School
University of North Carolina,
    Chapel Hill
Chapel Hill, NC 27514

Naomi Quinn
Department of Anthropology
Duke University
Durham, NC 27706

Debra Skinner
Department of Anthropology
University of North Carolina,
    Chapel Hill
Chapel Hill, NC 27514

Eve E. Sweetser
Department of Linguistics
University of California, Berkeley
Berkeley, CA 94720

Geoffrey M. White
Institute of Culture and
    Communication
East-West Center
1777 East-West Road
Honolulu, HI 96848

Introduction

1
Culture and cognition[1]

Naomi Quinn & Dorothy Holland

Undeniably, a great deal of order exists in the natural world we experience. However, much of the order we perceive in the world is there only because we put it there. That we impose such order is even more apparent when we consider the social world, in which institutions such as marriage, deeds such as lying, and customs such as dating happen at all because the members of a society presume them to be. D'Andrade (1984a:91) contrasts such culturally constructed things with cultural categories for objects such as stone, tree, and hand, which exist whether or not we invent labels for them. An entity such as marriage, on the other hand, is created by "the social agreement that something counts as that condition" (ibid.) and exists only by virtue of adherence to the rules that constitute it.

Such culturally constituted understandings of the social world point up not only the degree to which people impose order on their world but also the degree to which such orderings are shared by the joint participants in this world, all of whom behave as though marriage, lying, and dating exist. A very large proportion of what we know and believe we derive from these shared models that specify what is in the world and how it works.

The cognitive view of cultural meaning

The enigma of cultural meaning, seemingly both social and psychological in nature, has challenged generations of anthropologists and stimulated the development of several distinctive perspectives (see Keesing 1974 for an early review). Each of these ideational traditions in anthropology has had to address the same question: How are these meaning systems organized? Any convincing answer to this question should be able to account for at least the following properties of culture. It must be able to explain the apparent systematicity of cultural knowledge – the observation, old to anthropology, that each culture is characterized, and distinguished from others, by thoroughgoing, seemingly fundamental themes. Such a theory of culture also ought to explain how we come to master the enormous amount of cultural knowledge that the people of any culture have about the world and demonstrate in their daily negotiations with it (D'Andrade

1981). Moreover, the large base of cultural knowledge we control is not static; somehow, we extend it to our comprehension of particular experiences as we encounter them. Given the uniqueness, sometimes radical and sometimes small, of these myriad daily experiences, cultural meaning systems must be adapted to the contingencies and complexities of everyday life. A theory of the organization of cultural knowledge must explain the generative capacity of culture. The approach in this volume makes progress and offers promise in accounting for all these properties of culture.

The papers in the volume represent a cognitive approach to the question of how cultural knowledge is organized. For nearly three decades, cognitive anthropologists have been pursuing the question of what one needs to know in order to behave as a functioning member of one's society (Goodenough 1957:167). This school of anthropology came to stand for a new view of culture as shared knowledge – not a people's customs and artifacts and oral traditions, but what they must know in order to act as they do, make the things they make, and interpret their experience in the distinctive way they do.

It is this sense of culture that is intended in the title of the present volume: *Cultural models* are presupposed, taken-for-granted models of the world that are widely shared (although not necessarily to the exclusion of other, alternative models) by the members of a society and that play an enormous role in their understanding of that world and their behavior in it. Certainly, anthropologists of other persuasions have arrived at the idea of "folk models" as a way of characterizing the radically different belief systems of nonwestern peoples (e.g., Bohannan 1957; Holy & Stuchlik 1981a). What is new in the present effort is an attempt to specify the cognitive organization of such ideational complexes and to link this organization to what is known about the way human beings think.

Cultural models, talk, and other behavior

In practice, Goodenough's original mandate to investigate the knowledge people need in order to behave in culturally appropriate ways has been translated into a narrower concern for what one needs to know in order to *say* culturally acceptable things about the world. The relation between what people say and what they do has not gone entirely unconsidered by cognitive anthropologists. For example, this concern surfaces in an ongoing tradition of natural decision-making studies of which Geoghegan (1969), Gladwin and Gladwin (1971), Johnson (1974), and Fjellman (1976) are early representatives. In this line of research, behavioral decision models constructed with the help of informants' accounts of how they make decisions are then used to predict their actual choices. (See Nardi 1983 and Mathews in press for recent critiques of this approach from a perspective that would insist on the role of cultural knowledge in framing, not just making, decisions.) For the most part, however, cognitive anthropologists have specialized in talk.

This definition of the research task – explaining what people need to know in order to say the things they do – is simply taken for granted by the linguists with whom cognitive anthropologists exchange ideas, and it is a conventional research strategy in other branches of cognitive science as well. In artificial intelligence, for example, apart from an occasional robotic *tour de force,* the major methodological and theoretical challenge has been to build computer programs capable of story comprehension and other kinds of linguistic processing. This definition of the task is a legacy of earlier attempts to solve the machine translation problem. Artificial intelligence workers attempting machine translation discovered that language cannot be understood, much less translated, without reference to a great deal of knowledge about the world. The preoccupation of subsequent artificial intelligence research with this problem has captured the interest of cognitive anthropologists similarly concerned with what people have to know in order to use language.

It has been colleagues from the more materialist traditions in anthropology, and indeed from some of the ideationalist traditions within the discipline as well, who have been at pains to point out the limitation of a research program for validating cultural models solely on the basis of linguistic behavior. These anthropologists observe that people do not always do what would seem to be entailed by the cultural beliefs they enunciate (for cognitive anthropologists' own critique of this issue, see Lave et al. 1977; Frake 1977; Clement 1982). Do cultural models, they want to know, influence more than talk, and if so how? Harris (1968) has proposed that cultural beliefs are epiphenomena altogether, reflecting the political economic circumstances that they arise, *post hoc,* to rationalize. From a wholly different perspective, Levi-Strauss (1953) had earlier characterized native models as "home-made" ones, to be treated as repositories of false knowledge. The influence of his view can be gauged by the stance adopted in the work of anthropologist Barbara Ward (1965; 1966). Citing Levi-Strauss, she felt obliged to apologize for her interest in Hong Kong fishermen's native models of society, about which she wrote.

A third, related strain in anthropological thought reflects this same tendency to discount the role, in people's behavior, of the cultural beliefs reflected in their talk. In this formulation, models for talking are separated, analytically, from models for doing. Paralleling Ryle's (1949) distinction between "knowledge how" and "knowledge that," and Geertz's (1966) distinction between "models for" and "models of," Caws (1974) presents an oft-cited argument for a tripartite typology of models (see also Holy & Stuchlik 1981b:19–21). In addition to the scientist's "explanatory model," Caws proposes two types of native models: "representational" and "operational." The former are indigenous models of their world that people can more or less articulate; the latter are indigenous models that guide behavior in given situations and that tend to be out of awareness. Representational models, from this view, are not necessarily operational nor are the latter necessarily representational; thus, inconsistencies between what people say and what they do need not be cause for puzzlement. Holy (1979) applies this distinction in his attempt to resolve a long-standing debate in social anthropology over the reported disparities between Nuer descriptions of their kinship system and Nuer kinship behavior "on the ground."

Our vision of the role and importance of cultural models is at odds with the views of Harris and Levi-Strauss and that articulated in social anthropology by Caws. We do not assume that cultural models always translate simply and directly into behavior. Indeed, the papers in this collection by Hutchins, Linde, and Price move toward a more precise understanding of the situations in which cultural models are invoked to rationalize and sometimes disguise behavior for other people and for ourselves. Nor do we expect cultural conceptualizations of the world to be the sole determinants of behavior. The work in this volume does suggest, however, that cultural models – which we infer from what people say – do relate to their behavior in complex, powerful ways. We are only beginning to specify the nature of these relations. Keesing is right, in his paper in this volume, to urge that cognitive anthropologists like ourselves take an active role in the emerging interdisciplinary study of "humans-in-societies." By linking meaning to action, cognitive anthropologists could substantiate Keesing's argument that "how humans cognize their worlds constrains and shapes how humans-in-societies reproduce them." We think it is a crucial first step to show, as these studies do, how cultural models frame experience, supplying interpretations of that experience and inferences about it, and goals for action. When interpretation and inference call for action, as discussed by Lutz with regard to the goals embodied in Ifaluk emotion words, and by White with regard to the dual conceptual and pragmatic functions of proverbs, then cultural understandings also define the actor's goals. (See also Jenkins 1981; Nardi 1983; Quinn 1981; Salzman 1981; and White 1985 for complementary views.)

THE RELATION OF TALK TO ACTION AND AWARENESS

Seen as simultaneously interpretative and goal-embodying, cultural knowledge is not productively analyzed into "models of" and "models for," into "representational" and "operational" knowledge. Rather, in our view, underlying cultural models of the same order – and in some cases the same underlying cultural model – are used to perform a variety of different cognitive tasks. Sometimes these cultural models serve to set goals for action, sometimes to plan the attainment of said goals, sometimes to direct the actualization of these goals, sometimes to make sense of the actions and fathom the goals of others, and sometimes to produce verbalizations that may play various parts in all these projects as well as in the subsequent interpretation of what has happened. Complexity in the relationship between what people verbalize about what they do and the execution of other, nonverbal activities is inherent in part because speakers so frequently undertake complex tasks with many goals that may or may not include producing a veridical verbal description of what they are about. Just to pose some possibilities in which verbal accounts are decidedly not veridical to the behavior they purport to describe, people may sometimes be concerned, simultaneously, to manage their affairs in a way advantageous to themselves and to present their goals in a favorable light; or to carry out their plans while hiding their true objectives from onlookers. In producing verbalizations, it is not so much that speakers invoke a different order of conceptualization of the activity about which they speak; it is rather that they invoke those cultural understandings pertinent to performing the linguistic part of the overall task at hand – say, in the task of presenting one's actions in a favorable light, a shared model of the good person for whom one wishes to be taken; or, in the task of concealing one's plans, a shared model of plausible intentions with which to detract attention from one's real motives. Even when people are not wholly concealing or misrepresenting their behavior in what they say about it, they are characteristically called on to construct *post hoc* accounts of that behavior that are comprehensible, plausible, justifiable, and socially acceptable to themselves and other audiences, and that require a certain amount of smoothing, patching, and creative amendment to these ends.

Moreover, the multiple cognitive tasks and subtasks required to meet one's varied goals must often be executed simultaneously; the task demands of nonverbal behavior and those of concurrent verbal behavior may diverge, creating a further complexity in the relationship between the two. A waiter bent on getting a good tip, for instance, might be attempting to provide customers with swift, faultless service, silently anticipating their requests before these can be voiced, while at the same time keeping up a line of niceties and flattery. Even such ordinary daily activities as are involved in doing one's job are multifaceted in nature, often requiring verbal expression and other action at once – sometimes in coordination, other times for independent purposes. Again, this is not to agree to the assumption that there exist, in the mind of the individual performing those different cognitive tasks simultaneously, two orders of cultural model. It is simply to acknowledge that these differing tasks draw on a variety of cultural knowledge available for different purposes at different times. Indeed, talk itself involves such complex skills and understandings. As Sweetser (this volume) points out, even a single utterance may have multiple purposes. Her paper on lies and Kay's on hedges in this volume point up this complexity especially well; talk, as they demonstrate, may use much specialized cultural knowledge about linguistic utterances as well as other cultural knowledge about the nonlinguistic world being talked about.

It is also a misleading simplification to imply, as Caws has, that one set of models (those guiding behavior, in his formulation) are out of awareness, whereas another set (those said to guide description) are not. It is no doubt true that some knowledge is more habitually, hence more readily, put into words than other knowledge; that some knowledge but not other knowledge is tidily "packaged" in memory, hence easily retrieved for the telling; and that some knowledge is under conscious and voluntary control whereas other pieces are less available for introspection and articulation. Hutchins, in this volume, provides an instance of the latter case: a case in which inferences attributed by the analyst to the speaker in order to account for her interpretation of a Trobriand myth, appear to be out of the awareness of the speaker herself, Hutchins presumes, because they are so painful as to be repressed.

At another extreme, some linguistic outputs, but by no means most, have the "canned" quality of well-worked and well-rehearsed rationalizations or idealizations. Perhaps ethnographers are especially likely to be proffered such accounts. Much of people's cultural knowledge, however, is likely to be somewhere in between these two extremes of accessibility and inaccessibility – as D'Andrade (this volume) found for the American college students he interviewed about the way the mind works. These interviewees could not provide a comprehensive, well-organized view of the entire cultural model of the mind but could certainly describe how it operates when they were asked questions about specific examples. Models such as this one of the mind, which people use in a variety of tasks such as making inferences and solving problems (for a different example, see Jorion 1978), will be brought into awareness and made available to introspection and articulation to varying degrees depending on the precise demands of those tasks for such introspection or articulation.

Equally, knowledge embodied in cultural formulations that Caws might want to call "representational," cannot easily be distinguished from "operational" models with regard to the function he assigns the latter, of guiding behavior. Well-articulated cultural models of the world may also carry "directive force" (a term borrowed from D'Andrade 1984a). An obvious example, provided by White in this book, is that of proverbs. Proverbs promote enactment of the dictums they contain, White argues, precisely because their formulaic and linguistically economical construction signals cultural wisdom. This claim on wisdom is enhanced by present tense verb forms, which give them a timeless, enduring quality, and by their disallowance of exceptions or hedges, which grants them a seeming universal validity.

Cultural models, then, are not to be understood in either–or terms. That various anthropologists have proposed to sort cultural understanding into a kind for thinking and a kind for doing and to associate talking with the former may reflect more about the mind–body duality in our own western cultural model of the person than it does about how cultural knowledge is actually organized.

TALK AS ACTION

Were its only claim to be able to account for what people say, the present enterprise would still be an important one. The dismissive materialist stance that cultural models influence little more than talk neglects the pivotal social function of talk itself. As modern sociolinguistics teaches us, talk is one of the most important ways in which people negotiate understanding and accomplish social ends. Of course, discourse can be crucial to the efforts of individuals to create inner meaning for themselves, as illustrated vividly by Hutchins's analysis, in this book, of a Trobriand woman's attempt to comprehend her own experience in the terms of a familiar myth. However, these shared cultural understandings also figure large in the creation of social meaning. In Trobriand litigation, which is the subject of Hutchins's (1980) recent book, spoken claims and counterclaims are consequential acts.

For the college-age women whom Holland and Skinner describe in this volume, labeling another woman's fiancé a *nerd* is not just inconsequential chatter. The illness stories Price collected from poor Ecuadorian city-dwellers (this volume) reveal the efforts to which people will go in order to establish public, legitimated accounts of their behavior (see also Early 1982). Lutz (this volume) details a case in which the future course of kin relations depends on the accepted interpretation of an incident, an interpretation that emerges as the kinspeople involved talk to one another, proposing and negotiating different possible emotional definitions of the event (see also Frake 1977; Young 1981). Other papers in the collection suggest how cultural models undergird such varied kinds of talk as negotiations about the justification for anger, marital disagreements, proverbial and other advice about the solution to everyday problems, and inquiries into suspected lies. Such talk, in turn, influences social relations among people and the subsequent actions they take toward one another. Talk is itself a kind of act, and speech acts can have powerful social consequences.

THE DIRECTIVE FORCE OF CULTURAL MODELS

How do cultural models, whether invoked to persuade another or to order one's own inner experience, motivate behavior? The papers in this collection reveal differential sources of motivational force: One basis is in the authority and expertise with which cultural models may be invested, another in the intrinsic persuasiveness these models themselves have for us.

White's analysis of proverbs, as mentioned, suggests that linguistic forms can grant a certain amount of persuasiveness to knowledge by packaging it as "cultural wisdom." Relatedly, Linde shows how explanatory systems for human behavior that are devised by one group of culturally designated experts – academic psychologists – have come to provide us with models for making our own life choices. This is so even though neither ordinary people nor the "expert" psychologists themselves agree on a single explanatory system. Cultural understandings would seem to gain force from their identification with expert knowledge and cultural wisdom, in spite of the availability of alternative, equally expert explanatory systems and contradictory, equally wise-sounding admonitions.

Even though expert validation and cultural authority play a role in the persuasiveness of cultural models, explanatory adequacy in the face of our experience can also be compelling. This effect is perhaps best illustrated in the present collection by Kempton's example of an informant who switches from a "valve" theory to a "feedback" theory of home heating in mid-interview, after realizing that the first of these analogies was contradicted by her memory of how an observable heating device actually worked. Kempton shows elsewhere in his paper how acceptance of one or another of these alternative theories has consequences for thermostat settings. Collins and Gentner's paper, on the other hand, cautions against any conclusion that evidence drawn from real-world analogies is automatically compelling, showing as it does that a thinker such as their Subject *PC,* who relies heavily on analogies to phenomena he has observed or heard about, may shift among these local analogies without checking their consistency – failing to develop a coherent view of evaporation and often giving inaccurate answers.

This tendency of individuals to check their understandings against expert opinion and test them against experience highlights the co-existence of alternative, often conflicting cultural renditions of that world. In the pages of this book, it appears that individuals find it relatively easy to entertain different theories of how the thermostat works and even abandon one theory for another; to combine components of different analogies in their attempted explanations of evaporation; to invoke conflicting proverbial advice for the solution of different problems; and to adopt one or another contradictory folk theory of language depending on which one best fits the linguistic case at hand.

The latter example, of two contradictory folk theories of language, prompts Kay (this volume) to observe that cultural models are not to be thought of as presenting a coherent ontology, a globally consistent whole, in the way that the expert's theory is designed to be. Cultural models are better thought of, in Kay's view, as resources or tools, to be used when suitable and set aside when not. That there is no coherent cultural system of knowledge, only an array of different culturally shared schematizations formulated for the performance of particular cognitive tasks, accounts for the co-existence of the conflicting cultural models encountered in many domains of experience. What is not accounted for, in this view, is the degree of apparent systematicity, best characterized as a thematicity, that does seem to pervade cultural knowledge as a body. In the final section of this introduction, we argue that this thematic effect arises from the availability of a small number of very general-purpose cultural models that are repeatedly incorporated into other cultural models developed for special purposes. This account of cultural thematicity does not rule out the kind of contradiction arising among variant cultural models that Kay and other volume authors describe.

Some cultural understandings people have, such as the models of mental processes, emotional states, marital commitment, career choice, gender relations, and kinship obligations described in this book, have a different feel from our models of heating devices. The metaphor of conceptual models as tools to be taken up and put down at will does not fit these other cultural models very well. They are compelling in a way that does not depend on what the experts say and often seems highly resistant to revision in the face of apparent contradiction. Largely tacit and unexamined, the models embed a view of "what is" and "what it means" that seems wholly natural – a matter of course. Alternative views are not even recognized, let alone considered. But more than naturalness, these cultural models grant a seeming necessity to how we ourselves live our lives.

How do ideas gain such force? Partially, the answer lies in what we accept as the typical and normal way of life, judging from the lives of our fellows. When we look around us, we find confirmation for our own lives in the beliefs and actions of other people; cultural models that have force for us as individuals are often the historically dominant models of the time. This is so even though such cultural understandings have certainly undergone historical change, often radical, and certainly have contemporary competitors in any given historical moment.

But the force cultural understandings can have is not simply a matter of people's conformity to the dictums popular in their time. In considering the directive force of cultural meaning systems, D'Andrade (1984a:97) returns to the ideas of Melford Spiro (1961), who argued persuasively that much socially required behavior comes to be inherently motivating for individuals, most often because it directly satisfies some culturally defined need (what Spiro called "intrinsic cultural motivation") or sometimes also because it realizes some strongly held cultural norm or value ("internalized cultural motivation," in Spiro's term). As D'Andrade (ibid.:98) summarizes, "through the process of socialization individuals come to find achieving culturally prescribed goals and following cultural directives to be motivationally satisfying, and to find not achieving culturally prescribed goals and not following cultural directives to be anxiety producing." D'Andrade adapts this argument to a cognitivist view of cultural meaning. He suggests that culturally acquired knowledge need not be purely representational, as the term *cultural knowledge* connotes, but may draw on socialized-in motivation as well. This directive force is "experienced by the person as needs or obligations to do something" (ibid.).

Thus, in D'Andrade's (ibid.:98) example, the cultural meaning of success for Americans, accomplishment may be rewarding because it is both instrumental in the satisfaction of culturally shaped needs for personal recognition and achievement and an objective that has come to be valued in its own right. Both sources of directive are learned as part of the understanding of success and what it entails. This inner motivation to be successful, along with external sanctions for making a living and providing for one's dependents, and social pressure toward conformity with the image and the life-style that mark success, together and in interaction overdetermine the motivational component of this cultural meaning system. As D'Andrade (ibid.) muses, "perhaps what is surprising is that anyone can resist the directive force of such a system." This complex of meaning and motivation is an American preoccupation even though, for most Americans, what constitutes success in our society is actually unattainable.

In the course of human socialization, directive force seems to become attached to those understandings, such as the meaning of success for Americans, that are most closely bound up with the sense individuals have of themselves and the sense they make out of their lives. Perhaps such understandings, including culturally provided understandings about oneself and one's place in life, organize our knowledge of what D'Andrade (n.d.:23) has described as "highly general conditions which people want to bring about or avoid." Cultural models of self and life organize what are, literally, vital understandings. These understandings – however differently they may be delineated in different cultures – become, again in D'Andrade's (ibid.) words, "the most general source of 'guidance,' 'orientation,' and 'direction' in the system."

Socialization experiences may differ sharply in the degree to which they endow a given cultural model with directive force for an individual. Thus, "where there's a will there's a way," to the degree that this common proverb frames a model of the self as the agent of one's fate, may have special force for individuals whose socialization has led them to think of themselves as the sole or primary agents of their own fate. Other individuals, who learn from a quite different socialization experience that they are relatively powerless and blameless with regard to their own fate, may, like the interviewee quoted in Linde's paper in this volume, find behavioral psychology a particularly persuasive interpretation of their lives.

Consider another example. Just as Americans learn to think of themselves and their lives in terms of success, many American women grow up with the teaching that marriage is the measure of a woman's success in life. If this lesson is amplified, as it was for one of Quinn's interviewees whose mother conveyed to her a personal sense of failure for having been unable to hold on to a husband, then the idea of marital success becomes conceptually powerful in the extreme. Thus, as D'Andrade (n.d.:23) points out, what he calls "lower-level schemas," such as the model of marriage in this example, act as goals only when "recruited" by some more general "upper-level schema which is currently functioning to 'guide,' 'orient' and 'direct' the flow of action," such as the model of the successful life in this example. Cultural models of all kinds gain directive force when they are recruited, whether in the course of uniquely individual experiences or those more widely shared, by understandings of oneself and one's life.

Consideration of the potential directive force of cultural models brings us to Keesing's concern with the ideological force of some of these models and their use as instruments of ideological hegemony. Social life, as Spiro (1961) saw, depends on the fit between what is socially required and what is individually desired. So, too, the designs of those who would rule society, and those who would benefit from this control over others, depend upon the willingness of the populace to fill its role in these plans. Therefore, states and other agencies promulgate ideology persuading people to do what they otherwise might question or resist doing. In spite of the resources and power that may be brought to such attempts at persuasion, it is not always effective. To be successful, ideologies must appeal to and activate preexisting cultural understandings, which are themselves compelling. Even though ideologues may mold and adapt cultural models to their own devices, and often show a great deal of genius for doing so, they do not create these cultural ideas *de novo,* nor are they able to guarantee the power of any given cultural model to grip us. Specifically, Lewontin et al. (1984:64) observe that to be convincing, an ideology must pose as either legitimate or inevitable. For "if what exists is right, then one ought not to oppose it; if it exists inevitably, one can never oppose it successfully." These ideas about what is right and what is inevitable are largely given by cultural models of the world. The point made by Lewontin et al. leads to a further observation: Among alternative versions of what is legitimate and what is inevitable, a given ideology is most compelling if its rightness engages the sense one has of one's own personal uprightness and worthiness, or if its inevitability engages the view one has of one's own inherent needs and capacities. These matters lie at the heart of our understanding of ourselves and our place in life. They also are largely cultural matters. Perhaps the contribution cognitive anthropology is poised to make (and *poised* may be slightly too optimistic a word) toward the study of "humans-in-society" is this: insight into those conditions under which cultural models are endowed with directive force and hence with ideological potential.

A short history of methodological strategy

The point from which the previous section departed, cognitive anthropology's focus on linguistic phenomena as the behavior to be accounted for, has proved to be a richly productive strategy, as the papers in the present volume illustrate. In the course of the enterprise, it will be seen, the original view of the relationship of language to culture, with which cognitive anthropology set out, has undergone significant modification.

Our cultural understanding of the world is founded on many tacit assumptions. This underlying cultural knowledge is, to use Hutchins's (1980:12) words, "often transparent to those who use it. Once learned, it becomes what one *sees with,* but seldom what one *sees.*" This "referential transparency" (ibid.), we note in the previous section, causes cultural knowledge to go unquestioned by its bearer. At the same time, this transparency has posed an absorbing methodological problem for the analyst: how, and from what manner of evidence, to reconstruct the cultural models people use but do not often reflect on or explicitly articulate. The problem has remained central to cognitive anthropology, but approaches to it have changed.

Early efforts sought to describe the semantic structure of lexical domains. If analysts could recover or reconstruct what one needed to know in order to label pieces and portions of the world correctly in the native's own language, it was reasoned, then the resulting model would capture an important part of those people's culturally constructed reality. Such analyses produced the formal taxonomic and paradigmatic descriptions for which the emerging enterprise variously called "ethnoscience," "ethnographic semantics," and "the new ethnography" became known and with which cognitive anthropology, evolved out of these earlier efforts, has been persistently associated long after its practitioners began exploring networks of semantic relations, schemas for decision making, and other alternatives to taxonomic and paradigmatic models (D'Andrade n.d.:19).

The semantic structures recovered in these earliest analyses did provide insight into the organization of some domains of the lexicon. However, the organization of lexicon was soon recognized to offer only limited insight into the organization of cultural knowledge (D'Andrade 1976; D'Andrade et al. 1972; Good & Good 1982; Howe & Scherzer 1975; Lave et al. 1977; Randall 1976; White 1982). Notwithstanding the primacy attributed to referential meaning in the western positivist/empiricist tradition, what one needs to know to label things in the world correctly did not prove to be the most salient part of cultural meaning. Formal semantic analysis did not uncover the cultural models that individuals invoked for the performance of such naturally occurring cognitive tasks as categorizing, reasoning, remembering, problem solving, decision making, and ongoing understanding, but gave only such partial and selective glimpses of those models as had come to be embedded in the lexical structure. In the tradition of formal semantic analysis, special tasks were devised that induced subjects to rely on lexical structure for their performance; as Randall (1976) first pointed out, however, naming and discrimination tasks such as these are infrequently encountered in the ordinary course of life.

Even the "psychologically real" analyses of people's judgments of semantic similarity, which followed on the heels of formal semantic analysis, proved to be of limited insight into the organization of cultural models.

Such analyses revealed that people brought something more in the way of cultural understanding than word knowledge or even "encyclopaedic" knowledge, to use Sperber's (1975:91–94) term, to their improvisations of these unfamiliar sorting tasks. But what this something more was still had to be filled in.

Several papers in this volume represent the culmination of this methodological tradition. Both the paper by White and that by Holland and Skinner show how additional analysis of natural discourse must be introduced to make sense of the results of multidimensional scaling (and by implication other multivariate analyses) of semantic similarity judgments. Holland and Skinner's paper is a particularly telling critique of the tradition in cognitive anthropology that has relied exclusively on the interpretation of such semantic similarity results. Their analysis argues that the items composing the lexical domain of gender labels used by college students are related in an interesting but oblique way to these students' presupposed knowledge of gender relationships. The terms label individuals who violate cultural expectations about the course of normal relationships between males and females. To understand these labels, one must understand the presumed relationship. An interpretation based on labels of gender types alone, then, would be missing the central assumptions of the cultural model. Lutz makes a similar point in her paper about Ifaluk emotion words: The meaning of these words cannot be fully grasped from an analysis of the words alone; one must have an understanding of the Ifaluk ethnotheory of emotion that underlies them.

This is not to argue that semantic similarity-based multidimensional scaling analyses and other such techniques should be discarded. People do sometimes use semantic similarity of terms to accomplish such natural tasks as inferring information about acquaintances (D'Andrade 1965; 1974). Moreover, both White and Holland and Skinner demonstrate the utility of the method of analysis as a preliminary step in recovering cultural models. Elsewhere than this book, D'Andrade (1984b; 1985) has made the same use of these scaling techniques; he shows the considerable advantage of such analysis for sketching in the broad outlines of a large domain of American culture, that of person perception. Such an approach is highly efficient but relatively crude. It necessarily sacrifices depth for scope; description of how particular parts of the model work for rapid identification of key components and orientation of these components relative to one another. Such scope is important because, as is discussed further in the final section of this introduction, cultural models appear to interpenetrate one another, some of general purpose playing a role in many other more special-purpose models. Thus, for example, in this volume, assumptions about relations among thought, intention, and action, which figure in a folk model of the mind argued by D'Andrade to be widely shared by Americans, are shown by White to underlie our model of problem solving. Assumptions about difficulty, effort, and success, which

D'Andrade (1984b) has shown to be part of a shared American model of task performance, play a role in Americans' model of marriage, as described by Quinn (1985, this volume). In Samoan thought, Clement (1982) has found notions of valued social identities to underlie understanding of mental disorders. A sweeping view identifies these interconnections. Thus, a methodological division of labor seems to be emerging. Multivariate analyses of semantic similarity judgments, techniques by which a relatively large quantity of data can be efficiently collected and effectively reduced, are used to sketch in a map of the territory and orient it relative to other domains, while different methods provide the higher resolution needed to explore a given terrain closely.

New approaches to the investigation of cultural models, then, reflect a recognition that the relationship between a model and any regularities in the terminology of semantic domains referenced by this model is likely to be complex and indirect at best. Consequently, there are no mechanical procedures by which the former can be derived from the latter. Now, word meaning and, indeed, all of language are viewed as holding possible clues to the underlying cultural knowledge that enters into linguistic and other behavior. Reconstructing the organization of this cultural knowledge, however, requires kinds of linguistic data richer in such clues than the data provided by naming and sorting tasks, and it requires eclectic exploitation of all possible sources of such data.

The major new data sources that cognitive anthropologists have adapted to the task of reconstructing cultural models, represented in this volume, are two: systematic use of native-speaker's intuitions, and analysis of natural discourse. For many nonanthropologist practitioners of cognitive science, of course, neither method is new. The former is exemplified in the volume papers by Lakoff and Kövecses, by Sweetser, and by Kay, all linguists for whom the method of developing one's analytic model out of one's native-speaker's intuitions, and verifying this model against further intuitions, is a matter of disciplinary canon. Using his own native speaker's intuitions represents a methodological departure, however, for anthropologist D'Andrade, who draws not only on his intuitions about the language of mental processes, but also on a long tradition of introspection about such matters by philosophers.

What all these papers suggest is that the intuitions of native speakers about their language are heavily dependent on the intuitions of these natives as culture-bearers. Sweetser, for example, demonstrates elegantly how our judgment that some speech act is or is not a *lie*, depends on cultural assumptions about the simplified worlds of communication and mutual assistance in which such acts occur. Kay shows that the co-existing, alternative folk theories of language that lie behind the two hedges, *loosely speaking* and *technically*, depend on cultural assumptions about the nature of truth and the authority of experts, respectively.

It is of interest that neither Sweetser, on the one hand, nor D'Andrade on the other are comfortable with a cultural analysis validated solely against their native-speaker's intuitions. Sweetser goes on to show that the model she constructs on the basis of her own introspection and the accounts of linguistic philosophers can parsimoniously account for experimental findings of Coleman and Kay (1981), who elicited subject's judgments as to whether a lie had been told in each of a series of systematically varied hypothetical cases. D'Andrade demonstrates that interview responses to questions about mental events are explicable in terms of his model of the mind. These efforts at independent verification of analyses derived from native speaker's intuition, against the linguistic responses of other speakers, can be interpreted as attempts to satisfy alternative standards of evidence that co-exist in multidisciplinary enterprises such as the one in which this group of cognitive scientists is joined. This strategy of building accounts from native speaker's intuitions and then testing them against other, independent observations can be expected to become a methodological hallmark of future investigations into cultural knowledge.

The models developed in other papers rely heavily on another method likely to become a mainstay of the new enterprise. This is an eclectic kind of discourse analysis fashioned, as necessary, out of borrowed parts. An important source of inspiration for this methodological approach has been Linde, a linguist whose earlier work on discourse types (1978; n.d.) has influenced most of the anthropologists in the group. Many of these papers – most explicitly, those of Hutchins, Kempton, Quinn, Collins and Gentner, and Linde herself – show how the type of discourse Linde calls *explanation* can be exploited to reveal the cultural models that underlie speakers' reasoning. Kempton, for example, infers the underlying folk theories of home heating devices that informants hold from the metaphors they use, as Quinn infers from interviewees' metaphors the underlying propositions they are asserting about marriage. Collins and Gentner are able to identify a limited number of schemas or "component models" that recur in their subject's explanations of evaporation. Likewise, Linde uncovers a small number of recurrent "explanatory systems" identifiable by characteristic themes in American interviewees' explanations of their occupational choices, such as the "split self" theme, which is part of the Freudian explanatory system, and the "non-agency" theme, which is characteristic of the behaviorist explanatory system. Price's paper mines another discourse type discussed by Linde, *narrative,* in Ecuadorian stories about illness episodes, to reconstruct cultural understandings about familial roles from their "traces" in these narratives: what narrators highlight, elaborate, leave unsaid, mark with counter-examples, and comment on in affective propositions.

Another powerful influence on several of the anthropologists in this group has been Hutchins's (1980) book on Trobriand land litigation. Hutchins demonstrated how explanation in natural discourse could be decoded to reveal cultural schemas for the propositions on which the argument of the discourse was based. Schemas, in Hutchins's usage, state propositional relations in terms of variable ranges, so that a given schema serves as a "template" from which any number of propositions can be constructed (ibid.:51). Trobriand litigation over land transactions, however, is a special-purpose discourse that uses a limited set of such schemas composed of highly technical information about the specific rights in land that may be transferred as a result of particular prestations. Could his approach be used to discover the schematic structure underlying more general-purpose explanation (Quinn 1982a)? Three papers in this volume, by Lutz, Quinn, and Hutchins himself, would seem to answer "Yes."

Lutz analyzes word definitions, natural instances of word use, and more general propositional statements elicited from interviewees to reveal the "basic level schemas" that enter into the Ifaluk cultural model of emotion and how these schemas concatenate to form statements and inferences about common situations and their associated emotions.

Quinn's analysis identifies stable proposition-schemas and schemas of chained propositions used in reasoning about marriage. As she shows, it is necessary first to decipher the metaphorical speech in which propositions are cast, the referencing of earlier propositions by later ones, and the causal constructions linking one proposition with another, in order to reveal the common underlying schemas in this talk.

Hutchins cracks an even less obvious code, showing that mythic schemas, as disguised representations of their repressed thoughts and fears, enable Trobrianders to reason about their relations to deceased relatives. Key to his interpretation is the identification of the propositional structure of the myth with an analogous structure outside the myth, in a "relevant bit of life."

Thus, although it is fair to say that much of the original ethnoscientific enterprise was driven by a seemingly powerful method – semantic analysis – and constrained by the unforeseen limitations of that method, the same is not true of modern cognitive anthropology. Current efforts are more intent on theory building than on the pursuit of any particular methodology. The theoretical question is: How is cultural knowledge organized? The methodological strategy is to reconstruct the organization of this shared knowledge from what people say about their experience. To this strategy, cognitive anthropology has adapted some of the time-honored methodological approaches of linguistics.

An account of cultural knowledge from artificial intelligence

This volume presents some initial answers to the question: How is cultural knowledge organized? In doing so, it makes a contribution, not to the field of cognitive anthropology alone, but to the multidisciplinary enterprise of cognitive science. Cognitive science asks: How is knowledge organized? However, the central role of culture in the organization of this everyday understanding has only recently begun to be appreciated by cognitive scientists. Efforts within artificial intelligence to model understanding by computer confront culture when, as is often the case, the task solution to be modeled depends on preexisting knowledge of the sort human beings draw on so readily.

Robert Abelson (1975:276) has referred to the difficulty of incorporating this knowledge into computer simulations as the "size problem," concluding that "there is too much common sense knowledge of the world in even the humblest normal human head for present computer systems to begin to cope with." Recognizing that most artificial intelligence has avoided the problem either by dealing with very restricted domains, or by modeling very general cognitive mechanisms that work in principle but never operate in actual situations, Abelson himself has attempted, with Roger Schank (1977), to design a more knowledgeable understander. Because theirs is arguably the most thoughtful attempt, from this quarter of cognitive science, to build cultural knowledge into understanding, and because their formulation is widely known to cognitive science audiences, a brief discussion of their work will be useful in order to say why anthropologists find it lacking and to compare it with the approach represented in this volume.

Schank and Abelson (ibid.) begin with the notion of *scripts* as basic building blocks of our everyday understanding. Scripts, derived from daily routine, are standardized sequences of events that fill in our understanding of frequently recurring experiences. The "restaurant script," now famous in cognitive science circles, guides the customer through the series of interchanges required to get a meal at a restaurant – getting seated, ordering, paying, and even sending unacceptable food back to the kitchen or adjusting the size of the tip to reflect the quality of service received. All this is mundane, but undeniably cultural, knowledge. (A strikingly similar approach to cultural knowledge of routinized events has been offered by anthropologist Charles Frake, who provides an analysis of such a routine in another culture; see Frake 1975; 1977.)

The cultural models to be described here bear an intriguing resemblance to Schank and Abelson's scripts. Their enactment is not tied to a concrete physical setting, as is that of the restaurant script. They do, however, have two features that Abelson (1981:3) has singled out to characterize scripts:

> The casual definition of a script is a "stereotyped sequence of events familiar to the individual." Implicit in this definition are two powerful sources of constraint. One is the notion of an event sequence, which implies the causal chaining of enablements and results for physical events and of initiations and reasons for mental events. . . . The other constraint generator comes from ideas of stereotypy and familiarity. That an event

sequence is stereotyped implies the absence of fortuitous events. Also, for events to be often repeated implies that there is some set of standard individual and institutional goals which gives rise to the repetition.

The papers in this volume illustrate how our knowledge is organized in culturally standardized and hence familiar event sequences that tell, for example, how marriage goes (Quinn); or how anger is engendered, experienced, and expressed (Lakoff & Kövecses); or under what circumstances a lie has been told (Sweetser); or what to expect in a relationship between two young adults of opposite gender (Holland & Skinner); or that wishes give rise to intentions and intentions to actions (D'Andrade). These "stories" include prototypical events, prototypical roles for actors, prototypical entities, and more. They invoke, in effect, whole worlds in which things work, actors perform, and events unfold in a simplified and wholly expectable manner. These events are chained together by shared assumptions about causality, both physical and psychological, as Abelson's characterization of scripts suggests. Abelson's casual definition of a script has much in common with what we here call a "cultural model" (or sometimes, a "folk model") to capture both its dynamic role in guiding expectations and actions and its shared possession by the bearers of a culture.

To this point, the account of shared knowledge rendered by Schank and Abelson is not dissimilar to our own. Beyond scripts, however, the two accounts begin to diverge. The first difference is one that would strike any anthropologist. Schank and Abelson are not explicit about the cultural nature of the knowledge they invoke. They write of "well-developed belief systems about the world" (ibid.:132); however, they tend to attribute such belief systems to pan-human experience of how the world works (ibid.:119) rather than questioning whether some of these belief systems might be unique to our own culture. Without trying here to settle the big question of cross-cultural universals in human thought (a question D'Andrade and Sweetser address in this volume), we assert that many of Schank and Abelson's examples invoke knowledge peculiar to Americans.

Cultural knowledge is key to the higher-order structures that embody goals in Schank and Abelson's formulation. As their inventors were the first to point out, all is not scripts. There is more to understanding than knowing how get a meal at a restaurant and how to execute the numerous other scripts and plans for carrying out all our daily objectives. As Schank and Abelson are led to ask, how do these goals themselves arise? How are story understanders and other observers of the everyday world able to assess actors' goals and predict their future goals? Schank and Abelson's answer is that related goals are bundled together in "themes." These themes are said to generate actors' goals as well as other people's inferences about these likely goals. It is possible to make such inferences about the goals of other people, presumably, because knowledge of themes, no less than knowledge of scripts, is shared.

Anthropologists found this account at once provocative and unsatisfactory. Themes generate related goals. But how are they related? Schank and Abelson (ibid.) propose three types of theme: "role themes," like WAITRESS or SHERIFF; "interpersonal themes," like MARRIED or LOVER; and "life themes," like SUCCESS or LUXURY LIVING. Each of these labels conjures up to the anthropologist a vast store of cultural knowledge. However, merely naming themes MARRIED or SUCCESS begs the question of how this shared knowledge of being married or achieving success organizes the goals we associate with these respective themes. Perhaps because Schank and Abelson supply examples drawn from their own cultural knowledge, which has a seeming naturalness for them, they take for granted in their theoretical formulation the same complex knowledge that ordinarily goes unquestioned in their everyday lives.

Schank's (1982) more recent reformulation of the theory of scripts is much more sophisticated about how knowledge must be hierarchically organized and continually modified in memory in order to account for such processes as reminding and the generalization of learning. At the same time, however, Schank's newer account more glaringly exposes the inadequacy of a theory of the organization of knowledge that gives an insufficient role to how human beings acquire most of their knowledge, especially their most general understandings. Failing to make a place in his account for knowledge that is culturally shared and transmitted, Schank is left with the awkward supposition that an individual's understanding of the world is accumulated through the painstaking generalization of knowledge from one firsthand experience to another. It is difficult to imagine how people could learn as much as they know, even by the time they reach adulthood, from personal experience alone.

Many of Schank's favorite examples, such as that of learning a different routine for ordering, paying, and eating in fast-food restaurants than that followed in regular restaurants, may represent the kind of detailed knowledge of setting-specific conventions that is, in fact, normally picked up in personal encounter with each new setting. However, others of his examples are less readily assimilated to this model of learning from actual experience. Knowledge of the "societal conventions" (ibid.:98) surrounding the idea of CONTRACT, for instance, is said to be generalized from successive experiences in which services are procured – meals at restaurants, visits to doctors' offices, home visits from plumbers, and the like. It is implausible to suggest that people learn all they need to know about such complex cultural matters as are embedded in CONTRACT or MARRIED or SUCCESS (e.g., that MARRIED has something to do with the other two) solely from successive experiences with actual contractual relations, marriages, and personal successes. Indeed, we know that individuals have sizable expectations about such things before ever experiencing them personally. Moreover, as Schank stresses, what happens to different people and how they respond to these experiences differs; if direct experience were the only source of knowledge, then each individual's understanding of the world would diverge from that of every other individual. Indeed, this is what Schank is led to conclude: "There is no reason," he notes (ibid.:224), "why structures that are based on experience should bear a relationship to any other person's structures." But of course, even allowing for their unique individual perceptions of the world, people somehow do end up with considerable shared knowledge. To pursue one of Schank's examples, the homeowner who calls a plumber about a leaking pipe and the plumber who comes to replace it can negotiate a contract between them, even though they have never met one another before, grew up in different parts of the country, and have entirely different class and ethnic backgrounds. How this comes to be is left unexplained in Schank's formulation.

The research presented here assumes that individuals are heir to a great deal of knowledge about the world that they do not necessarily draw from firsthand experience. Cultural knowledge is typically acquired to the accompaniment of intermittent advice and occasional correction rather than explicit, detailed instruction; but it is learned from others, in large part from their talk, nonetheless (D'Andrade 1981). This is perhaps most clearly illustrated by highly abstract ideas, such as the theory of relativity, philosophical arguments about the meaning of existence, or cultural conceptualizations of self and group identity, which are transmitted and perpetuated through language and could hardly be learned without it (Holland 1985:406–407). There is perhaps no experience, however concrete or however novel, that is not informed in some way by the culturally transmitted understandings an adult individual brings to that experience.

The work in this book goes on to address the question: How does this received knowledge organize our understanding? Cultural models, as conceived by this volume's authors, play the conceptual role blocked out by "themes" in Schank and Abelson's original formulation. Cultural models frame our understanding of how the world works, including our inferences about what other animate beings are up to, and, importantly, our decisions about what we ourselves will do. With Lutz (this volume), we want to claim that many of our most common and paramount goals are incorporated into cultural understandings and learned as part of this heritage.

An account of cultural models from prototype theory

Our view of cultural models has obvious connection to ideas about *prototypes,* which have figured importantly in cognitive scientists' recent discussions of knowledge representation. Event sequences played out in "simplified worlds" (Sweetser's term, this volume) appear to serve as prototypes for understanding real-world experience. The notion that schematic structures, or *schemas* of some kind, systematically organize how experience is understood, has wide acceptance in cognitive science, including cognitive anthropology (Casson 1983). That prototypes (e.g., the most representative members of a category) might serve as schemas for categories of things, is an appealing implication of Rosch's experimental research on categorization (fully reviewed in Rosch 1977; as Rosch stressed in a 1978 assessment of this work, however, the identification of prototype effects is not to be mistaken for a theory of mental representation accounting for these effects). Anthropologists are perhaps more familiar with the prototype notion from its original application to color categories in the work of Paul Kay and his associates (Berlin & Kay 1969; Kay & McDaniel 1978). The extension of the notion from its earliest application to color and such physical objects as birds and furniture, to prototypical event sequences, has reached anthropology through linguistics.

Linguists first came to see the necessity of incorporating cultural knowledge into their accounts of word use. Perhaps the single most-cited example of a folk model, at the conference from which this volume grew, was the analysis of *bachelor* provided by linguist Charles Fillmore (1975; 1982). Fillmore had argued that traditional "checklist" definitions of words such as *bachelor* were inadequate. In the checklist view, a bachelor is a man who has never been married (Katz & Fodor 1963:189–190). However, as Fillmore pointed out, this definition utterly fails to explain why we do not consider, for example, the Pope to be a bachelor, or a wolf-boy grown to maturity in the jungle. (Or, we might be tempted to add if we were linguists, a male victim of brain damage who has been in a coma since childhood.)

This critique of the traditional linguistic approach to word definition parallels anthropologists' dissatisfaction with componential analysis of lexical sets discussed in an earlier section: Both accounts appear to leave out a crucial part of what speakers have to know in order to use a word or a system of terminology. The alternative Fillmore proposed is that the word *bachelor* "frames," in his term, a simplified world in which prototypical events unfold: Men marry at a certain age; marriages last for life; and in such a world, a bachelor is a man who stays unmarried beyond the usual age, thereby becoming eminently marriageable. (Fillmore might have noted that the bachelor's female counterpart, the spinster, suffers a different fate.) Here is an example of a folk model presumed by a single word.

A similar analysis, of the word *orphan,* has been offered by the linguist Ronald Langacre (1979). Quinn (1982b) has argued that a cultural model of difficult enterprises underlies the polysemous meanings of the word *commitment,* as this word is used in reference to marriage. Fillmore has elsewhere (1977) suggested that a set of related verbs from the domain of commerce can be understood as elements in "the scene of the commercial event," which is activated by use of one of these words, such as *buy* or *pay.* Several of the volume papers emerge directly from this linguistic tradition, an approach Fillmore has labeled "frame semantics." Sweetser's analysis of *lie* is perhaps the most sustained linguistic analysis of the simplified world required to explain use of a single word. Kay's reconstruction of the folk theories about language and speech that inform use of *loosely speaking* and *technically* extends this tradition to the analysis of hedges. The paper by Lakoff and Kövecses can be viewed as extending the same linguistic approach to another feature of language, metaphor. They show that American English metaphors for *anger* are structured in terms of an implicit cultural model of human physiology and emotion, which they delineate.

Understandably, linguists are most concerned with the important implications of underlying cultural models for their theories of word definition, metaphor, polysemy, hedging, and other linguistic phenomena (but see Lakoff 1984). Anthropologists tend to orient their analyses in the opposite direction, treating linguistic usages as clues to the underlying cultural model and working toward a more satisfactory theory of culture and its role in such nonlinguistic tasks as reasoning (Hutchins 1980; and the papers by Hutchins, by Lutz, and by Quinn in this volume), problem solving (Kempton this volume; White this volume), and evaluating the behavior of others (D'Andrade 1985; Holland & Skinner this volume; Price this volume). However, the different questions that draw linguists and anthropologists should not obscure the common insight that brought together this particular group of linguists and anthropologists in the first place: that culturally shared knowledge is organized into prototypical event sequences enacted in simplified worlds. That much of such cultural knowledge is presumed by language use is as significant a realization to anthropologists as to linguists. For the latter, these cultural models promise the key to linguistic usage; for the former, linguistic usage provides the best available data for reconstruction of cultural models.

The forms cultural knowledge can take

How is the knowledge embodied in cultural models brought to the various cognitive tasks that require this knowledge? Lakoff (1984) offers some extremely helpful starting suggestions about types of cognitive models, observations that are as applicable to the culturally shared cognitive models described in this volume as to the more idiosyncratic cognitive models individuals devise.

PROPOSITION-SCHEMAS AND IMAGE-SCHEMAS
Lakoff (ibid.:10) makes a useful distinction between what he calls *propositional models* and *image-schematic models*. Consonant with the work of Hutchins (1980), which demonstrates the utility of a notion of culturally shared schemas for propositions and sets of linked propositions, we adopt the term *proposition-schema* to refer to Lakoff's "propositional model," and for parallel syntax, *image-schema* to refer to Lakoff's "image-schematic model." Image-schemas and proposition-schemas, then, are two

alternative forms in which knowledge may be cast. (Since a cultural model may be recast in one or the other type of schema, or may use the two in combination, it seems clearest to reserve the term *model,* in the present discussion, for the entirety of a prototypical event sequence embedded in a simplified world and to talk about "schemas" as reconceptualizations of given cultural models, or components of such models, for particular cognitive purposes. The reader should beware, however, of the differing and conflicting uses of *model* in related literature, including some papers in this volume; as is typical of new theoretical endeavors, this one has not yet gotten its terminology under control.[2]). Indeed, we argue, proposition-schemas and image-schemas seem suited to different kinds of cognitive tasks.

In the present volume, various papers illustrate proposition-schemas, with D'Andrade's describing perhaps the most complex set of related proposition-schemas, those of Lutz and Quinn showing how fixed schemas of related propositions may be used in reasoning, and that of White showing how the proposition-schemas underlying proverbs may be invoked for problem-solving. Proposition-schemas specify concepts and the relations which hold among them (Hutchins 1980:51; Lakoff 1984:10). As Quinn points out for reasoning about marriage, in the discourse type Linde calls *explanation,* the causal assumptions connecting proposition to proposition are often dropped out, making these connections seem "empty." In fact, the reasoner, and any listener who shares the same knowledge, can fill in the missing information as necessary for clarification. The capability, afforded by proposition-schemas, of dropping out this detailed knowledge allows speakers to present relatively lengthy arguments and arrive at their conclusions with reasonable economy. Much more generally, the stable, culturally shared proposition-schemas available for instantiating such causal chains not only facilitate the task of communicating familiar inferences about the world but also allow these inferences to be made swiftly and accurately in the first place.

This is an implication of the ability shown by Quinn's American interviewee, Lutz's Ifaluk informants, and the Trobriand litigants in Hutchins's (1980) study alike to work readily through relatively complex reasoning sequences. It is brought home in a study by D'Andrade (1982), who demonstrates the dramatic improvement in American university students' performance of a reasoning task requiring a complex contrapositive inference, when abstract logical values are replaced with familiar concrete relationships such as that between rain and wet roofs. Presumably, that causal relation, like the relation Americans recognize between marital difficulties and impending divorce, and that the Ifaluk recognize between the emotion of *ker* and subsequent misbehavior, is inferred from a readily available proposition-schema. Further, Lutz suggests, the structure of proposition-schemas may enable children to learn the content of cultural models in stages, first mastering abbreviated versions of proposition-schemas – or

"chunks" in Hutchins's (1980:115–116) terminology – in which interven-
ing links in a complex chain of causality are omitted and only later
understood.

Image-schemas lend themselves to quite different uses. Lakoff (1981)
regards image-schemas as gestalts just as visual images are. However, they
are much more schematic than what we ordinarily think of as visual imagery, and they may contain not just visual components but also kin-
aesthetic information of all kinds. The examples he provides – "Our
knowledge about baseball pitches includes a trajectory schema. Our
knowledge about candles includes a long, thin object schema" (Lakoff
1984:10) – make clear that image-schemas convey knowledge of physical
phenomena, such as shape and motion.

In the present volume, Lakoff and Kövecses provide an example – of
anger conceptualized image-schematically in terms of hot liquid in a container. Kempton's informants provide another: For some of these people,
the "valve" theorists, home thermostats are imagined as faucet-like devices;
for others, the "feedback" theorists, as on–off switches. The labels Collins
and Gentner give to the various "component models" (our "image-
schemas") on which their subjects draw to imagine how evaporation
works – the "sand–grain" model, the "random-speed" model, the "heat-
threshold" model, the "rocketship" model, the "container" model, the
"crowded room" model, and so forth – graphically convey the image-
schematic nature of these components that subjects combine into a runable
model of the process by which molecules might be conceived to behave
in the water at the outset of evaporation, escape from the water into the
air, behave in the air, return to the water, change from liquid to vapor,
and vice versa.

Two of these studies suggest strongly, if they do not demonstrate con-
clusively, that image-schemas are actually being used to perform the
cognitive task that is verbally described for the investigator, rather than
just being used to construct the verbal account of that task (a cognitive
task in its own right, but a different one). The reports Kempton's informants give of their thermostat adjustment habits agree with his predictions, based on which of the two image-schemas household residents are
using. Collins and Gentner compare the content of subjects' verbal protocols to the adequacy of their explanations for mundane observations,
such as why you can see your breath on a cold day. The answers given
by the two subjects illustrate two divergent tendencies, which seem to
reflect the greater success of the first subject in reasoning from image-
schemas. The second subject was able to give fewer correct answers and
often fell into inconsistencies. From his protocols this appears to be
because, unlike the first subject, he had not established a stable set of
image-schemas with which to work through the hypothesized evaporation
process and against which to check his reasoning for inconsistencies.
Rather, he invoked a different component model for every answer and

relied frequently instead on isolated analogies to different phenomena he happened to have seen or heard about.

More extensive evidence that image-schemas indeed enter into the performance of a task comes from Gentner and Gentner (1983). They argue that subjects use one of two different analogies for explaining electricity. This study shows convincingly that choice of analogy has consequences for reasoning: Subjects using each characteristically make different kinds of mistakes. The nature of these mistakes would seem to favor the interpretation that subjects are reasoning from image-schemas of the physical-world analogy they use. For example, subjects who adopt the "teeming crowd" model of electricity are predictably better able to understand the difference between parallel and serial resistors, which they view as gates. These people correctly respond that parallel resistors (viewed as two side-by-side gates) give more current than a single resistor; serial resistors (viewed as two consecutive gates) less. An image-schematic interpretation would argue that such subjects gain an advantage by being able to manipulate these "gates" mentally and visualize how electricity, like a racing crowd, might make its way through them. Subjects who use the "flowing fluid" model, on the other hand, typically err in their explanations of parallel and serial resistors, viewing resistors as impediments to the passage of a fluid. These latter people conclude that both combinations of resistors constitute double obstacles and thus that both result in less current.

Image-schemas seem well-adapted to thinking about not only physical relations but logical ones as well, when that logic is amenable to reconceptualization in spatial terms. Johnson-Laird and Steedman (1978), for instance, have argued that subjects solve difficult syllogisms by conjuring up Venn-diagram-like schematic relationships among groups of imaginary entities and then consulting these mental diagrams to read off the overlap between groups. Image-schemas would seem to permit the scanning and manipulation required by certain kinds of complex reasoning.

THE ROLE OF METAPHOR IN SUPPLYING IMAGE-SCHEMAS

Lakoff (1984:10) goes on to argue that metaphor plays an important role in cognitive modeling, mapping proposition-schemas and image-schemas in given domains onto corresponding structures in other domains. Such mappings have a characteristic direction, as Lakoff and Johnson (1980:56–68) observed: Metaphors appear to introduce information from physical-world source domains into target domains in the nonphysical world. Why this should be so has not been made entirely clear. Lakoff and Johnson (ibid.:57, 61–62) sometimes seem to be suggesting that the concepts metaphors introduce are more readily understandable because they are grounded in our bodily interaction with the physical environment. However, Holland (1982:292–293; see also Butters 1981) points out that this is demonstrably not the case for Lakoff and Johnson's prime example, the metaphor ARGUMENT IS WAR. Lakoff and Johnson assert that we understand war more readily because of its basis in our evolutionary history as human animals, equipped for physical conflict. Holland responds that our understanding of modern war, far from resting on a conception of primal physical combat, is just as culturally given as our notions about argument; and argument is the more directly apprehended experience for most Americans.

We suggest, rather, that the advantage of metaphors from the physical world rests on the nature of physical experience itself, and the manner in which physical properties and relations are apprehensible to human beings: – a view that Lakoff and Johnson (1980:58, 60–61) at other points seem to be developing. The present discussion about the role of image-schemas in understanding allows us to be more precise. Image-schemas are constructed out of physical properties and relations, and the advantage of metaphors drawn from domains of the physical world is that these source domains provide the material for image-schemas. Metaphor is important to understanding, then, because it enables image-schematic thought. Thus, it does not really matter whether WAR is grounded in actual experience or genetic memory of physical combat, or known indirectly from depictions of such combat. What makes it a useful metaphor for ARGUMENT is that, unlike the latter, war is largely culturally defined for us in terms of physical space – battlegrounds, battle lines, routes of retreat, demilitarized zones, and so forth – occupied by physical occurrences – troop advances, cross-fire, body counts, and so forth. The metaphor allows the largely intangible social dynamics of argument to be reconceptualized in the image-schematic terms provided by the tangible events of war.

The result of any such mapping, from physical experience in the source domain to social or psychological experience in the target domain, is that elements, properties, and relations that could not be conceptualized in image-schematic form without the metaphor can now be so expressed in the terms provided by the metaphor. Such a result is achieved, for example, by the metaphor of anger as a hot fluid in a container, which can be envisioned as boiling, producing steam, rising, and exerting pressure on its container, which, as a consequence, can be imagined to explode. Similarly, the image-schema of marriage as an entity allows it to be conceptualized as a manufactured object more or less well constructed and hence more or less likely to fall apart; and the image-schema of a problem as a protrusion on the landscape allows it to be reduced, conceptually, from the size of a mountain to the more realistic, and hence surmountable, size of a molehill. Like other image-schemas, metaphorically derived image-schemas are gestalts that make multiple relations more immediately apprehensible. These gestalts can then be scanned to arrive at entailments among related elements and manipulated to simulate what would be entailed under different conditions.

In their paper, Collins and Gentner decompose the process by which novices – struggling to explain a physical phenomenon, evaporation, about which they have probably never before been asked – generate their explanations by analogy and the image-schemas it provides. The subjects manipulate image-schemas, or as these authors put it, "run mental models" to simulate what might happen under various conditions.

Collins and Gentner argue convincingly that subjects perform mental simulations in new domains by partitioning the system they are trying to understand (here, evaporation) into a set of component processes. Then models (in our terms, image-schemas) can be mapped analogically onto each component process from some known domain. For example, sometimes subjects use a "heat-threshold" model of the process of molecular escape from the water to the air; this model (incorrectly, as it happens) has molecules popping out of the water like popcorn when they reach a certain temperature. Collins and Gentner show, then, how analogies are used to supply image-schemas that can be set into imaginary motion and mentally observed in action. Interestingly, they provide an example of the importation of image-schemas from physical-world source domains to a target domain that is also in the physical world but that cannot be conceptualized image-schematically in its own terms, because its physics is unknown to the subject and unavailable for direct observation. (That they choose to call these mappings "analogies" rather than "metaphors" may simply be that mappings from one physical-world domain to another are less typical of what we have learned to treat as metaphor than mappings from a domain of physical experience to a domain of nonphysical experience.) Just as do intangible social and psychological experiences, this unknown and invisible physical phenomenon requires translation for image-schematic conceptualization.

Given this special role of well-understood physical-world domains in providing image-schematic representation for other domains of experience, then these authors' description of how people run mental models of an unknown physical process constructed from their knowledge of other physical processes takes on a special significance. Perhaps because subjects are aware that there exists a well-specified scientific account of evaporation, one they perhaps should know, they are willing to work harder at the attempt to produce an explicit and coherent explanation of it than, say, D'Andrade's (this volume) interviewees, who are not attempting to approximate an accepted "scientific" account of mental processes. Close analysis of the full, extended responses given by subjects as they think through explanations for this relatively complex and unfamiliar physical phenomenon is a strategy that allows Collins and Gentner to describe the reasoning process in fine detail. Their paper reveals the ability of mental models research from psychology to specify a cognitive process, reasoning from image-schemas, which may prove central to linguistic and anthropological accounts of cultural models in all domains of experience. Here is a crucial link between two lines of research.

Many of the papers in this volume illustrate Lakoff and Johnson's (1980) claim that ongoing understanding often relies on the rich mapping potential of metaphor. However, Quinn's paper and that of Lakoff and Kövecses suggest that metaphors are extended, not willy-nilly from any domain to any other, but in closely structured ways (see also Holland 1982:293–294). A multiplicity of metaphors for marriage or for anger or for types of men (Holland & Skinner 1985) fall into a handful of classes. What appears to constrain these metaphors to these classes is the underlying cultural model in the domain to which they are mapped: The classes from which speakers select metaphors they consider to be appropriate are those that capture aspects of the simplified world and the prototypical events unfolding in this world, constituted by the cultural model. Chosen metaphors not only highlight particular features of the cultural model; as we discuss, they also point to entailments among these elements. Thus, one husband's metaphor of marriage as a "do-it-yourself project" at once suggests for him the durable quality of something made in this manner – "it was very strong because it was made as we went along" – and implies, additionally, the craft and care and effort that must go into such a thing to make it well. Speakers often favor just such metaphors, which allow two or more related elements of the source domain to be mapped onto a corresponding set of related elements in the cultural model (Quinn 1985) and a comment on that relation to be made. At the same time, other metaphors that fail to reflect, or even contradict, aspects of the cultural model in the target domain to which they are mapped are likely to be rejected. Quinn (ibid.) gives an anecdotal example in which marriage was likened to an ice-cream cone that could be eaten up fast or licked slowly to make it last longer – a metaphor in such clear violation of our understanding of marriage as an enduring relationship that it bothered and offended members of the wedding at which it was voiced.

THE ROLE OF METONYMY IN STRUCTURING
CULTURAL MODELS

In Lakoff's (1984) formulation, metaphor does not exhaust the possible devices for structuring our understanding; metonymy has a central role to play. A *metaphoric model* maps structures from one domain to another; what Lakoff terms a *metonymic model* structures a domain in terms of one of its elements. Something is gained by this substitution of part of a category for the category as a whole: the former "is either easier to understand, easier to process, easier to recognize, or more immediately useful for the given purpose in the given context" (ibid.:12). Thus, for example, the social world in which some men are bachelors is structured, not by our full knowledge of the many possible courses men's lives may take, but by what Lakoff calls a *typical example* of a male life course. This life course, treated as canonical for men, provides the presupposed world within which *bachelor* is an applicable term.

Typicality is not the only metonymic relation that may hold between a domain and some element in this domain. Again, the papers in this volume provide examples of several types of metonymic model treated by Lakoff (ibid.:12–15). Just as there exists in our minds, against the backdrop of a typical male life course, a stereotype of the sort of man who would deviate from this course to remain a bachelor (ibid.:21), so Holland and Skinner's data argue that their interviewees, conceptualizing interactions between college men and women in terms of how such a relationship typically proceeds, understand individuals who violate the expectations engendered by this canonical relationship in terms of (largely) negative *social stereotypes*. These social stereotypes of various kinds of inept and exploitative men are quite different from interviewees' notions of the (proto)typical man. Price discusses how knowledge about social roles is embedded in *salient examples,* remembered illness episodes that are used to characterize appropriate social role behavior both by exhibiting instances of that behavior and, more dramatically, by elaborating counterexamples. The proposition-schemas about marriage that Quinn enumerates exemplify another type of metonymy – *ideals.* Even though Americans might agree that most marriages are difficult, they would probably not agree that most marriages are enduring. This proposition-schema, that MARRIAGE IS ENDURING, derives not from any notion of the statistically dominant pattern, but from an ideal of the successful marital enterprise. Just as a successful marriage is enduring, a happy marriage is mutually beneficial, and a real marriage is lived jointly (Quinn 1985). Finally – in an example that constitutes an addition to Lakoff's list of metonymic types – Hutchins shows that a myth can be understood as a *symbolic reformulation* of events in life, a culturally given yet disguised representation that serves as a defense mechanism against realization of painful and unacceptable sentiments.

Lakoff's discussion gives us a better sense of why cultural models have the prototypical nature they do: They are constructed out of various types of metonymy. In his words, (1984:11),

> Prototype effects are superficial phenomena. They arise when some subcategory or member or submodel is used (often for some limited and immediate purpose) to comprehend the category as a whole.

In either proposition-schematic or image-schematic form, by way of metaphor or not, cultural models draw on a variety of types of idealized events, actors and other physical entities in these events, and relations among these, all of which are available to our understanding of ordinary experience: the typical, the stereotypical, the salient in memory, the mythic, the ideal successful, the ideal happy, and so on. Just as Fillmore has pointed out that simplified worlds provide the context of our understanding, Lakoff has drawn our attention to the fact that these presupposed worlds are simplified in different ways and that the different types of simplification put our understanding in different perspective.

Any given cultural model may be constructed out of several types of metonymy. We have seen, for example, that the American cultural model of marriage, depending on the metonym in focus, allows propositions about the ideal successful marriage, the ideal happy marriage, and what can be considered a "real" marriage, as well as what the typical marriage is like. All of these ideas are part of the cultural understanding of marriage. Moreover, as is discussed in the final section, the several metonymic types can stand in causal relation to one another, such prototypical causal links yielding the relatively complex chains of event sequences that characterize cultural models. These complexities are constructed out of simple metonymies.

Our discussion of the prototypical nature of cultural models applies equally to our models of these models. Linde (this volume) discusses the interaction between the models of culturally designated "experts," or scientists, and the models of the "folk." Folk models of the world incorporate expert knowledge, as Linde's analysis of life stories shows. Conversely, as suggested by Kay's (this volume) observation that each of the two folk theories of language he identifies has its counterpart in an academic linguistic theory, the former penetrate the latter. As analysts, we cannot expect our "explanatory models" of cultural models, to adopt Caws's (1974) term for them, to be of a wholly different order than the cultural models we seek to explain. Simplification, by means of metonymy, is a feature of both. Nonetheless, by constantly questioning how cultural knowledge is organized, we aspire to a kind of analysis that can be successively improved to capture the native model and the tasks, explanatory and otherwise, to which it is brought by the native user. Not only do we hope to recognize and make explicit the cultural assumptions in our own analytic models, we also hope to minimize the kind of distortion of other people's cultural models that Keesing (this volume) cautions against, that arises from a too-facile reading of metaphysical theories of the world out of formulaic ways of talking.

Cultural models and human cognitive requirements

Given the observation that cultural models are composed of prototypical event sequence set in simplified worlds, we can begin to say something more about the organization of such models and the properties that make them readily learned and shared. In the simplified worlds of cultural models, complicating factors and possible variations are suppressed. In the world of Fillmore's bachelor, males are either old enough to marry or not; and if of marriageable age, they are either already married or yet unmarried – there are no problematic thrice-married divorcés, Sweetser (this volume) points out. As we have seen, the papers in the present volume provide many additional examples of presupposed worlds defined by such simplifying assumptions. In Americans' folk model of the institution, MARRIAGE IS ENDURING; in the folk model of communication that informs our understanding of lying, INFORMATION IS HELPFUL; in our cultural model of the mind, WISHES GIVE RISE TO INTENTIONS; in Americans' model of the emotion of anger, AN OFFENSE TO A PERSON CAUSES ANGER IN THAT PERSON; in the different world of Ifaluk emotion theory, JUSTIFIABLE ANGER IS CAUSE FOR SUICIDE.

Even further, these worlds are ordered and simplified by implicit presuppositions about how such propositions may be linked one to another. In the Ifaluk model of emotion (described in more elegant notation by Lutz, this volume) because MISBEHAVIOR IN ONE PERSON LEADS TO JUSTIFIABLE ANGER IN ANOTHER, and because JUSTIFIABLE ANGER CAN LEAD THE ANGRY PERSON TO REPRIMAND THE PERSON WHO MISBEHAVED, and because A REPRIMAND CAUSES FEAR AND ANXIETY IN ITS RECIPIENT, then it follows that JUSTIFIABLE ANGER IN ONE PERSON OVER ANOTHER'S MISBEHAVIOR PRODUCES FEAR AND ANXIETY IN THE OTHER. In our own culture (Lakoff & Kövecses, this volume), because AN OFFENSE TO A PERSON PRODUCES ANGER IN THAT PERSON, and because RETRIBUTION CANCELS AN OFFENSE, then predictably, ANGER DISAPPEARS WHEN RETRIBUTION IS EXACTED. The predictable sequence of events, played out in the simplified world of the cultural model, allows that world to be characterized not only by proposition-schemas but also in terms of a smaller number of more complex schemas that specify sets of such propositions and the causal relations in which they stand to one another. It is these "causal chainings," to use Abelson's phrase quoted in an earlier section, that give the events occurring in cultural models their quality of unfolding stories. What we need to learn and remember and communicate about the world is vastly reduced by being packaged in such units.

Further, these models articulate with one another in a modular fashion. As D'Andrade (this volume) makes explicit, a given schema may serve as a piece of another schema. D'Andrade uses Fillmore's example of the commercial transaction to make this clear. To know whether BUYING is taking place, one must invoke the other terms of the relationship to judge whether PURCHASER, SELLER, MERCHANDISE, PRICE, OFFER, ACCEPTANCE, and TRANSFER are involved. Each of these components, in turn, is constituted by a complex schema; but one need not know details of each event such as how the price was actually set or whether it was fair, to know that a sale has taken place. The significance of this latter point, D'Andrade argues, is that this hierarchical organization of cultural knowledge is adapted to the requirements of human short-term memory. To perform any particular cognitive task, such as judging whether something has been sold by one person to another, an individual need invoke and hold in mind only a small set of criteria – a number not exceeding the limits of short-term memory storage.

The nestedness of cultural models one within another lends a further, far-reaching economy to cultural knowledge. This hierarchical structure in which models of wide applicability recur as elements of models in many domains of experience has implications for long-term memory as well. These general-purpose models considerably reduce the total amount of cultural knowledge to be mastered. A component model such as BARGAINING – a possible way in which price can be set – presupposes and draws on the BUYING schema within which it is nested. In the same way, nested within the cultural model of anger that Lakoff and Kövecses describe is a more widely applicable cultural model of exchange and balance in human affairs; this more general model includes a schema that yields the proposition RETRIBUTION CANCELS AN OFFENSE. In Quinn's model of American marriage, the proposition-schema, MARRIAGE IS MUTUALLY BENEFICIAL, makes sense in terms of the more widely applicable schema for social relationships, VOLUNTARY RELATIONSHIPS ARE MUTUALLY BENEFICIAL; and, since marriage is distinctive among voluntary relationships in that THE BENEFITS OF MARRIAGE ARE FULFILLMENT OF NEEDS, the knowledge that MARRIAGE IS MUTUALLY BENEFICIAL can be filled in by a further model, of need fulfillment, general to our understanding of the self.

Reliance on general-purpose models for filling in knowledge is perhaps even more striking in the case described by Collins and Gentner, in which subjects were called on to answer questions on a subject – evaporation – about which they were untutored in the scientific model and had available no ready-made common-sense theory. In this situation, the interviewees fell back on their understanding of other physical phenomena and attempted to apply very general principles such as that of a heat threshold or that of molecular attraction drawn from their models of these other phenomena.

Clearly, complex proposition-schemas such as those for bargaining, retributive justice, mutual benefit, need fulfillment, and molecular attraction have application across multiple domains of our experience. The capability of such general-purpose cultural models for filling in the details of other cultural models creates a further simplification. This was demonstrated by Quinn's (this volume) interviewee, who was able to reason about the benefits, difficulty, and enduringness of marriage without having to explain the implicit theory of need fulfillment she knows she shares with her addressee. A great deal can be taken for granted.

Parenthetically, it is just these cultural models of wider applicability, serving as modular components of many other models, that give a culture its distinctiveness. As D'Andrade points out in his volume paper, understanding a culture depends on knowledge of at least these widely incorporated models. Anthropologists have long attempted to capture the distinctiveness of one culture from another in concepts such as that of "cultural themes," or "cultural belief systems," or differing "world views." However, such accounts have typically failed to specify the range of domains in which a given theme, alleged to be central to a culture, applies. Nor have they been able to explicate how such central premises articulate with particular domains of knowledge in which they figure (Clement 1976). The theory of cultural models under construction here promises to identify pervasive cultural premises and to reveal the structural linkages between these premises and the more circumscribed models specific to emotion, problem solving, the mind, gender relations, and the myriad other topics of cultural knowledge.

The account emerging from this volume, then, is one in which cultural understanding is organized into units smaller and simpler in construction and fewer in number than might have been supposed. It is an account that offers a beginning solution to Abelson's "size problem," the problem of how we can learn and use as much knowledge as human beings do. The prototypical scenarios unfolded in the simplified worlds of cultural models, the nestedness of these presupposed models one within another, and the applicability of certain of these models to multiple domains all go far to explain how individuals can learn culture and communicate it to others, so that many come to share the same understandings.

Notes

1. This introduction has benefited immensely from the long, careful readings and comments given an earlier draft by Roy D'Andrade, Edwin Hutchins, Paul Kay, Richard Shweder, and Geoffrey White, as well as from the briefer but telling reactions of Ronald Casson, Susan Hirsch, Alice Ingerson, John Ogbu, and Laurie Price. There are points on which each of these people would still disagree with us. On other points, years of talk with Roy and Ed have sometimes made it difficult to know where our ideas end and theirs begin. Both of them have contributed to our thinking about numerous matters.

2. Also variant in these papers is the plural form of *schema*. The editors recommended to the authors that all adopt a regularized plural, "schemas," in place of the Latin plural, "schemata," which is grammatically correct but awkward for many English speakers. There is precedent for both variants in the cognitive science literature. However, one author, Paul Kay, argued that technically, "schemas" was improper usage. We have honored his wish to use the longer form in his paper.

References

Abelson, R.
  1975. Concepts for representing mundane reality in plans. *In* Representation and Understanding: Studies in Cognitive Science, D. G. Bobrow and A. Collins, eds. New York: Academic Press. Pp. 273–309.

1981. Constraint, construal, and cognitive science. *In* Proceedings of the Third Annual Conference of the Cognitive Science Society. Berkeley: University of California. Pp. 1–9.

Berlin, B. and P. Kay
1969. Basic Color Terms: Their Universality and Evolution. Berkeley: University of California Press.

Bohannan, P.
1957. Justice and Judgment among the Tiv. London: Oxford University Press.

Butters, R.
1981. Do "conceptual metaphors" really exist? Southeastern Conference on Linguistics Bulletin 5(3):108–117.

Casson, R.
1983. Schemata in cognitive anthropology. Annual Review of Anthropology 12:429–462.

Caws, P.
1974. Operational, representational, and explanatory models. American Anthropologist 76(1):1–11.

Clement, D. H.
1976. Cognitive anthropology and applied problems in education. *In* Do Applied Anthropologists Apply Anthropology? M. Angrosino, ed. Athens, Ga: University of Georgia Press. Pp. 53–71.
1982. Samoan folk knowledge of mental disorders. *In* Cultural Conceptions of Mental Health and Therapy, A. J. Marsella and G. White, eds. Dordrecht, Holland: D. Reidel Publishing Company. Pp. 193–215.

Coleman, L. and P. Kay
1981. Prototype semantics: The English verb *lie*. Language 57(1):26–44.

D'Andrade, R.
1965. Trait psychology and componential analysis. American Anthropologist 67(5,2):215–228.
1974. Memory and the assessment of behavior. *In* Measurement in the Social Sciences, H. Blalock, ed. Chicago: Aldine-Atherton. Pp. 159–186.
1976. A propositional analysis of U.S. American beliefs about illness. *In* Meaning in Anthropology, K. H. Basso and H. A. Selby, eds. Albuquerque: University of New Mexico Press. Pp. 155–180.
1981. The cultural part of cognition. Cognitive Science 5(3):179–195.
1982. Reason versus logic. Paper presented at symposium, The Ecology of Cognition: Biological, Cultural, and Historical Perspectives, April, Greensboro, N.C.
1984a. Cultural meaning systems. *In* Culture Theory: Essays on Mind, Self, and Emotion, R. Shweder and R. LeVine, eds. Cambridge, England: Cambridge University Press. Pp. 88–119.
1984b. Cultural models and person perception. Washington, D.C.: Progress Report to the Anthropology Program, National Science Foundation.
1985. Character terms and cultural models. *In* New Directions in Cognitive Anthropology, J. Dougherty, ed. Urbana: University of Illinois Press. Pp. 321–343.
n.d. Culture and personality: A false dichotomy. Unpublished manuscript, Department of Anthropology, University of California, San Diego.

D'Andrade, R., N. Quinn, S. B. Nerlove, and A. K. Romney
1972. Categories of disease in American–English and Mexican–Spanish. *In* Multidimensional Scaling, Theory and Applications in the Behavioral Sciences, Vol. 2: Applications, A. K. Romney, R. N. Shepard, and S. B. Nerlove, eds. New York: Seminar Press. Pp. 9–54.

Early, E. A.
1982. The logic of well being: Therapeutic narratives of Cairo. Social Science and Medicine 16(4):1491-1498.
Fillmore, C.
1975. An alternative to checklist theories of meaning. *In* Proceedings of the First Annual Meeting of the Berkeley Linguistics Society, C. Cogen, H. Thompson, G. Thurgood, K. Whistler, and J. Wright, eds. Berkeley: University of California. Pp. 123-131.
1977. Topics in lexical semantics. *In* Current Issues in Linguistic Theory, R. W. Cole, ed. Bloomington: Indiana University Press. Pp. 76-138.
1982. Towards a descriptive framework for spatial deixis. *In* Speech, Place, and Action, R. J. Jarvella and W. Klein, eds. New York: John Wiley and Sons. Pp. 31-59.
Fjellman, S.
1976. Talking about talking about residence: An Akamba case. American Ethnologist 3(4):671-682.
Frake, C. O.
1975. How to enter a Yakan house. *In* Sociocultural Dimensions of Language Use, M. Sanches and B. Blount, eds. New York: Academic Press. Pp. 25-40.
1977. Plying frames can be dangerous: Some reflections on methodology in cognitive anthropology. Quarterly Newsletter of the Institute for Comparative Human Development 1(3):1-7.
Geertz, C.
1966. Religion as a cultural system. *In* Anthropological Approaches to the Study of Religion, M. Banton, ed. A.S.A. Monographs 3. London: Tavistock Publications. Pp. 1-46.
Gentner, D. and D. R. Gentner
1983. Flowing waters or teeming crowds: Mental models of electricity. *In* Mental Models, D. Gentner, and A. L. Stevens, eds. Hillsdale, N.J.: Lawrence Erlbaum Associates. Pp. 99-129.
Geoghegan, W.
1969. Decision-making and residence on Tagtabon Island. Language-Behavior Research Laboratory Working Paper No. 17. Berkeley: University of California.
Gladwin, H. and C. Gladwin
1971. Estimating market conditions and profit expectations of fish sellers in Cape Coast, Ghana. *In* Studies in Economic Anthropology, G. Dalton, ed. Anthropological Studies No. 7. Washington, D.C.: American Anthropological Association. Pp. 122-142.
Good, B. J. and M.-J. D. Good
1982. Toward a meaning-centered analysis of popular illness categories: 'Fright-illness' and 'heart distress' in Iran. *In* Cultural Conceptions of Mental Health and Therapy, A. Marsella and G. White, eds. Dordrecht, Holland: D. Reidel Publishing Company. Pp. 141-166.
Goodenough, W. H.
1957. Cultural anthropology and linguistics. *In* Report of the Seventh Annual Round Table Meeting in Linguistics and Language Study, P. Garvin, ed. Monograph Series on Language and Linguistics, No. 9. Washington, D.C.: Georgetown University. Pp. 167-173.
Harris, M.
1968. The Rise of Anthropological Theory. New York: Thomas Y. Crowell Company.

Holland, D.
1982. Conventional metaphors in human thought and language. Review article, Metaphors We Live By, by G. Lakoff and M. Johnson. Reviews in Anthropology 9(3):287–297.
1985. From situation to impression: How Americans get to know themselves and one another. In Directions in Cognitive Anthropology, J. Dougherty, ed. Urbana: University of Illinois Press. Pp. 389–411.
Holland, D. and D. Skinner
1985. The meaning of metaphors in gender stereotyping. North Carolina Working Papers in Culture and Cognition No. 3. Durham, N.C.: Duke University Department of Anthropology.
Holy, L.
1979. Segmentary lineage structure and its existential status. In Segmentary Lineage Systems Reconsidered, L. Holy, ed. Queen's University Papers in Social Anthropology 4. Belfast: Queen's University. Pp. 1–22.
Holy, L. and M. Stuchlik
1981a. The Structure of Folk Models. A.S.A. Monographs 20. New York: Academic Press.
1981b. The structure of folk models. In The Structure of Folk Models, L. Holy and M. Stuchlik, eds. A.S.A. Monographs 20. New York: Academic Press. Pp. 1–35.
Howe, J. and J. Scherzer
1975. Take and tell: A practical classification from the San Blas Cuna. American Ethnologist 2(3):435–460.
Hutchins, E.
1980. Culture and Inference: A Trobriand Case Study. Cambridge, Mass.: Harvard University Press.
Jenkins, R.
1981. Thinking and doing: Towards a model of cognitive practice. In The Structure of Folk Models, L. Holy and M. Stuchlik, eds. A.S.A. Monographs 20. New York: Academic Press. Pp. 93–119.
Johnson, A.
1974. Ethnoecology and planting practices in a swidden agricultural system. American Ethnologist 1(1):87–101.
Johnson-Laird, P. and M. Steedman
1978. The psychology of syllogisms. Cognitive Psychology 10(1):64–99.
Jorion, P.
1978. Marks and rabbit furs: Location and sharing of grounds in coastal fishing. Peasant Studies 7(2):86–100.
Katz, J. and J. Fodor
1963. The structure of a semantic theory. Language 39(2):170–210.
Kay, P. and C. McDaniel
1978. The linguistic significance of the meanings of basic color terms. Language 54(3):610–646.
Keesing, R. M.
1974. Theories of culture. Annual Review of Anthropology 3:73–97.
Lakoff, G.
1981. Introductory remarks. Paper presented at conference, Cognitive Science, Language, and Imagery, May, Berkeley, California.
1984. Classifiers as a reflection of mind: A cognitive model approach to prototype theory. Berkeley Cognitive Science Report No. 19. Berkeley: University of California Institute of Human Learning.
Lakoff, G. and M. Johnson
1980. Metaphors We Live By. Chicago: University of Chicago Press.

Langacker, R. W.
 1979. Grammar as image. Paper presented at conference, Neurolinguistics and
 Cognition, Program in Cognitive Science, March, University of California,
 San Diego.
Lave, J., A. Stepick, and L. Sailer
 1977. Extending the scope of formal analysis. American Ethnologist 4(2):321–
 339.
Levi-Strauss, C.
 1953. Social structure. In Anthropology Today, A. L. Kroeber, ed. Chicago:
 University of Chicago Press.
Lewontin, R. C., S. Rose, and L. J. Kamin
 1984. Not in Our Genes: Biology, Ideology, and Human Nature. New York:
 Pantheon Books.
Linde, C.
 1978. The organization of discourse. Ch. 4 in Style and Variables in English,
 T. Shopen and J. M. Williams, eds. Cambridge, Mass.: Winthrop Publishers.
 Pp. 84–114.
 n.d. The creation of coherence in life stories. Unpublished manuscript in
 preparation, Structural Semantics, Palo Alto.
Mathews, H.
 (in press). Predicting decision outcomes: Have we put the cart before the horse
 in anthropological studies of decision making? Human Organization.
Nardi, B.
 1983. Goals in reproductive decision making. American Ethnologist 10(4):
 697–715.
Quinn, N.
 1981. Marriage is a do-it-yourself project: The organization of marital goals.
 In Proceedings of the Third Annual Conference of the Cognitive Science Society, Berkeley: University of California. Pp. 31–40.
 1982a. Cognitive anthropology comes of age in the Trobriands. Review article,
 Culture and Inference: A Trobriand Case Study, by E. Hutchins. Reviews
 in Anthropology 9(3):299–311.
 1982b. "Commitment" in American marriage: A cultural analysis. American
 Ethnologist 9(4):775–798.
 1985. American marriage through metaphors: A cultural analysis. North Carolina
 Working Papers in Culture and Cognition No. 1. Durham, N.C.: Duke University Department of Anthropology.
Randall, R.
 1976. How tall is a taxonomic tree? Some evidence for dwarfism. American
 Ethnologist 3(3):543–553.
Rosch, E.
 1977. Human categorization. In Studies in Cross-cultural Psychology, Vol. 1,
 N. Warren, ed. London: Academic Press. Pp. 3–49.
 1978. Principles of categorization. In Cognition and Categorization, E. Rosch
 and B. Lloyd, eds. Hillsdale, N.J.: Lawrence Erlbaum Associates. Pp. 27–48.
Ryle, G.
 1949. The Concept of Mind. London: Hutchinson House.
Salzman, P. C.
 1981. Culture as enhabilmentis. In The Structure of Folk Models, L. Holy and
 M. Stuchlik, eds. A.S.A. Monographs 20. New York: Academic Press. Pp.
 233–257.
Schank, R.
 1982. Dynamic Memory: A Theory of Reminding and Learning in Computers
 and People. Cambridge, England: Cambridge University Press.

Schank, R. and R. Abelson
  1977. Scripts, Plans, Goals and Understanding: An Inquiry into Human Knowledge Structures. Hillsdale, N.J.: Lawrence Erlbaum Associates.
Sperber, D.
  1975. Rethinking Symbolism. Cambridge, England: Cambridge University Press.
  (First published in 1974 as Le Symbolisme en Général.)
Spiro, M.
  1961. Social systems, personality, and functional analysis. *In* Studying Personality Cross-Culturally, B. Kaplan, ed. New York: Harper and Row Publishers.
  Pp. 93–127.
Ward, B. E.
  1965. Varieties of the conscious model: The fishermen of South China. *In* The
  Relevance of Models for Social Anthropology, M. Banton, ed. A.S.A. Monographs 1. London: Tavistock Publications. Pp. 113–137.
  1966. Sociological self-awareness: Some uses of the conscious models. Man
  1(2):201–215.
White, G.
  1982. The ethnographic study of cultural knowledge of 'mental disorder.' *In*
  Cultural Conceptions of Mental Health and Therapy, A. J. Marsella and G.
  White, eds. Dordrecht, Holland: D. Reidel Publishing Company. Pp. 69–97.
  1985. Premises and purposes in a Solomon Island ethnopsychology. *In* Person,
  Self and Experience: Exploring Pacific Ethnopsychologies, G. White and J.
  Kirkpatrick, eds. Berkeley: University of California Press. Pp. 328–366.
Young, A.
  1981. Rational men and the explanatory model approach. Culture, Medicine
  and Psychiatry 6(1):57–73.

PART I
Presupposed worlds, language, and discourse

2

The definition of lie

AN EXAMINATION OF THE FOLK MODELS
UNDERLYING A SEMANTIC PROTOTYPE[1]

Eve E. Sweetser

This paper investigates how the semantic structure of one English word
depends on, and reflects, our models of relevant areas of experience. As
a linguist, my original concern was with the problems posed by the word
lie for traditional semantic theories; but these problems led inexorably to
the cultural models of informational exchange that motivate the existence
of a semantic entity meaning *lie*.[2] I begin by posing the semantic problem
and go on to the cultural solution.

George Lakoff (1972), Fillmore (1977), and Coleman and Kay (1981)
have argued against traditional generative and structuralist "checklists"
of semantic features that constitute necessary and sufficient conditions
for set-membership in the category denoted by a word. Lexical categories
can have better or worse members, or *partial* members.[3] Kay and
McDaniel (1978) have shown that color categories lack necessary and sufficient conditions; *red* is a gradient quality whose category-boundaries
are best described by fuzzy set theory rather than by traditional set theory.
Checklist feature-definitions, which do not allow for color's being "sorta
red," must be replaced by a theory capable of dealing with fuzzy set-
membership. Prototype semantics views word-meaning as determined by
a central or prototypical application, rather than a category-boundaries.
Clear definitions can thus be given for words with fuzzy boundaries of
application. We define the best instance of a word's use, and expect real-
world cases to fit this best example more or less, rather than perfectly or
not at all.

Coleman and Kay (1981) show that prototype theory is needed to explain the usage of the verb *lie*.[4] As is natural in prototype semantics (but
not in traditional set-membership semantics), lying is a matter of more
or less. Clear central cases of lies occur when all of Coleman and Kay's
proposed conditions are fulfilled; namely, (a) speaker believes statement
is false; (b) speaker intends to deceive hearer by making the statement;
and (c) the statement is false in fact. Conversely, a statement fulfilling
none of a-c is a clear nonlie. But when only one or two of a-c hold,
speakers are frequently confused and find it difficult to categorize an action as lie or nonlie. Further, these conditions (unlike checklist-features)

differ in weight, (a) being strongest and (c) weakest in influencing speakers' categorization of acts as lies.

Prototype semantics has been attentive to the grounding of language in the speaker's world. Kay and McDaniel found physical perceptual reasons for color–term universals; Rosch (1978) and Mervis and Rosch (1981) demonstrate that linguistic categories depend on general human category-formation abilities. Fillmore (1977) discusses some ways in which the *social* world shapes word–meaning. *Bachelor* is a classic difficult case: Why is it difficult to say whether the Pope, or a thrice-married divorcé, can be called a bachelor? The answer, Fillmore says, is that *bachelor* depends on a simplified world-view in which people are marriageable at a certain age, mostly marry at that age, and stay married to the same spouse. In this simplified world, a bachelor is simply any unmarried male past marriageable age; *outside* the simplified world, the word *bachelor* just does not apply. *Bachelor* necessarily evokes a prototypical schema of marriage within our cultural model of a life-history.

I argue that like *bachelor, lie* is inherently grounded in a simplified or prototypical schema of certain areas of human experience. This, I suggest, is why Coleman and Kay found that *lie* needs a prototype definition. Basing my analysis on their experimental findings, I motivate those findings by relating them to work on discourse pragmatics and conversational postulates. It is necessary to examine folk understandings of knowledge, evidence, and proof; our cultural model of language (or at least of lying) cannot be analyzed independently of beliefs about information. I hope to show that *lie* has a simpler definition than thas been thought, in a more complex context; since the cultural–model context for a definition of *lie* is independently necessary, our analysis is simplified overall.

A cultural model of language

Is there a simplified "prototypical" speech–act world, as there is a simplified marriage history? Although such a world has not been examined in detail, Kay (1983) suggests that the word *technically* evokes a "folk theory" of language use that assumes that experts are the arbiters of correct word-use. Grice's (1975) conversational maxims, and Searle's (1969) felicity-conditions, are constraints on the appropriateness of utterances – speakers are assumed to follow these rules in the default situation.

Kay's folk theories, Grice's maxims, and Searle's felicity-conditions all describe parts of our cultural understanding of discourse-interaction. Grice's "Be as informative as necessary," for example, is a maxim of which speakers are conscious; one can criticize an interlocutor for informational insufficiency. But informational content is irrelevant to a speech activity such as joke-telling. Robin Lakoff's (1973) work on politeness rules and Goffman's (1974) work on frame semantics show that conversation often has its primary purposes at the level of social interaction; making someone happy, or negotiating the interaction–frame, may be a more important goal than informativeness. The maxim of informationality is thus binding precisely to the degree that we consider ourselves to be operating in a simplified world in which discourse is informational, so that the default purpose of an utterance is *not* joking, politeness, or frame–bargaining. Our covert discourse–purposes are only made possible by a cultural model that establishes our overt purpose as informational; frame–bargaining, and most indirect speech, depend on having "direct" speech say something else.

I sketch some relevant aspects of our folk understanding of informational language-use and then use this cultural model to explain the meaning of *lie* as presented by Coleman and Kay. First, let us posit two basic principles as parts of our model of general social interaction rather than of our specific model of speech acts. These principles, which are assumed to operate in the default case (like Gricean maxims), are (1) Try to help, not harm and (2) Knowledge is beneficial. Together, the two principles yield the result that giving knowledge (since it is beneficial) is part of a general goal of helping others. Thus, in cases in which (2) is true, (1) translates at least partly as (3) Try to inform others.

The rules just proposed constitute the cultural motivation for a folk understanding of language as informational. Before going on to a folk theory of knowledge and information, one issue needs clarification: the status of these cultural models, or folk theories. What does it mean to say that language is assumed to be informational in the "default" case? I do not mean that purely informational discourse is statistically more common than, or acquisitionally prior to, other kinds of discourse; indeed, it would be hard to separate discourse modes cleanly, since one utterance may have multiple purposes. However, the informational mode is the "direct" mode on which indirect speech is parasitic; and it may be viewed as more basic in the sense that all discourse involves the conveyance of information (if only about a speaker's intentional state), whereas not all discourse participates in all of the other purposes of language use. Our cultural model presents this "basic" discourse–mode, which is a vehicle for other modes, as being *in its pure form* the unmarked mode, the *norm*.

Unlike maxims and conditions, this cultural model does not constitute rules of language use, but rather beliefs about what we do when we use language. These beliefs in turn make general social rules applicable to the domain of discourse: Grice's maxim of informationality is the manifestation of a general "Help not harm" maxim, in a simplified (folk–model) world in which information is always helpful. Now, on to our cultural model of information.

A folk theory of information and evidence

Any truth-conditional semantics assumes that we can "know" the propositional content of "true" statements; this begs the vexed question of what knowledge is. I intend to pass over the philosophers' view of knowledge and instead examine our cultural idea of what *counts* as knowledge, since this is what underlies our understanding of lies and truths in discourse.

Clearly, we do not imagine that all our beliefs can be proven logically. Nonetheless, we consider our beliefs sufficiently justified, and we are not really worried that their truth is not known from logical proof (few of "us" speakers know formal logic) or personal experience. Evaluation of evidence is thus frequently an important issue: "knowledge" is not so much a relationship between a "fact" (= true proposition) and a knower as a socially agreed-on evidential status given by a knower to a proposition.

Rappaport (1976) demonstrates just how "social" the difference between *statement* and *truth,* between *belief* and *knowledge,* really is. He observes that a normative standard of truthfulness in informational exchange is essential to ensure that our belief–system (and our social existence) is not constantly undermined by distrust of new input. (Actual statistical likelihood of a random statement's truth is irrelevant to this norm.) He argues that a central function of liturgy and ritual is to transform a statement or belief into accepted, universal truth – that is, into something that can be unconditionally believed and treated as reliable.

Rappaport is mainly concerned with social "facts," not with such falsifiable information as "Ed is in Ohio." But let's remember that knowledge has many socially acceptable ("valid") sources – and that we do not in fact tidily separate messy socially based knowledge from clean falsifiable facts. We know promises can get broken – yet certain ritual aspects of oaths and promises still make us treat them as extratrustworthy, maintaining our social norm of truthfulness. Or, take a modern scholar who "knows" Marx's or Adam Smith's economic teachings – this "knowledge" may seem to a cynic as faith-based as religious belief, but that does not prevent a whole community of social scientists from acting on it as fact. Hard scientific knowledge and evidence often turn out to be as paradigm–dependent as social-science argumentation. What is crucial is not whether scientists always have objectively true hypotheses, but that any society agrees on a range of socially acceptable methods of justifying belief; without such agreement, intellectual cooperation would be impossible.

What counts as evidence or authority is thus a cultural question. In reply to a college student's scoffs at a medieval philosopher who appealed to classical authority, I once heard a professor ask how the student "knew" what Walter Cronkite had told him. Many natural languages formally mark with evidential markers the difference between direct and indirect (linguistically or logically mediated) experience, and/or between various sensory modalities as sources of a statement's information. Some priority or preference seems to be given universally to both direct experience (especially visual) and culturally accepted ("universal") truths. But failing these best sources of universal truth or personal experience, we trust some input more than others; and we constantly make (nonlogical) deductions based on our observations of correlations in the world. We do not bother to distinguish these generally trustworthy deductions from "fact" except when observed correlations break down and deductions fail.

Whatever our rules of practical everyday inference are like, we trust them, in the default case. Thus, belief is normally taken as having adequate justification, and hence as equivalent to knowledge, which would entail truth. Gordon (1974) demonstrates the close, complex relationship of belief and knowledge in our cultural understanding; he shows that, in adult as well as child use, factivity of verbs such as *know* is not fixed, especially if the person said to "know" is not the speaker. A theory of knowledge as a cultural status given to certain beliefs is more compatible with this flexibility than is a theory of knowledge as a link between an objective fact and a person's mind.

In our cultural model of knowledge, the default case is thus for belief to entail justification and hence truth. Conversely, untruth will entail lack of evidence and impossibility of belief. Let us combine these entailments with the informational model of language. I start with a norm-establishing "meta-maxim":

(0) People normally obey rules (this is the default case).

Our general cooperative rule is:

(1) *Rule:* Try to help, not harm.

Combined with a belief such as (2), we can instantiate (1) as a Gricean conversational rule of informativeness, as in (3):

(2) Knowledge is beneficial, helpful. (*Corollary:* Misinformation is harmful.)
(3) *Rule:* Give knowledge (inform others); do not misinform.

Our model of knowledge and information gives us the following proof of (6) from (4) and (5):

(4) Beliefs have adequate justification.
(5) Adequately justified beliefs are knowledge (= are true).
(6) ∴ Beliefs are true (are knowledge).

(6) allows us to reinterpret our helpfulness–rule (3) yet *again:*

(7) *Rule:* Say what you believe (since belief = knowledge); do not say what you do not believe (this = misinformation).

The hearer, in this cultural model, is presumed ready to believe the speaker; why refuse help from a speaker who is assumed to be not only helpful but also well-informed (having well-justified beliefs)? Putting together the whole chain of entailments, we reach the startling conclusion that (in the simplified world of our cultural model) the speaker's saying something entails the truth of the thing said:

(a) *S* said *X*.
(b) *S* believes *X*. (a) plus (7) and the meta-maxim)
(c) ∴ *X* is true. (b) plus (6))

Logically (outside our model), or statistically, this conclusion is rubbish. But as a folk model of language by which we all operate from day to day, it makes good sense – in fact, it seems doubtful that we could ever live our lives questioning the truth of every statement presented to us. We question truth if we fear that our simplified discourse–world is too far from reality: when our source might be ill-informed (a broken link between belief and justification), naïve (breaking the entailment between justification/ evidence and truth), or might want to deceive us (invalidating our assumption that folks are out to help, and so wish to inform correctly). Note that even in these cases, the usual cultural model is in effect: We know our interlocutor *expects* us to take what is said as an instance of information–giving. But in general, we take people's word.

The next section examines cases in which we should not take someone's word; we now look at lying in the simplified discourse–setting established by our cultural understanding of linguistic exchange as informational.

Prevarication in a simplified world

Coleman and Kay proposed three components of a prototype–definition of *lie:*

1. Speaker believes statement to be false.
2. Speaker said it with intent to deceive.
3. The statement is false in fact.

Now, in the simplified world we have outlined, any one of these conditions would entail the others. In particular, if we assume both a folk model of evidence in which a speaker's belief constitutes evidence of truth and a model of discourse as informational (intending to be believed), then we find that a factually false statement must be known to be false by the speaker, and (if made) must be intended to induce (false) belief and thus to deceive. The reasoning runs as follows:

> *Premise: X* is false.
>
> So *S* did not believe *X,* since beliefs are true.
>
> Therefore *S* intended to misinform, since we know that in order to inform one says only what one believes.

Further, assuming that even *un*informative speakers do not randomly discuss areas in which they have no beliefs (people act *purposefully*), we can go beyond "*S* did not believe *X*" to assert "*S* believed *X* to be false." We do not premise the meta-maxim that *S* is obeying the rules, since *S*'s obedience to the Cooperative Principle is precisely what we are trying to prove or disprove.

Figure 2.1 gives a taxonomy of speech settings; the box on the right encloses the idealized informational–discourse world. *Lie* must be defined within this restricted world; outside of this world, the word lacks application. Only within this world can the hearer properly link utterance with informativeness, sincerity, and factual truth. The feature [+ Truth Value Relevant] on the tree indicates that the informational–exchange view of language is in effect; when truth value is relevant, knowledge is beneficial

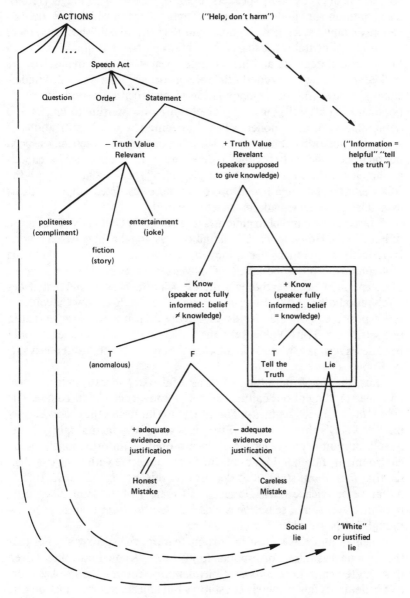

Figure 2.1. A taxonomy of speech settings

and informing helpful. [+ Know] indicates that our folk theory of knowledge and evidence is in effect; when belief is justified and hence true, the speaker can be assumed to have knowledge about what is said.

Thus, we can define *lie* as a false statement, if we assume the statement occurs in a prototypical (informational) speech setting. This definition is elegant and would also help explain why native speakers tend to define *lie* as a false statement. Not only is this the first definition given "out of the blue" by many speakers, but it is (according to Piaget (1932)), also common for children to pass through a stage in which *lie* is used to denote any false statement. Wimmer and Perner's (unpublished data) more recent experimental work shows that children up to age nine class "good faith" false statements and lies as alike, even when they themselves are tricked into being the "good faith" false informer. Four-year-olds understand sabotage (physical manipulation to obstruct a precondition of an opponent's goal) well; but five-year-olds are only starting to understand manipulation of an opponent's belief–system. The social motivations of such manipulation entail an understanding of the speech setting as social interaction. Children only come to differentiate lies from other falsehoods as they learn the sociocultural background of speaking and acquire the folk theories that are a backdrop to the more restricted adult use of *lie* as a false statement made in a certain world.[5]

A fascinating parallel to child usage is found in Gulliver's explanation of lying to the Houynhnms. His definition, "saying the thing which is not," is perfectly comprehensible to him, but proves incomprehensible to the Houynhnms, precisely because (as Gulliver says) they have little experience of deception in any area; they lack the sociocultural background that makes a falsehood a lie. Adult English speakers (like Gulliver) have a complex set of possible discourse–worlds (cf. Figure 2.1); it is not strange that in one setting (+ Truth Value Relevant, − Know) a false statement should be called a *mistake,* whereas in another setting (+ Truth Value Relevant, + Know) a false statement is a *lie.*

Thus, the simple definition of *lie* as a false statement is natural given an understanding of our cultural model of knowledge and discourse. The taxonomy of speech settings in Figure 2.1 also motivates the order of Coleman and Kay's three features. First, it is clear why factual falsity is the least important feature. Outside of the prototypical (informational) speech environment, falsehood is not particularly connected with lying (we shall see that *lie's moral* status also depends on this setting; for now, suffice it that we experience a false statement differently when factors like truth–relevance vary). In a sense, *lie* is closer to *tell the truth* than to *joke,* although jokes are often factually false.

Coleman and Kay's most important feature, the speaker's belief that the statement is false, corresponds to my + / − Know branching: Given that a statement *is* false (*another* Coleman/Kay feature), the speaker's correct belief in its falsity merely constitutes full and correct information (the informational part of our simplified cultural model of discourse). Being the first tree-branching above the box enclosing the simplified world, this feature is most important in speakers' judgments as to whether we are in that world (and hence whether the term *lie* applies). The next tree-branching, $+/-$ Truth Value Relevant, corresponds to Coleman and Kay's "intent to deceive"; a falsehood can only intend to deceive if truth value is assumed to be relevant (information = beneficial) – not if we are joking or story-telling. This branching is above the $+/-$ Know branching and farther from the break between the simplified world and other worlds – so it is a less important feature in a definition that crucially depends on that break.

Coleman and Kay's least important feature is the definitional one: factual falsity. In the environment of their experiment, which actively stretched speakers' consideration beyond the prototypical informational setting, falsehood does not distinguish lies as a unified class. Within the simplified world, however, truth value criterially distinguishes between the two possible kinds of speech act – hence falsehood becomes the defining characteristic of *lie,* and native speakers reasonably cite it as such.

Thomason (1983) (who also tries to ground Coleman and Kay's analysis in the speech setting) adds two more features to the semantic prototype of *lie:* "unjustifiability of belief" and "reprehensibleness of motive." However, he himself remarks that unjustified belief in the truth of X directly conflicts with "speaker believes X is false," which he retains; how could both be part of the meaning of *lie?* Under my analysis, the general maxims enjoining us to inform will also condemn misinformation, even if not deliberate. Thus, unjustified statements will automatically be judged as *like* lies in some ways (without changing our definition of *lie* = false statement in prototypical informative setting). Mere unjustified (sincere) belief does not, however, greatly contribute to my actual *classification* of even a *false* statement as a lie. Furthermore, if "unjustified belief" were part of a definition of *lie,* then even *true,* sincere, unjustified statements would have to be considered lies to some degree: not a promising result of an admittedly self-contradictory definition of *lie.* The informationality maxims give a more general, coherent explanation of any perceived likeness between lies and unjustified statements. We shall see that Thomason's proposed feature of reprehensibility also follows from a more general understanding of informational exchange and is superfluous to a definition of *lie.*

Notice how rules and maxims change form as they change setting: The general "Help don't harm" is manifested as "Inform others" in the setting in which information/truth is the most relevant beneficial factor. In the domain of politeness, the same general supermaxim is manifested as R. Lakoff's (1973) politeness rules. This model agrees, I think, with our experience: Both information and politeness are considered good and helpful (in their contexts), although in fact the two may conflict when we are unsure which setting takes priority.

A lie, then, is a false statement made in a simplified informational-exchange setting. All rules enjoining veracity are in effect, and the speaker is a fully knowledgeable imparter of information to a credulous hearer. *Lie* has a simple definition within a matrix of cultural models that are independently necessary. The prototype seems to be in the context, rather than in the definition itself. Speakers have difficulty judging whether an action is a lie when they are not sure the action's setting sufficiently matches the prototypical setting specified by the cultural model of informational exchange.[6] The next section fits a larger sector of English vocabulary into the cultural model we have outlined; I then go on to motivate our moral condemnation of lying in terms of our cultural models as well.

Less simplified worlds, less simple words

English has words for false nonlies, or palliated/justified lies. These words mark deviations from the simplified world of the cultural model; thus, examining the deviations may elucidate the model. Common terms include *white lie, social lie, exaggeration, oversimplification, tall tale, fiction, fib,* and (*honest* or *careless*) *mistake,* some of which appear in Figure 2.1.

First, as stressed in the previous section, a lie is not committed if truth is irrelevant. Thus *jokes, kidding,* and *leg-pullings,* which exist in a world where humor rather than information is the basic goal, are outside the informational model and cannot be considered lies. Of course, every culture also has a model for humor, and humorous discourse (like all speech) uses some aspects of the informational model. When we cannot decide which model predominates in a given situation, we ask the common (and intelligible) question, "*How* serious was that remark?" Seriousness characterizes contexts, not statements; the same remark may be serious or not, depending on context. Since interlocutors constantly negotiate context (including the predominance of informational or humorous goals), one may ask about a statement's seriousness, meaning the speaker's perception of its micro-discourse context.

Tall tales, fiction, and *fantasy,* when not referring to literature, palliate falsehoods by looking at them as literary, rather than as prototypically informational. The discourse in question is looked at more as a story (with a goal of artistic entertainment) than as facts with relevant truth values. Grandpa's *tall tales* of fifty-foot snowfalls in his childhood are fun and harmless. Similar claims in a history book, however, would be *mistakes,* to say the least. Tall tales of huge fish I caught are *lies* if we are still on the fishing trip and I convince you there is fish for dinner when there is not. I personally only use *fantasy* and *fiction* to refer to literature (or to internal, unspoken fantasizing). When *fantasy* refers to a false statement, however, it seems not only to mean a more artistic story than the truth, but also to include an element of *self*-deception that further palliates the offense of deceiving others. Any departure from the prototypical informational setting, such as weakened truth–value relevance (literary, not informative goals) or less complete control of facts by the speaker, can make the difference between our judging a falsehood as a lie (within the simplified informational world) or as something else (in some other world), such as a tall tale.

Mistakes are cases in which, without speakers' knowledge, the normal chain of entailment from belief to truth breaks down. Both speaker and hearer think they are in the simplified world delineated by cultural models of knowledge and evidence, but there is an unknown deviation. For an *honest mistake,* in particular, the entailment between belief and evidence *does* hold: The speaker has normally sufficient reason to believe what was said. *Carelessness* is charged if the broken entailment is between belief and evidence – the speaker should have realized the evidence was insufficient, but failed to. Speakers are responsible for evaluating evidence, so we blame irresponsibility where we would not blame an honest mistake. In either case, however, we assume that the rules *ought* to hold: *Mistake* marks a *disruption* of our simplified informational world's assumptions, rather than an agreed-on *suspension* (in favor of other goals), as in the case of *joke. Lie,* on the other hand, denotes a wrong moral choice, with no disruption or suspension of the informational model.

As further indication that speech acts are subcases of actions (rather than some separate, parallel category), note that the same word *mistake* denotes both an unintentional falsehood and a wrong turn taken, or a typo. Ideally, we should be able to justify *any* act, speech or otherwise; the graver the consequences, the higher the standards for justification. But blameless wrong choices do occur; and if we did our best with available information and resources, unintentional harm can be forgiven. The category *mistake* is a recognition of human frailty as an allowable out.

In *exaggerations, oversimplifications, understatements,* and other *distortions,* the informational–exchange rules are more or less consciously bent, rather than suspended or disrupted. Such cases do not strictly follow the dictates of our cultural model; we feel we are being less informational (less truthful) than we might be, hence less helpful. But distortions are not necessarily in direct opposition to truth; they may indicate a subjective personal reaction better than the strict truth could, and hence be truthful at another level. Or, it may be more informational for an expert to oversimplify than to fail totally to communicate with a nonexpert. Many such distortions are indisputably literally false. Whether we judge them as lies depends on (1) whether the setting is prototypically informational and (2) if so, whether they advance or obstruct the informational goals of interaction.

White lies and *social lies* are generally like lies, but they occur in settings in which information might harm rather than help. They are still called lies: even nonreprehensible, deliberate misinformation counts as a lie. In these cases, the entailments of speaker's knowledge, evidence, and intent to be believed (seriousness) still hold; likewise the supermaxim "Help don't harm" holds; but the usual helpfulness of truth cannot be assumed.

For a social lie, the politeness maxims have superseded the injunction to truthfulness. Truth is seen as more harmful to the social situation than minor misinformation would be. In the case of white lies, truth might harm in some other, sometimes more direct, way: Some people would call it a white lie to tell a dying person whatever he or she needs to hear to die in peace. Some speakers would also call a (less altruistic) lie told in self-defense a white lie if it helped them and hurt nobody else. As with politeness, self-defense is clearly only supposed to be allowed to supersede the informational mode if the consequences of the resulting deception are small. The compounds *white lie* and *social lie* show in their two elements the conflicting worlds in which the actions take place (it is a lie as an informational utterance, but it is *also* a social utterance). Figure 2.1 puts them under more than one heading to show this dual categorization.[7]

There are lies which most people would think justified by some higher good achieved but which would not be called white lies, since their informational consequences are too major (however moral) for us to diminish their status as lies. I would think it moral to lie to the Gestapo about the location of a Jew, but I would call that an unqualified lie. The informational paradigm is fully, even saliently, in effect in this instance – it is only that we feel our uncooperativeness to be justified.

Last and least, a *fib* is a small or inconsequential lie, and thus a palliated offense, since the seriousness of an offense of lying is a function of its harmful consequences. However, a fib is nonetheless an offense (though minor) in that it is considered to have at most only a selfish and unimportant reason for overriding the usual motivations for veracity.

This brings us to the question of the importance of a falsehood or a deception. As Coleman and Kay observe, we can only judge major versus minor deviations from the truth in terms of human consequences. They contrast an error in the millions column of a city's population (a deception) with an error in the ones column (no deception, because it has no serious consequences). It is clearly only felt allowable to override the truth-is-beneficial maxim when the truth–violation could have no negative consequences as serious as the negative results of truthfulness. A social lie cannot be justified as polite (hence helpful) if it gravely and harmfully misinforms. When truth is more important than politeness, the informational mode cannot be overridden. This merely repeats that our judgement of a lie depends on the extent to which the relevant cultural models are in effect.

Knowledge as power: the morality of lying

The cultural models relevant to lying also help explain the generally accepted reprehensibility of lies. Coleman and Kay, noting that a lie is no more or less a lie because of reprehensible motives on the speaker's part (consider my Gestapo example as a case of a real lie with good motives), decide that such motives are typical rather than prototypical of lying. That is, lies tend in the real world to be selfishly motivated, just as real surgeons currently tend to be male; but one cannot claim that maleness is in any way part of the *meaning* of *surgeon*.

Placed in the framework of cultural models of discourse and information, the variable reprehensibility of lies follows naturally. To the extent that information really is beneficial at a higher level, and false information harmful, a lie will harm. General social judgements will condemn deliberate harmful actions.

Thomason (1983) disagrees that lies are typically reprehensibly motivated; he suggests that social lies are the most common sort of lie and are nonreprehensible. I differ with him; social lies are rarely altruistic, though their element of selfishness may not be deeply harmful; and their statistical predominance is unprovable, as a valid survey is surely impossible in this domain. Coleman and Kay correctly reflect a folk understanding that deceit usually profits the deceiver, to the listener's detriment. Thomason's wish to include reprehensibility in the prototype of *lie* shows that he shares this folk belief in a deep connection between deceit and harmfulness.

This deep judgment of falsehoods as *inherently* harmful goes beyond what we can so far predict from cultural models examined; our informational–exchange model would ask us to condemn falsehood only *when*, in fact, truth is beneficial and misinformation harmful, so that the simplified world is in effect. I now turn to an examination of the cultural links between information and power, in order to explain why a stigma of immorality attaches to even well-intentioned prevarication. Let us first examine what we do in making an "ordinary" informational statement, true or false.

R. Lakoff's (1973) Rules of Politeness, now recognized as a necessary part of our understanding of speech acts, are:

1. Don't impose. (*Formality*)
2. Give options. (*Hesitancy*)
3. Make interlocutor feel good; be friendly. (*Equality/Camaraderie*)

Lakoff says (2) explains why a direct command is less polite than an indirect command with the surface form of a request or of a query about the hearer's willingness or ability to do the task. Indirect forms give the hearer options besides obedience or disobedience; the hearer can negatively answer a query about ability without having to refuse compliance directly. Alternatively, indirectness allows compliance without implicit acceptance of the felicity–conditions of a command and recognition of the speaker's authority. Hedged commands avoid assuming ungranted authority over an addressee. Without details of the motivation, Lakoff also says that the same factors make it more polite to qualify assertions with "I guess" or "sorta." This seems a puzzle at first: Why should it be more polite to guess than to assert, or to make a hedged assertion rather than an unhedged one? Statements have so many purposes that the issue is messier than for commands, but the answer (as Lakoff at least implicitly noticed) is that a statement *does* something to the hearer, just like other speech acts. It pushes at the hearer's belief-system. An informative speaker requires a hearer ready and willing to believe, or information cannot be imparted. This cooperative hearer grants the speaker a good deal of power to push around certain aspects of his or her belief system.[8]

English reflects the equation of knowledge with power, in the uses of a group of hedges that mark the evidential status of statements. Some examples of evidentiality-hedges are: *to the best of my knowledge; so far as I know; if I'm not mistaken; as far as I can tell; for all I know; as I understand it; my best guess is; speaking conservatively; at a conservative estimate; to put it mildly; beyond question.*

The literal use of these hedges is to limit the speaker's normal responsibility for the truth of assertions. An assertion has the precondition (Searle 1969) that the speaker be able to provide evidence for its truth. Or, in terms of our cultural models of information and evidence, in an informational setting a hearer knows that a cooperative speaker will only state justified beliefs. However, even reliable-looking evidence can turn out to be insufficient. Evidentiality-hedges allow the hearer access to the evidence-evaluation and thus transfer some of the speaker's evaluative responsibility to the hearer. They avoid potential charges of carelessness or irresponsibility by not allowing the hearer to over- or undervalue the evidence supporting the hedged assertion. (Cf. Baker 1975 on some related hedges that signal and excuse potential discourse violations.)

G. Lakoff points out (personal communication) that responsibility-transfer goes even further. Not only can we qualify a statement's evidential status, but we can also evade personal responsibility for the original (prequalification) statement. For example:

> to the best of *our current knowledge*
>
> to the extent to which this phenomenon *is understood at all*
>
> so far as *can be judged from work to date*
>
> according to the *current consensus in the field*

This last set of hedges makes criticism or disagreement difficult; whereas if the speaker had simply evidentially qualified his or her personal evaluation, the hearer could easily disagree (though not accuse the speaker of irresponsibility or prevarication). At the opposite end of the spectrum, hedges such as *speaking conservatively* commit a speaker to an assertion's high evidential status (another example is *all the evidence points to the conclusion that*). Evidentiality-hedges, then, allow the speaker to modify the normal degree of responsibility for a statement's truth by qualifying its evidential status. Unqualified statements presumably take on a default level of responsibility, varying with context.

However, evidentiality–hedges have another function besides the meta-linguistic evaluation usage just described; they also function as pragmatic deference–markers. However sure a student may be of one of the following assertions, he or she might have *social* motivation to mark uncertainty with an evidentiality–hedge:

> But, Professor Murray, *as far as I can tell,* this parallels Andrews' example, which suggests another interpretation.

> Professor Jones, *if I'm not mistaken,* haven't Smith's recent results made the Atomic Charm hypothesis look dubious?

When social authority is low, the right to push people's belief systems is correspondingly low. Especially if our hearer may be unwilling to listen and change opinions, we have to be socially careful; we have no more authority to command belief changes than any other action against the will of our interlocutor.

Evidentiality–hedges thus hedge both kinds of authority that underlie an assertion: informational authority (evidence) and social authority (we cannot as readily command belief–systems of people higher on the social scale). This is a natural pairing, considering our understanding of assertion as manipulation of belief systems. In a prototypical informational exchange, the hearer is as ignorant and credulous as the speaker is knowledgeable and ready to inform. Who has the upper hand in such an exchange – the knowing and manipulative speaker, or the ignorant and passive learner? Teaching (a relatively one-way exchange, at least in early stages) has aspects of authority even without a surrounding institutional power-structure. To a lesser degree, any assertion has the same inherent power structure.

In further support of this analysis, note that a person with both kinds of authority can lay aside *either* kind with an appropriate evidentiality-hedge. A professor who wants to get a point out of a student rather than giving the answer may thus lay aside *both* aspects of authority, in a statement like:

> But *as I understand it,* semantics is the study of meaning – so how does it strongly depend on spelling, Mr. Smith?

Too many such hedges from the professor would sound sarcastic, since it is insincere to deny the existence of one's power position while leaving its broader social presence unchanged.

As further evidence that speakers link assertion with (a) request for belief and (b) assumption of an authority position, consider the following hedges:

> *(Please) believe me:* . . .
>
> *I don't ask anyone to believe this,* but . . .
>
> *I can't expect you to believe me,* but . . .

These hedges mark unreasonable belief–requests, tacitly assuming that an *ordinary* belief–request is just a matter of course. *I can't expect you to believe me* needs to be stated, even though our normal right to such an expectation passes unnoticed and unstated.

Phrases like the *strength* of an assertion, or the *authority* for a statement, are not random. Both social and informational authority structure our discourse world, and the strength of an assertion depends on both. If either kind of authority is extremely strong, it may overcome opposition from the other: An undergraduate who is *very* sure of a fact may correct a department chair, and a dean may feel freer than a student to speculate, having more social protection from contradiction.

Thus, our cultural model of information as power motivates evidentiality's relationships with politeness and authority. Incidentally, Grice's (1975) maxims are often cited as barring assertions that are obvious or well known to the hearer because they are useless and uninformative. However, I have not seen it overtly said that obvious statements are also often *insulting*. Their rudeness cannot be deduced from their uninformativeness but follows directly from viewing them as unwarranted assumptions of informational authority ("I know better than you").[9] This view may help explain the Coleman example (P. Kay, personal communication) "Crete is sort of an island," where *sort of* appears to hedge neither the choice of the word *island* nor the precision of the truth–value, but the *act* of asserting is weakened to avoid rudeness.

Conversely, Jef Verschueren (personal communication) points out to me that the idea of informational authority gives added motivation (besides Lakoff's rules) for seeing questions about ability or willingness as politer than direct commands. Question form has the inherent courtesy of giving the addressee a presumed informational authority. It is no huge politeness to assume an individual is the best authority on his or her own wishes and abilities. The contrary assumption, however, is *ipso facto* particularly counter to the rules of politeness, unless either camaraderie or unusual social authority overrides politeness. A direct command thus indicates presumed unconcern for whether the addressee *has* opinions, let alone what they are – and in a domain in which that person is the evident authority (i.e., his or her own internal state).

Verschueren also drew my attention to the contrast between an indirect but less polite "The window's open" (in a rude tone, to hearer who sees the window) and a direct but more polite request or command "(Please) close the window." Here I feel, the chosen mode of indirectness is more insulting than a direct command – the statement implies either (1) that the hearer is so unaware of the obvious that the assumption of informational authority is warranted OR (2) even greater social authority than a command; the hearer is expected not only to obey, but also to deduce and meet the speaker's wishes before they are stated (the *hearer* does not seem to mind the open window).[10] For me, the politeness–contrast reverses (as expected) if "The window's open" is said courteously, to a person who somehow (mental absorption? a physical barrier?) just has not noticed but might reasonably share the speaker's concern. These examples demonstrate the complex interplay between informational and social authority in determining politeness.

From the preceding discussion, lying emerges as serious authority-abuse. Authority relations structure the prototypical informational exchange, the setting in which *lie* is defined. As we get further from the simplified world in which the credulous hearer depends on the speaker for some crucial information, truth becomes less relevant and falsehood less reprehensible. In the simplified world, however, (barring major reversal of social authority and morality judgments, as in the Gestapo example), falsehood constitutes a deliberate use of authority to harm someone in a weaker, dependent informational position. We thus naturally judge it as immoral, barring exceptional extenuating circumstances.

As salient examples of our view of lying as authority–abuse, let me cite the anger of patients lied to by doctors, or of children systematically lied to by adults (e.g., about sex). Doctors in particular derive much of their authority from large amounts of knowledge that is not otherwise accessible to patients. By refusing information or misinforming, they can control important decisions for patients. To a lesser degree, any possessor of information can influence or control less knowledgeable hearers. To the extent that we feel people should control themselves, lying is immoral because it undermines the potential for self-determination.[11] This deep identification of lying with power abuse may explain why for some people all lies retain some reprehensibility, however good the motive.

Deception and lying

Lies are only a subclass of deception. Any deception, in that it induces false beliefs in a credulous hearer, is a culpable abuse of informational authority and naturally liable to the same moral charges leveled at a lie. But oddly enough, speakers often feel less immoral if they manage to deceive rather than to lie straight out. Victims conversely feel that such a deception is a dirtier trick; they cannot complain of being lied to and resent the deceiver's legal loophole.

There thus seems to be a further folk belief that literal truth and *real* truth (honest information-transmission) are prototypically connected. A literally true statement thus retains vestigial legality (if not morality), even if it misleads, whereas a deliberate factually false statement retains some stigma of reprehensibility, even with strong moral justification. Folklore gives magical power to literal truth, and a common folk theory is that law also emphasizes literal truth rather than informativeness (I do not know about modern perjury laws). Some people would find lying to the Gestapo immoral; yet most of them would think it laudable to *mislead* villains, saving an innocent victim. In any case, complete dissociation between literal and "real" truth, or between the latter and morality, is regarded as highly atypical.

A common way to mislead is to imply, but not overtly state, the false proposition to be communicated. The overt statement and the false proposition are often linked by Gricean conversational implicature; the utterance is irrelevant or insufficient in context, unless the hearer also assumes the unspoken falsehood. In such cases, the speaker *could* without self-contradiction go on to cancel the deceitful implicature. Taking a case from Coleman and Kay: "Mary, have you seen Valentino lately?" Mary: "Valentino's been sick with mononucleosis all week." Mary *could* go on, "But I've visited him twice." Part of people's disagreement about the morality of misleading (and about whether it constitutes lying) may be genuine disagreement about the degree to which a conversational implicature constitutes a "statement" and hence makes the speaker responsible for having said it. As Thomason says, some speakers are so sure the implicature was present that they include it in a restatement: "Mary said *No,* Valentino had been sick."

The plot thickens as the implicatures become more closely bound to the linguistic form. Such implicatures seem to me to be closer to statements than Mary's implicature about Valentino. Thus, I would predict that an utterance such as "*Some* of my students cut class," (used when not one showed up) would impress speakers as closer to a prototypical lie than Mary's statement.

An even more difficult case is that of *presupposed* falsehoods. How close to lies are statements such as "He's *only* a sophomore, *but* he got into that course," used of a student at a two-year college where sophomores are the most privileged students, and said to deceive the hearer about the nature of the college or the course? I personally rate these examples high. I hope in the future to investigate what constitutes "stating," as well as what constitutes lying. Our cultural model of representation is essential to our understanding of misrepresentation.

Cross-cultural parallels

Anthropologists interested in cultural models, or linguists interested in culturally framed semantics, now ask "How universal or culture-bound are the cultural models we have just examined?" I have used English data (like Coleman and Kay); studies of French (Piaget) and German (Wimmer and Perner, above) child language agree with each other and are highly compatible with my proposed analysis of the English verb *lie*. These linguistic communities also share the accompanying moral judgements of lying, probably due to shared understanding of power structures and informational exchange. However, a first glance at more distant cultures shows a startling degree of surface variance as to the morality of misleading or lying. Ochs Keenan (1976) discusses the frequency (and acceptability) of vague or misleading answers to questions in a small Malagasy-speaking community. Gilsenan (1976) states that successful lying is a major positive status–source for males in a Lebanese Arabic-speaking community. In what respects do these groups differ from English speakers?

My answer is that, on examination, these cultures differ from ours much less than the isolated statements above might indicate. At least, the differences are not in their understanding of informational exchange, evidence, or abuse of informational power.

Ochs Keenan's Malagasy community, while agreeing with English speakers that information-giving is cooperative and useful, has a different idea of when a hearer has a *right* to such cooperation. Europeans or Americans might think of their own contrast between "free goods" (any stranger gets a reply to "What time is it?") and other facts (e.g., one's age, or middle name) that need a reason to be told. Malagasy speakers place an even higher power–value on information than do English speakers (news is rare in small communities) and naturally hoard precious and powerful knowledge; questioners cannot expect as broad a spectrum of free goods in such a society, and day-to-day informational demands have less right to expect compliance. Malagasy speakers are not uncooperative when refusing information could seriously harm (e.g., if asked "Where's the doctor?" by an injured person). Our classic informational–exchange setting is just not in place as often as in an English-speaking community; since Malagasy speakers all know this, their equivocations do not manipulate unsuspecting addressees. The Malagasy community shares basic cultural models of information and truth with English speakers, but evokes them under different circumstances.

We might note here that lying to enemies is often culturally accepted. Many English speakers think such lies less immoral than lies to trusting friends, who are "owed" more sincerity (Coleman and Kay cite speakers who, extending this scale, said Mary did not "owe" John the truth about Valentino, as they were not engaged). In some cultures, lying may be forbidden primarily *within* the group; but such a culture does not lack our judgment of lies as harmful. Rather, their rule about who should not be harmed is different.

Gilsenan's Lebanese village is an even more complex case. He states that this community thinks lying immoral, probably for the same reasons we do. Community members caught lying lose status and *honor*. However, certain restricted kinds of undetected lies told by adult males can be extremely status–productive.

First, verbal self-presentation is highly competitive for Lebanese men, so false (or unfalsifiable) boasts are profitable, though detection causes corresponding status–loss. Conventional verbal competition gives noninformational aspects to Lebanese boasts (though not as formalized as, e.g., Turkish, or urban black American, boys' boasting or insults). English speakers might lie competitively in other areas, and less conventionally; but the Lebanese view of lying is not in serious conflict with our own.

The second way a Lebanese man can gain status by lying is to lead another man "up the garden path" and subsequently reveal the deception. He must avoid detection, or it may be difficult to prove he did not mean to deceive permanently. A "garden path" is crucially *not* real lying, since it achieves its goal only by eventual truth–revelation. Thus, such deceptions do not show a different idea of *lying* from ours; but why do these play–lies give status?

Gilsenan explains that *discernment* is a major source of prestige for Lebanese men: A reputation for telling truth from falsehood is valued especially in religious leaders, but also in any adult male. He tells of a visiting religious leader who upstaged the village religious leader (a man with a long-built reputation for discernment, even omniscience). A village man, resenting the intruder, perpetrated and then publicly revealed a successful minor hoax on him; he left, discredited. Lebanese "garden-path" lies are usually less important, but do cause real status – gain or loss – unlike American April-fools or leg-pulling.

Lebanese society evidently has conventionalized competitive uses of informational power; men overtly gain power by forcing false beliefs on others or by seeing through false claims (exposing the author as nonauthoritative, dishonorable, or simply unsuccessful at one-upping). Serious use of this power by lying would be immoral, but one can conventionally display power without using it – as a martial arts victor does not kill but shows that he has overcome his opponent and *could* kill. A martial arts victor's status need not indicate corresponding cultural approval of actual killing or assault; nor should status given by "garden paths" be taken as indicating general social approval of lying.

Very different cultures emerge from this discussion as possessing saliently similar understandings both of lying and of the general power and morality dimensions of informational exchange. This similarity presumably stems from universal aspects of human communication. Where cultures differ appears to be in *delimitation* of basic "informational exchange" settings and in *conventional use* of the relevant power parameters. Folk models of knowledge and informativeness (and the corresponding semantic domains) may universally involve strong shared elements.

Conclusions

A lie is simply a false statement – but cultural models of information, discourse, and power supply a rich context that makes the use of *lie* much more complex than this simple definition indicates. Definitions of morally, informationally, or otherwise deviant speech acts follow readily from a definition of a simplified "default" speech world. The cultural models in question not only underlie a whole sector of our vocabulary but also motivate our social and moral judgments in these areas; they further appear to have strong shared elements cross-culturally.

Cultural models underlying linguistic systems are a fairly new area of analysis, though a few people were ahead of the rest of us (Becker 1975 is a good example). However, collaboration among linguists, anthropologists, and other social scientists in this area looks increasingly fruitful. My own preference for this approach stems from both its intuitive plausibility (ethnographers, if not grammarians, have long known that word-meanings are interrelated with cultural models) and its explanation of a long-term paradox facing semantic analysts. Word–meaning has orderly aspects that make us feel that it *ought* to be simply formalizable; yet we all know from bitter experience how readily the complexities of meaning elude reductionistic formal analysis. If the analyst's intuitive feeling that definitions are simple is right, then perhaps much of the fuzziness and complexity lies in the context of meaning, rather than in the meaning itself. A better understanding of cultural models (aided by research such as that represented in this volume) is important to lexical semantics: Words do not mean in a vacuum, any more than people do.

This paper leaves many unresolved problems. It is insufficient to discuss *one* cultural model or folk theory of speech (here, our default model of literal discourse as informational) as if it were largely independent of all the other models relevant to verbal interaction. Our folk understanding of knowledge also needs more investigation. On the linguistic front, in which cases can we expect the fuzziness of fuzzy semantics to be ultimately locatable in the sociophysical world (or in our perception of it), or in the fit between the world and a cultural model; and in which cases, if any, can we expect inherently fuzzy semantics? This last question can be answered only as we learn more about the relationship between linguistic and social (even metaphorical) categorization. Just now, I must be content with showing that a simpler semantics of *lie* follows from an analysis of the cultural models relevant to prevarication.

Notes

1. Only members of the Berkeley linguistic community will understand how much this work owes to their ideas and support. However, my intellectual debt to my advisors, Charles Fillmore and George Lakoff, should be evident. Linda Coleman and Paul Kay, original inspirers of this project, were patient and intelligent critics throughout. I have also benefited from the insightful comments of Susan Ervin-Tripp, Orin Gensler, David Gordon, John Gumperz, Dorothy Holland, Mark Johnson, Naomi Quinn, John Searle, Neil Thomason, Jef Verschueren, Jeanne Van Oosten, and the participants in the Princeton

Conference on Folk Models. An earlier version of the paper was presented in the symposium Folk Theories in Everyday Cognition, organized by Holland and Quinn for the 80th Annual Meeting of the American Anthropological Association, 1981.

2. The term *folk theory*, which I originally used throughout, emphasizes the nonexpert status of such a theory or model; *cultural model*, which I am now adopting, stresses the fact that our cultural framework models the world for us. I have retained the word *folk* in contexts where I find it particularly useful.

3. For a recent and complete survey of work on linguistic categorization, see G. Lakoff (in press).

4. Coleman and Kay presented subjects with a series of short fictional scenarios, asking the subjects to judge in each case (1) whether a lie had been told in the interaction described and (2) how sure the subject felt about this judgment. The actions described in the scenarios varied independently with respect to deceptiveness, factual falsity of statements made, and speaker's belief of the content of the statements.

5. Susan Ervin-Tripp has suggested to me that young children are simply "behaviorists," judging acts by result, not by intent. Before children can state their intentions, they are bound to get rewarded and punished behavioristically. Four- to nine-year-olds are certainly not insensitive to intentions but may remain behaviorists enough to class lies with other false statements.

6. Paul Kay has brought to my attention a playful usage that seems odd in the context of either a feature *or* a prototype analysis of *lie:* "Do you know, I thought I told the truth the other day, but it turns out I lied to you: I'm so sorry." This usage seems to me parasitical on serious usage in that the speaker jokingly attributes to a past speech act his or her *current* mental knowledge–space (in Fauconnier's [1985] sense of *mental space*). Since past acts are not actually judged in the light of subsequently gained knowledge, we find this amusing.

7. Lakoff (in press) comments that *social lie* and similar collocations pose problems for the theory of complex categories. A prototypical social lie is not necessarily a prototypical lie. Without proposing a new theory of complex categories, I feel it is clear that *social lie* is not an intersection of the categories *lie* and *social act*. Rather, it is viewed simultaneously (and perhaps somewhat contradictorily) as a member of two categories that we do not usually understand as interacting at all.

8. Social rights and responsibilities are reciprocally arranged: If the Speaker has the right (authority) to say *X,* then the Hearer has a duty to believe it. If *H* has a special right to hear (to know) *X,* beyond the general right to information, then *S* has a correspondingly more important duty to tell *X* to *H.*

9. Paul Kay has suggested to me that the rudeness of telling someone what they already know is best compared to the rudeness of giving an unnecessary or redundant gift. However, such gifts are only rude *if* they imply an unwarranted power–assumption. If I give you a paperback you own a copy of, I'm only rude if I thereby (unjustifiably) purported to extend your literary horizons; but if I pay for your bus ticket (which you are presumed capable of buying), then I'm rude unless you asked for help with change. All valuable resources, like information, confer power on their owners.

10. Forman (n.d.), in a (somewhat astonishingly) still unpublished paper, "Informing, Reminding, and Displaying," elucidates the informational uses of apparently noninformative statements; he would categorize this as an example of informative reminding.

11. Bok (1979) provides a treatment of the social issues involved in lying and decep-

tion. One case she analyzes is that of a woman who was the only likely kidney donor for her daughter and overtly willing. Perceiving severe repressed fears in her, doctors falsely told her that she was not physically compatible enough with her daughter to be a good donor. This deception robbed her of the chance to confront her fears and make her own decision about giving the kidney. Bok also notes that deception is less frightening if we ourselves have authorized the deceivers and are aware of their tactics. Unmarked traffic control cars voted into use by the community are less threatening than if the police use them without citizens' input.

References

Baker, C.
   1975. This is just a first approximation but. . . . *In* Papers from the Eleventh Regional Meeting of the Chicago Linguistic Society. Chicago: Chicago Linguistics Society. Pp. 37–47.
Becker, A.
   1975. A linguistic image of nature: The Burmese numerative classifier system. Linguistics 1975 (165):109–121.
Bok, S.
   1979. Lying: A Moral Choice in Public and Private Life. New York: Pantheon Books.
Coleman, L. and P. Kay
   1981. Prototype semantics: The English verb 'lie.' Language 57(1):26–44.
Fauconnier, G.
   1985. Mental Spaces. Cambridge, Mass.: M.I.T. Press.
Fillmore, C. J.
   1977. Topics in lexical semantics. *In* Current Issues in Linguistic Theory, R. Cole, ed. Bloomington: University of Indiana Press. Pp. 76–138.
Forman, D.
   n.d. Informing, reminding, and displaying. Unpublished manuscript, Department of Linguistics, University of California, Berkeley.
Gilsenan, M.
   1976. Lying, honor, and contradiction. *In* Transaction and Meaning: Directions in the Anthropology of Exchange and Symbolic Behavior, A.S.A. Essays in Social Anthropology, Vol. 1, B. Kapferer, ed. Philadelphia: Institute for the Study of Human Issues. Pp. 191–219.
Goffman, E.
   1974. Frame Analysis: An Essay in the Organization of Experience. New York: Harper and Row, Publishers.
Gordon, D. P.
   1974. A developmental study of the semantics of factivity in the verbs 'know,' 'think,' and 'remember.' Ph.D. dissertation, University of Michigan. (Published as Natural Language Studies, No. 15. Ann Arbor: University of Michigan Phonetics Laboratory.)
Grice, H. P.
   1975. Logic and conversation. *In* Syntax and Semantics, Vol. 3, Speech Acts, P. Cole and J. Morgan, eds. New York: Academic Press. Pp. 113–127.
Kay, P.
   1983. Linguistic competence and folk theories of language: Two English hedges. *In* Proceedings of the Ninth Annual Meeting of the Berkeley Linguistics Society. Berkeley: University of California. Pp. 128–137.

Kay, P. and C. McDaniel
   1978. The Linguistic Significance of the Meanings of Basic Color Terms.
   Language 54(3):610–646.
Lakoff, G.
   1972. Hedges: A study in meaning criteria and the logic of fuzzy concepts. *In*
   Papers from the Eighth Regional Meeting of the Chicago Linguistic Society.
   Chicago. Pp. 183–228. (Reprinted in Journal of Philosophical Logic 2:458–
   508, 1973.)
Lakoff, G.
   In press. Women, Fire, and Dangerous Things: What Categories Reveal about
   the Mind. Chicago: University of Chicago Press.
Lakoff, R.
   1973. The logic of politeness: Or minding your P's and Q's. *In* Papers from
   the Ninth Regional Meeting of the Chicago Linguistic Society. Chicago:
   Chicago Linguistic Society. Pp. 292–305.
Mervis, C. and E. Rosch
   1981. Categorization of natural objects. Annual Review of Psychology 32:89–
   115.
Ochs Keenan, E.
   1976. On the universality of conversational implicatures. Language in Society
   5(1):67–80.
Piaget, J.
   1932. The Moral Judgement of the Child. M. Gabain, trans. New York: Har-
   court Brace.
Rappaport, R. A.
   1976. Liturgies and lies. *In* International Yearbook for the Sociology of
   Knowledge and Religion, Vol. 10, G. Dux, ed. Freiburg, Germany:
   Westdeutscher Verlag. Pp. 75–104.
Rosch, E.
   1978. Principles of categorization. *In* Cognition and Categorization, E. Rosch
   and B. Lloyd, eds. Hillsdale, N.J.: Lawrence Erlbaum Associates. Pp. 27–48.
Searle, J.
   1969. Speech Acts. Cambridge, England: Cambridge University Press.
Thomason, N. R.
   1983. Why we have the concept of 'lie' that we do. Unpublished Ph.D. dissertation. University of Oregon.

3
Linguistic competence and folk theories of language
TWO ENGLISH HEDGES[1]

Paul Kay

In the ordinary sense in which we say that words like *chair* and *table* are ABOUT furniture, hedges are words about language and speech. There is nothing remarkable in this; language is part of our environment, and we have words about most things in our environment. The linguistically interesting aspect of hedges is that, although they are about language, they are not exactly used to talk about language as we would say that *chair* and *table* are used to talk about furniture or, for example, *gerund* and *entailment* are used to talk about language. When we use a word like *chair* or *table* or *gerund* or *entailment,* chairs, tables, gerunds, and entailments do not become *ipso facto* part of what is said. With hedges it is different; when we use a hedge like *loosely speaking,* the notion of "loose speech" which this expression invokes becomes part of the combinatorial semantics of the sentence and utterance in which it occurs. A familiar (if probably vacuous) combinatorial semantic rule is

> (SR) If adjective *a* denotes class *A* and noun *n* denotes class *N,* then the denotation of the expression *an* is the intersection of the classes *A* and *N.*

I wish to claim that the notion of "loose speech" is part of the combinatorial semantics of sentences containing the expression *loosely speaking* in the same way in which the notion of class intersection is claimed by proponents of (SR) to be part of the combinatorial semantics of an expression like *red chair.*

A hedged sentence, when uttered, often contains a comment on itself or on its utterance or on some part thereof. For example, when someone says, *Loosely speaking France is hexagonal,* part of what they have uttered is a certain kind of comment on the locution *France is hexagonal.* In this sort of metalinguistic comment, the words that are the subject of the comment occur both in their familiar role as part of the linguistic stream and in a theoretically unfamiliar role as part of the world the utterance is about. Such metalinguistic reference seems unaccounted for (and perhaps unaccountable for) in standard theories of semantics that are based on a context-free, recursive definition of truth for sentences, and in which linguistic objects and world objects (or objects in a model) belong to disjoint realms. The problem, I believe, goes beyond that of indexicality as usually conceived, and although it would be interesting to investigate in detail the relation between the kinds of facts to be discussed here and discussions of indexicality within model theoretic semantics (e.g., Kaplan 1977), that comparison will not be attempted. The omission might be justified by appeal to limitations of space, but such a plea would be less than candid, as I suspect that the phenomena I will describe constitute a principled set of exceptions to any theory of natural language meaning that makes a rigorous separation between truth conditional meaning for linguistic types (i.e., sentences), normally called *semantics,* and other aspects of meaning, frequently called *pragmatics* (see, for example, Gazdar 1979:2f). The latter claim would, to be sure, require considerable clarification before a demonstration could be begun. In this chapter I must content myself with presenting a few facts and some timid empirical generalizations.

The principal conceptual tool I will employ for stating these empirical generalizations will be that of *folk theory*. The term is borrowed from anthropology. In describing the system of knowledge and belief of another culture, an anthropologist speaks of that culture's folk theory of botany, the emotions, language, and so on. Anthropologists discover such folk theories by analysis of the use of words in the native language. The guiding idea is the familiar one that any natural lexicon implies a tacit, structured conceptualization of the stuff that the words of that lexicon are about. What the words we shall be concerned with here are about is language and speech, and the folk theory we shall be looking for is the tacit and mostly unconscious theory of language and speech we invoke when we employ certain parts of the lexicon of English.

The present essay is thus in the first instance lexicographical. But we will see that in the domain of hedges, lexicography is inseparable from combinatorial semantics because the schemata or folk theories that constitute the semantic content of the hedges as lexical items serve as combinatorial structures for putting together the meaning of the sentences in which the hedges occur. Hence, world knowledge about language – what I have called folk theories of language – may at times be part of knowledge OF language.

Knowledge of a language, linguistic competence, is commonly distinguished from knowledge of the world. Linguists do not generally consider it a matter of interest that the language we are competent in is also in our world and therefore a thing of which we have world knowledge, that is, a folk theory. Certainly linguists do not often ask whether world knowledge of language bears some special relation, that other sorts of world knowledge do not bear, to the knowledge that constitutes linguistic competence. Perhaps the question is not posed because the answer is considered obvious, namely No. The facts to be considered below suggest, however, that the folk theory of language presupposed by various hedges should be interpreted both as world knowledge ABOUT language and as knowledge OF language – i.e., as part of linguistic competence.

The data to be considered in this chapter concern two hedges, *loosely speaking* and *technically*. The concept *folk theory* will figure in the analysis of the meaning of each of these expressions. The comparison of the two analyses will reveal a not altogether obvious difference between the folk theories that constitute our tacit knowledge of the world (as realized in word meanings) and consciously formulated theories: folk theories, like conscious theories, answer to a requirement of local consistency but, unlike conscious theories, folk theories answer to no requirement for global consistency.

Loosely speaking

The hedge *loosely speaking* may be employed in the service of a variety of semantic and/or pragmatic functions which, from a traditional point of view, appear disconcertingly diverse. Let us consider some of the possible semantic–pragmatic roles of *loosely speaking* in the response of Anthropologist *A* to Layman *L* in the following dialogue.

(1) *L:* Where did the first human beings live?
     A: Loosely speaking the first human beings lived in Kenya.

First, believing the evolutionary process to be inherently gradual, *A* may consider the expression *the first human being* to be semantically ill-formed and hence devoid of the capacity for nonvacuous reference. If *A* had this problem, believing that *the first human being* could not possibly refer to anything, he might reply more fully

(2) *A:* Strictly speaking, one can't really talk about "the first human beings," but loosely speaking, the first human beings . . .

Secondly (and alternatively), *A* may think that *the first human beings* is a normal referring expression, but not the one that picks out exactly the entity about which he wishes to assert *lived in Kenya*. For example, *A* may consider it important to distinguish in this context *the first human beings* and *the first human beings known to science*. If this were *A*'s reason for hedging with *loosely speaking*, his fuller answer might be along the lines

(3) *A:* Strictly speaking, we can only talk of the first human population known to science, but loosely speaking, the first human beings . . .

A's problem may be not with *the first human beings* but rather with *in Kenya*. A third motivation for *loosely speaking* could then be that *A* considers the unhedged sentence *The first human beings lived in Kenya* to have a reading which presupposes the modern nation of Kenya to have existed at the time the first human beings were alive. Such fastidious pedantry might motivate a longer reply along the lines

(4) *A:* Loosely speaking, in Kenya; strictly speaking, in the place now called Kenya.

Fourthly, and perhaps most typically, *A* may think that the unhedged sentence *The first human beings lived in Kenya* oversimplifies or otherwise distorts the pertinent facts, but is nonetheless the best he can do given the exigencies of the conversational situation. Sometimes the demands of Gricean Quantity (Say no more than necessary) and Manner (Be brief) require a sacrifice in Quality (Tell the truth). In our present example, the relevant facts might involve sites not only in Kenya but also in Uganda and Tanzania, fossils of uncertain relation to each other, and so on. *Loosely speaking* can be and probably often is used to apologize for this sort of deficiency in Quality, induced by the demands of Quantity and Manner. The fuller version of *A*'s reply could be something like

(5) *A:* Loosely speaking in Kenya. Strictly speaking, we are dealing here with a complex situation involving sites mainly in Kenya, but also in Tanzania and Uganda, and with a set of fossils which may not all represent the same species . . .

Examples (2–5) illustrate four distinct kinds of "loose speech" that the hedge *loosely speaking* may reflect in (1): (i) the use of an incoherent description in an act of reference (2); (ii) the use of a coherent but "wrong" description in an act of reference (3); (iii) the utterance of a sentence that (the speaker feels) permits an unintended interpretation that contains a false presupposition (4); and (iv) the utterance of a sentence that is defective in Gricean Quality, that is, in truth (5).

What, then, does *loosely speaking* mean? George Lakoff (1972) gives the example

(6) (a) A whale is a fish. (FALSE)
     (b) Loosely speaking, a whale is a fish. (TRUE)

and argues that the semantic function of *loosely speaking* is that of a predicate modifier which, through selection of certain features of meaning internal to the intension of a category word like *fish,* maps it into another category–type intension. But we see that this cannot be correct, since in (1) *loosely speaking* does a variety of things that have nothing to do with the modification of a category word. Furthermore, it may do several of these things simultaneously: in uttering his part of (1), *A* might be bothered by any combination of the factors discussed in connection with (2–5) [except of course those combinations containing both (2) and (3), since these happen to be mutually exclusive]. Thus the semantic scope of *loosely speaking* must be at least as broad as the entire sentence it accompanies, for example, in (6)(b) the sentence *A whale is a fish.* Since presence or absence of *loosely speaking* in a sentence such as (6) may affect our judgment of its truth, the classical view holds that *loosely speaking* must make a contribution to the semantics of the SENTENCE in which it occurs. Since the scope of *loosely speaking* must be at least as broad as the whole sentence it accompanies, its scope must be that whole sentence, and one is tempted to conclude that the semantics of *loosely speaking* is a function from sentence intensions to sentence intensions – that is, from the set of worlds in which whales are fish (the null set in some theories) to the set of worlds that are like this one with respect to the fishiness of whales. But nothing of this sort can be right because, as we saw in connection with (2), *loosely speaking* sometimes functions to comment directly on the FORM of the sentence it accompanies.

Moreover, when (6)(a) is changed to (6)(b) by the addition of *loosely speaking* the reason that our judgment changes from false to true is not that a false proposition P ($= A$ *whale is a fish*) has been changed into some true proposition P'. Rather, we abstain from judging (6)(b) false because we understand (6)(b) both to assert the sentence *A whale is a fish* and to express a reservation regarding the adequacy of that assertion. If the dimension of adequacy is taken to be that of truth (tightness of "word-to-world fit") as seems to be the relevant dimension in the case of (6)(b), then we have no trouble accepting a judgment of true. In the general case, however, the dimension of adequacy directly addressed by the hedge *loosely speaking* need not be that of truth: the loose speech referred to may involve laxness in obedience to the rules of language, as in (2) and perhaps (3) or even looseness with respect to stylistic canons, as in (4). Of the four examples, (2–5), only (5) directly concerns truth, and even in this case, we do not experience (1) as expressing some proposition P', which is distinct from but closely related to *The first human beings lived in Kenya,* and which is exactly true.

The empirical claim about *loosely speaking* that I have attempted to develop may be summarized as follows:

(7) For any sentence S of the form *loosely speaking P,* where P is a declarative sentence, an utterance of S constitutes two acts:
(i) an act of asserting P,
(ii) an act of warning that (i) is in some way a deviant (loose) act of assertion.

Probably the most typical way for an assertion to be deviant is in terms of Quality, but, as we have seen, an assertion may have other kinds of defects about which *loosely speaking* warns.

If (7) is even approximately correct, expressions such as *loosely speaking* present an interesting challenge to current formal theories of semantics and pragmatics. If *loosely speaking* means what (7) says it means, this is surely its literal meaning (not figurative, ironic, *et cetera*). Although (7) specifies the literal meaning of *loosely speaking,* (7) does not consist of a specification of truth conditions of either S or P, but rather expresses a warning to the addressee that he should be wary in his acceptance of the assertion of P. If (7) is correct, literal meaning and truth conditions cannot always be the same thing, not even almost the same thing.

It is not obvious how the meaning of an expression like *loosely speaking* is to be captured in a theory of the generally accepted kind, where the truth conditional meaning of a sentence is established in terms of a possible world semantics independent of pragmatic considerations, and no feedback from pragmatic reasoning to literal meaning is countenanced. But even supposing that with sufficient ingenuity we could develop an account of *loosely speaking* within this kind of framework, it is not clear that we should wish to do so. If we look at the different kinds of semantic-pragmatic functions that may be accomplished by *loosely speaking* [illustrated, though by no means exhausted, in (2–5)], we find that they constitute, from the traditional view, a disparate collection. Another way to view the same matter is to notice – as the reader may already have done – that (7)(ii) is stated far too broadly. *Loosely speaking* doesn't point to just any kind of deviance in an act of asserting. For example, acts of assertion that deviate because they contain uninterpretable indexicals or because they fail to answer a question just posed are not examples of "loose speech."

(8) (a) Jack and John were running and $\left\{ \begin{array}{c} \text{*loosely speaking he} \\ \text{one of them} \end{array} \right\}$ fell down.

   (b) A: When did Mary get her car tuned up?
       B: *Loosely speaking, because the engine was knocking.

I have spoken informally of the various kinds of "loose" speech represented by examples (2–5), and in this informal usage I think lies the key to the semantic unity of the expression *loosely speaking*. I suggest that what enables us to speak informally about "loose" speech in connection with all of these examples is what constitutes the actual semantic unity of the expression *loosely speaking*. In every utterance of a sentence like (1), the linguistic act of asserting that the first human beings lived in Kenya is talked ABOUT (in the same familiar sense in which we say that in the utterance of a sentence like *Trout eat flies* trout are talked about). That is, when we say *Loosely speaking P* we bring to bear part of our world knowledge of what it is to assert something, or, as I would prefer to say, we bring to bear part of our folk theory of language and speech – the part that concerns assertion. We have knowledge, beliefs and schematizations of language and speech just as we have knowledge, beliefs and schematizations of everything else in our experience. When we use a hedge like *loosely speaking* in an utterance we use it to talk about some other part of that same utterance, and so at one level we use our world knowledge of language and speech in the same way we use our world knowledge about zoology when we employ the word *trout* or *fly*. *Loosely speaking* interprets the utterance in which it occurs as a world object according to a particular folk theory of utterance, which is part of our larger folk theory of language and speech.

To speak loosely is to assert something not quite true. Typically, loose speech is speech that would be true in a world slightly different from the one we are describing, but in some cases we characterize our speech as loose if it fails to achieve precise truth because of some defect in its construction. Expert theories of language and speech normally make a strict distinction between locutions that don't (quite) state propositions and locutions that state propositions that aren't (quite) true; but not all parts of our unconscious folk theory of language and speech insists on this distinction; *loosely speaking* appears to invoke such an area of the folk theory.

Technically

Technically, used as a hedge, has a meaning that may be roughly glossed "as stipulated by those persons in whom Society has vested the right to so stipulate." Thus when we say, *Technically, a whale is a mammal,* we appeal to the fact that systematic biologists have decreed that, whatever we common folk may say, whales are mammals. One line of evidence for this analysis of *technically* comes from pairs of synonyms – or near synonyms – of which only one member belongs to an authoritative jargon; in such pairs only the member from the jargon takes the hedge *technically.*

(9) (a) Technically, that's a rodent. (order *Rodentia*)
     (b) *Technically, that's a varmint.

(10) (a) Technically, that's an insect. (order *Insecta*)
      (b) *Technically, that's a bug.

The (b) versions may be heard as attempts at humor, precisely because the words *varmint* and *bug* not only belong to no technical jargon, but, on the contrary, are markedly colloquial.

Further, if we hear a sentence like

(11) Technically, street lights are health hazards.

our reaction is to wonder WHO has decreed that street lights are health hazards and BY WHAT AUTHORITY. If we learn that the Surgeon General of the United States has done so, even if we reject his arguments and therefore question the wisdom of the stipulation, we cannot legitimately deny the claim expressed in (11). If, on the other hand, we learn that an individual genius has proclaimed street lights to be health hazards on grounds we consider impeccable, we will surely agree that street lights are in fact health hazards, but we may well deplore that the claim expressed in (11) is not the case.

Lakoff (1972) attributes to Eleanor Rosch a revealing example similar to the following,

(12) Technically, a TV set is a piece of furniture.

pointing out that the sentence can have different truth values in different contexts, if there exist in society two distinct bodies with the authority to make such stipulations about TV sets and furniture. For example, moving companies might designate TV sets as furniture, while the insurance industry excludes TV sets from furniture.

Given this account of the meaning of *technically,* we may ask whether *technically* displays the two properties of hedges, previously discussed, that provide problems for standard formal semantics. These, it will be recalled, are (a) that the lexical meaning of a hedge may become one of the organizing schemata of the combinatorial semantics of the sentence in which the hedge occurs, and (b) that a hedged sentence may contain a metalinguistic comment regarding the way in which a word or phrase of the sentence is being used in that sentence.

Regarding property (a), if we sketch the logical structure of (12) in terms of our intuitive account of *technically,* we get something with the rough structure of (13), in which we find that the effect of the word *technically* is not confined to a single element but is distributed throughout the quantificational and predicational structure of the sentence.

(13)   There is an *x* such that Society has authorized *x* to stipulate the meaning
         of *TV set,* and Society has authorized *x* to stipulate the meaning of *furni-
         ture,* and *x* has stipulated the former to be included in the latter.

The precise wording of (13) is not intended to be taken literally; the point of (13) is just that most of the "logical syntax" of (12) comes from the word *technically.* The lexical meaning of *technically* provides the structural skeleton of the meaning of sentences, like (12), in which it occurs. In this respect, *technically* acts like "logical" words (e.g., *all, and, not*) are supposed to act. But we noted that *technically* is a substantive, world-knowledge-embodying word; in fact it is precisely by virtue of the folk theory it embodies regarding language, society, and the social division of linguistic labor that *technically* achieves its organizing function in sentence like (12). Semantics and mere lexicography find themselves confounded.

That *technically* displays property (b) – regarding metalinguistic comments in which the linguistic item(s) MENTIONED are simultaneously USED as regular linguistic counters – is not apparent from the examples so far given (9–12). One reason for this is that since the target words (e.g., *TV set* and *furniture* in (12)) appear with the generic indefinite article, the examples conduce to a straightforward interpretation in which these words are mentioned, but not also used. Consider, however, the following.

(14)   The movers have come for your furniture, which technically includes TV sets.

Here the word *furniture* is both used and mentioned: *furniture* is used in the ordinary way as the lexical head of a definite noun phrase, *your furniture,* to pick out a set of world objects; *furniture* is simultaneously mentioned as the topic of a metalinguistic comment, which informs us that, by stipulation of relevant authorities, the extension of *furniture* includes TV sets.

Comparison of loosely speaking and technically

In the case of each of the two hedges considered, I have sought to explain both its lexical meaning and its combinatorial semantic function in terms of an implicit folk theory of language and speech. The discussion of *loosely speaking* hinged on the notion of truth, implicitly defined in terms of a metatheory in which there is a linguistic system disjoint from the world whose elements (words, sentences) may be combined to represent objects and states of affairs in the world via the meanings or intensions of those elements. The sentence *Snow is white* is true . . . . This general schematization of language is familiar as an informal sketch of the basic intuitions that lie behind the formidable accomplishments of that tradition of semantic theorizing descended from Frege via Tarski to the modern proponents of model theory, including in particular the various versions most relevant to linguists arising from the work of Richard Montague. In this framework, words may refer to or represent world objects because the former have intensions that may be matched by the actual properties of the latter.

This conscious theory of language, and particularly of reference, has recently been opposed by the baptismal–causal theory of Kripke (1972) and Putnam (1975). The reader may have noticed that in discussing the meaning of *technically,* I had recourse to Putnam's phrase "the division of linguistic labor" (1975:145ff). The part of the folk theory of language which *technically* invokes seems in its main lines to agree with the theory of Kripke and Putnam, especially Putnam's version. On this view, a word refers, not via an intension it contains, but on account of someone having once stipulated that henceforth this word shall designate some ostensively presented thing or thing–type. Putnam's idea that we have unconscious recourse, in using a word like *gold,* to the notion of some expert or official who has the right and the knowledge to diagnose real world gold in a presented sample is especially close to the account I have given above of that aspect of the folk theory of language which underlies the use of *technically.*

Thus when we use *loosely speaking,* we are taking a Fregean view of language and, moreover, because of property (a), we are organizing the semantics of our utterance in accord with Fregean notions. On the other hand, when we use the hedge *technically,* we are taking a Putnamian view of language and are organizing the semantics of our utterance along Putnamian lines. If a natural language like English has a formal semantics that employs logical schemata such as conjunction, negation, etc., to compose the meaning of a sentence from the meaning of its parts, then we must number among that same array of structure-composing schemata such substantive folk beliefs about language as those implicitly underlying the explicit theories of reference associated with scholars like Frege and Putnam. These are the combinatorial semantic schemata invoked by *loosely speaking* and *technically* respectively.

Folk theories

I have written throughout this chapter in terms of a single folk theory of language and latterly pointed out that this "theory" differs from conscious theories in that it is not internally consistent. I could as easily have written that English encodes a variety of different folk theories of language. The distinction would have been merely terminological and the same conclusions would have been reached. There are two points here: the first is that a folk theory does not present a globally consistent whole the way a conscious, expert theory does. This should surprise no one, since it is precisely the conscious reflection characteristic of expert theorizing that is generally considered to produce its global coherence. The second point is that folk theories are not "believed" in the way conscious theories are but are used or presupposed as the occasion of thought or communication demands. The penetration of these folk theories of language into the semantic structure of language, via hedges, appears to present several challenges to the generally accepted framework of much current semantic theory.

Notes

1. Reprinted with permission of the Berkeley Linguistics Society from the *Proceedings of the Ninth Annual Meeting* (Berkeley 1983).
2. The present paper is based on a much longer work on hedges which is still in progress but part of which has been made semi-public in a typescript ms. (Kay, n.d.) of which the subtitle was "hedges revisited." The word *revisited* referred to the well known paper of George Lakoff (1972). In Kay (n.d.) I discuss in detail Lakoff's approach to hedges and my own agreements with and divergences from that approach; space does not permit a recapitulation of that discussion here. Also in that (n.d.) paper there are references to personal communication and advice from many people whose contributions cannot be recited here, although all have helped shape my view of the subject. I must acknowledge, however, a very general intellectual debt to Charles Fillmore and George Lakoff.

References

Gazdar, G.
   1979. Pragmatics. New York: Academic Press.
Kaplan, D.
   1977. "Dthat." *In* Syntax and Semantics, Vol. 9, Pragmatics, Peter Cole, ed. New York: Academic Press. Pp. 221–44.
Kay, P.
   n.d. The role of cognitive schemata in word meaning: Hedges revisited. Unpublished manuscript, Department of Linguistics, University of California, Berkeley.

Kripke, S.
  1972. Naming and necessity. *In* Semantics of Natural Language, D. Davidson and G. Harman, eds. Dordrecht, Holland: D. Reidel Publishing Company. Pp. 253–355.
Lakoff, G.
  1972. Hedges: a study in meaning criteria and the logic of fuzzy concepts. *In* Papers from the Eighth Regional Meeting, Chicago Linguistic Society. Chicago: Chicago Linguistic Society. Pp. 183–228. (Reprinted in Journal of Philosophical Logic 2:458–508, 1973).
Putnam, H.
  1975. The meaning of meaning. *In* Mind, Language and Reality. Cambridge, England: Cambridge University Press. Pp. 215–271.

4

Prestige and intimacy

THE CULTURAL MODELS BEHIND AMERICANS' TALK
ABOUT GENDER TYPES[1]

Dorothy Holland & Debra Skinner

". . . I can't believe we're talking about this!"

Margaret, an informant in a study of college-age women, said this in the
midst of a "talking diary" interview. Earlier, the interviewer had limited
herself to questions that a friend or new acquaintance might ask: What's
been happening since I talked to you last? How are your classes going?
Who is this Alice that you're talking about? When did you join volleyball
club? Then, at a point in the interview, Margaret began to describe a skit
about "jocks," "frat guys," "Susie Sororities," and other campus types.
For a time, Margaret answered the interviewer's questions about the different types and how they could be identified and then interrupted herself:

Margaret: . . . I can't believe we're talking about this!
Interviewer: Why?
Margaret: I don't know. You just don't sit around talking about it that much
with anybody. It's just kind of there.
Interviewer: So it's not the sort of thing you'd sit around in your dorm room
and talk about to your roommates?
Margaret: No, you allude to it more than anything else.
Interviewer: What do you mean, allude?
Margaret: You know, little things, like, "Oh, you're wearing your add-a-beads
today." Things like that.
Interviewer: And that's all you have to say?
Margaret: Yeah, it's understood.

As might be expected, our participant–observation and interview data
from a group of college-age Americans shows such types to be a conventional way of talking about other people. One hears words like *jock* or
hunk or *freak* in conversations about who John so-and-so is, what he's
like, what he's likely to do, and why he treated Mary or whomever the
way he did. One also hears arguments about whether specific individuals
can be described accurately as a "chauvinist" or whatever category has
been proposed and sometimes, caricatures of men in general—as in
Margaret's skit—couched in these terms. Names like *jerk* and *bitch* are
also popularly used as insults and others like *honey* and *sweetheart* appear in compliments and endearments.

A striking aspect of this talk about other people is that a great deal of knowledge about gender-marked types is taken for granted. Women assume, for example, that telling another woman, "He's an asshole," will be taken as advice to avoid the male approaching them in a bar. They assume that other women know why calling a "jock" an "ass" to his face would be a risky thing to do or why referring to someone as a "hick" is relevant to a description of him as insensitive.[2]

Margaret and our other informants know implicitly what a number of scholars from a variety of disciplines (e.g., Agar 1980; Labov & Fanshel 1977; Rice 1980; Schank & Abelson 1977) have labored to make explicit; namely, with members of one's own cultural group, descriptions are constructed in conventional ways according to unspoken expectations and implicit common knowledge. The hearer is expected to infer missing information cued only by the information that is included and by the genre in which the information is presented. Margaret was chagrined by the interviewer's ignorance of types of men and women, knowledge that she, Margaret, had taken for granted in describing her skit to the interviewer. Not only was she startled by the interviewer's questions, but she also found them difficult to answer. It was hard work to make the information explicit.

Our purpose in this paper is to describe the understandings of male/female relations that Margaret and the other American women in our study take for granted when they converse with one another. We refer to this body of shared implicit knowledge about gender-marked types and about ways to talk about these types as a *cultural model*. Focusing on the manner in which these cultural models of gender are grasped by individuals, we are also interested in how this knowledge of gender types is mentally represented. Does Margaret simply know a list of definitions of *jock* and *frat guy* and other types of males and females, for example, or is her understanding organized in some other way?

A partial account of what women know about the types of males they talk about

STUDY A

In the first set of interviews we collected – the Study A-1 interviews – female informants were asked to list types of males. Male informants were asked to list types of females. Next, they were asked to describe the different types and to tell when someone might use such a term. Those 42 interviews revealed what is easily corroborated by listening to everyday conversation: Americans have an extremely rich vocabulary for talking about males and females. There are hundreds of terms for males and hundreds of terms for females. Furthermore, the vocabulary is colorful. Many of the words are derived by metaphorical extension from the domain of animals, the domain of foods, the domain of objects, occupations, or by metonymic construction. New names are easy to make up and, as *turkey, libber,* and *feminist,* indicate, easily assimilated into common cultural knowledge (Holland & Davidson 1983; Holland & Skinner 1985).

An obvious way to present this American cultural knowledge of gender types is simply to list and describe or define all of these different kinds of males and females. We could even present the definitions in an economic fashion as in the ethnoscience tradition (see, for example, Tyler 1969 or Spradley 1972) by organizing and presenting the terms according to their taxonomic and paradigmatic relations. Tempting though this "dictionary definition" solution might seem, a decade of developments in cognitive anthropology, linguistics, and psychology suggests that this ethnosemantic approach cannot adequately describe how individuals organize their knowledge about gender types. As D'Andrade and associates have demonstrated, dictionary definitions often omit the very attributes of the topic that people think are the most important (D'Andrade et al. 1972). Studies of person and social types, in particular, show that what is important to people about these types is not what one must ascertain about persons to accurately classify them but rather what one must know in order to know how to behave toward them (Burton & Romney 1975; Harding & Clement 1980; White 1980).[3] For Ixil–Maya speakers discussed in Harding and Clement, for example, the important things about social roles are associated wealth, local affiliations, and their relationship to the civic–ceremonial complexes[4] – attributes that might not be included in dictionary-type definitions of the roles (see also Keesing 1979).

Rejecting dictinary-type definitions as a means of describing the cultural model of gender, we turned first to the "cognitive–structure" approach used in the Burton and Romney, Harding and Clement, and White studies. In the Study A–2, interviews informants were asked to do more systematically and more comprehensively what they do on a limited scale in conversation: They were asked to compare and contrast types of males and types of females according to whatever criteria they considered important. If we could find out the bases for comparison and contrast, then we would have an idea of the implicit propositions about gender types that organize women's thinking about men, and vice versa.

From the Study A–1 interviews, we selected 41 male types and 41 female types.[5] We wrote each subtype on a card and asked the respondents to sort the 41 types according to similarity and then to describe the similarities they saw among the types they had put into each pile. The reasons they gave for their sortings were recorded verbatim.

Important characteristics of gender-types. In the Study A–2 interviews, the respondents were allowed to compare and contrast the types according to whatever criteria seemed important to them. In most studies of gender stereotypes, the respondents are not allowed as much freedom; they are given a list of personality traits such as rational, warm, nurturant, and independent and asked to say which traits are characteristic of males, which of females (Rosenkrantz et al. 1968; Spence, Helmreich, & Stapp 1975). If we had been willing to assume that the cultural model of gender is organized according to personality traits, we could have asked respondents to tell us which traits are associated with which types. However, since our Study A–1 interviews showed no exclusive emphasis on personality traits, and since more general studies (e.g., Bromley 1977) show that other characteristics of persons are considered important, we wanted to give respondents freedom to emphasize whatever aspects they considered important. (See Holland & Davidson 1983 for more discussion of the difference between most gender stereotype research and our own.) As it turned out, a variety of characteristics were described, as the following examples show:[6]

1341 [*jock*] a male who is impressed by his own physical prowess – like a matinee idol . . . a physically attractive or physically impressive athlete. People also use it [*jock*] to indicate a physically able and mentally deficient male

0931 [*chauvinist pig*] a guy who believes women are inferior

0131 [*dude, athlete, jock, macho, stud, hunk, Don Juan, playboy, egotist, frattybagger*][7] guys that think they are real cool, woman-pleaser types, conceited type people

0831 [*turkey, nerd, jerk, prick*] all derogatory; terribly insecure

2231 [*wimp, sissy, homosexual, queer, gay, hippie*] they all seem queer. Seem like terms for homosexual except *hippie* doesn't fit. They're all strange, socially unacceptable. They're all fags.

0631 [*man, guy, fellow, gentleman, boyfriend, fiance, lover, sweetheart*] they connote a more positive image . . . the most positive image of all the cards. They connote a kind of "boy back home": a more traditional role of a male as I think of it ideally.

Personality traits are mentioned frequently. Also mentioned are comments on looks, on specific attitudes, on the kind of a date the type makes, on sexual preference, and on many other specific mannerisms and background characteristics.

Our next task was to identify any themes or dimensions that underlay the multifaceted descriptions we had been given. We used a procedure that translates the measures of similarity from the sorting into a visual display. In the visual display that was created by a technique called multidimensional scaling, types that were often sorted together by the respondents were placed close together; types that were seldom sorted together were placed far apart.[8] This multidimensional scaling procedure was used to produce Figure 4.1, which indicates how male types were sorted by females, and Figure 4.2, which indicates how female types were sorted by male respondents.

Multidimensional scaling is primarily an aid to visualizing the patterns of comparison and contrast. It is also useful as a basis for estimating the

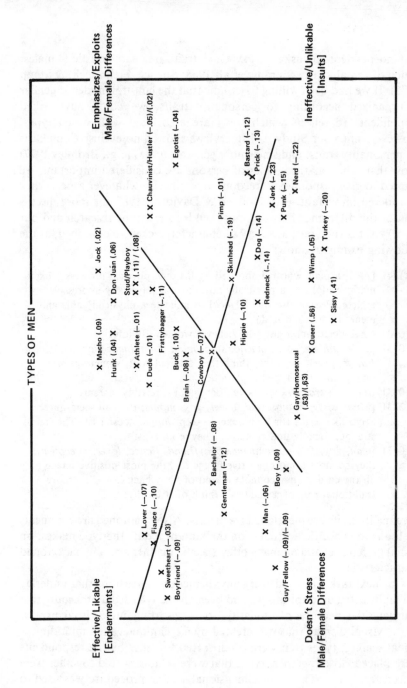

Figure 4.1. Three-dimensional representation of male social types (Stress = .147)

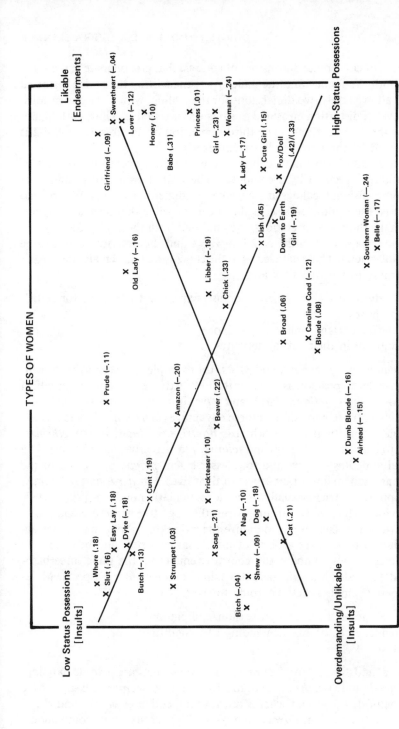

Figure 4.2. Three-dimensional representation of female social types (Stress = .138)

number of conceptual dimensions of contrast that predominate in the sorts. For both the female and the male types, the sorting data were distorted if we allowed only two dimensions for the scaling; with three dimensions, the level of distortion measured as *stress* was acceptable. Thus, both figures show three dimensions. (The third dimension on Figures 4.1 and 4.2 is indicated by the numbers in parentheses.)

The multidimensional scalings are carried out according to a set of algorithms executed by a computer. The next steps are to examine the multidimensional scalings and interpret the dimensions of comparison and contrast the respondents seemed to be using when they sorted the types. To make these interpretations, we analyzed both the explanations given by the respondents in the A-2 interviews and the descriptions from the A-1 interviews. These data led us to the conclusion that females type males according to whether they are:

1. likely to use their position or attractiveness to females for selfish purposes,
2. ineffectual and unlikable, and/or
3. unusual in their sexual appetites

Chauvinists, playboys, and *jocks,* for example, are seen as types who use their social position as males or their attractiveness to women for selfish purposes; *guys, fellows, boys,* and *gays,* in contrast, are seen as being unlikely to try to capitalize on these advantages. *Jerks, nerds,* and *turkeys* are inept and unattractive, whereas *boyfriends, financees, sweethearts,* and, to a lesser extent, *guys* and *fellows,* are attractive and effective. The sexual appetites of *gays* and to a lesser extent *playboys,* are out of the ordinary and an important aspect of their lives. For *nerds* and *skinheads,* the opposite is true; sexuality is not a particularly notable aspect of their behavior. What we are arguing from the cognitive–structure analysis is that women focus on and organize their thinking about male types according to these three aspects of male characteristics and behavior.

Males do not compare and contrast females on the same three bases just described, although there are some complementary aspects. Males compared female types according to their:

1. prestige as a (sexual) possession/companion
2. tendency to be overdemanding and engulfing
3. sexiness

Bitches and *scags,* for example, are types that are overdemanding; *girlfriends* and *sweethearts* and, to a lesser extent, *women,* are supportive and helpful. *Foxes* and *whores* are sexually enticing; *prudes* and *dykes* are sexually repelling. *Foxes* and *dolls* are high-status sexual companions, whereas *whores* and *easy lays* are low status. These characteristics are important to males about females.

Summing to this point: Study A has provided partial information on the cultural models of gender types for our samples. As a cognitive entity, a cultural model may be defined as learned mental representations of some aspect of the world – in this case, gender types. These mental representations or schemas actively guide attention to components of the world and provide inferences about these components and their various states and form a framework for remembering, reconstructing, and describing experiences. (For a related conceptualization of *schema,* see, for example, Neisser 1976 or Rice 1980.)

Study A provided the broad outlines of the characteristics that females are guided to look for in types of males, and vice versa. These models tell females what to pay attention to about new males they meet, what to be on guard about in males they already know, and what questions to ask about newly identified types of males.

Limitations.   On the basis of Study A, we felt we had correctly grasped the characteristics of male and female types that were important to the respondents. We also felt that based on what we had learned about these important characteristics and what we had learned about the conventions for naming types, we could correctly predict how the respondents would react to types we had not included in the interviews and even how they would be likely to react to names of newly identified types. Using a method such as Burton's (1972), we could have undertaken a validation of our interpretations and predictions; however, we were concerned about certain limitations of our approach and decided instead to examine another source of data.[9]

The type of analysis we had done – cognitive–structure analysis – did not adequately present the total amount of information we had learned from the interviews. Cognitive–structure analysis is predicated on the idea of underlying "dimensions of meaning" as the organizing structure for the set of terms – in this case, gender types. The question of how these dimensions are mentally grasped by informants has received little explicit attention in the literature (see D'Andrade 1976 for an exception), but the implication is that the dimensions or characteristics of importance can be described accurately as single attributes or features of meaning.

We had difficulty in finding and, as is discernible from the labels affixed to Figures 4.1 and 4.2, did not manage to isolate in every case, a single attribute or descriptor that seemed to capture the sense of the "characteristic" the respondents were talking about as the basis for their comparisons of the different types of males and females. Even when we did use two attributes or a descriptive phrase, we found it was not clear from our descriptions how women integrated "ineffective" and "unlikable" as co-occurring characteristics, for example, or why "exploitation of male/female differences" should not also be coupled with "unlikable." Furthermore, we realized that our descriptions of the characteristics as simple attributes were also limited because these attributes did not offer any insight into the affect our respondents displayed when they discussed the different types. There was information from the interviews that illuminated these questions, but clearly that information was not being effectively conveyed by the cognitive–structure analysis that presented the "characteristics" as though they were simple attributes. A more accurate way of describing the "characteristics" had to be found.

A SECOND LOOK AT STUDY A

We returned to the A–1 and the A–2 interviews to find out how the respondents had communicated a sense of what *jocks* or *wimps* or *broads* are like. We reread the 460 or so descriptions of individual types in the A–1 interviews and the 250 or so explanations for the groupings of types in the A–2 inerviews.

In both sets of interviews, the descriptions were strikingly similar and included a variety of information. Some descriptions were limited to single descriptors reminiscent of the attribute-like features we had first looked for to describe the "dimensions" from the multidimensional scaling. These single descriptors often had to do with character, mood, or personality:

0231 [*sissy*] a male who is effeminate
0431 [*bastard*] a male who is mean
0331 [*turkey, nerd, jerk, frattybagger*] these are people who are just plain stupid
1031 [*stud*] a guy who is horny

Other single-focus descriptions contrasted with these in that they depicted not the type's inner state, but rather his acts or behavior:

0731 [*hustler*] a male who takes advantage of a person
0931 [*pussy*] a guy who doesn't stand up for what he believes in or who is a coward
0931 [*pimp*] a man who prostitutes women

Another large set of the descriptions were unlike the ones just quoted in that they included more than one type of information. They contained information about the type's inner state *and* information about his behavior *and* other information, such as females' reactions to him.

0431 [*boy, dude, dog, wimp, hippie, turkey, punk, nerd, jerk, prick, skinhead*] these are losers – all the names that you call really queer dates. They're usually immature or ugly, or think they're cool, but aren't at all. They try to impress girls, but actually make fools of themselves.
2231 [*redneck, dog, turkey, punk, nerd, jerk, skinhead, cowboy, brain*] I think of little 98-pound weaklings – jerks. They're all ugly little jerks that you'd never want to be seen with, or never want to talk to. You cannot get rid of them.
1131 [*couchwarmer*] a guy who is too cheap to take you out so he takes you to his home all the time.

0431 [*lover, athlete, jock, macho, stud, egotist, bastard, hunk, Don Juan, playboy*] these are the typical jock-type, good looking but they know it. Can get any type of girl they want because girls usually go for them. They're popular.

0331 [*Don Juan, playboy*] implies someone who likes to play around – women are attracted to them but they don't set up a serious relationship.

0331 [*ladies' man*] a friendly man who is deceitful. Ladies' man and macho man are variations on the same theme – one tends to have larger biceps.

1331 [*boyfriend, fiancé, lover, sweetheart*] these are all subtitles of what we would call the man who is showing the romantic side of a man in relation to a woman.

0431 [*sissy, homosexual, queer, gay*] they're the type you find in my dancing class. They're just all gay, pretty unmasculine, talk with a lisp.

The respondents were clearly not limiting their thinking to a single characteristic of the male types they were describing. In order to convey their sense of the social types, they were providing, it might be surmised, the outlines of a social drama, or sometimes, a scene from the drama. In the scenes – which are sometimes described as though they were being visualized – the male type plays a role in an encounter or a relationship with another person, usually a female. He is her date or perhaps her friend or her would-be lover. His style of playing the role is different from how an ordinary male would play the role. In the descriptions, the unusual aspects of his style are communicated by an account of his actions or a description of his intentions, personality traits, or beliefs, He is friendly, but deceitful; he thinks he is cool, but actually makes a fool of himself. Sometimes, we also are told the female's reactions to such males (e.g., "women are attracted to them," or "they can get any girl they want").[10]

The recognition that the respondents were constructing their descriptions of gender types from social scenes or perhaps scenarios made it clear why trying to describe the characteristics of the types as single attributes was a difficult and perhaps impossible task. In trying to represent the information conveyed to us by the respondents as single attributes, we had undertaken the task of describing a gestalt of social information and action in a few words. Although the multidimensional scaling had assisted us in our identification of the key behaviors and characteristics of the different types, it did not help us in the identification and description of the taken-for-granted social world in which these characteristics are significant.

The realization that the respondents were thinking of the types in terms of social dramas rather than single attributes prompted further study. The aim of Studies B and C – analyses of two other sets of data – was to uncover premises about the social worlds associated with the scenarios: What makes types such as *jocks* or *wimps* so special that they are labeled as different from ordinary males? What were the respondents assuming about normal relations between males and females that made these types stand out?

Besides the implications of our reanalysis of Study A, the work of linguist Fillmore also encouraged us to pursue the examination of this taken-for-granted world of male/female relations. We noted a similarity between the kinds of *scenes* that Fillmore (1975:124) argues are associated with linguistic frames and the descriptions given us by the respondents. Fillmore has presented his proposed *frame semantics* by elucidating the meaning of words such as *orphan* and *widow*. He (1975:129; 1982:34) has argued that the meaning of *bachelor,* for example, is integrally related to a conceptualization of a social world in which such things as bachelors exist. *Bachelor* cannot simply be defined as an unmarried male, for the role of *bachelor* is not relevant to all the social worlds in which unmarried males are found. Is Pope John Paul II a bachelor? Is a trice-married, presently divorced man a bachelor? Fillmore says that the category of *bachelor* is not relevant to these cases because the worlds of the Pope and the trice-married, divorced man deviate from the conceptualization we have of the social world in which bachelors exist.

A complete analysis of the type suggested by Fillmore is given by Sweetser (this volume) for the word *lie.* She shows that the meaning of *lie* is not detachable from a conceptualized social world in which communication between individuals follows a culturally standardized, normative pattern. In this simplified world, the telling of false information has certain consequences, such as harm to the recipient of the lie, and thus is clearly a reprehensible act. Perhaps, we reasoned, the exploitation of male/female differences has particular poignancy to the women in our sample because of the implications of exploitation in the simplified world in which *Don Juans, machos, hunks,* and *chauvinists* are relevant characters. Perhaps females attach importance to ineffectiveness and insensitivity in males because this characteristic poses a difficult problem for what is taken for granted to be the normal course of male/female relationships.

STUDIES B AND C

Studies B and C were conducted in the same locale as Study A with the same age population two years after the completion of Study A. Studies B and C consisted of participant–observation research and tape-recorded one-to two-hour interviews. The 23 informants of Study B and the 10 informants of Study C were each interviewed an average of 8 and 5 times, respectively. The participation–observation research was useful because it revealed the extent to which the same kind of talk about males and females that occurred in the interviews was also occurring in the everyday activities of the informants.

The Study B interviews primarily consisted of "talking diary" interviews in which the informant was asked to describe what had been happening to her since the interviewer had last seen her. In the course of these interviews, which took place over a year-long period, the respondents frequently talked about encounters and relationships with males. As suggested by the excerpt from the interview with Margaret at the beginning of the paper, the "talking diary" interviewers tended to stay within the bounds of questions the women were accustomed to answering and talking about with their peers.

The Study C interviews provided a more out-of-the-ordinary task for the informants. They were asked to tell about their first and then subsequent memories of someone, usually someone with whom they had had a relatively long relationship. After they had told about the memories as they wished, the interviewer asked in-depth questions about their impressions of and reasoning about the individual, often requiring the informant to make explicit information or beliefs about males and females that she would have otherwise taken for granted.

In searching through these interviews for relevant passages, we looked for passages in which the gender of the other was of explicit significance to the informant's reasoning about the other person. Any passage which included reference to the gender-marked social types that had been identified in Study A–1 was automatically consulted. Our guiding questions were: What do our informants assume about ordinary relationships between males and females? and What are the taken-for-granted worlds in which these male and female types interact? As it turned out, this taken-for-granted world is a world of prestige and intimacy gained and lost.

The taken-for-granted world of male/female relationships

In the taken-for-granted world of male/female relations, from the perspective of the women in our study, a male earns the admiration and affection of a female by treating her well. Intimacy is a result of this process. The female allows herself to become emotionally closer, perhaps as a friend, perhaps as a lover, perhaps as a fiancée, to those attractive males who make a sufficient effort to win her affection. Besides closeness and intimacy, the process of forming a relationship also has to do with prestige. When a male is attracted to a female and tries to earn her affection by good treatment, her attractiveness is validated and she gains prestige in her social group. For his part, the male gains prestige among his peers when he receives admiration and affection from and gains intimacy with females.

Normally, prestigious males are attracted to and establish close relationships with prestigious females, and vice versa. Sometimes, however, a male can succeed in winning the affection of a female whose prestige is higher than his own. However, the more attractive she is, the more he must compensate for his lack of prestige by spectacular efforts to treat her well. Correspondingly, females sometimes do form close relationships with males who have higher prestige than they do. When the male is more attractive or has higher prestige than the female, she often must compensate by giving her affection to him without his doing anything to earn it.

Several aspects of this world can be illustrated by interpretations that informants made of their experiences with males. It should be noted that although the interpretations included in the following sections pertain primarily to romantic relationships, our data indicate that friendships between a male and a female are interpreted in terms of the same taken-for-granted world.

THE INGENIOUS BEAU

Karla had an "official boyfriend," Christopher.[11] Meanwhile, another guy, Alex, was doing things like showing up at her door with the gift of an egg, dyed purple. For a visit to listen to records, he appeared dressed in a costume befitting the punk-rock genre, a costume he had creatively assembled from castaway clothes and a dead carnation. What meaning could this bizarre behavior have? Karla interpreted it as an effort to win her affection:

Karla: . . . if you want to get down to brass tacks, the main crux of the problem [with the relationship with Christopher] right now is this new guy. Because I must say he fascinates me, he fascinates me more than anyone I've ever known and furthermore he's making the most interesting efforts to get me.

Alex was treating Karla well. Being well treated by a male means being shown special considerations and courtesies; having one's values, desires, and feelings taken seriously; and being appreciated for one's qualities and accomplishments. Some other examples of such treatment besides the creative efforts of Alex included things, in Karla's eyes, like wearing a jacket on a casual date and being pampered when one is feeling sick.

Another informant, Diana, gives additional examples in a life history interview. She begins by talking about how attractive females want to date attractive males and then switches to the kind of treatment she expects from males.

Interviewer: How about dates . . . any more to add on dates? What was important to you?

Diana: Well, if you were fairly nice looking you wanted to date a good looking guy, I mean, that was probably all part of our ego, we wanted to have the best looking date or things like that . . . of course you wanted to be attractive to them [males] you know. Like I said, you wanted them to think that you were pretty . . . .

Interviewer: Did you want them to think anything else?

Diana: Of course you wanted them to think you had a good personality, that you weren't just beauty and no brains. But it was important to me for someone to respect my values and most of my friends were the same. Of course, there's, in every community there's a few girls that don't have such strict moral values, but we wanted to make sure that the guys that we went out with did respect that or we wouldn't go out with them any more. All my friends were about the same in that respect; we wanted our dates to respect us and treat us like ladies, not like one of the fellows.

Interviewer: What would constitute being treated like a lady?

Diana: Well not only respecting our moral values, but to me, at least, maybe it was because I was in the role of the female where you were old-fashioned and so on, but it was important for them to open the door for me, seat me if we went out to eat, to open car doors for me, just common courtesy that a lot of times you don't even think about.

KARLA THE GERM

Bad treatment is being ignored, being unappreciated or scorned, and being treated like an object rather than a person. In describing her relationship with Christopher, Karla recounted a phase of their relationship in which she became disgruntled with how Christopher was treating her. The situation came to a crisis when she returned to school after a holiday and promptly came down with a bad case of the flu. Instead of being solicitous, Christopher tried to avoid her:

Karla: Well I was . . . feeling so horrible that night about nine o'clock that I put on my pajamas and went to bed, and Christopher comes by at 9:30 to see me. And he says, "What are you doing in bed?" Well [when I told him], he just kind of like turned pale. And I thought that it would be nice, very nice of him [*laughs*] to sort of well, you know, bring me a little chicken soup, tell me to have a nice day, send me a little card. I really wanted that, but instead he just, . . . he wasn't exactly rude, but he sort of got out of the room as fast as he could cause he's so scared he'd get it, and I can understand that, his practice schedule, he plays with a university group, if he got sick it would screw him up a lot, but I don't like being treated like I have germs, whether I have them or not. . . .

Later that week, Christopher took her to a play even though he was still afraid of catching the flu from her:

He didn't say this, but he went out with me anyway, but he was just kind of like on edge all night long because of that and I think that's why he started making some nasty remarks. . . . So that made me angry and that's why we had our big fight. . . .

Interviewer: How did uh, why did you . . .

Karla: I said, "Why, how dare you treat me like a germ?" And he asked me to explain this, so I did and I told him that I had not had a good time that evening [*laughs*] and, I said that, well . . . it was earlier in the evening in the restaurant that he had made the nasty comment about my family. I said, "Christopher, how can you sit there and say something like that, and act like your family and your family's background is so much better than mine when this very evening, Christopher, you have behaved with no class whatsoever?" . . .

Karla interpreted Christopher's behavior as bad treatment, treatment that suggested that she was nothing more than an object – a germ. She thought that he had overestimated his own attractiveness or prestige relative to hers and that he had no right to expect her affection if he continued to treat her in a condescending manner. Eventually, she let him know she was angry.

Although Karla changed her interpretation after another talk with Christopher, she initially took his behavior as meaning that he considered his prestige to be higher than hers. In subsequent passages, she described how she responded by challenging and bringing about a change in his definition of their relative positions. Evidence of the negotiation about relative prestige or attractiveness and its significance is also evident in the following passage.

THE UPPER HAND

"I just don't want him to get the upper hand on me. . . ."

Karen is describing a guy she has just started to date. She has been talking about the times he calls for dates and how much he likes her. She goes on to explain that she has not been completely straightforward with him:

Karen: . . . I just don't want him to get the upper hand on me, you know. Like I play games with him . . .
Interviewer: Could you give an example?

In response to this question, Karen discusses in a very oblique way how northerners' (Hal, the new guy that she is dating, is a northerner) morals are different from those of southerners (Karen is from North Carolina). She describes northerners' sexual morals as being more "open and carefree."

Interviewer: When you said that part about you didn't want him to get the upper hand, could you talk a little more about that?
Karen: I didn't want him to think that I was really crazy about him and that he could just use me, you know, maybe if he knew I'd want to go out with him and stuff like that. So that's why I just sort of let him, in fact I was trying to get it with him, you know, get the upper hand with him, but it didn't work. He's the same way, you know.
Interviewer: How did you try to do that and why didn't it work?
Karen: Well, you know, I'd tell him – he'd say something about going out and I'd say, "Well just . . . we probably will, but it's a little early right now." I'd do stuff like that, and he'd ask me, he asked me if I had, um, well the first night he asked me if I had a boyfriend back home and I didn't say anything, and he says, "Well, I figured you did." And, I said, "Well . . ."; I didn't say anything, you know. I just told him that I dated a couple of guys, you know. I didn't tell him if I still saw them or not, you know.

She goes on to explain other ways in which she tries to give Hal the impression or allows him to infer that she has other boyfriends, including such subterfuges as sometimes leaving the dorm when she thinks he is going to call.

Here, Karen has read a lot into Hal's pattern of calling and asking her out and making overtures to her. She has interpreted his behavior as a preliminary move in a negotiation in which she and he work out whether his prestige or attractiveness is higher than, equal to, or lower than hers. If she appears to have an active social life, then her prestige as an attractive female is in evidence and he will not be able to treat her badly by taking her for granted and not calling when he says he will or, perhaps, although she does not directly say this, expecting her to become sexually intimate faster than she would choose to. If, on the other hand, his prestige is high, as evidenced by the fact that she finds him extremely attractive, then he will be able to exploit her and treat her badly if he wants to. She would rather that her prestige be seen as higher than his so she acts to bring about that interpretation.

Women judge whether their friends' relationships make sense in terms of the treatment they receive from males. Whether bad treatment is understandable to other women comes up a number of times in our data. From the cultural model, a female may form a relationship with a very attractive male even though he treats her badly. An example of the application of this idea comes from Diana. Diana has been having a number of run-ins with Donny, her boyfriend, who attends a university in a nearby city. Their calls often end in recriminations and tears on Diana's part. Her friends on the hall constantly point out to her that Donny is being mean, that he's just a "jerk." Diana's reply to them can be summarized in her words: "It must be love." She implies that she finds him so attractive that she is willing to sacrifice good treatment for the sake of being around him. Her friends are not convinced. They think he's not worth the trouble he causes Diana; he does not seem all that attractive to them.

Problematic males

These stories describe experiences that the informants interpret according to a set of assumptions about normative relationships between males and females. In the taken-for-granted world constituted by these assumptions, arrogance in a male has special implications and getting involved with an "asshole" has predictable consequences. Arrogance, as elaborated below, has implications for a male's assessment of his own status relative to that of the females around him; the ineffectiveness or insensitivity of an *asshole* is problematic because of the way he is likely to treat females. This taken-for-granted world, in other words, provides the background against which several basic types of males pose a special challenge or problem for females. These types were foreshadowed by the dimensions identified in the multi-dimensional scaling. The problematic males are those who are arrogant and use their position or attractiveness as males for their own selfish purposes in interactions with females, are insensitive and unlikable, and have unusual sexual appetites.

ARROGANT AND SELFISH MALES

From our informants' interpretations, males who think they are "God's gift to the earth," "who think that anyone without a penis doesn't exist," "who are arrogant and out for themselves," and "who are good looking, but know it" are problematic because they are likely to assume that they do not have to earn a female's admiration and affection and intimacy; they are likely to expect these things from females simply on the basis of their looks or other claims to high prestige.[12] They are likely to be able to exploit their attractiveness and prestige for their own selfish purposes, treating females in a bad or demeaning manner, and not suffer for their behavior. Examples of how informants see these *jocks* and other types are provided by the data.

Annette and Sam.   In one of her interviews, Karen told about an encounter she summarized as follows:

Karen: A friend of mine [Annette] invited us, invited several of us to a party at a dorm. And, she told us that there'd be . . . , a couple of people there that she really liked a lot, guys, that is . . . well, they're on the basketball team, you know, big jocks and stuff like that, you know, and . . . when we got there, um, the main one she wanted to see . . . I mean, he just, he didn't even hardly acknowledge her presence. He practically didn't even speak to her. . . . And, it just sort of messed up the whole party – mainly for her, and because of that, it messed it up for all of us.

The remainder of the interview was devoted to questions about this episode:

Interviewer: What were your expectations when you went to the party?
Karen: . . . I expected to meet a couple of the players, and . . . I expected, you know, some real nice guys. And I thought that well, they'd be real glad to see her, and you know, just real friendly and everything. And, but, they, they didn't.
Interviewer: What . . . how did they act when they came? I guess there were two of them that came at different times.
Karen: Yeah. One of them [Robert] was real nice to her and glad to see her and all, you know. That wasn't the main one she wanted to see, the one she wanted to see [Sam] acted real stuck-up, you know, as if she wasn't even there.
Interviewer: Oh, how did he do that?
Karen: He, he ignored her. And, I mean, he saw her several times . . . she'd be standing practically beside him, and he wouldn't say anything . . . this other girl came and he just talked to her practically the rest of the night.

Later, the interviewer asks Karen why she thinks Sam acted as he did:

Karen: I don't know if he was, if he, if, I don't know if maybe she just had it in her head that he liked her, or if he was just, if he didn't want her around, and he was just trying to talk to this other girl or something. But he did act, he acted sort of too good for her, you know?

The interviewer asked for more detail about why Sam acted as he did:

Karen: . . . maybe because he was a big jock on campus or something, that he
thought, that, you know, she was just an average girl, and he was too good
for her, or something. But, um, I didn't look at him that way until he walked –
you know, he walked in, and then he just sort of carried himself like, you know,
everybody's looking at me. And, I didn't like that at all about him. And, um,
he, he was just, it just seemed like he was standing there waiting for people
to come and talk to him, you know. Instead of him acknowledging anybody
else. . . .

Karen talked about how upset Annette was and said she thought perhaps
if Annette could talk to some other guy, she would feel better.

Interviewer: What? Why would that make her feel better?
Karen: Um, uh, she probably, I don't know, I guess just to boost her confidence
back up, or to make her feel like she's really somebody. Instead of what he,
I mean he made her feel like she wasn't even alive. . . .

Annette continued to be upset about the incident, and Karen explained
that Annette was trying to reason out why Sam acted as he did:

Interviewer: What were some of the ways she reasoned it out?
Karen: Um, well, she thought at first maybe because he was with that girl, he
didn't want to talk to anybody else. And, but then, he was talking to other girls
that were walking by, and um, then she was thinking, maybe he was mad at
her, but she didn't know why, you know, she was just thinking of different stuff
like that.
Interviewer: Did you think of any things like that too?
Karen: Uh, not really, I, I, it's gonna sound terrible. I thought, well he just didn't
want to, didn't want to see her at all, cause he just didn't, I don't know, what
I thought was that, he was like I said before, he was some big jock on campus,
you know, and he just wanted the real, um, just certain girls around him, you
know.
Interviewer: What . . . what kinds?
Karen: Real pretty, you know, real – (I think Annette's pretty, too) – and he
just, you know, to make him look that much more better, you know. That's
what I was thinking, after I, after I saw what he was doing to her.
Interviewer: Why would, why do you think that he would want that, would want
these girls?
Karen: I guess to help his image, you know, make him look that much more
better.

In Karen's interpretation, Annette is treated badly. Her presence is not
even acknowledged by Sam. The situation is an embarrassing one because
Annette has revealed her attraction to Sam yet he has ignored her; she
has been shown to be less attractive or of lower prestige than Sam. She's
just an average girl.

In Karen's eyes, Sam's attractiveness is diminished. She says, "I didn't think he was attractive anymore." Her inclination is to demean him, to label him as a lower status male, an unattractive type:

Karen: . . . I wanted to tell him, he, you know, what he did to her, you know, that he was acting like an ass.

She does not call him an "ass," however, because she did not think Annette would have wanted her to and because he was around a group of people and she did not want to "make a fool" of herself either. Obviously, other people, such as the woman he was talking with, did not think Sam was an ass.

   Another part of this story contrasts Sam with Robert. Attractive males do not necessarily exploit their attractiveness for their own ends; they are not necessarily demeaning to females who have less prestige than they do. Robert was nice. He treated Annette very well and even went out of his way for Annette's friend, whom he had just met:

Karen: Oh, I like him [Robert] a lot, yeah. Cause he, cause he made her laugh and, he was just, so, he was real nice to all of us. And, um, well, one of my friends wanted a beer, you know, but there was this real long line, so he just walks right up. He takes a cup and goes and breaks in front of everybody, you know, and gets it and brings it. He takes a cup and goes back to her, you know. That really impressed me, there, cause he didn't know her, he didn't have to do that. You know. And um, that's just the type of guy he was, you know, just real friendly and nice to everybody.

Robert was attractive and he treated Annette, his friend, in a way that earned her affection and admiration (and Karen's, too). Even though he was attractive and did not have to do things for Annette, he did. The difference between him and Sam, as Karen interpreted it, was that Robert just wanted to have a good time whereas Sam wanted to make himself look better.

   Not only was Sam guilty of demeaning Annette, he, in Karen's interpretation, was also using females to further his own ends. He was not sincerely trying to earn their affection and admiration and giving them good treatment in return. He was simply using them to get what he wanted – in the case of the party, increased evidence of his own attractiveness:

Karen: . . . you know it's just like they're [guys like Sam] they're out for themselves, you know, just to make, "I just want to be seen." You know, it's like they're just using the girl or something. . . .

INEFFECTIVE AND UNLIKABLE MALES

In contrast to males who are problematic because they are attractive but prone to treat women badly, there is a second type whose labels are used as insults. Karen, for example, fantasized insulting Sam by telling him he was acting like an "ass." Diana's friends claimed Donny was acting like a "jerk." *Jerks, nerds, turkeys,* and *asses,* among others (see Figure 4.1) constitute this second type of problematic male. These males are both unattractive and insensitive and thus unlikely to receive a female's admiration and affection. Lacking sensitivity to what females want, these low-prestige males are neither attractive to women nor are they effective at pleasing females and thereby earning their affection. Two accounts from the data illustrate interpretations of experience in which this type of male plays a part.

Patty and the hick.   Patty was asked to describe someone whom she knew from her work. She picked Erve, a colleague, at the school in which she teaches. As a potential friend, she found Erve wanting:

Patty: . . . And I mostly don't care for him very much. Part of it is the fact that he's a real Okie kind of person, in a derogatory sense, and I mean it that way, he's a real hick. . . .

Patty goes on to list many things she dislikes about Erve, including his lack of a sense of humor, the strange things he says in the middle of conversations, the way he usurped the position of the coach, the tactless way he deals with the students, his disruption of the faculty lunches by his topics and styles of conversation, the fact that he asked her her age but did not tell his, and so forth. Furthermore, he did not seem to realize that she disliked him:

Patty: . . . and the other thing that now tops it off is for some reason he's decided I'm his friend and he will come and talk to me, and there's a period of the day, it's usually about twenty minutes of three . . . when everybody fades out and you can get something done, and he will come in there if he hasn't got anything to do and he will talk a blue streak, and I feel resentment about that. And I'm a passive–aggressive person so I never say anything. I just sit there and feel, and he's not long on sensitivity, so he never picks up the vibrations . . . I disagree with just about everything I seem to have noticed about him.

At a later point in the interview, Patty further elaborates the idea that Erve is oblivious to her desires and feelings:

Patty: . . . But in an annoying situation, I will put up with the situation rather than make waves. However, to someone who knows me, the air is absolutely thick with unharmonious vibrations.
Interviewer: And he doesn't?
Patty: No, he does not pick up on those things at all. There are people who will receive such feelings and ignore them and there are people who do not receive, and he is a nonreceiver.

In describing his lack of attention to her feelings, she reiterated a situation in which she had complained to him about his treatment of a student and he had simply made a joke of her statement as though he did not understand she was angry:

Patty: . . . I was really peeved. I did it quite pleasantly, but anyone with a grain
of sensitivity would have noticed that I was peeved. Carl [another teacher] knew
that I was peeved; Alice [the principal] knew that I was annoyed and they heard
me say the words in the same tone of voice that this guy did.

Erve, in short, is remarkable in his lack of sensitivity.

Patty also points out in the interview that Erve has a lower-class style
about him, is "uncivilized," and has very parochial tastes in many aspects
of life. Her comments, plus those of other informants and respondents
in Study A, suggest that lower-class males are thought to be insensitive
to females and therefore are not likely to treat a female well. Upper-class
males are more likely to know how to respond to a female and thus are
more likely to be able to earn the admiration and affection of females.
Other sources of insensitivity are stupidity and meanness of character.

Rachel and Edward.   The main problem with the kinds of males who
get classified as "jerks" and "nerds" and so forth is that they are often
obnoxious. They are so insensitive that they cannot even tell they are unattractive to the female and so they often act as if the relationship were
a closer one than what the female wants. Erve, for example, apparently
could not sense Patty's negative opinion of him. He would come to her
room and talk to her for long periods of time despite the fact that she
did not want to talk to him. Another example of a male persevering in
trying to get closer to a female is given by Rachel in her description of
a painful and frustrating weekend with Edward.

Rachel had been friends with Edward for many years. They had been
planning to go on a weekend camping trip with two other friends. At the
last minute, Edward casually phoned Rachel to tell her that the other
friends had decided not to go and that he and Rachel should stay at his
university instead of going to the mountains. Rachel was annoyed. She
did not want to be alone with him for such a long time. However, because
it was too late to arrange anything else and because she really wanted to
go somewhere, she went to see him. The entire weekend turned out to
be a frustrating struggle over the closeness of their relationship, with
Edward indicating he wanted them to be closer and Rachel indicating she
wanted the relationship to be less close. This struggle had been going on
for quite a while:

Rachel: . . . several periods during our relationship he's wanted to get closer than
I wanted to get. I don't know, he's a really great guy and I feel real close to
him, deep down, but personality-wise, we just have a lot of conflicts, and I don't
know, he requires a lot of patience from me. To be around him I have to kind
of say, "Okay. You're going to be around Edward, really put yourself down
on his level." And he really needs me, as a friend, I feel like, and he tells me
that. So I'm just not as enthusiastic about our relationship as he is. Lately, he's
just, he's been, every time we've been together, which is several times a month,
he'll bring up this stuff about, you know, he just can't help the way he feels

and he can't stand it anymore, blah, blah, and I've told him how I felt, I can't change my feelings and I'm really tired of talking about it. . . .

Rachel's assessment of Edward is that he speaks in a "hicky way" and is not "attractive to the opposite sex." His ideas have not developed much beyond what they were many years ago when they first became friends:

Rachel: . . . he seems very immature to me now. Sometimes I feel like he must have been dropped on his head when he was a baby, I mean, he's really slow sometimes.

That Rachel does not feel attracted to Edward is a problem in the face of his efforts to win her affection:

Interviewer: How does it make you feel that he wants the relationship to be closer, whatever?

Rachel: It makes me feel real sad because I don't feel that way at all, and I know how much it means to him and there's really nothing that can be done about the situation, so it hurts me that he feels that way and it seems kind of like a hopeless situation right now, because he really can't get along too well right now without our friendship, but it's painful for him to have the friendship too. It also repulses me too because I can't stand the sight of us being more than friends. I'm just not attracted to him, and [then there's] our personality differences, it just never entered my mind at all.

Despite his efforts to treat her well, Rachel is not attracted to Edward, and because of his perseverance in his attempts to get closer, she becomes irritated by his lack of acceptance of her feelings. Although he cares for her and does things for her, he is not attractive enough or sensitive enough for her to want a closer relationship with him. Rachel attributes his disregard of her negative feelings to his family background and possibly his fundamentalist religious upbringing. She says he may have gotten the mistaken idea that males can earn a female's closeness, or at least that he can win hers, simply by dint of will power. Not only was Edward's attractiveness not sufficient for how close he wanted the relationship to be, but he also had the problem of not being able to accept that he was pursuing a lost cause. This made him even more unattractive in Rachel's eyes because she found his overtures obnoxious and irritating.

Erve and Edward are problematic types for two reasons: (1) they are not very attractive or likable, and (2) they are also handicapped by a lack of awareness or lack of character to the point that they are, in some situations, at least, unable to tell what a female would like. For the more insensitive types of unattractive males who cannot tell what a female wants, there is little chance of earning an attractive female's affection, admiration, and intimacy by treating her well.

Unattractive, insensitive males would not be a problem if they understood their situation and acted on that understanding, but they are often so "out of it" that they fail to understand their position. They act as though they are attractive and capable of earning a female's admiration and affection. They hang around females who are more attractive than they are and are obnoxious because the female has to "put them off."

In both Study B and Study C, we found cases in which such names as *jerk, ass, asshole,* and *creep* were used as insults. In Study A, as well, respondents often indicated that these were insulting and derogatory names. It is now clear why this is the case: These names refer to types who are neither attractive nor adept at treating females well. They refer to men who are on the bottom of the prestige ranking; they are the least likely of males to earn females' admiration and affection. Their insensitivity makes them treat females as poorly as *jocks, Don Juans* and *egotists* are likely to do, but they do not have the redeeming quality of these latter types of being attractive in some way. Their prestige is especially low because they do not even know when they are disliked. They make "fools" of themselves by pursuing attractive females who are not at all interested in them. This factor of prestige is why Karen could not call Sam an "ass" and not look like a fool herself. By calling Sam an "ass," Karen would have been indicating that his prestige was low and that therefore it was unlikely he could earn the admiration of a female. Clearly, Sam did not have this problem. Not only was he known as a "big jock on campus," he was also at the party with a female.

MALES WHO HAVE (UNUSUAL) SEXUAL APPETITES
From the Study B interviews, we know that talking about the sexual aspects of one's current relationships is an indication of intimacy or closeness. Most of our informants did not feel close enough to us to discuss sex and sexuality in their own personal relationships. The ones who did discuss these topics in the interviews had moments of embarrassment, and even the very articulate ones had difficulty in finding words to describe their interpretations. Where sex and sexuality are talked about on a more impersonal level as a topic of conversation or as a target for joking, however, the informants were less reticent. The "horny" and "oversexed" person, for example, was caricatured even in our presence for comic effect.

Because of the informants' reticence and difficulty in talking about the aspects of their relationships that had to do with sex and sexuality, we have only a few in-depth accounts that present information relevant to informants' views on types of males who are problematic because they are sexually unusual or extraordinary. Because of this limitation, we include only one of the few relevant stories plus list a set of assumptions that have been pieced together from the data:

1. Males have a natural desire for sexual intimacy with females, and vice versa.
2. Besides desiring sexual intimacy for its own sake, males also want to demonstrate their sexuality.
3. It is the female's prerogative to decide the extent of sexual intimacy she has with a male.

4. As with affection, admiration, and other forms of intimacy, females are more prone to choose to be sexually intimate with a male if they find him attractive.

Males who have unusual sexual appetites are those who prefer to have intimacy with other males. Also unusual are heterosexual males who have an unnaturally high level of desire and/or a strong need to demonstrate their sexuality. These males are problematic in terms of the presupposed world of male/female relations because both types are likely to provide little prestige or intimacy to females. Homosexual males focus on males and, although they can be friends with females, they are not suitable romantic partners for females. They are, in fact, competitors for other males. Sexually aggressive heterosexual males are even more problematic. They are prone to treat females in an uncaring manner because sex or their sexuality is of foremost importance to them, not the female and her concerns. They may become overly focused on sex and disregard aspects of the female that are important to her own self-identity. Or, the attractive ones may take advantage of their attractiveness, accepting intimacy from a woman with no intent to treat her well. Or, they may make overtures that cause her to have to make decisions about intimacy before she is ready. Karla, for example, in describing a "pass" a man made at her on their second date, recounts how she assessed what she considered to be a fast invitation to intimacy:

Karla: I guess for about two weeks there, I was looking around for a surrogate for my old boyfriend. And [after this incident] I started looking on him as somebody who would be more of a challenge, someone who'd be kind of fun to play with because I realized this attitude which would lead him to ask me that sort of question on the second date would also make him rather interesting to deal with, and so I was not put off from dating him at all, I just realized that I'd have to be rather clever about it.

As Karla interprets it, males who have a strong sex drive or a high need to prove their sexuality are more of a challenge than males who do not. Relating to them is riskier because the pace is faster and more difficult to control than is the case in a normal relationship. Also, there is greater risk of being treated badly.

Summary of the cultural model of gender types

For American women, at least the ones in our samples, there is a standard, taken-for-granted way in which close male/female relationships – both romantic and friendship – come about. The male demonstrates his appreciation of the female's personal qualities and accomplishments by concerning himself with her needs and wants, and she, in turn, acts on her attraction to him by permitting a close, intimate relationship and by openly expressing her admiration and affection for him.

In the prototypical relationship, the two parties are equally attractive and equally attracted to one another. However, if the discrepancy in relative attractiveness is not too great, adjustments are possible. A relatively unattractive male can compensate for his lesser standing by making extraordinary efforts to treat the woman well and make her happy. A relatively unattractive female can compensate by scaling down her expectations of good treatment. When sufficient compensation is not in evidence or when the more attractive partner seems to be the one who is compensating, the relationship does not make sense and people say to one another: What does he see in her? or, Why does she put up with him?

Don Juans, turkeys, gays, and other types of males are singled out and talked about in relation to this taken-for-granted world of male/female relationships. These types have characteristics that lead them to cause problems for women. Attractive, popular males who are arrogant or self-centered, for example, take advantage of their attractiveness to women to gain affection and intimacy without intending to enact the friendship or romantic relationship that would normally follow mutual attraction in the taken-for-granted world. They treat the woman badly, which puts her in an uncomfortable position (like that of Annette) of being shown to be less attractive than the male. The woman has revealed her affection and admiration for the male with nothing to show in return.

In contrast to *Don Juan, jock,* or *chauvinist* types, there are the *jerks* and *nerds,* who are not adept at pleasing a female. Unattractive males of this type, the "losers," are particularly problematic because they often pursue a female who is more attractive than they are. Since they are not only unattractive but also inept at earning her affection by treating her well, they are engaged in a futile pursuit. Yet they hang around, impervious to her disinterest and unaware that she is more attractive than they. Eventually, they become obnoxious.

Sexually different males also create anomalies in the taken-for-granted world of male/female relationships. Both homosexual males and males who are heterosexual but overly focused on sexual activity render the meaning and value of physical or sexual intimacy between males and females problematic. Homosexual males do not want intimacy with females and therefore cannot be romantic partners for females. Relationships are a priori arrested at the level of friendship. Males who are overly sexually aggressive, on the other hand, force females to a decision about intimacy before the relationship has progressed very far. They are also unlikely to carry through with the relationship because for them there is less involvement with the female as an individual, a person.

Discussion

Two questions were posed at the beginning of the paper: What do Americans leave unspoken when they talk about gender types? and How is this implicit knowledge mentally organized? The preceding section summarizes the implicit knowledge that the women in our samples take for granted about male/female relationships and about types of males who are likely to cause a relationship to go awry. Here, we outline the implications of our research for the cognitive organization of knowledge about gender types. The final section of the paper discusses the questions of the susceptibility of the cultural model to change and its likely distribution in the American population.

THE COGNITIVE ORGANIZATION OF CULTURAL KNOWLEDGE ABOUT GENDER TYPES

Our studies indicate that individual Americans understand talk about *jerks, wimps, he-men, chicks, broads,* and their behavior by thinking of these characters in relation to a taken-for-granted relationship between males and females. In the prototypical sequence of events described in detail in the previous section, a male and a female are attracted to one another and develop a close relationship in which they become friends and/or romantic/sexual partners. Cognitively associated with this taken-for-granted course of male/female relationships are scenarios of disruption in which one or another of the participants causes the relationship to abort or go awry. Most gender-marked types, it turns out, are types who cause such disruptions.

This organization of knowledge according to prototypic events and scenarios is not what we had originally anticipated. At the start of our study, as explained, we rejected the hypothesis that knowledge about gender types is cognitively organized as a list of definitions of *fox, doll, scag,* and so forth. We turned instead to an analysis of the cognitive structure or similarity structure of the set of types. Researchers customarily assume that this type of analysis, which is usually carried out with the aid of multidimensional scaling, identifies key attributes of a domain (e.g., gender types) and that these key attributes organize and orient people's thinking about the domain. Such an analysis presumes that knowledge about gender types is basically organized according to a set of attributes.

Our studies indicated, however, that such an approach was of limited utility for gender types. When the people in our sample were asked which types were similar, they did not perform this task by explicitly focusing on important attributes of the types. Rather, they related the types to a set of scenarios in which the prototypical male/female relationship is disrupted. We found, in other words, that respondents compared types of males and females according to their fit to scenarios. Furthermore, in order to explicate the scenarios, we found it necessary to consult additional data, from which we inferred the underlying taken-for-granted world of male/female relationships. The multidimensional scaling did assist us in identifying an important aspect of the cultural model, namely, the groupings of problematic types of males and females. Cognitive–structure analysis did not, however, provide us with a means of or a motivation for presenting the scenarios that seemed to be an integral part of our respondents' thinking about these different gender types. Nor did it provide us with the information about the taken-for-granted world we needed to understand the scenarios and their emotional poignancy. Nor did it prepare us for the description of scenes that respondents sometimes seemed to picture as a means of capturing the nature of the type.

Without knowledge of the scenarios, we would have been at a loss to explain why respondents thought some terms for gender types could be used as insults whereas others could not. The multidimensional scaling approach offered no indication why calling a male a "Don Juan" or a "playboy" or a "jock" or some other type who is likely to take advantage of a woman is usually not considered to be insulting whereas calling someone a "creep," a "turkey," a "jerk," or some other type of ineffectual male is. We had to learn more about the taken-for-granted world of male/female relationships to know that even though males who use their attractiveness to exploit women may be avoided because they are dangerous, they are not as low in prestige as males who are unlikable and ineffective. Males of the latter category are unattractive. A woman who refers to a male as an "asshole" is indicating that he is unattractive relative to herself. She is indicating that she finds him "beneath her." The same is not necessarily the case for a woman who refers to a male as a "Don Juan." She is not necessarily insulting him. Although she may avoid him for fear that he will take advantage of her, she is attesting to his attractiveness, and, in fact, may be admitting that he is more attractive than she is.

In a similar vein, the present analysis illuminates rather than obscures, as does cognitive–structure analysis, the implications of categorizing someone according to a gender type. As Boltanski and Thevenot (1983) have pointed out, social–classification systems are different from nonsocial classification systems because, in applying them, one is also classifying oneself. In typing a male, a female is typing others and herself. This reflexive quality of categorization by gender type is both explained by the cultural model and apparent from the scenarios that include both the male and the female. Relationships between males and females reflect on both parties because of the assumptions in the cultural model that attractive males will choose to be with attractive females, and vice versa, and that attractive females can expect better treatment from males than can less attractive females. To classify a male is to make claims about the male and implicitly about oneself and about other women who have a close relationship with him. In calling Donny a "jerk," the women on Diana's hall were doing more than saying something about Donny. They were saying that they would not put up with his behavior and that they would not be associated with him. Classifications reveal one's standards and sensitivities and therefore one's assessment of one's own attractiveness and claims to prestige.

In short, we argue that the cognitive organization of gender knowledge is insufficiently illuminated by an approach such as cognitive–structure analysis, which assumes that there is a set of key dimensions or attributes onto which sets of similar gender types are mapped. Our informants associate type names with a prototypic male/female relationship and with scenarios of interactions that they sometimes seem to visualize, not just attributes, as would be expected from cognitive–structure analysis. Furthermore, although people do know important attributes of the different gender types and can say which types are similar and which dissimilar, they also know more – a lot more. They have knowledge of a taken-for-granted world to which these types are relevant and thus they know how the various attributes are interrelated. They know not only that some gender names are insulting but also the basis for and the emotional intensity of the insult. Similarly, they appreciate the reflexivity of categorizing other people by these terms. It is possible that a neophyte (perhaps a child, an anthropologist, or a freshman) begins to learn gender types by memorizing what a cognitive–structure analysis reveals – similar types and their important attributes – but it is also likely that the neophyte would eventually infer the more fundamental parts of the cultural model. She would form an idea of the normal or prototypical course of male/female relationships and come to see the named gender types as actors in this prototypical world. She would go beyond the limited organization of knowledge revealed by the cognitive–structure analysis.

INERTIA OF THE CULTURAL MODEL

If our argument is valid and the cultural model does organize the extensive amount of knowledge that we claim it does, then the difficulties of radically altering the model become apparent. The world posited by this cultural model is simply taken for granted as the world to which new experiences are relevant. Not only are new males seen as participants in this world, but they are also seen as possible variations on the small number of problematic types already identified. Gathering information on each new male or female one meets is unnecessary; one need check for only a small number of characteristics. However, the price of this cognitive economy is a bit of rigidity in interpreting the world and a certain slowness in recognizing or learning new models.

Cognitive constraints are important forces for the inertia of the cultural model; even more important are the constraints that derive from the social nature of the model. Verbal descriptions of individuals as gender types are understood by listeners in light of the cultural model. Comments such as "Wearing your add-a-beads, eh?," are heard against the backdrop of the extensive implicit knowledge organized by the cultural model. Even new names for new types are interpreted according to this model; one guesses what the type is like – extensive explanation is unnecessary (Holland & Skinner 1985). The shared cultural model vastly facilitates communication; experiences can be rapidly communicated to other people if described according to the conventions of the cultural model. Again, however, economy has a price. It is easy to communicate about the familiar but difficult to communicate about the unfamiliar. Even though it is certainly possible and perhaps even easy for some individuals to think up or recognize new gender types, communicating a concept of a truly new, radically different type of male or female to other people is a formidable task. Talk about types, new or old, is assumed to be talk that can be interpreted according to the cultural model. Even if the individual manages to think "outside" the cultural model (which may in fact happen quite frequently), he or she still will face considerable difficulty in communicating the alternative models to other people. Because it provides the backdrop for interpreting and the conventions for talking about experiences, the cultural model is a social entity not easily altered by a single individual.

Along these lines, one wonders if truly radical changes can be made in the model by the mere introduction of a new type, such as a *feminist,* or, as the men in our samples labeled the type, a "libber." Elaborating or introducing a new type is a relatively mild attack since the bedrock of the model, the taken-for-granted, prototypic relationship of males and females is, at best, challenged only indirectly and the new type is easily distorted to fit the existing model. Because the conventions for talking about females and males as types are so much an integral part of the cultural model described here, it is likely that totally new ways of talking about or describing or representing male/female relations may be an easier means through which to introduce new models of these relations. The essays of feminist social scientists, for example, or more likely the self-analysis talk learned in therapy could provide the new discourse genre.

THE DISTRIBUTION OF THE CULTURAL MODEL ACROSS SOCIAL
SPACE AND HISTORICAL TIME

The samples consulted in this study can tell us little about the distribution of alternative cultural models of gender over time and across social groups in the United States. The samples were predominantly composed of respondents who are white, southern, and middle class. Furthermore, most of the Study B and Study C data come from women who are young and unmarried.

Young, unmarried women attending universities such as those where our studies were conducted are usually participants in a social system that is closer to what Coleman (1961) and others such as Schwartz (1972) and Eisenhart and Holland (1983) have associated with adolescence or youth than it is to adult society. This youth society emphasizes social identities based on gender and, to a lesser extent, social class. Much of youth culture is devoted to the elaboration of gender relationships and gender types (see Davidson 1984 and Holland & Eisenhart 1981 for further detail on the peer groups of the women in our samples). The importance of gender-marked social types such as those described in this paper, in other words, may be a function of the age of the group studied.

Similarly, the dynamics of attractiveness and intimacy posited by the cultural model may be particularly stressed in youth as opposed to adult culture. Once the women in our samples have married and had children and/or permanently joined the labor force, they perhaps will learn a different perspective on male behavior. A male's potential behavior in and contribution to a household economy and family relationships or his behavior in the workplace may become more important to these women than the male's potential for providing intimacy and proof of one's attractiveness as a woman. Yet, we are reluctant to assume that the cultural model of gender has no currency in the thinking and talking of participants in adult society. Our interviews with an albeit limited sample of older women suggest that the cultural model continues to be important in the interpretation of experiences that occur in the formation of friendship and (extramarital) romantic relationships with males and in the interpretation of certain relationships in the workplace. Males who systematically treat female co-workers differently from male co-workers are interpreted according to the cultural model described here.

Perhaps even more intriguing than the question of the distribution of the cultural model across age groups is its relevance to our samples' male counterparts. The cultural model of gender described may be "role-centric." Unlike scientific models, which are supposedly constructed from a detached perspective, the cultural model provides for the interpretation of males from the point of view of the female in a (potential) male/female relationship. It is also the case that when the women in our samples talk extensively about particular males, they are usually talking to other women. For these reasons, it might be expected that males' cultural models of gender could differ from that of the females and that males' models tend to take the perspective of the male in the relationship. Unfortunately, we lack in-depth interviews from the males and so have been restricted in our description of the males' perspective. The data from males in the Study A interviews do suggest, however, that males share with females a concern for attractiveness and intimacy although from a different vantage point. Complementary to females' concern about good treatment, for example, males are sensitive to their vulnerability to the demands of females; they worry about becoming involved with a female who is too demanding, too "bitchy."

FUNDAMENTALS OF SOCIAL CATEGORIZATION

In our study, we ignored the question of alternative models of gender that may exist in different age, class, ethnic, and regional groups in the United States because we were concerned with a prior question; namely: How do individuals cognitively grasp the cultural models that inform their talk about gender types? Our work is an answer, from the perspective of cognitive anthropology, to the question of which aspects of the cultural model of gender are fundamental, basic, and stable versus which aspects are superficial and likely to be transient. In general, the process of identifying a cultural model involves determining fundamental versus surface elements of the complex of beliefs and knowledge (see also Clement 1982). The distinction between fundamental and surface elements of a belief system, is, of course, a necessary precursor to meaningful cross-(sub)cultural comparison.

Because of the limited availability of comparable research on social types, it is unwise to anticipate future generalizations about the cognitive fundamentals of cultural models of social types. Recognizing the perils, however, we would speculate that the organization of cultural knowledge will be similar for other social types, at least in American culture, to what we have found in the case of gender. We suspect that the implicit knowledge that informs the talk of other subgroups about gender types and the talk of all groups about other social types such as types of children, or types of hospital patients, or general role terms as described in Burton and Romney (1975) and in Harding and Clement (1980), may all conform to the pattern we have noted in the American cultural model of gender types. We suspect that the type names refer either to roles (e.g., *boyfriend, fiancé, bachelor, date*) in the taken-for-granted world or, more likely, to styles of enacting these roles (e.g., *Don Juan, jerk, wimp*) that disrupt the prototypical course of the relationship to which they are relevant.[13] On the other hand, we seriously doubt that the content of the prototypic relationship and therefore the problematic social types will be the same from one culture to another.

Notes

1. Because this paper draws on three separate research projects, there are many people and agencies to thank. First are the many individuals who participated in the studies as respondents, as informants, and as interviewers. Second, several sources of funds made it possible to collect and analyze a large amount of data: a grant from the National Institute of Education (NIE-G-79-0108), a National Research Service Award (1-F32-MH08385-01), grants from the University Research Council of the University of North Carolina at Chapel Hill (1-0-101-3284-VP376, 1-0-101-3284-VP497), and a Kenan leave from UNC. An earlier version of this paper was presented at the Princeton Conference on Folk Models; comments made by conference participants were extremely helpful. A version was also read in the departmental colloquium series at the University of North Carolina. Thanks go to the insightful comments of participants at that colloquium as well as to a helpful critique by Luc Boltanski.
2. Because the samples in Studies B and C (described below) included only two males, the paper focuses on women's perspectives of men.
3. Holland's pre-1982 publications are under the name of Clement.
4. The Ixil have suffered serious hardship and decimation in the recent and currently on-going government reprisals in Guatemala. As a result, the cultural and social systems of the Ixil have changed considerably since these data were collected (B. N. Colby, personal communication).

5. We selected types that were mentioned frequently. Otherwise, we attempted to include a wide range of types.

6. The codes indicate the following: The first two digits are unique identifiers for each respondent. The third digit refers to age, with code "3" indicating 18 to 25 year-olds. Codes "4" and above are older. A code of "1" in the fourth digit indicates a female respondent.

   The respondents for the A–1 interviews included 13 females aged 18 to 25 and 13 females who were 40 or older. The corresponding figures for the male respondents were 8 and 8, respectively. For the second interview, all the respondents, 16 males and 26 females, were all between the ages of 18 and 25. All the respondents were residing in North Carolina at the time of the interview. The implications of the sample limitations are discussed below.

7. In the A–1 interviews, respondents described one gender type at a time. In the A–2 interviews, the sorting interviews, they described the grouping of types they had formed.

8. From the sorting data, we calculated similarity measures among all pairs of items using the formula suggested by Burton (1975). These similarities measures were then analyzed using a nonmetric multidimensional scaling program developed by Kruskal (1964a; 1964b) as modified by Napior.

9. Since completing the present paper, we have tested our ability to predict reactions to types not included in our A–2 interviews and to types whose names we created. Our predictions, which were based on the cultural model described in this paper and on conventions we had noted in the names for the types, were largely borne out (Holland & Skinner 1985).

10. In some cases, the description is not about the type of person to which the term refers, but rather is about a type of person who would use such a term or the kind of situation in which the term would be used:
    1231 [*buck, macho, stud, chauvinist, egotist, bastard, prick, hunk, Don Juan, playboy*] what a female chauvinist pig would think of males – stereotypical attitudes.
    (cm Case 6 in Fillmore 1982:34)
      Another example of this kind of assessment was given by a local professional who looked over the names collected in Study A–1. He said his clients would be disdainful of the terms we had been given for homosexuals. He summarized their opinion in a retort, "Only a wimp would call a fag, a 'gay.'"

11. All names are pseudonyms. Furthermore, a few details from the passages have been changed to protect the anonymity of the informants.

12. In the campus cultures of the two universities where these studies were carried out, one big source of prestige for males is participation in athletics, particularly on the University varsity squads.

13. Marilyn Strathern's (personal communication 1984) observations of the Hagen of New Guinea must be noted as a possible counterexample. Hagen males talk about females as gender-marked types, but they do so in the context of exchange and transaction, not in the context of interpreting problematic behavior in a cross-gender interpersonal situation.

References

Agar, M.
1980. Stories, background knowledge and themes: Problems in the analysis of life history narrative. American Ethnologist 7(2):223–240.

Boltanski, L. and L. Thevenot
    1983. Finding one's way in social space: A study based on games. Social Science
       Information 22(4/5):631–680.
Bromley, D. B.
    1977. Personality Description in Ordinary Language. New York: John Wiley
       and Sons.
Burton, M.
    1972. Semantic dimensions of occupation names. In Multidimensional Scaling:
       Theory and Applications in the Behavioral Sciences, Vol. 2, Applications,
       A. K. Romney, R. N. Shepard, and S. B. Nerlove, eds. New York: Seminar
       Press. Pp. 55–71.
    1975. Dissimilarity measures for unconstrained sorting data. Multivariate
       Behavioral Research 10(4):409–423.
Burton, M. and A. K. Romney
    1975. A multidimensional representation of role terms. American Ethnologist
       2(3):397–407.
Clement, D.
    1982. Samoan cultural knowledge of mental disorders. In Cultural Conceptions
       of Mental Health and Therapy, A. J. Marsella and G. M. White, eds.
       Dordrecht, Holland: D. Reidel Publishing Company. Pp. 193–215.
Coleman, J.
    1961. The Adolescent Society. New York: Free Press.
D'Andrade, R. G.
    1976. A propositional analysis of U.S. American beliefs about illness. In Mean-
       ings in Anthropology, K. H. Basso and H. A. Selby, eds. Albuquerque:
       University of New Mexico Press. Pp. 155–180.
D'Andrade, R. G., N. R. Quinn, S. B. Nerlove, and A. K. Romney
    1972. Categories of disease in American–English and Mexican–Spanish. In
       Multidimensional Scaling: Theory and Applications in the Behavioral Sci-
       ences, Vol. 2, Applications, A. K. Romney, R. N. Shepard, and S. B. Nerlove,
       eds. New York: Seminar Press. Pp. 9–54.
Davidson, D.
    1984. Transmission of gender-specific knowledge in women's peer groups. Un-
       published master's thesis. University of North Carolina, Chapel Hill.
Eisenhart, M. and D. Holland
    1983. Learning gender from peers: The role of peer groups in the cultural trans-
       mission of gender. Human Organization 42(4):321–332.
Fillmore, C. J.
    1975. An alternative to checklist theories of meaning. In Proceedings of the
       First Annual Meeting of the Berkeley Linguistics Society, C. Cogen, H.
       Thompson, G. Thurgood, K. Whistler and J. Wright, eds. Berkeley: Univer-
       sity of California. Pp. 123–131.
    1982. Towards a descriptive framework for spatial deixis. In Speech, Place, and
       Action, R. J. Jarvella and W. Klein, eds. New York: John Wiley and Sons.
Harding, J. and D. Clement
    1980. Regularities in the continuity and change of role structures: The Ixil Maya.
       In Predicting Sociocultural Change, S. Abbott and J. van Willigen, eds.
       Athens, Ga.: University of Georgia Press. Pp. 5–26.
Holland, D. and D. Davidson
    1983. Themes in American cultural models of gender. Social Science Newsletter
       68(3):49–60.
Holland, D. and M. Eisenhart
    1981. Women's peer groups and choice of career. Final report to National In-
       stitute of Education, Washington, D.C.

Holland, D. and D. Skinner
  1985. The meaning of metaphors in gender stereotyping. North Carolina Working Papers in Culture and Cognition No. 3. Durham, N.C.: Duke University Department of Anthropology.
Keesing, R.
  1979. Linguistic knowledge and cultural knowledge: Some doubts and speculations. American Anthropologist 81(1):14–37.
Kruskal, J. B.
  1964a. Multidimensional scaling by optimizing goodness of fit to nonmetric hypotheses. Psychometrika 29:1–27.
  1964b. Nonmetric multidimensional scaling: A numerical method. Psychometrika 29:115–129.
Labov, W. and D. Fanshel
  1977. Therapeutic Discourse: Psychotherapy as Conversation. New York: Academic Press.
Neisser, U.
  1976. Cognition and Reality. San Francisco: W. H. Freeman and Company.
Rice, G. E.
  1980. On cultural schemata. American Ethnologist 7(1):152–172.
Rosenkrantz, P., S. R. Vogel, H. Bee, I. K. Broverman, and D. M. Broverman
  1968. Sex-role stereotypes and self concepts in college students. Journal of Consulting and Clinical Psychology 32:287–295.
Schank, R. and R. Abelson
  1977. Scripts, Plans, Goals and Understanding: An Inquiry into Human Knowledge Structures. Hillsdale, N.J.: Lawrence Erlbaum Associates.
Schwartz, G.
  1972. Youth culture: An anthropological approach. Addison-Wesley Module in Anthropology, No. 17. Reading, Mass.: Addison-Wesley Publishing Company.
Spence, J. T., R. Helmreich, and J. Stapp
  1975. Ratings of self and peers on sex role attributes and their relation to self-esteem and conceptions of masculinity and femininity. Journal of Personality and Social Psychology 32:29–39.
Spradley, J., ed.
  1972. Culture and Cognition: Rules, Maps, and Plans. San Francisco: Chandler Publishing Company.
Tyler, S. A., ed.
  1969. Cognitive Anthropology. New York: Holt, Rinehart and Winston.
White, G.
  1980. Conceptual universals in interpersonal language. American Anthropologist 82(4):759–781.

5
A folk model of the mind[1]

Roy D'Andrade

A cultural model is a cognitive schema that is intersubjectively shared by a social group. Such models typically consist of a small number of conceptual objects and their relations to each other. For example, Rumelhart (1980), following Fillmore (1977), describes the schema – and cultural model – of *buying* something as made up of the *purchaser,* the *seller,* the *merchandise,* the *price,* the *sale,* and the *money.* There are several relationships among these parts; there is the interaction between the *purchaser* and the *seller,* which involves the *communication* to the *buyer* of the *price,* perhaps *bargaining,* the *offer to buy,* the *acceptance of sale,* the *transfer* of *ownership* of the *merchandise* and the *money,* and so on. This model is needed to understand not just *buying,* but also such cultural activities and institutions as *lending, renting, leasing, gypping, salesmanship, profit making, stores, ads,* and so on.

Cognitive schemas tend to be composed of a small number of objects – at most seven plus or minus two – because of the constraints of human short-term memory (Miller 1956; Wallace 1961). For example, to judge if some event is an instance of "buying" something, the person making the judgment must decide whether there has been a *purchaser, seller,* some *merchandise* with a *price,* an *offer,* and an *acceptance,* along with the appropriate *transfer.* Since all these criteria must be held in mind simultaneously to make this judgment with any rapidity, the criteria cannot exceed the limits of short-term memory.

The number of objects a person can hold in mind at any one moment is limited, but these objects may themselves be complex schemas (Casson 1983). In the *buying* schema, for example, the part labeled *bargaining* is itself a complex schema that involves a *potential purchaser* and *seller,* an *initial price,* a series of converging *bids* and counter *offers,* and possibly a *final agreement.* Through hierarchical organization, human beings can comprehend a schema containing a very large and complex number of discriminations. The amount of work involved in unpacking a complex cultural schema can be quite surprising.

One consequence of the hierarchical structure of schemas is that certain cultural models have a wide range of application as parts of other models.

The cultural model of *money,* for example, has a wide range of application, serving as a part of many other models. Although it is unlikely that anyone knows all the models of any culture, to have a reasonable understanding of a culture, one must know at least those models that are widely incorporated into other models.

A schema is *intersubjectively shared* when everybody in the group knows the schema, and everybody knows that everyone else knows the schema, and everybody knows that everyone knows that everyone knows the schema (the third "knowing" is necessary because although you and I may both know the money is hidden in the teapot, for example, and I may know that you know (I saw you hide the money there), and you may know that I know (you caught a glimpse of me when I was spying on you as you hid the money), yet because I do not know that you know that I know, I cannot assume that your seeing me look at the teapot would tell you that I was thinking about the money. However, when everybody knows that everybody knows that everybody knows, then anyone's glance toward the teapot is understood by all, including the one giving the glance, as a potential reference to the money.

One result of intersubjective sharing is that interpretations made about the world on the basis of the folk model are treated as if they were obvious facts of the world. The spectators at a baseball game all see that a particular pitch, thrown over the head of the catcher, was obviously a *ball,* and so obviously a ball, that one would have to be blind to miss it. Of course, those people who do not know the game of baseball, seeing only the catcher trying to catch something thrown to him, cannot make such an interpretation and do not experience any such fact.

A second consequence of the intersubjective nature of folk models is that a great deal of information related to the folk model need not be made explicit. For example, in describing a game of baseball in which at the bottom of the ninth the score was tied, the bases were loaded, there were two outs, and the count was two and three, the narrator has only to say that the pitch was so far over the head of the catcher that he couldn't even catch it. People who know baseball do not need to be told the pitch was a ball, the ball gave the batter a walk, the walk forced a run home, the run gave the game to the team at bat, and the game was over. The narrator, speaking to someone who knows baseball, can reasonably assume that what obviously must happen (given the rules of baseball) does not need to be stated.

One cultural model with a wide range of application in American and European culture is the *folk model of the mind*. This model can be called a "folk" model both because it is a statement of the common-sense understandings that people use in ordinary life and because it contrasts with various "specialized" and "scientific" models of the mind (see Keesing this volume). This model is widely incorporated in a variety of other cultural models, such as categories of criminal acts, the classification system found in ordinary language character terms (D'Andrade 1985), categories of speech acts (D'Andrade & Wish 1985), and the cultural model of *commitment* involved in marriage (Quinn 1982) and so on.

An interesting characteristic of many kinds of cultural models is the quality of awareness of the model displayed by informants. In the case of the model of the mind, for example, most informants do not have an organized view of the entire model. They *use* the model but they cannot produce a reasonable *description* of the model. In this sense, the model is like a well-learned set of procedures one knows how to carry out rather than a body of fact one can recount. This difference corresponds to the distinction made in artificial intelligence circles between "procedural" knowledge, such as knowing how to ride a bicycle, and "declarative" knowledge, such as knowing the history of France (Rumelhart & Norman 1981). However, the folk model of the mind does not seem to be a completely procedural system since informants can partially describe how the model operates when asked questions about specific examples.

One issue raised by the attempt to make explicit the folk model of the mind is the question of the empirical basis – the accuracy – of the model. At one extreme, it might be argued that this folk model of the mind is based on "obvious" facts of human experience. That is, one might argue that people can perceive their internal states and processes just as well as they can perceive trees and birds, and so the folk model is simply a description of what is there – perhaps it could not even be described differently. At the other extreme, one might argue that by their nature, internal states and processes are so difficult to perceive that the folk model has no more relation to reality than has the Azande model of witchcraft. Cross-cultural information about folk models of the mind in other cultures is potentially relevant to a resolution of this problem. Some comparison of the model presented here for American–European ("western") cultures and Lutz's Ifaluk material on ethnopsychology are presented in the last section of this paper. At this point, it is sufficient to note that this folk model cannot appropriately be applied under all circumstances; it generally is not thought to apply to such special conditions as "hypnosis," or to various mental disorders such as "psychosis" and "depression." Indeed, it seems that when the model does not apply to how someone is acting, people consider the person to be in an "abnormal" state. Thus, the model seems to act as a standard for determining "normality."

I have found the work of linguistic philosophers, such as Anscombe, Vendler, and Searle, to be very helpful in developing a description of the western folk model of the mind, although sometimes it is difficult to decide if philosophers are describing how our folk model of the mind *is* or how it *should be* (see, for example, Ryle 1948, who did not like the western folk model of the mind at all). Also, philosophers are willing to criticize a folk model with respect to its internal consistency and its logical compatibility with other models in the same culture – a move anthropology has yet to make (but see White this volume). Work done by Edwin Hutchins in an unpublished paper on how people generate explanations of ongoing behavior has also been very helpful, although the model developed by Hutchins differs considerably from the model presented here (Hutchins, n.d.).

The initial model appears in the next section. It is followed by a summary of the major propositions of the model and a set of interview questions designed to test these propositions, along with illustrative interview responses. The informants were five college and high school students who had never had courses in psychology. The interview material presented here has been selected on the basis of clarity and explicitness. None of the interview material from the five informants contradicted the model, although some of the material could not be derived from just the model given here. In addition, some material from daily life and from literature that illustrates use of the model is presented.

In the last section of this paper, this folk model is contrasted briefly to the scientific models of the mind found in academic psychology and psychoanalytic theory, and then related to a nonwestern folk model of the mind described by Catherine Lutz, with some concluding speculations about cross-cultural similarities and differences.

The model of the mind

The folk model of the mind is composed of a variety of mental processes and states. These processes and states, as indicated by English verbals, are:

a. *perceptions:*
    i. simple state – see, hear, smell, taste, feel
    ii. achieved state – spot, sight, notice
    iii. simple process – look, observe, watch, listen, touch
b. *belief / knowledge:*
    i. simple state – believe, know, remember, expect, assume, doubt, imagine, suspect, recall
    ii. achieved state – understand, realize, infer, learn, find out, discover, guess, conclude, establish, forget
    iii. simple process – reason, think about
    iv. accomplished process – figure out, plan
c. *feelings / emotions:*
    i. simple state – love, like, fear, hate, blame, approve, pity, sympathize, feel sad, feel happy
    ii. achieved state – forgive, surprise, scare
    iii. simple process – enjoy, be frightened, be angered, be bored, mourn, emote
d. *desires / wishes:*
    i. simple state – want to, desire, like to, feel like, need

    ii. achieved state – choose, select
    iii. simple process – wish, hope for
e. *intentions:*
    i. simple state – intend to, aim to, mean to, plan to
    ii. achieved state – decide to
f. *resolution, will, or self-control:*
    i. simple state – determined to, resolve to
    ii. achieved state – resolve to
    iii. simple process – force oneself to, make oneself, strive

The distinctions of *state* and *process* and the subdistinctions of *achievement* and *accomplishment* are based on the time schema of the verb (Vendler 1967). When we inquire about a process, we ask, "What are you doing?" and the answer is, "I am looking/thinking/enjoying . . ."; that is, one is carrying out a repetitive set of internal actions. When we inquire about a state, we do not ask what the person is ". . . ing," rather we ask "Do you see/believe/like. . . ?" Outside idiomatic use, we do not say, "I am seeing/believing/liking. . . ." Both the state and process occur in time, but a process is something marked by an *iteration* of some action and thus admits continuous tenses.

In many cases, one can treat the same internal events as either a process or state. "I have been thinking about the tie-up on the freeway" references the process of thinking, whereas "I believe we should avoid the freeway" places oneself in a particular state of belief. This semantic distinction indicates that the folk model has two different ways of regarding the mind – as a collection of "internal states" versus a set of "internal processes." A typical illustration of this distinction is the "sleeping person" example: Whether Joan is awake or asleep, we can say she knows the multiplication table, fears nuclear war, probably intends to go shopping this weekend, and so on. But only if she is awake can we say she is calculating the answer to 11 times 15, worrying about nuclear war, planning to go on a trip, and so on. Thus, the mind is treated both as a *container* that is in various states and conditions, thereby having large number of potentialities simultaneously, and also as a *processor* engaged in carrying out certain operations, thereby being limited to a small number of concurrent actions.

Further, states are linked to processes in that typically someone is in a particular state because some process has or is occurring. Thus, John *sees* Bill because he is *observing* Bill; Sally *believes* Lisa is her friend because she went through the process of *assessing* her relation to Lisa and finally *concluded* she was a real friend; and Roger has been *frightening* his cousin, which is why his cousin *fears* him.

There is another relevant time distinction in English verbs based on the notion that certain processes and states are defined by a climax or terminal point that marks the end of the state or process. When such ter-

Table 5.1. *Characteristics of internal states*

Perception	Belief	Feelings	Desires	Intentions	Resolutions
cause outside mind	cause inside mind	cause inside and outside mind	cause inside and outside mind	cause inside mind	cause inside mind
takes simple objects	takes prop. object	takes either	takes prop. object	takes prop. object	takes prop. object
self usually agent	self usually agent	self usually object	self usually agent	self always agent	self always agent
not controllable	usually controllable	usually not controllable	not controllable	controls itself	control of control
count noun	count noun	mass noun	count or mass	count noun	count noun
have many at once	have one at a time	have many at once	perhaps have many at once	perhaps have many at once	perhaps have many at once

minal points define a state, they are called *achievements*. When they define a process, they are called *accomplishments*. For both achievements and accomplishments, we ask, "How *long did it take* to . . . ." Generally, we do not ask how long a simple state or process takes – we do not say, "How long did it take to believe that . . . ." For the simple states and processes, the event is treated as homogeneous across the entire period through which it occurs. Once one begins the process, one is truly in the process even if it is concluded abruptly. Thus, even if one *thinks* for only an instant, one has *been thinking*. However, no matter how long one has been at it, one does not *realize* something until that very moment when the light dawns (Vendler 1967).

There are a number of ways in which the various processes/states differ from each other. Table 5.1 summarizes a collection of these differences.

In Table 5.1, the *resolution* category is almost indistinguishable from the *intentions* category. In general, what appears to distinguish resolutions from intentions is that resolutions are second-order intentions – intentions to keep certain other intentions despite difficulty and opposing desires.

The first distinction in Table 5.1 involves the concept of cause: the idea that certain events are thought to bring about other events. Except in pathological cases, what one sees, hears, and/or senses is understood to be caused by various events and objects external to the mind. What one knows or believes is usually considered to be a creation from within, a result of the operation of the mind itself. What one feels emotionally is more problematic. Sometimes emotions are treated as something caused – at least in the sense of being "triggered" – by external events ("E.T. is so charming I couldn't help liking him.") At other times, emotions are treated as internally generated by the person ("Thinking about the game made Charley nervous.") Desires, like emotions, are also seen as both internally and externally caused. Intentions and resolutions, however, are treated as directly caused only from within.

Whether caused from the outside or created inside, according to the folk model one is generally aware of what one perceives, thinks, feels, desires, and intends. Of course, sometimes one can see something and not be fully aware of what one saw, or have some feeling or desire about which one is confused, but these are treated rather like problems that can be resolved by turning one's full attention to the situation.

Perceptions, thoughts, feelings, and so on in verb form vary in the kinds of objects they take. There appear to be two major kinds of objects: *simple* objects and *propositional* objects. Simple objects are objects like "cats" and "disasters" – they are things and events *in* the world, not thoughts *about* the world. Propositional objects, on the other hand, are not "things" – they are "thoughts" or "beliefs," such as the belief that there is likely to be a nuclear holocaust. Perception verbs usually take simple objects – we see John, hear about the war, notice a mistake. However, what one believes or knows, wishes or hopes for, aims to do or resolves to do normally involves some proposition about the world. In philosophy, states such as knowing or intending that take propositional objects are called "intentional states" (Kenny 1963). Stative verbs – that is, simple states and achieved states – of feeling and emotion can take either simple or propositional objects; for example, "Tom fears that Sue lost her wallet" *versus* "William is afraid of lightning." In the first case, it is a propositionalized state of affairs (something imagined or thought) that is the object of Tom's fright; in the second, it is an external physical event that causes William's fear. It seems to be the case that feelings and emotions are sometimes treated in the folk model like perceptions that take simple objects and sometimes like cognitions that take propositional objects.

Emotions also differ from the other internal states in that some emotions do not need an object of any kind: I may feel anxious or sad or happy not about anything, but just in general.

Anscombe (1963) and Searle (1975; 1980) have pointed out that there are different "directions of fit" for various internal states. Perceptions and thoughts should fit the world, that is, should correspond to how the world is. But in the case of desires, intentions, and resolutions, it is the world that someone wants to bring to fit whatever state of affairs is represented.

Perceptions, thoughts, feelings, desires, and intentions also differ in their relation to the self. With verbs of perception, thought, desire, and intention, the self is typically depicted as the active agent rather than the passive experiencer. However, one can say "the thought struck me," or "the urge to have a cigarette overwhelmed me," where the self is treated as something reacting to other parts of the mind. In the case of feelings and emotions, the typical verbal form is for the self to be a passive experiencer. Thus, we say that things bother, frighten, and bore us. Another common form is the use of the verb *feel* (e.g., "She feels happy"), in which the emotion is treated as something that produces a sensation experienced by the self. For many emotions, one can use either agentive or experiential verb forms: to fear versus to be afraid, to hate versus to feel angry, and so on.

Even though the self can be treated as the experiencing object of most internal states, the self is always the agent of intentions. Intentions do not overwhelm us, or bother us – intentions are the very core of the active self. The folk model treats the self as an area of focus that can expand and contract, but the limit of its contraction lies outside the core act of intending.

The self is also portrayed as able or unable to control various mental operations. One cannot directly control what one will perceive: One cannot turn the perception of blue to red or round to square under normal circumstances. Thoughts, on the other hand, are considered to be under control by the self: One can choose what one wishes to think about. However, it is acknowledged that sometimes it is difficult to stop thinking about something, especially if there are strong emotional promptings of some sort. Feelings, like perceptions, are not considered to be under one's direct control. One may be able to modify one's feelings by thinking of one thing rather than another, or by engaging in various activities, but according to the folk model, one cannot will one's self to hate or not to hate, to love or not to love someone, or even to enjoy something (but one can try). The situations seem less clear with respect to desires; but overall, they operate with respect to self-control like emotions: There seems to be no way to make oneself not want something or to want something one has no desire for. With respect to intentions, the idea of self-control is redundant since intentions *are* self-control. In intending to do something, we (our self) decide what we shall do.

An important aspect of emotions is marked in the folk model by the categorization of emotions by mass nouns rather than count nouns. In English, a count noun is something that can be numerically quantified – one can have one house, two houses, and so on. A mass noun, on the other hand, does not have the defined edges that make counting possible – one can have lots of money, sand, or anger, but in ordinary talk one does not have two monies, two sands, or two angers. In poetry, one can say "a grief ago," thus, treating "grief" as something countable; but in most discourse, emotions are usually not treated as discrete, quantifiable things – one feels sad, not the third sadness today. Further, like water and color, emotions can blend together, so that one feels several feelings at the same time. This is not true of propositional thoughts – one can have only one at a time, and even though they can get mixed up, they do not blend. Desires, like feelings, can occur simultaneously, and perhaps in some way can blend, but this seems less clearly worked out in the folk model.

In the folk model of the mind, the different kinds of internal states and processes are organized into a complex causal system, described in the next sections.

ACTIONS AND INTENTIONS

Complex human actions are assumed to be voluntary unless something indicates otherwise. A voluntary action is one in which someone did something to accomplish some goal. Given the question, "Why did John raise his hand?" one can answer, "To get the teacher's attention," if it is understood that raising one's hand is a way of getting a teacher's attention. It is unusual for someone to explain an act simply by saying that the *act* was intended: for example, the sentence "John raised his hand because he intended to" sounds odd unless there was some reason to suppose that John might have raised his hand involuntarily – perhaps because his hands were attached to strings that could be used to pick up his hand. Since in the folk model actions do not occur without intentions, and since, following the Gricean maxims, we do not say what is obvious, normally we do not explain an action by saying it was intended.

Anscombe (1963) has pointed out that intentions may be formed either prior to the act or as the act is being carried out. When one turns the wheel of a car in an emergency to avoid an accident, one *intends* to turn the wheel. The action and intention occur together (See also Searle 1980).

INTENTIONS AND DESIRES

Why do people have one rather than another intention? The normal expectation based on the folk model is that people intend to do those things that they desire/want/need/wish to do. The term *desire* highlights the affective aspect of this state ("He felt no desire for a cigarette"); the term *wish* highlights the conceptual aspect ("He wished that he had told the truth"); the term *need* highlights the physical or emotional necessity of obtaining satisfaction ("He needed a drink in the worst way"); and the term *want* appears to light evenly each of these aspects.

A desire may be directly satisfied by some action (e.g., "Susan kissed John because she wanted to") or the desire may be indirectly satisfied by the action (e.g., "Susan kissed John because she wanted to make Bill jealous"). In this example, we explain why someone did something by attributing some want or wish or desire or need to the actor without explicitly mentioning any intention. The intention can be assumed because it naturally follows from what is desired.

Do people have intentions without any kind of wish, want, need, or desire as their cause? Not normally, but it is recognized that sometimes one does something intentionally without understanding why – without understanding what it could be one wants. "I told him I would go, but I don't know why I did – I certainly don't want to go." This is a puzzling state of affairs since intentions are supposed to be connected to desires. When the actor experiences intentions without wishes, it is as if there was a failure in perception. The connection should be there – why can't I see it?

Sometimes people do things not because they want to, but because they have been coerced. "Bill gave the robber his money because the robber threatened to shoot him if he didn't." The conventional analysis of this situation is that although Bill did not want to hand over his money, he did want to continue living, and his desire to continue living was stronger than his wish to keep his money. Thus, the intended act is still based on a wish, but one that is indirectly rather than directly related to the action.

Are desires really different than intentions? Or, are intentions just very specific desires? According to the folk model, desires and intentions are different things, since I may have a wish to visit China without having formed any intention to visit China. One can have desires about which one intends to do nothing. Intentions are like desires in that both have as their objects desired future states of affairs, but in an intention the decision to act has been made.

Nevertheless, it would sound strange to talk about desires that do not become intentions even when all the conditions required to satisfy the desire are present – if I really want to go to China, and the means were available, and there were no drawbacks to going, would I not act on the wish? According to the folk model, I would if I *really* wanted to go to China. But then it would no longer be just a wish – it would also be my aim, goal, intention, decision, to go to China. According to the folk model, desires naturally become intentions under the right conditions.

Desires also have an emotional component, and, as discussed, the self is often treated as the object acted on by a wish (e.g., "The desire for a cigarette overwhelmed me"), but the self is rarely if ever treated as the object of an intention. A sentence such as "The intention to have a cigarette overwhelmed me" sounds wrong.

There is considerable question in the philosophic literature about whether desires have a unique emotional component. Is there a distinct feeling that is desiring, or is desiring simply the anticipation of some specific feelings, or is it a particular characteristic of certain feelings? If "John wants to see Susan," is there a distinct feeling of wanting involved, or is the wanting just the anticipatory enjoyment of Susan's company, the anticipation of not feeling lonely? The boundaries here do not seem to be clearly marked.

One can answer a question about why someone wants something with a means–end formulation – John wants to see Susan because he wants to give her a present because he wants to impress her because he wants her to go with him to the dance because . . . . At some point in the means–end hierarchy, we come to such ultimate wants as staying alive, being happy, and/or avoiding unpleasant feelings. Are these ultimate wants

based really on feelings of some sort, or are they self-causing? The boundaries here are also not clearly marked.

FEELINGS AND DESIRES

Another answer to the question of why John wants to see Susan is "Because
he misses her," or "Because he enjoys her company." In these explanations, a desire is causally related to some feeling or emotion (The term
feeling is somewhat more general than the term *emotion*. "Pain," for example, is usually not called an "emotion," but it certainly is a feeling.)
In general, feelings and emotions are thought to lead to desires. If John
gets angry, we will wonder what he will want to do about whatever it is
that is making him angry. If John is angry because Bill did not help him
when he needed help, John's anger may result in his deciding not to speak
to Bill, or in his wanting to telling Bill off, or in his intention to wait to
get even with Bill (Lakoff & Kövecses, this volume).

The emotion or feeling behind a desire need not be immediately experienced. John might want to see Susan because he thinks he would enjoy meeting her. Here, the feeling is anticipated. Is the anticipation of
a feeling also a feeling (attached to a thought), or is it just a thought?
Similarly, John might want to see Susan because he thinks one *ought* to
visit old friends. Here, what seems to be anticipated is some feeling of
guilt if the act is not done. In these cases, the folk model does not seem
to be clear as to whether the anticipation also "carries" feeling.

Feelings generally give rise to desires, but does every feeling give rise
to a desire? Can one feel sad or angry or happy without it; leading
to any identifiable desire? On this point, intuitions differ. However, we
do expect that there will be a relation between the kinds of feelings a person has and the kinds of desires these feelings engender: Feelings of anger,
for example, are expected to lead to desires that involve destruction or
harm, whereas feelings of love are expected to give rise to desires that involve protection and care.

The connection between feelings and desires does not seem to be as tight
as the means–ends relation between intentions and wishes. Within broad
constraints, there are many possible desires that can result more or less
expectably from the same feeling. One reason the connection between feelings and desires is looser than the connection between desires and intentions is that the means–ends relations are located in different worlds. The
means–ends relation between desires and intentions is located in the actor's
understanding of the external world. If one wants to acquire a million
dollars, certain intentions are reasonable – one might decide to buy a lot-
tery ticket, apply for a job at Brinks, or study the stock market, for example. The constraints here are in the understood causal structure of the
world – certain things might lead to acquiring a million dollars; other things
would probably not. The assumption of the folk model appears to be that
the causal structure of the external world affects a person's understand-

ing of that casual structure – however imperfectly – and thereby affects
what intentions will follow from what wants.

In the relation between feelings and desires, however, the causal structure is the mind of the individual. Why did John's anger at Bill lead him
not to want to speak to Bill, rather than wanting to tell him off, or wanting to do any one of a number of other things? How will telling Bill off
affect his feelings? Will he really feel better? The answer to such questions lies in a causal structure that is John's mind. Someone who does
not know John can only make a guess based on the assumption that John
reacts the way other people do. John himself may not know the answers
to any of these questions.

In general, feelings do not seem to be clearly demarcated in the folk
model. There are specific emotions, like love, amusement, irritation, and
fright, that give rise to various desires. There also are general sentiments
such as liking or enjoying something, or disliking something, or being
pleased by something, or being made uncomfortable by something, which
are given as explanations for desires (e.g., "He wants to go to the game
because he likes to watch football.") How are these sentiments related to
specific feelings? Some feelings are thought to be pleasant, others unpleasant – the so-called "hedonistic tone" of the various emotions seems well
agreed on. Is the unpleasantness of fright a separate feeling that comes
with being frightened, or is it simply a characteristic of fright, along with
such other characteristics of fright as high arousal, and anticipations of
disaster? If the unpleasantness of fright is just a characteristic of fright
and not a separate feeling, how about the enjoyment of listening to music?
Is that not a separate feeling? These questions have been much debated
in philosophy. (For a review of these issues, see Kenny 1963.)

What seems to be the case with regard to the folk model is that sometimes "pleasure," "enjoyment," "liking," "displeasure," "dislike," "anticipation," and so on, are treated as feelings in their own right and sometimes
they are treated as characteristics of other feelings. The equivocation of
the folk model on this issue may be due to some innate difficulty that
human beings have in perceiving the boundaries of feelings. The amorphous nature of feelings, indicated in the treatment of emotions as mass
nouns rather than as count nouns, seems to lead to feelings being conceptualized in contradictory ways. This may be why the folk model is also
equivocal with respect to whether wishes involve a unique kind of feeling, whether anticipations are also feelings, and whether there are wishes
that are not based on feelings. (On the other hand, our experience of the
"amorphous nature" of feelings may be due to the vagueness and ambiguity
of the model we use to understand them, not to their actual lack of structure. It would be of psychological interest to know which hypothesis is
true.)

One interesting aspect of feelings is that they are thought to cause
various involuntary visceral responses – turning pale or flushing, trem-

bling, fainting, sweating, for example – although the degree of individual and situational variation in the manifestation of these responses is considered to be very great.

BELIEFS AND FEELINGS

In the folk model, acts, intentions, desires, and feelings are connected in a simple causal chain. There are no direct feedback loops: Intentions do not lead directly to desires, nor do desires lead directly to feelings. We would not explain Tom's desire to go to Spain by saying it was his intention to visit Europe, nor would we explain Howard's hatred of Wimbledon by saying he wished to avoid seeing tennis matches. However, if reversed, these explanations sound sensible: We explain Tom's intention to go to Spain by saying he wants to visit Europe, and we explain that Howard wishes to avoid Wimbledon by saying he hates tennis.

Beliefs, however, are expected to influence feelings, and feelings are expected to influence beliefs. Here, there is a two-way causal relationship. Someone who believes he or she has lost a friend is likely to feel sad. And someone who is sad is likely to think about the time he or she lost a friend and believe the world is a grimmer place.

Even though there is a two-way causal connection between beliefs and feelings, the path from beliefs to feelings is not conceptualized exactly the same way as the path from feelings to beliefs. Feelings and emotions are considered reactions to the world, mediated by one's understanding of the world. These emotional reactions are treated as innate human tendencies, modified in each case by the particulars of experience and character. The causal connection whereby experience – what one believes has happened – arouses feeling is considered to be strong and immediate.

The effect of feelings and emotions on belief, however, is not considered to be as strong as the effect of belief on feelings. Feelings are portrayed as "coloring" one's thinking, "distorting" one's judgment, "pushing" one to recall certain things, confusing one, for example. The image here seems to be of a force which is a sort of perturbation of the medium. One imagines a swimmer caught in a current.

By itself, just the process of thinking is not considered to have much power to arouse the emotions. "Just thinking" about nice things or bad things may have some emotional effect, but we expect such effects to be small except in pathological cases. It is only in its role as the formulator of what one believes or as the interpreter of perceived events that the process of thinking has major effects on feeling and emotion. Thinking is considered a part of how one comes to believe that things are a certain way, and it is to what is believed to be the case that people respond with emotion.

In some mental states, feeling and belief blend together into a single entity. Thus, "approval" is a state that combines both belief and feeling. One cannot say that someone approves of something but has no feeling about it, or that someone approves of something but has no belief about it. Perhaps one can think something is good in some way without feeling anything, and perhaps one can like something without consideration or thought about it. But if one disapproves of something, one does so because of certain things one thinks and because one feels a certain way.

Like approval and disapproval, wonder and doubt also meld together feeling and belief. Related terms, like *anticipation* (discussed above) and *surprise,* may also be used in the sense of a combined feeling and thought, although the affective component seems weaker here (Vendler 1972).

BELIEFS, DESIRES, AND INTENTIONS

Belief also has a two-way causal relationship with the perception of external objects and events. The major direction of causation runs from perception to belief: Seeing or hearing certain things leads me to believe certain things. I see the car go by, so I know (am justified in my belief) that a car went by, and I realize that traffic is still moving. However, belief is not considered just a reflex of perception. People can believe things to be true that they never experienced, and they can even believe they "saw" things happen that did not happen. Perception is not considered an error-free process in the folk model, and belief is often thought to be one reason for an erroneous perception. For example, if I believe that Jim is a bad person, I may perceive his "bumping" into Tom as a deliberate attack although an unbiased observer would have seen only an accident.

In the folk model, beliefs are also causally related to each other: One belief can give rise to another, inconsistency between different beliefs may bring about various attempts to escape from the dilemma and so on. The general interrelatedness of beliefs is indicated in the folk model concepts of inference, evaluation, and judgment, in which a particular proposition is finally accepted or rejected after searching among other propositions for confirming or disconfirming evidence.

Thus, beliefs are treated in the folk model as having causally complex relations to both feelings and perception. The feedback loops in which belief affects feeling, which, in turn, affects belief, and in which perception affects belief, which then affects perception, give the portrayed machinery of the mind a complexity and flexibility it would not have if the causal chain were depicted as running solely in one direction.

Even though the main line of causation in the folk model runs from perception to belief to feeling to desire to intention to action, belief also has a special direct relation to desire and intention. This relation is based on the fact that the states of intention and desire have propositional or intentional objects – that is, they are directed toward the world through the medium of thought, or through framing propositions. One wishes something or another were the case, and the formulation of something being the case is a thought. To want there to be a better world presupposes the mental formulation of the notion of a "better world."

Since what one can desire, wish for, or want depends on what one can think, thought enters directly into wishes, but not in a causal sense. According to this account, cats can wish to catch birds because they can conceive of catching birds, but it is unlikely that cats wish to have souls because it is unlikely that they can formulate the notion of having a soul. Thus, in the folk model the quality of one's wishes depends on the quality of one's thoughts – evil he who evil thinks.

Intentions are, in this regard, like wishes: Any intention takes as its object a state of affairs formulated in a thought. However, there is a further relation between intentions and thoughts in the folk model, which is expressed in the notion of "planning." For example, suppose one wishes to visit Italy and decides to visit Rome during the coming summer. This intention cannot be carried out without further specification of action, which means planning. Such specifications involve working out what means of travel to take, where and when to make reservations, when to leave, where to stay and so on. Planning consists of thinking out a feasible set of actions to accomplish the intention or goal. Once the plan is made, each of the conceived actions becomes a subgoal or subintention, which itself may require more planning before the initiating intention can be accomplished.

The folk model treatment of desire and intention as states that take propositionally framed objects or states of affairs means that what can be wanted, aimed for, and planned depends on what is known, or believed, or understood. There is a further effect here, and this is that since what is wanted, aimed for, and planned are things thought of, one may "deliberate" about these wants, aims, and plans. These deliberations may, in turn, lead to other feelings, such as guilt or doubt, or other wishes, which may counter the original wish, or may involve various second-order intentional states, such as resolution or indecision. Were this feedback loop, in which one can think about what one feels, desires, and intends, not present in the folk model, there would be no mechanism of self-control in the system, and hence we would have no basis for concepts of responsibility, morality, or conscience.

Even though the normal situation is one in which a person can, through thought, intervene between the wish and the intention so that self-control is possible, according to the folk model there are abnormal situations in which either the wish is so strong or the capacity to think and understand what one is doing is so diminished (perhaps because of drugs, fatigue, strong feelings, etc.) that self-control cannot be expected.

Since what one desires and intends are things about which one has a belief or thought, a thought potentially attached to some desire or intention can trigger that desire or intention. If a set of circumstances lead one to realize that one has a good chance of winning a million dollars, one may suddenly discover that one very strongly desires a million dollars.

Here, the causal relation is of a special kind. Thoughts are not considered to have the power of creating desires or intentions out of nothing, only the potential of "triggering" off a preexisting desire or intention (Searle 1980). The chance of winning a million dollars could not set off a great desire for money if one really did not care about money.

The difference between "creating" and "triggering" appears to center on the contrast between making something that did not exist versus activating something that is already present. The difference is not always clearly marked in the folk model: Sometimes emotions, for example, are treated as things "triggered" by experience, and at other times as things "created" by experience. The difference seems to depend on how the person's natural state is characterized: a tiny annoyance "sets off" the anger of people known to be irritable, although it might take an outrageous event to "make" a mild-tempered person angry.

In sum, in the folk model, the cognitive processes of thinking, understanding, inferring, judging, and so on have extensive feedback relations with all the other kinds of internal states. By itself, the thinking process is considered to have only a small amount of power; but as the process by which beliefs are formed, and as the process through which different internal states interact, thoughts play a central role in the operation of the mind. According to the folk model, if the process of thinking or the capacity to think is badly disturbed, persons cannot be held accountable for their actions – they do not know what they are doing. This central role of thought also has the consequence that mental illness in the folk model is considered to be primarily a loss of cognitive capacity (C. Barlow, unpublished data).

OTHER ASPECTS OF THE MIND

The description just presented does not cover all of the material included in the western folk model of the mind. No analysis has been given, for example, of kinds of ability, such as intelligence, creativity, and perceptiveness, or kinds of strengths, such as will power and stability. (A good start on the analysis of these aspects of the mind is presented in Heider's *Psychology of Interpersonal Relations* 1958.) What is attempted here is the description of the most basic elements of the model, elements needed before further analysis can be carried out. Thus, the concept of *intelligence* for example, assumes that the mind includes a process of thinking, and that people vary in the degree to which they can apply this process to certain kinds of problems to arrive at solutions. However, the specific ideas about intelligence held by Americans go considerably beyond the material presented here. Sternberg, et al. (1981), for example, studied folk concepts of intelligence and found that Americans distinguish three major kinds of intelligence, which might be glossed "knowledge about things," "problem-solving ability," and "social intelligence."

Summary of major propositions and interview material

1. Perceiving, thinking, feeling, wishing, and intending are distinct mental processes.

    The best evidence for this proposition is the existence of the semantically different verbal terms for these internal states and processes. Some of the semantic features of these terms are given in Table 5.1.

2. One is usually conscious of what one perceives, thinks, feels, wishes, and intends to do. However, many internal states and processes are indistinct and hard to delimit.

    Q. Could it be the case that someone sees something and isn't aware of what they see?

    A. Yes. You might see a situation and you think it is one thing and it is really something else.

    Q. Can you see something and not be aware that you're seeing anything at all?

    A. You'd better say it again. You lost me.

    Q. Can you see something and not be aware that you saw it at all?

    A. I don't know how.

    Q. Could someone think something and not be aware they thought it?

    A. Yeah.

    Q. How could that happen?

    A. Because your mind is so cluttered with all kinds of things. I'm not aware of half the stuff I think or things that are embedded in there. They sometimes come up and bother me later and I have to sit there and think about it and try to sort out what's the matter, why I can't do something.

    Q. Could you think something was true, believe it, but not know that you believed it?

    A. No, that sounds silly. Sorry.

    Q. Could you have a real feeling or emotion about something and not be aware you have that feeling?

    A. Yes.

    Q. Could you be angry at somebody and not know it?

    A. Yes. But it might come up later and you would realize it.

    Q. Could you be sad and not know it?

    A. You could be any kind of feeling and not know it.

    Q. Is that the way it usually works?

    A. No. Usually you know how you feel. At least a little.

    Q. Could you wish for something, desire something, and not know you wished for it?

    A. Yes, that is definitely true.

    Q. Can you give me an example of how that would work?

    A. Well, let's say I want to play really well in a concert, but it is so deep down that I don't know I want to play really well, but in fact that gets in my way, that wanting to play really well. I just don't let myself play naturally.

Q. Could someone intend to do something and not be aware they intend to do it?

A. I think so.

Q. You sound a little hesitant. Could you intend to go to France and not realize it?

A. No, not something concrete like that.

Q. How about intending to get married to someone but you don't know it.

A. No, that sounds silly. Maybe you could have a very general intention like intending to do well and not know it. But that would be just like wanting to do well. Not something specific.

Q. How come you can have specific feelings and not know you have them, but you can't have specific intentions and not know you have them?

A. I don't know.

3. The process of thinking is controlled by the self in much the same way one controls any action.

Q. Suppose somebody named John can't keep his mind on his homework. What might account for such a situation?

A. He's got his mind on something else probably.

Q. Why might he have his mind on something else?

A. Because the something else is more appealing or more important at the time.

Q. What can he do about it?

A. Well, he could either go do something about the thing he's worried about or thinking about and do his homework, or he could force himself to get it out of his mind and then do his homework.

Q. How do you force something out of your mind?

A. You have to relax because you can't do anything about the other situation right then. You just have to relax and put your mind to what you are doing.

Q. What does he have to do to put his mind to what he is doing?

A. You have to focus it, you have to look at what you're doing, you have to be completely absorbed in what you're doing. You can't be floating around somewhere else. You can't be sitting apart and watch what you are doing, you have to do it.

4. The process of perception is not controlled by the self except in so far as one can direct one's attention toward or away from something.

Q. If you don't like something you see, or something that you hear, like loud music, or you don't like what you're tasting, what can you do about it?

A. You can either ignore it or try to change what you don't like.

Q. If you were tasting something and didn't like the taste, could you just make it not taste so bad by will power?

A. No, I don't think you could. I mean if it tastes bad, it just does. You either spit it out or you swallow it.

Q. How about hypnosis? Could somebody hypnotize you so you would think "Oh, this tastes great."

A. Yes, you could.

    Q. How does that work?

    A. I don't know how hypnosis works. Sorry.

5. The process of feeling some emotion about something or desiring something is not directly controlled by the self but can sometimes be manipulated indirectly by changing one's environment or what one thinks about.

    Q. Suppose you were afraid of heights and wanted to get rid of this fear. What could you do?

    A. If it were me, I'd face it. If I were afraid to do something, I'd just go right through it and face it.

    Q. I'm not sure whether you're saying you can make the fear go away or whether going through it makes the fear go away.

    A. You go through the fear and the fear dissolves, because you realize it's not so bad as you thought.

    Q. Suppose you were angry at someone. What could you do to get rid of the anger?

    A. Get mad at them.

    Q. How does that work?

    A. You either start arguing or start picking on the person.

    Q. How does that make the anger go away?

    A. Because you are venting your frustration.

    Q. Then you don't feel so angry?

    A. Not really. It sort of half goes away. But it is still kind of there.

    Q. How does picking on the person make the half go away?

    A. Because you are mad and all frustrated and it's all inside and you have to vent it somehow. Being nasty at the person you think you are mad at helps you let it out.

6. One does not speak of controlling one's own intentions, since when one intends to do something one is controlling oneself.

    Q. How does the sentence "John can't control what he intends to do" sound to you?

    A. A little odd. How could John control intent? It doesn't make sense.

7. One can perceive many things at once, feel a number of emotions at the same time, and perhaps desire more than one thing at a time. Feelings can blend together. But one can only think one propositional thought at a time or picture one image at a time.

    Q. Is it possible to feel sad and angry at the same time?

    A. Yeah.

    Q. Is it possible to feel sad, angry, and excited at the same time?

    A. Yes, that's easy.

    Q. Could someone feel something which was a blend of love and fear?

    A. Yeah, I guess so.

    Q. Could you think about two different things at the same time, like prime numbers and your favorite colors?

    A. Yeah.

    Q. You could think two different thoughts at the same time?

A. Yeah, I could think all the prime numbers in red.
Q. Can you blend ideas about things?
A. What do you mean?
Q. Well, you gave an example of prime numbers which are red, right? Put them together in a picture. But could you do it just with thoughts?
A. No. It would be a mix up.

8. In English, the self is typically treated as the object or experiencer of emotions (and also physical sensations). The other mental processes typically treat the self as the subject or agent who does the process, but, except in the case of intentions, it is possible for the self to be the object of all the mental processes.

Q. I'm going to read some sentences and I want to know how they sound to you – tell me which ones sound normal and which ones do not. O.K.?
A. O.K.
Q. "John is often threatened by his feelings."
A. Normal.
Q. "John is often threatened by his thoughts."
A. Normal.
Q. "John is often threatened by his wishes."
A. Yeah.
Q. You sound a little hesitant . . . .
A. Yeah, I was hesitating. Because I guess I think of wishes as desires and if you had said "desires," I would have said "yes" right away.
Q. "John is often threatened by his intentions."
A. That doesn't sound right. I can't make it click.

9. Most things that people do – outside of reflex actions like sneezing – they do because of some intention or goal they have in mind.

Q. When somebody does something, do they usually have an intention in mind?
A. Yes.
Q. Are there some things that people do that they don't have any intention in mind when they do them?
A. Yeah, like sneezing or your heart beating; it just goes on.
Q. Like buying a car?
A. No.

10. Why does someone have certain intentions rather than others? One reason is that some intention is a subgoal considered necessary to reach another, more general goal. Another reason is that one wants or desires something, and that is why one intends to do something – to get what one wants.

Q. Suppose John intends to buy a horse. What might be some explanations for that?
A. He could want a horse, to ride a horse, or might want it for his farm for a work horse. Or he might want it for his kids.

11. Not every desire or wish gives rise to action, or the intention to do something. However, if one has an opportunity to do something, and

there is nothing preventing one from doing it like a conflicting desire or an outside force, and one does not even form an intention to try to do it, then one does not really desire it.

Q. John says he wants to see *Key Largo*. He had a chance to go, but he didn't take it, although he didn't have any reason not to go. What could explain such a situation?

A. I can understand that. I do it all the time.

Q. What could explain such a situation?

A. You just get obstinate. Even though you want to do something really badly, its like there's this part of you that thinks, "I don't want to do it." Sort of like a mule; it justs sits there and doesn't want to go and fights you – I guess your intentions.

Q. O.K., in that case some part of John didn't want to go. But if there wasn't a counterwish, could it be the case that he just didn't go even though he wanted to?

A. That's like a contradiction. Because that doesn't make too much sense. There would have to be a reason why the person didn't do it if they wanted to do it. There'd have to be some reason like that or just a simple reason like they couldn't do it. It wouldn't be that they just wouldn't do it.

12. One often does things one does not wish to do because one has to, or because it is right, or because other people want one to, or because one is paid. In such cases, one wish prevails over another wish – the wish to stay alive, or be a good person for example. One does something one does not wish to do because there is something else one wishes for even more strongly.

Q. Last night, John said he didn't want to study, but he did. What could explain such a situation?

A. He probably had to. He probably had classes and things to do. I mean, nobody likes to study. So he made himself – he disciplined himself and did it. It had to be done.

Q. O.K. So he doesn't want to study because that's work, but he wants to study to do something – to pass the course or something. So he has opposing wishes?

A. Exactly.

Q. Why did one wish win over the other?

A. I guess because it was stronger for him.

13. Sometimes – but rarely – one does something without knowing why. That is, one does not know what desire or wish leads to the action.

Q. John stole Bill's socks. Now he says he doesn't know why he did it. Could John be telling the truth?

A. That's an old line. They're trying to get out of it. They know why they did it deep inside and they are trying to hide from it.

Q. You think they really know?

A. They probably have to really dig to find out.

Q. So they might not be really aware of it when they say it?

A. They're not really aware. Maybe they really believe they don't know why they did it.

14. Is every nonreflex act the result of some wish or desire? Probably, but not surely.

    Q. Can one just do something for no reason at all - nothing intended or wanted?

    A. Really no reason at all? I'd say there should be some reason somewhere. Otherwise, it's silly.

    Q. Could the reason be trivial?

    A. Could be trivial, could be anything. But there should be a reason.

15. Why does someone have certain desires rather than others? Some desires are for things that are needed in order to get something else one desires. Some things are desired because they make one feel good, or one likes them, or they are pleasurable. Some things are desired because one is in some emotional state such as anger or love. Some things are desired because one thinks doing those things is right.

    Q. Why do people want things?

    A. They enjoy it, it gives them pleasure.

    Q. What are some other reasons?

    A. Some sort of honor they would receive. Something that makes them good either in their own eyes or makes them feel they're better in other people's eyes.

    Q. Could one be in love and not wish to do anything about it? Not have it give rise to any kind of wish?

    A. Not in my movie.

    Q. Could you be angry and not have it give rise to some wish to do something?

    A. I guess not.

    Q. Could one be afraid and not wish to do anything?

    A. If you're afraid, you might just want to stay still and be safe and you wouldn't want to do anything.

    Q. But then you are trying to be safe, you want to be safe.

    A. Yes, so that's wanting something.

    Q. Could you be sad and not want to do anything?

    A. Yes. You're just all despondent. Just sitting there. I guess that is sort of doing nothing.

16. Most feelings are either pleasant or unpleasant. (Most events give rise to some feelings - so most events are either pleasant or unpleasant.)

    Q. Do people have feelings which are neutral - neither pleasant nor unpleasant?

    A. No.

    Q. Can you always tell if a feeling is either pleasant or unpleasant?

    A. Not at first. Sometimes it's unpleasant at first and then it changes.

17. Feelings and emotions are primarily reactions based on one's understanding of events. But sometimes there is a lack of fit between one's understanding and what one feels - either the amount of feeling is disproportional to the experienced event, or the kind of feeling is incongruous with the nature of the event.

    Q. What are some things that might make a person feel sad?

A. Somebody dies. Or you forget really important things you believe in, and suddenly it comes back to you, it can make you sad because you forgot it and you separated yourself from it.

Q. What about anger?

A. Frustrating kinds of things that you can't do anything about, like work or your boss is always picking on you.

Q. What about fright?

A. Well, anything can make you afraid. I mean, just a scary movie or something like that.

Q. Could you feel sad even though nothing happened?

A. Yes.

Q. Could you feel angry even though nothing happened?

A. No.

Q. Could you feel happy even if nothing happened?

A. Sometimes I read something and I'm happy, or I think about something that makes me happy. Does that count as something happening?

Q. Yes.

A. Well, then "no" for all of them. You can't just sit there and have a feeling.

Q. Could someone feel sad if only a minor thing happened, like seeing a child drop a piece of candy?

A. Sure.

18. What one believes and knows influences how one perceives the world.

Q. Two people watch an argument between a policeman and a taxi driver. One of the watchers says it was almost a fight. The other onlooker says it wasn't serious at all. How could you explain this difference?

A. They have different ideas about what serious is.

Q. Suppose they both mean by serious that there was almost a real fight?

A. Well, if it was obvious one way or the other, I don't know. That's like disagreeing on whether something is blue or red.

Q. Well, suppose it wasn't that obvious?

A. Well, maybe one of the watchers knew the taxi driver, and the other didn't.

19. One can affect one's feelings just by thinking about certain things rather than other things. However, the degree of influence here is weak.

Q. If one wants to change one's feelings, say if one feels sad and wants to feel more cheerful, what can one do?

A. If you're sad and you want to feel cheerful, you can go out and do something constructive or active or something you would feel cheerful about.

Q. Could you just think about something and make yourself feel more cheerful?

A. Yes.

Q. Does that always work?

A. No, sometimes it does.

Q. How come it doesn't always work?

    A. Because maybe your sad thing is too hard to get out of your mind by just thinking about something else.

20. What one feels also influences how one thinks. Feelings may sometimes stimulate one to think in certain directions, or block thinking about certain things, or even completely wipe out the ability to think.

    Q. If you felt very angry, or very frightened, could it affect how you think?

    A. Yes.

    Q. Would it make your thinking better or worse or what?

    A. Worse. It could affect how you think about a person for the worse so you just see one thing about the person, like if you are very angry. You don't even want to think about the good parts of them.

    Q. Is everyone the same about this?

    A. I don't know.

21. Sometimes, what one thinks and what one feels fuse together into a single response, as in approving of something, or wondering about something.

    Q. Can someone approve of something, yet not have any feelings about it?

    A. No. If they approve, they approve, and that's a feeling.

    Q. Could they approve of something and not have any thoughts or opinions about it?

    A. No, if they approve, they approve. Approve is an opinion and a thought.

22. What one believes is strongly influenced by what one perceives. One believes that what one perceives to have happened actually happened – unless there are special reasons to think one is hallucinating, or led by ambiguity to imagine things.

    Q. John thinks that UFOs visit Del Mar, because he said he saw one land at the racetrack. What could account for John's opinion?

    A. He has an eye problem or he has a big imagination or maybe he really saw one.

    Q. Would it surprise you to know that John was a strong believer in UFOs even before he saw one land at the racetrack?

    A. No. He probably looks at UFO pictures in magazines and then thinks he sees one in real life. It could happen.

    Q. What could happen?

    A. You could imagine it. You could have an image so strong in your mind that you see maybe a plane or just a flash in the sky and suddenly your mind just inserts the whole picture there. That happens to me. When you have something strong, you can see just part of it and your mind sees the whole thing right there.

23. Thoughts are related to each other. Sometimes, one thought leads to another; sometimes one recognizes inconsistency between thoughts; sometimes one can figure out something from other things one knows or believes.

    Q. Sometimes someone says they didn't know something at first, but then they figured it out. What do they do when they "figure out" something?

    A. That's a hard question. They go over a problem in their mind, and somewhere there is something that will click. They go over it in their mind, and there's a bunch of little things over here that are just maybe unconnected. And they see the connection. I can't explain it.

24. In order to wish for something, or desire something, or intend to do something, one must be able to conceive of that something.
    Q. Could a goldfish wish to discover the theory of relativity?
    A. I don't know. I doubt it. Because a goldfish isn't developed to the point where they could think thoughts like that.
    Q. Is everything you wish for something you can think of?
    A. Yes.
    Q. Could you wish for something you couldn't think of?
    A. It depends on what you mean by "think of." Maybe you could wish for something you couldn't remember very well. You can't wish for something you can't think about.

25. Thinking about something can trigger a wish or desire if the wish or desire is already there – either one already knew that one had the desire, or one realizes after thinking about it that one has the desire.
    Q. If you just think about eating something good, could it make you want to eat something even if you weren't really hungry?
    A. No, not if you really weren't hungry. But you might stimulate yourself by thinking about something if your were just a little bit hungry to really want to eat a certain thing.

26. Since one is usually aware of what one desires and what one intends to do, one can think about one's desires and intentions, plan things, change one's mind, select the better rather than the worse course of action, and in general control one's self.
    Q. How come people have the ability to control themselves, at least some of the time?
    A. The brain sends a message to the body, like to your finger, and it moves. I don't know how.
    Q. How about self-control, like controlling oneself when one is on a diet. How does somebody keep from having ice cream for dessert?
    A. How can I keep myself from having ice cream tonight? I tell myself – my brain told my other brain that I didn't want it. I mean, I wanted to be thin more than I wanted the taste of ice cream in my mouth.
    Q. So it's like you spoke to yourself?
    A. Yes. My bad half was held in by my good half.

27. If one can't think clearly for any reason, one cannot control one's self very well, and one is not fully responsible for what one does.
    Q. What could account for the fact that there are some people who don't seem to be able to control themselves, even when they want to?
    A. They have psychological problems.
    Q. What does that mean?
    A. That means that there is something bothering them, I think. They are all mixed up. They have problems.
    Q. Could you expect someone to control themselves if they couldn't think clearly?

> A. No, not really. If you didn't know what was happening and you didn't
> know what you were doing, there would be no way to get back.
> Q. Should a person like that be punished if they did something wrong?
> A. No, it's not their fault if they didn't know what was happening.

The interview data collected so far support the major propositions
presented here for the folk model of the mind. It should be understood
that these propositions are a theory, not a simple description, of what
Americans – and probably most Europeans – believe about the mind. The
usefulness and validity of such a theory will not be established on the basis
of one person's interviews of several informants, but rather on the results
obtained across a range of investigators, informants, and kinds of data.

Some idea about the historical depth of this folk model can be obtained
from earlier novels and plays. Even though writers of novels and plays
do not usually state the propositions of the folk model of the mind explicitly, they do use the model in constructing character and plot, and they
sometimes comment on the reactions of their characters to events in very
revealing ways. For example, in *Emma*, a novel by Jane Austen published
in 1816, there is a description of Emma's and Emma's father's reaction
to the recent marriage of Miss Taylor, who had been Emma's governess
and companion (1969:17).

> She [Emma] had many acquaintances in the place, for her father was
> universally civil, but not one of them who could be accepted in lieu of
> Miss Taylor for even half a day. It was a melancholy change; and Emma
> could not but sigh over it, and wish for impossible things, till her father
> awoke, and made it necessary to be cheerful.

The tacitly understood propositions here seem to be that "melancholy"
is a natural reaction of the experience of loss, and that "sighing" is a natural
expression of such a feeling, and further, that the experience of loss and
the resulting sadness create a "wish" for something that will remove the
sadness, along with thoughts about this "something." Austen (ibid.: 17)
continues:

> His spirits required support. He was a nervous man, easily depressed;
> fond of everybody that he was used to, and hating to part with them;
> hating change of every kind. Matrimony, as the origin of change, was
> always disagreeable; and he was by no means yet reconciled to his own
> daughter's [Emma's sister] marrying, nor could he ever speak of her but
> with compassion, though it had been entirely a match of affection, when
> he was now obliged to part with Miss Taylor too; and from his habits
> of gentle selfishness and of being never able to suppose that other people
> could feel differently from himself, he was very much disposed to think
> Miss Taylor had done as sad thing for herself as for them, and would
> have been a great deal happier if she had spent all the rest of her life at
> Hartfield. Emma smiled and chatted as cheerfully as she could to keep
> him from such thoughts; but when tea came, it was impossible for him

not to say exactly as he had said at Dinner: 'Poor Miss Taylor! I wish she were here again. What a pity it is that Mr. Weston ever thought of her!'

Emma's father is also subject to the same emotional reaction to the loss of Miss Taylor, but Austen treats him as a person who is emotionally predisposed to such reactions, so that Miss Taylor's marriage easily "triggers" his response. Because Emma knows her father is like this, she acts cheerful. We "fill in" the needed connections – Emma does not want her father to be unhappy, and believes (or at least hopes) that being "cheerful" will, by creating a happy environment for him, keep away his depression and anxiety, and so this wish of Emma's results in her intentionally acting in a cheerful manner. We also understand that Emma has the strength to keep to her intention despite her own sadness.

Emma's father, on the other hand, lacks strength of character. His feelings and desires influence his thoughts inappropriately; his self-centeredness leads him to think that other people feel the same about events as he does – even when this is obviously not the case – and his feelings and confused understanding lead him to think of his daughter's and Miss Taylor's marriages as unfortunate events even for them. Desires and emotions can, according to the model, influence belief, but they should not. A "strong" person does not let feelings and wishes distort reality, but a weak person is liable to.

Overall, reading Jane Austen and other early English novelists, one is impressed with how little obvious change there is in the folk model of the mind in the past 200 years. But at much greater time depths, the implicit connections that knit together actions and reactions in stories are harder to discern, and it is difficult to tell if the difficulty lies in translation, or in a failure to appreciate the cultural understandings about the meaning of events, or in a change in the model of how the mind works (see, for example, the discussion of Achilles in Friedrich 1977).

Another, more modern example of the use of the folk model of the mind: a 7-year-old child and her mother had the following conversation:

Mother: Rachel, you're making me mad!
Rachel: I didn't mean to make you mad.
Mother: Well, you sure seem to be trying.
Rachel: But I didn't mean to. If I didn't mean to, how could I be trying?

Here, Rachel uses the connection in the folk model between intentions and actions. "Trying" is an action undertaken to bring about a particular intention – what one "means to do." Therefore, if there was no intention on Rachel's part to make her mother mad, by definition she could not have been "trying" to make her mother mad. (This example also illustrates nicely the ability of people – even young people – to reason effectively when using a well-understood cultural model. For a nonwestern example, see Hutchins 1980.)

The folk model and science

It is not possible to contrast the folk model presented here with a single scientific model, since there is no one theory of the mind held by all psychologists. There are, however, certain general trends within academic psychology with which the folk model can be compared. Based on an examination of several popular undergraduate psychology texts, it seems that the current academic vocabulary is a blend of folk terms plus the addition of specialized terms. The typical text contains chapters on vision, audition, taste and touch, cognition and memory, learning, motivation, emotion, intelligence, personality, and mental disorders. The material on vision, audition, taste, and touch is heavily physiological, although various kinds of illusions are discussed in which conscious experience is contradicted by physical facts.

One major disagreement between the folk model and the academic model involves "motivation." Although the term *motivation* has its roots in the folk model, it has come to have a specialized meaning in psychology. Motivation, unlike emotions, desires, and intentions, does not refer primarily to a phenomenological state or process – that is, it is not something primarily defined by the conscious experience of the person. Instead, motivation refers to a condition of deprivation or arousal of the "organism" that is only variably correlated with phenomenological experience. High motivation is likely to result in a person's thinking about the objects that would "satisfy" or "reduce" the motivation, emotional arousal (not necessarily of any specific kind), the experience of desire to do various actions that have led in the past to satisfaction, the formation of relevant intentions, and the carrying out of such actions if given the opportunity. Most psychologists consider motivation to be a real rather than hypothetical state of the person, but not a state that the person is necessarily aware of. The conscious mental states caused by motivational arousal may have some function in directing the final action the person takes, but these conscious mental states are typically considered to be neither necessary nor sufficient conditions for motivational arousal.

The psychoanalytic theorists are also greatly concerned with motivation. Psychoanalytic theorists place more emphasis on motivational conflicts than do academic psychologists and are more interested in how the motivational situation influences thought and feeling through repression, isolation, displacement, denial, sublimation, and other mechanisms of defense. Psychoanalytic theory also differs from the folk theory in that it emphasizes unconscious states. The folk model allows that it is possible for someone to desire something or have some feeling of some kind but not know it, but such conditions are considered atypical. Psychoanalytic theory also distinguishes between two forms of thought – primary process thought and secondary process thought – but the folk model makes no such distinction.

Even though both the academic and psychoanalytic models modify the folk model, it is clear that these are modifications of an already existing conception of the mind. The general tenor of the academic model is to place emphasis on what can be described physically – hours of deprivation, the neural pathways, peripheral responses and so on – with the hope that the mental states and processes of the folk model will eventually be reduced to a physical science vocabulary and simply ignore those parts of the folk model that cannot now be physically described. For example, until recently, there was a complete avoidance in modern psychology of the term *consciousness* – a process that is difficult to handle within a physical science model. In the past decade, this has begun to change. Sperry (1982:1225), for example, states:

> . . . one of the most important indirect results of the split-brain work is a revised concept of the nature of consciousness and its fundamental relation to brain processing. The key development is a switch from prior noncausal, parallelist views to a new causal, or 'interactionist' interpretation that ascribes to inner experience an integral causal control role in brain function and behavior. . . . The events of inner experience, as emergent properties of brain processes, become themselves explanatory causal constructs in their own right, interacting at their own level with their own laws and dynamics. The whole world of inner experience (the world of the humanities), long rejected by 20th century scientific materialism, thus becomes recognized and included within the domain of science.

Sperry's position does not appear to be the majority position of research psychologists, who continue to carry the hope that the folk model eventually can be completely physicalized without the use of "emergent properties." However, with the rise of modern cognitive psychology, much greater attention has been given to the problem of consciousness, its function, and physical bases (Mandler 1982; Natsoulas 1978).

The situation is quite different with regard to the psychoanalytic model, which considers consciousness, intentions, and the self as things of interest in their own right. However, the conscious mental states and processes are considered to be only a small part of the picture – and not the part where the main action is. Despite the shifts in psychoanalytic thinking from its early days, it has not changed in considering unconscious states and processes to be the center of the causal system.

Thus, even though the academic and psychoanalytic models have their origins in the folk model, both are deeply at variance with the folk model. That is, the folk model treats the conscious mental states as having central causal powers. In the folk model, one does what one does primarily because of what one consciously feels and thinks. The causal center for the academic model is in the various physical states of the organism – in tissue needs, external stimuli, or neural activation. For the psychoanalytic model, the causal center is in unconscious mental states. Given these differences in the location of the casual center of the operations of the mind, the three models are likely to continue to diverge.

The west versus Ifaluk

The American–European folk model also contrasts with the folk models recorded by anthropologists for nonwestern peoples. Recently, Catherine Lutz presented a summary of the ethnopsychological knowledge system of the people of Ifaluk (Lutz 1980; 1982; 1983; 1985; see also this volume). Ifaluk is a small atoll, only one-half square mile in area, located in the Western Caroline Islands of Micronesia. The island was previously studied by Burrows and Spiro (1963). The present population is 430 persons. Most of the islanders are monolingual speakers of a Malayo–Polynesian language. The culture of this small society is distinctive for its strong values on nonaggression, cooperation, and sharing.

The folk model used on Ifaluk contrasts with the model presented here for American–European – or "western" – culture in a variety of ways. However, the general framework of both models is similar. In both models, there seems to be a similar division of internal states into thoughts, feelings, and desires. In the model used on Ifaluk, there is a distinct class of emotion terms, for which a general correspondence to English emotion terms can be found, although the particular blends of affective tone differ from what we find in English. For example, the term *fago* refers to feelings of "compassion," "love," and "sadness"; and although it involves caring about someone, it is also judged by native informants to be semantically similar to words involving loneliness and loss (Lutz 1982). A similar affective blend is found in Samoan for the cognate term *alofa* (Gerber 1975). This particular blend is different from the American English term *love* and its cognates, which do not prototypically involve sadness and loss (but note the sadness of many love songs and stories).

Even though there appears to be an overall similarity between the models in the division of mental states and processes into thoughts, feelings, and wishes, on Ifaluk the distinctions are made much less sharply. The term *nunuwan,* one of the two major terms used to describe mental states (*niferash,* "our insides"), refers to "mental events ranging from what we consider thought to what we consider emotion" (Lutz 1985:47). The meaning of *nunuwan* appears to be somewhat like the special meaning of English of the word *feel* when used in the sense of "to think," as in, "I feel it is likely we will succeed." (As mentioned, several terms in English also blend thought and feeling, such as *approval* and *doubt.*)

The other primary term used on Ifaluk to describe internal states is *tip-* which Lutz translates "will/emotion/desire." When asked the difference between *nunuwan* and *tip-*, people say that the two are very similar. The distinction is that *tip-* has connotations of desire and movement toward the object: An informant said "Our tip- is what we want, like to chat with someone or to go visit another village" (Lutz 1985:48). It appears that *tip-* always takes a propositional object, unlike *nunuwan*. However, like *nunuwan*, emotion is held to be inherent in the experience of *tip-*. It is likely that intentions are also included within the semantic range of *tip-*, since there appears to be no separate term for intentions as part of "our insides."

In general, it would appear that the people of Ifaluk regard emotional experience as a central feature of the mind and emphasize the affective elements in the experience of both thinking and wishing. Lutz has traced out how the values of nonaggression, cooperation, and sharing are supported by the various conceptions of emotion. For example, one term, *metagu,* glossed "fear/anxiety," which is the feeling that occurs when one must be in the midst of a large group of people, or when one encounters a ghost or a shark, or when someone is justifiably angry with one, is considered a necessary part of socialization. A person who does not experience *metagu* is like a "shameless" person in English – that is, someone who will not have the proper constraints on his or her behavior. A child who does not experience *metagu* is considered to lack a primary inhibitor of misbehavior, and such a deficiency would indicate that parents failed to socialize the child properly – to display *song,* "justifiable anger" at the child's misdeeds, which is thought inevitably to elicit *metagu* in the person to whom the anger is directed (Lutz 1983).

The people of Ifaluk considered feelings to be natural responses to particular events, typically interpersonal situations of various kinds. Such eliciting events are considered a basic part of the definition of the emotion (Lutz 1982). Emotions are also thought to give rise to particular behavior; *fago,* for example, is thought to give rise to talking kindly, giving food, and crying.

In portraying emotions as natural reactions to experience and also as causes of behavior, the folk model of the people of Ifaluk is similar to the western model. However, the model used on Ifaluk appears to give more consideration to the dyadic aspect of emotion, where if *A* feels emotion *X* and expresses it, then these actions will cause *B* to feel emotion *Y*. Thus, if *A* feels *song, B* feels *metagu,* whereas if *A* feels *tang* (frustration/grief), *B* feels *fago* (Lutz 1982).

The model used on Ifaluk also agrees with the western model in distinguishing between emotions and physical sensations. Lutz (1985:49) states:

> Other aspects of 'our insides,' and ones which are distinguished from
> both nunuwan and tip-, are the states of hunger (*pechaiy*), pain
> (*metagi*), and sexual sensations (*mwegiligil*). These latter states are considered to be universal and unlearned human proclivities. Although their occurrence can lead to thoughts and feelings, they are considered an entirely different class of events from the latter. The Ifaluk further distinguish between these three states of physical sensation and the corresponding desires or drive-like states that follow upon the sensations. These include

'wanting food (or a particular food)' (*mwan*), 'wanting pain to end' (gar), and 'horniness' (*pashua*).

In the western model, this distinction between the physical state and the mental state for hunger, pain, and sex is not lexicalized nor does it seem to be a distinction that most people make in ordinary discourse.

The model used on Ifaluk also differs from the present western model in considering the mind to be located primarily in the gut, which includes the stomach and abdominal region. Thus, thoughts, feelings, desires, hunger, pain, and sexual sensations are all experienced in the gut. When people eat well, they say "Our insides are good," which means they have both good physical sensations and good emotions. Loss of appetite is typically regarded as a symptom of either physical or emotional distress. In extreme grief, people say "my gut is ripping," and others advise them not to "hate" their own "gut" (Lutz 1985).

According to the model used on Ifaluk, unpleasant emotions that are not expressed may cause illness. Individuals are advised to "throw out" their feelings in order to avoid illness. At funerals, people are advised to "cry big" in order to avoid illness. Expressing one's feelings (except angry feelings) is considered a sign of maturity and social intelligence as well as a way of staying healthy. Further, one's bad feelings can make other people ill. This is especially likely in the case of a mother and infant. It is said, "It is like the baby knows the 'thoughts/emotions' of its mother and becomes *nguch* 'sick and tired/bored' of the mother" (Lutz 1985:55).

This connection between emotionality and illness is also found in the western folk model: For example, it is thought people who are homesick or sad about the loss of a loved one sometimes "pine away," and that chronic anger can lead to a heart attack. The model used on Ifaluk, however, appears to make the connection between emotions and illness much more generally and explicitly, perhaps reinforced by the attribution of both physical and mental sensations to a location in the gut.

The model used on Ifaluk, like the western model, gives a central role to "thought" in the control of behavior. The concept *bush,* "crazy, incompetent," which is considered the opposite of *repiy,* "social intelligence," is widely used to refer to behavior that is deviant and appears to be due to a failure to perceive the nature of the situation correctly. All infants and children to about the age of 6 are considered *bush*. People we would label as psychotic are called *bush;* on Ifaluk this is manifested by their being unable to work and engaging in inexplicable behaviors, such as shouting or eating without table manners. Lutz reports the case of such a person whose "crazy" behavior consisted of saying repetitively "*my* knife, *my* lighter, *my* basket," etc. On Ifaluk sharing is strongly stressed as proper behavior, and the use of first person singular pronoun is felt to be rude in many contexts – and "crazy" in this one (Lutz 1985).

The ability to think correctly, especially on the part of children, is considered to be influenced by instruction. Children are given lectures in which a rule of proper behavior is gone over quietly and repeatedly. Lutz (1985:61) states:

> . . . children are believed to obey *when* and *because* they listen and understand language; intention and knowledge become virtually synonymous in this system. It is assumed that correct behavior naturally and inevitably follows from understanding, which should follow from listening. Although the concept of independent will is not absent (this is represented in the concept of tip-,) the greatest stress is placed on the connections between language, listening, understanding, and correct behavior.

Here, the connection between thought and desire found in the western model is reversed. In the western model, if one desires or intends to do what is good, then one must be able to conceive of what is good. In the model used on Ifaluk, if one can and does conceive of what is good, one must do what is good. However, there have been theologians in the western tradition who also argued that if one *truly* understood what was good, one would desire it.

Based on indirect evidence, there appears to be another difference between the model used on Ifaluk and the western model. In his interviews with a psychotic man, Spiro found that his assistants became disgusted with this man's reports of his hallucinations, saying he "talk lie, only talk lie" (Spiro 1950). Based on these reactions, it seems likely that the notion that someone might really see and feel what is not actually there is not part of their model of the mind.

Overall, however, the model used on Ifaluk and the western model seem to have similar frameworks. Thoughts, feelings, and desires are distinguished. Feelings are considered a natural response to experience, not under self-control, and also to have the power to move the person toward action. The emotions are distinguished from physical sensations. Understanding is required for appropriate behavior, and lack of understanding results in loss of control.

On the other hand, there are significant differences between the two models. The one used on Ifaluk fuses thought and feeling with regard to the upper-level term *nunuwan* and apparently does not distinguish desire from intention. In this model, the gut is thought to be the site of feeling and thinking rather than the head. The emotion terms blend affects in somewhat different ways than the western model. The interpersonal role of emotion is more distinctly conceptualized than in the western model, as is the role of emotion in physical illness and the therapeutic use of catharsis. An understanding of hallucinatory experience may be absent from this model. Finally, understanding what is right is treated as a necessary and sufficient condition for doing what is right, rather than being treated as simply a necessary condition.

Based on these two cases, it seems likely that the folk model of the

mind will turn out to be like the folk model for colors as described by
Berlin and Kay (1969). That is, certain salient areas of the experiential
field will be universally recognized, although the degree to which the total
field is differentiated and the exact borders and boundaries between areas
will vary cross-culturally. However, at this point no simple ordering of
basic concepts like the ordering found for color terms has been found for
the model of the mind. In some areas, the people of Ifaluk do not make
distinctions we do (e.g., the distinction between desire and intention), but
in other areas they make more distinctions that we do (e.g., they commonly distinguish between the physical sensations and the emotional desires
concerning sex, hunger, and the cessation of pain, but this distinction is
rarely made by us).

Speculations about cultural differences and similarities

Logically, it might have been the case that the Ifalukan materials could
not even be translated into the western model. Suppose they had an extremely different model of the mind, one that made none of the distinctions made in the western model. Since internal states and processes are
private, how could we ever learn anything about their model? However,
this is not what we find. The model used by the people of Ifaluk can be
translated. How is this possible?

   If it were the case that an ethnographer could not learn the model, one
would wonder how the children on Ifaluk could learn the model. This
raises a more general question: If these models are models of private experience, how are they ever learned, either here or on Ifaluk? Even if everyone's private experience is highly similar, how can someone else's words
be matched to anyone else's private experience?

   What in fact is the case is that neither model is *only* a model of private
experience. Both models use similar external, public events as identifying
marks in their definitions of internal states. Thus, thinking is like speech,
and speech is public. What are thoughts? One can say that thoughts are
like things one says to oneself, or images of what one sees with one's eyes.
Feelings are like those sensations that do have public elicitors; we know
how to tickle each other. Furthermore, as human beings, we have what
appears to be an innate communication system for emotions, signalled
by patterns of facial expression (Ekman 1971). Various autonomic responses are also available as public events for the definition of feelings.
Feelings are typically aroused by relatively specific external events. To
understand what wishes are, we have the public expression of requests
and commands: Wanting is the feeling that gives rise to the child's saying
"gimme, gimme." Intentions are related to such speech acts as promises
and threats; that is, to the accomplishment of events to which one has
given a commitment. The tight connection pointed out by Vendler (1972)
between speech acts and internal states is not fortuitous; the thesis pre-

sented here is that speech acts are one of the major classes of public events used as identifying marks of internal states and processes.

This cannot be the full answer to how we learn about internal processes, since even though types of speech acts and facial patterns may offer a means of identifying internal events, they do not account for our beliefs about the causal relations among these internal events, such as our belief that we can think what we want to but that we cannot make ourselves feel what we want to, or our belief that desires influence intentions but not the reverse. One answer to this issue is to say that these are universals of experience. Once one has categories such as "feeling" and "thought," identified by their relationship to various public events, one cannot escape noticing that one cannot decide what to feel but one can decide what to think. Such a hypothesis has a ring of plausibility but seems completely untestable.

Finally, one speculates about what generally might account for cultural differences in folk models of the mind. Perhaps differences in the social and interactional conditions of life give differential salience to some of the identifying public marks of internal states. The emphasis on emotional mental states in the model used on Ifaluk would seem to be related to the strong salience of such emotion-linked actions as aggression and sharing in daily life. However, such differences in salience would not explain why there are differences in the conceptualization of causal relations between various mental states, such as the notion that lecturing on what is good causes the hearer to understand what is good thereby causing the hearer to be well behaved. Nor would these differences in the salience of emotion linked actions explain why the people of Ifaluk believe the verbal expression of feelings, especially depressive feelings, keeps one from being made ill by those feelings. It seems likely that some part of this folk model, like most folk models, cannot be explained by variation in current social or ecological factors. Parts of most folk models are legacies from the past, and the information needed to discover whatever causes once operated to create these models is often not obtainable.

Note

1. Support for research reported in this paper was provided in part by a grant from the National Science Foundation (BNS 8005731). The author wishes to thank Paul Kay and Laurie Price for critical commentary on an earlier draft of this paper and Susan Lindner and Ronald Langacker for discussions concerning the semantics of mental states and processes.

References

Austen, J.
  1969. Emma. London: Collins. (First published 1816.)
Anscombe, G.
  1963. Intention. Ithaca, N.Y.: Cornell University Press.

Berlin, B. and P. Kay
  1969. Basic Color Terms: Their Universality and Evolution. Berkeley: University of California Press.
Burrows, E. and M. Spiro
  1963. An Atoll Culture: Ethnography of Ifaluk in the Central Carolines. New Haven, Conn.: H.R.A.F. Press.
Casson, R.
  1983. Schemata in cognitive anthropology. Annual Review of Anthropology 12:429–462.
D'Andrade, R. G.
  1985. Character terms and cultural models. In Directions in Cognitive Anthropology, J. Dougherty, ed. Urbana: University of Illinois Press. Pp. 321–344.
D'Andrade, R. G. and M. Wish
  1985. Speech act theory in quantitative research on interpersonal behavior. Discourse Processes 8:229–259.
Ekman, P.
  1971. Universals and cultural differences in facial expressions of emotion. In Nebraska Symposium on Motivation Series, J. K. Cole, ed. Lincoln: University of Nebraska Press. Pp. 207–283.
Fillmore, C.
  1977. Topics in lexical semantics. In Current Issues in Linguistic Theory, R. W. Cole, ed. Bloomington: Indiana University Press. Pp. 76–138.
Friedrich, P.
  1977. Sanity and the myth of honor: The problem of Achilles. Ethos 5(3): 281–305.
Gerber, E.
  1975. The cultural patterning of emotions in Samoa. Unpublished Ph.D. dissertation. University of California, San Diego.
Heider, F.
  1958. The Psychology of Interpersonal Relations. New York: John Wiley and Sons.
Hutchins, E.
  1980. Culture and Inference. Cambridge, Mass.: Harvard University Press.
  n.d. An analysis of interpretations of on-going behavior. Unpublished manuscript, Department of Anthropology, University of California, San Diego.
Kenny, A.
  1963. Action, Emotion, and Will. London: Routledge and Kegan Paul.
Lutz, C.
  1980. Emotion words and emotional development on Ifaluk atoll. Unpublished Ph.D. dissertation. Harvard University.
  1982. The domain of emotion words on Ifaluk. American Ethnologist 9:113–128.
  1983. Parental goals, ethnopsychology, and the development of emotional meaning. Ethos 11(4):246–262.
  1985. Ethnopsychology compared to what? Explaining behavior and consciousness among the Ifaluk. In Person, Self, and Experience: Exploring Pacific Ethnopsychologies, G. White and J. Kirkpatrick, eds. Berkeley: University of California Press. Pp. 35–79.
Mandler, G.
  1982. Mind and Body. New York: W. W. Norton and Company.
Miller, G.
  1956. The magical number seven, plus or minus two: Some limits on our ability to process information. Psychological Review 63:81–97.
Natsoulas, T.
  1978. Consciousness. American Psychologist 33(10):906–914.

Quinn, N.
  1982. "Commitment" in American marriage: A cultural analysis. American Ethnologist 9(4):775–798.
Rumelhart, D.
  1980. Schemata: The building blocks of cognition. *In* Theoretical Issues in Reading Comprehension; Perspectives from Cognitive Psychology, Linguistics, Artificial Intelligence and Education, R. Spiro, B. Bruce, and W. Brewer, eds. Hillsdale, N.J.: Lawrence Erlbaum Associates. Pp. 33–58.
Rumelhart, D. and D. Norman
  1981. Analogical processes in learning. *In* Cognitive Skills and Their Acquisition, J. Anderson, ed. Hillsdale, N.J.: Lawrence Erlbaum Associates. Pp. 335–359.
Ryle, G.
  1948. The Concept of Mind. London: Hutchinson House.
Searle, J.
  1975. A taxonomy of illocutionary acts. *In* Language, Mind, and Knowledge, Minnesota Studies in the Philosophy of Science, Vol. 7, K. Gunderson, ed. Minneapolis: University of Minneapolis Press. Pp. 344–369.
  1980. The intentionality of intention and action. Cognitive Science 4:47–70.
Spiro, M. A.
  1950. A psychotic personality in the South Seas. Psychiatry 13(2):189–204.
Sperry, R.
  1982. Some effects of disconnecting the cerebral hemispheres. Science 217:1223–1226.
Sternberg, R., B. Conway, J. Ketron, and M. Bernstein
  1981. People's conceptions of intelligence. Journal of Personality and Social Psychology 41(1):37–55.
Wallace, A.
  1961. On being just complicated enough. Proceedings of the National Academy of Sciences 47:458–464.
Vendler, Z.
  1967. Linguistics in Philosophy. Ithaca, N.Y.: Cornell University Press.
  1972. Res Cognitans: An Essay in Rational Psychology. Ithaca, N.Y.: Cornell University Press.

PART II
Reasoning and problem solving from presupposed worlds

6
Proverbs and cultural models
AN AMERICAN PSYCHOLOGY OF PROBLEM SOLVING[1]

Geoffrey M. White

Proverbs are generally regarded as repositories of folk wisdom. As stylized sayings that presume to represent the commonsensical in everyday life, they are a topic of special interest for this volume's focus on cultural models. The dictionary defines a proverb as "a short, pithy saying in frequent and widespread use, expressing a well-known truth or fact." Attention to just what "well-known truths" are, in fact, expressed by proverbs and how, cognitively and linguistically, they obtain their particular brand of meaning may provide some insight into the organization of cultural models that underlie them.

Proverbs are especially interesting because, like much of ordinary language, they accomplish both conceptual and pragmatic work (see Briggs 1985). On the one hand, proverbs offer succinct ("pithy") descriptions of events. A familiar expression such as "It only takes one bad apple to spoil the barrel" brings a number of salient and well-known propositions about people and social life to bear on a particular person or situation. In doing so, this proverb provides an interpretation of specific actions or events in terms of a general, shared model. But proverbial sayings amount to more than economical descriptions. They are essentially concerned with morality, with evaluating and shaping courses of action and thus are frequently used in contexts of legal and moral argumentation (see, for example, Messenger 1959; Salamone 1976). In the proverb just quoted, the evaluative claim is explicit: one bad apple threatening to corrupt other, good apples. In other sayings, evaluative implications may rest just beneath the surface, such as "You can't judge a book by its cover." In this saying, a prior evaluation (either good or bad) is corrected by reminding the listener of our assumptions about distinctions between appearances and reality.

Whether explicit or implicit, the evaluative assertions expressed in proverbs lend them directive force as recommendations for a desired course of action. The saying about bad apples ruining good ones may imply that some action should be taken to spare the threatened good apples, even though the overt form of the saying is that of a simple description of a state of affairs. This form of "indirect directive" is typical of many proverbs that overtly take the form of descriptions but that have the effect of suggestions, recommendations, or commands and the like.

Since the conceptual and pragmatic functions of proverbs are also handled routinely by ordinary language, why do so many languages and cultures around the world have a recognizable class of proverbial sayings?[2] I suggest that the answer lies partly in their peculiar form of indirection and partly in their communicative effectiveness. As compact expressions of important cultural knowledge, proverbs combine a cognitive economy of reasoning with pragmatic force aimed at influencing other people. To understand why proverbs rather than less formulaic language are used, it is useful to ask, 'What is the speaker trying to *do* with proverbs?' rather than simply 'What is he or she trying to *say?*' To do so, one might examine the situations in which proverbs are invoked to have some social effect, such as Hausa marital quarrels (Salamone 1976) or Yoruba child rearing (Arewa & Dundes 1964), where focused observation might record repeated uses of proverbs in particular contexts. However, understanding the social uses of proverbs also requires knowing something about the interpretive work done by both speaker and listener.

This paper is concerned primarily with the conceptual processes that underlie proverb meaning rather than with questions of social usage. The analysis is based on the assumption that certain key understandings make up a kind of kernel of proverb meaning, even though such meaning may be shifted or elaborated in particular contexts of use. The fact that proverbs represent generalized knowledge, applied to the interpretation of particular events, suggests that they may tell us something about enduring cultural models of experience. Dyer (1983) has noted that the abstract advice encoded in familiar sayings or "adages" plays an important role in understanding stories. Narrative comprehension frequently proceeds by using existing knowledge structures to process new information and draw inferences about the social and moral implications of what is said; in other words, to get the point. A closer examination of proverbial understanding as a cognitive process, then, may illuminate the organization of global knowledge structures.

Interlocutors comprehend proverb meaning through a process of inference that allows them to link the saying with prior understandings and to fill in unstated propositions. Even though this is so in much of natural discourse, proverbial sayings tend to be particularly figurative, partial, and indirect. To understand what is said when a proverb is uttered requires going beyond the utterance itself by using underlying assumptions to draw appropriate implications. So, for example, understanding a statement like "It only takes one bad apple to spoil the barrel" involves both a translation of metaphorical imagery as well as a cultural theory of moral corruption.

The fact that certain proverbs are frequently used suggests that they express key understandings about everyday life. If so, proverbs may provide a source of insight into cultural models in particular areas of common experience. This paper pursues this idea by examining a set of American English proverbs that may all be used in a similar way: to give advice to someone in a problematic situation, broadly conceived. By selecting sayings that can be used to counsel someone dealing with a personal quandary, the analysis focuses on certain American understandings about persons, problems, and purposeful behavior.

Proverbial understanding

Before looking more closely at proverbs of problem solving, it is necessary to consider briefly the linguistic and conceptual processes that enter into proverb meaning. Certain aspects of the linguistic form of proverbial sayings mark them as distinctive from other types of ordinary language, lending them their particular aura of veracity. For example, by using verb forms not qualified or marked by number or tense, proverbs acquire a timeless, enduring quality, seemingly not subject to the vicissitudes of circumstances or change. And, by using such quantifiers as *all, every,* and *no,* proverbs do not allow exceptions or hedges. Thus, one finds "Time heals *all* wounds" rather than, say, "Time heals *some* wounds," which would hardly provide a comforting bit of advice. Allowing exceptions or hedges would deny proverbs their claim to universal validity. Some proverbs also draw on hyperbole as a device for underscoring the obvious, commonsensical quality of an assertion. Thus, we have "Rome wasn't built in a day" rather than, say, "Rome wasn't built in six months" or, perhaps, "Salem village wasn't built in a day."

Perhaps the most characteristic feature of proverbs is their extensive use of metaphorical imagery to conceptualize and express social messages. It is significant that most proverbs are overtly metaphorical in their composition (but there are exceptions, such as "Where there's a will, there's a way"). The fact that most proverbs are constructed in this way suggests an important complementarity of function between the conceptual role of metaphor and the pragmatic uses of proverbs. If one views metaphor as a device for expressing abstract concepts in terms of other concepts more closely grounded in physical experience, then metaphorical imagery would seem to be an excellent vehicle for proverbial sayings that seek to express propositions taken to be self-evident on the basis of shared experience and that can thus be used to give advice, make recommendations, and so forth. When seen in this light, proverbs appear as a special case of the more general process of metaphorical understanding. As described by Lakoff and Johnson (1980:115):

> . . . metaphor pervades our normal conceptual system. Because so many of the concepts that are important to us are either abstract or not clearly delineated in our experience (the emotions, ideas, time, etc.), we need to

get a grasp on them by means of other concepts that we understand in clearer terms (spatial orientation, objects, etc.). This need leads to metaphorical definition in our conceptual system.

Lakoff and Johnson speak of metaphorical understanding as a way of interpreting abstract and loosely structured experiences by conceptualizing them in terms of other, more concrete and clearly formulated types of experience. Although neither type of experience is more "basic," the latter is more closely grounded in the physical realm of the body and environment.

Carbonell and Minton (n.d.) and others have described metaphorical understanding as a process of common-sense reasoning. They suggest that simile, analogy, and metaphor are all based on the same type of cognitive process (analogical reasoning) used to interpret new situations in terms of other, previously encountered and understood situations. The essential process in this type of reasoning is one of *mapping* aspects of a previously known and well-delineated ("source") domain to a newer and less well structured ("target") domain (see Collins & Gentner, and Lakoff & Kövecses, this volume).

This model of metaphor may also be extended to the process of proverbial understanding. As noted, most proverbs assert their truths about social and moral matters by linking features of social situations to other, more mundane domains with widely known and clearly defined conceptual entailments. Indeed, this is such an inherent part of proverbial understanding that some published collections of proverbs organize their contents in terms of types of source domain, such as "animals," "natural environment," "food," "fishing," "travel," and the like (see Brown 1970; Schultz 1980).[2]

A key question in models of analogical reasoning is 'How are mappings between domains constructed?' or, 'How are the relevant cross-domain similarities identified?' The ultimate answers to these questions will have to draw from pragmatic and contextual information not yet dealt with in cognitive theories of metaphor. However, for many metaphors in frequent use, the mapping is well known and hence does not have to be reconstructed each time any metaphor is used. This notion of "frozen" metaphors applies well to proverbs, which are among the most formulaic and standardized types of metaphorical usage. The fact that people are readily able to paraphrase proverbs out of context, to render their meanings in nonmetaphorical language without reference to particular denotata or instances of usage, strongly indicates the "frozen" quality of proverbial inference and the important role of prior cultural models in their interpretation.

Noting the prepackaged association of abstract, social meanings with concrete metaphors gives only a partial picture of the process of reasoning underlying proverb meanings. Proverbs are also used to pick out and communicate salient aspects of a social situation in terms of prior knowledge about similar situations. As in the use of metaphor generally, uncertain or ambiguous events can thus be understood and evaluated in terms of existing models of social experience. However, unlike the process of metaphorical understanding, most of the "action" in the process of proverbial understanding is concerned with drawing out behavioral and evaluative implications, with distilling a particular interpretation of a situation, rather than with constructing a mapping to link source domain with target domain. Thus, understanding what is meant by the assertion "The squeaky wheel gets the grease" does not concern interpreting the notion of "squeaky wheel" in terms of vocal assertiveness so much as making the inference that if such behavior leads to positive outcomes (getting "grease"), it is worth pursuing.

Proverbs function as effective communicative devices because they set up the listener to draw such practical inferences by expressing one or more key propositions embedded in a cultural model with known entailments. By instantiating certain elements of an existing model, other, related propositions are invoked through inference. In this way, the proverb user is able to formulate and communicate a point of view without verbally articulating all of its elements. Behavioral directives need not be stated overtly since any listener with common sense will draw the appropriate conclusions, given the premises asserted and/or implied by the proverb. At the same time, its metaphorical form brings those conclusions into sharper focus by formulating them in a domain in which propositions and their behavioral entailments are more tightly and obviously connected.

The interpretation of proverbs may be viewed as an interactive construction in which the speaker (1) perceives and evaluates a social situation in terms of an abstract cultural model, (2) articulates that point of view in a proverb expressing one or more interlinked propositions, which is then (3) interpreted by the listener, who expands on those propositions by locating them in the relevant cultural model and drawing appropriate inferences. Just what inferences are drawn will depend on the context of use, the abstract propositions expressed by a particular proverb, and the cultural model(s) in which they participate. Insofar as proverbial inference follows from the instantiation of pieces of a knowledge structure, proverbs offer a window onto the organization of generalized models of experience. The analysis in the next section examines the way informants interpret proverbs pertaining to human action and problem solving. By asking, 'What does one need to know or assume in order to interpret the meaning of a proverb?' one may begin to identify some of the key propositions and inferences that enter into the ethnopsychology of American problem solving.

An ethnopsychology of problem solving

My interest in proverbs began in the context of research on common sense reasoning about personal (social, psychological) problems. In the course of an earlier study of the ways different cultural groups explain and deal with adjustment problems (White 1982), we noticed that informants occasionally used idiomatic and proverbial sayings such as "Time heals all wounds" to formulate their views of problems and how to deal with them. It then occurred to us that there are a substantial number of common sayings that express culturally constituted understandings about how to respond to problematic circumstances. Guided by this assumption, we decided to survey the range of well-known sayings that, in our judgment, could be used as advice in dealing with a problematic situation. We then set out to examine these sayings more closely to see what kinds of conceptualizations they embody.

The notion of "personal problem" here is simply that of any type of everyday quandary or adversity that is of some social or psychological significance for the person or persons involved. Hence, cultural knowledge about such problems is general rather than specific; it pertains to the nature of persons and their relation to the world through thought and action. Sayings such as "Every cloud has a silver lining" are widely known and used because they may be applied to a wide range of activities and situations, rather than to one specific domain of experience. The understandings that underlie such proverbs make up some of the most basic premises of American ethnopsychology. These understandings are quite different from the sort of conceptualizations studied by cognitive psychologists doing research on problem solving, in particular on "task environments," where problems and solutions are well specified in the form of winning games, solving puzzles, or proving theorems (see, for example, Newell & Simon 1972). The common-sense reasoning about problems expressed in proverbs is primarily concerned with person–problem relations rather than problem–solution algorithms. As such, they draw on a rich body of knowledge about persons and social action. Sayings such as "The grass is always greener on the other side of the fence" represent conceptualizations of problem situations with an implicit agenda about how to evaluate and respond to them. In probing the meanings of proverbs such as this, the following analysis is led into a consideration of the ethnopsychological understandings required to interpret them.

METHODS

Assuming that certain proverbs pertain to the way people respond to everyday problems, we began by selecting a number of proverbs that could be used in roughly the same way: to give advice to someone dealing with a personal dilemma or quandary. By using this general context as a frame, we were able to select a set of proverbs that could be compared in order to draw out common or contrasting themes in cultural knowledge about persons and problems.

The approach taken here draws on both elicited data obtained from informants as well as the investigator's (and reader's) intuitive knowledge of proverb meanings. This strategy combines several types of formal and nonformal data that are constrained in different ways and that thus shed light on proverb meanings from different angles.

Although proverbs may seem to be simple, direct, and obvious when used in context, many appear more complex, indirect, and ambiguous when considered in light of the unspoken assumptions and contextual information that give them their meaning. It thus becomes interesting to ask a number of informants to paraphrase proverbs in order to see how they render their meanings in less metaphorical language and the extent to which they agree in doing so. We did this by selecting a set of 11 proverbs and asking 17 informants to explicate them. The resulting paraphrases carve out a range of possible interpretations for each proverb and point to similarities and differences in meaning among them.

To pursue the hypothesis that the proverbs we selected derive their meaning from a common underlying ethnopsychology, we next asked our informants to look for similarities among the sayings and to sort them into groups. We also asked informants to state briefly their rationale for grouping certain proverbs as similar, thus forcing the kind of abstract speculation in which we ourselves were engaged in interpreting proverb meanings.

Because the paraphrases and rationales given for grouping proverbs together are quite varied and complex, it is useful to examine the *overall* pattern of similarities among the sayings in order to identify those judged most similar or different. I have used multidimensional scaling as a way of graphically representing this pattern of proverb similarities in a visual model. We may then look more closely at the paraphrases and the rationales given for grouping proverbs together in order to reconstruct the conceptual basis for judging similarities among them.

SOME PROVERBIAL SAYINGS

In searching for candidate sayings, we discovered that it is quite difficult simply to retrieve proverbs from memory at will. They resist introspective recall. However, given the right set of circumstances, the appropriate proverb seems almost to leap to mind.[4] Our approach was to draw up a list of problem-solving proverbs by searching through published collections of English proverbs (Collins 1959; Ridout & Witting 1967; Stevenson 1948; Wilson 1970; see also Simpson 1982) and to supplement that list using ourselves and acquaintances as informants. Based on the criteria that a proverb be widely known, frequently used, and pertain (at least potentially) to personal adversity, we selected the 11 sayings listed in Table 6.1. This corpus is not intended to be either exhaustive or representative of the full range of American sayings about problem solving. The only claim is that the statements in Table 6.1 are a subset of sayings relevant to the ways Americans construe responses to problematic circumstances.

What can be said about these proverbs at first glance? As expected,

Table 6.1. *Eleven American English proverbial sayings*

1. Every cloud has a silver lining.
2. God helps those who help themselves.
3. The grass is always greener on the other side of the fence.
4. There's no use crying over spilt milk.
5. Where there's a will there's a way.
6. Necessity is the mother of invention.
7. Rome wasn't built in a day.
8. The squeaky wheel gets the grease.
9. You can't have your cake and eat it too.
10. Don't make a mountain out of a mole hill.
11. Time heals all wounds.

most of them are phrased in figurative language. With the possible exception of two of those listed ("God helps those who help themselves" and "Where there's a will there's a way"), all are overtly metaphorical. Common objects and events such as clouds, green grass, spilt milk, squeaky wheels, and eating cake are used to characterize problem situations in terms of more immediate, physical imagery. Although diverse, these images represent several more general types of metaphor: notions of mechanics and construction (squeaky wheels, building Rome), food (cake, milk), and visual imagery (green grass, silver linings).

The proverbs listed were chosen because they say something about relations between a person and a problem or goal. They presuppose a discrepancy between the state of the world and the state of the person (intentions, desires, actions and the like). Each saying evaluates the likelihood of achieving a goal or changing a problematic situation, and, in so doing, carries an implied recommendation about the appropriate response that will bring person and world back into alignment, creating a better fit between personal outlook and worldly circumstances. As a preview of the following analysis, note that the proverbs in Table 6.1 span at least two distinct types of recommended response: those encouraging an active attempt at changing the world (e.g., "The squeaky wheel gets the grease") and those calling for adjustment of the person (e.g., "There's no use crying over spilt milk").

PSYCHOLOGICAL INFERENCE

In order for these proverbs to carry implications for appropriate action, they require certain background assumptions about human psychology and action (see Kirkpatrick & White 1985). They acquire their meaning against a backdrop of cultural understandings about the organization of perception, feeling, and thought that mediate the interrelation of person and world. By drawing on a cultural model of the person, informants make

specific inferences about the actions that follow from proverbial assertions about a problem/goal, or a person's perception of it. The analysis
of proverb interpretation developed here indicates that certain elements
of the American cultural model of the mind described by D'Andrade (this
volume) and other notions about personal action described by Heider
(1958) and Hutchins (n.d.) underlie proverb meanings. In particular, D'Andrade's assertion that "the main line of causation in the cultural model"
runs from perception through thought and feeling to intention and action captures much of the structure of reasoning in these proverbs about
personal processes that mediate the fit between person and world.

Despite considerable variability in the specific propositions asserted by
different proverbs in Table 6.1, they draw on similar understandings about
human psychology and action to obtain their full meaning and force. Some
of these understandings surface in the paraphrases and judgments of
similarity, such that inferences about feelings and intentions are made
explicit as informants seek to articulate proverb meanings. These data,
discussed below, indicate that proverbial reasoning involves an inferential process that moves from (1) an assertion about some aspect of the
person or problem, to (2) an expansion of its psychological implications
based on a cultural model of the person, to (3) inferences about an appropriate response or course of action. A consideration of how informants
paraphrase proverb meanings illustrates these different facets or levels of
proverbial reasoning.

Seventeen native speakers of English, all students at the University of
Hawaii, were asked to paraphrase each of the 11 proverbs in Table 6.1.
The proverbs were presented written on 3″ × 5″ index cards, one to a
card. Informants were asked first to look at all the proverbs and ask questions about any that were unfamiliar. Except for three people who said
they did not know "The squeaky wheel gets the grease," all of the proverbs were well known. Once having reviewed the set of 11 sayings, informants were asked to paraphrase each one by briefly writing out its meaning in plain language.

The 17 distinct paraphrasings obtained in this way represent a range
of interpretations that capture several levels of inference associated with
each proverb. Depending on the particular proverb, the paraphrases span
all or some of the levels of proverbial reasoning outlined: (1) description
of the problem situation, (2) its psychological implications, and (3) a
recommended response or course of action. It appears that the paraphrases
are mostly pitched at levels (1) and (2), whereas the more abstract
judgments of similarity tend to be made on the basis of (3), the implied
recommendation, as seen in the following section.

This type of variation in the level at which explications of the same
proverb may be phrased is illustrated by examining all of the paraphrases
given for a single proverb. The saying "The grass is always greener on
the other side of the fence" provides a particularly good example of varia-

tion in paraphrases that reflect the structure of proverbial reasoning. Because this saying is less explicit about the relations between the state of the person and the problem situation than some of the other proverbs (for example, "Where there's a will there's a way"), it requires the listener to make inferences in order to draw implications for behavior (there is no use trying to move to the other side of the fence) from its basic proposition about the perception of a problem or goal (it only *appears* better on the other side of the fence).

Like the proverbs "Every cloud has a silver lining" and "Don't make a mountain out of a mole hill," the saying about grass being greener on the other side of the fence uses the notion of visual perception as a metaphor for thought. By asserting that a person has misperceived a problem or goal (has not *seen* the silver lining; has mistaken a mole hill for a mountain; has the illusion of grass being greener than it really is), these proverbs are in fact saying that a person's judgment or thinking about the problem/goal is flawed. In this way, the metaphor does its work of taking a potentially complex and ambiguous process (such as faulty reasoning) and describing it in terms of events that are more clearly delineated and accessible to public demonstration (such as determining what things look like). As might be expected, then, the greatest number of paraphrases of the proverb "The grass is always greener on the other side of the fence" focus on the act of misjudgment or misperception, saying that things either "seem better," "look better," or "appear more attractive" on the other side of the fence. Some informants extend the metaphor of sight into their paraphrase:

1. Other people's situation sometimes *look* better than they actually are.
2. Things *look* better with other people.
3. Things *appear* to be more attractive or better when you are not involved.
4. No matter what one has, he can always *see* something better he doesn't have if he *looks* for it.
5. People tend to *focus* on their own problems and on their neighbor's assets.

Other informants simply assert that things "seem better":

6. Things which are unobtainable always *seem better.*
7. That which you cannot have always *seems better.*
8. Our own condition always *seems bleaker* than what others have.
9. Someone else's things will *seem nicer* than yours not because they are better, just because they aren't yours.
10. Once we make choices, the choice not taken always *seems better.*
11. *Fantasy* of what we have or have not.

The paraphrases listed here all speak directly to the person's perception of problems or goals. In other words, they say something about the relation between person and problem situation that approximates the proposition asserted in the proverb itself. Other informants, however, chose to paraphrase the proverb's meaning by going beyond the information given in the proverb to say what such a situation would imply about the person's feelings and desires. Specifically, six informants rendered the meaning of the proverb by noting that people who continually see people or things elsewhere as better will not be *satisfied, content, or happy;* they will be *envious.*

12. One is rarely *satisfied* with what one has.
13. The common *dissatisfaction* one has with one's own state of affairs.
14. One is never *satisfied* with what one possesses or situation in which one is in.
15. *Contentment* is seldom achieved.
16. You will always be *envious* of what the other person has – used in a situation where someone is *never happy.*
17. It won't help to be *envious;* the other person's blessings may only look that way to you.

By drawing on a cultural model of the person that links certain kinds of perceptions or thoughts with specific feelings and desires, people are readily able to characterize the emotional state of a person for whom "the grass is always greener on the other side of the fence." The direction of inference here, from perception of situation to emotion is consistent with the general direction of inference in American ethnopsychology (D'Andrade, this volume) and in Ifalukian knowledge about the situational antecedents of emotion (Lutz, this volume):

PERCEPTION/THOUGHT ====> FEELING/DESIRE

However, note that feelings such as "satisfaction," "contentment," or "envy" point beyond emotional responses to things a person may want, "possess," or "achieve." In other words, they are also about goals and desires. When seen as desires (which, in D'Andrade's scheme, mediate feelings and intentions), it becomes more apparent that our informants' psychological inferences play an important role in reasoning about the intentions and actions expected to follow from a particular problem, perceived in a certain way.

These inferences about the feelings or desires of someone who sees greener grass on the other side of the fence imply, in turn, certain kinds of intentions and actions that follow from dissatisfaction. It is these further implications for behavior, also derived from an underlying ethnopsychology, that give these proverbs their directive force as sources of advice about a recommended course of action. Although informants did not, in general, refer directly to these behavioral implications when they paraphrased the proverbs, they did frequently point to this level of proverb meaning when stating reasons for similarity among them, as seen below. These different levels of meaning, then, extend the underlying chain of inference further in the direction postulated by D'Andrade to link perception and feeling with intention and action:

PERCEPTION/THOUGHT =====> FEELING/DESIRE
                    =====> INTENTION/ACTION

This type of inference chain gives an indication of one way by which people draw behavioral implications from statements about a problem situation. When depicted in this way, the course of reasoning underlying some of the proverbs in Table 6.1 resembles quite closely Hutchins's (n.d.) description of American common-sense reasoning about behavior. In his analysis, ordinary interpretations of action move backward from behavior to the attribution of intentions to inferences about some background problem that gives rise to those intentions:

BEHAVIOR =====> INTENTION =====> PROBLEM

If we postulate that a person's perception of some event as a problem (PROBLEM) leads to a desire (WANT) for change and ultimately to an attempt (TRY) to bring about change, it is possible to see how a proverb that questions perception can have implications for action. Proverbs asserting that a person's perception of a problem is flawed (such as "Every cloud has a silver lining," "Don't make a mountain out of a mole hill," and "The grass is always greener on the other side of the fence") discourage emotions and actions aimed at changing the situation by negating the premise that it is in fact a problem at all (~PROBLEM):

~PROBLEM =====> ~WANT =====> ~TRY
PERCEPTION/THOUGHT =====> FEELING/DESIRE
                  =====> INTENTION/ACTION

By asking what must be assumed in order to understand the behavioral implications of the remaining sayings, it is possible to identify a small number of ethnopsychological inferences that link a proverb's overt assertion with its implied recommendation for action.

Two of the remaining proverbs that are similar in meaning to those mentioned and were judged so by our informants ("You can't have your cake and eat it too" and "There's no use crying over spilt milk") also have the effect of discouraging attempts to change a problem situation. In these examples, however, the effect is achieved through a different course of reasoning. By asserting that a situation cannot be changed, these sayings imply that further attempts to do so are futile. They appear to draw on the underlying belief that, for a person to try to reach a goal or change a problematic situation, he or she must believe it is possible to do so.

Here again the proverbs rely on a basic element of American ethnopsychology for their intended meaning. In his analysis of "naïve psychology," Heider (1958) observed that ordinary explanations of behavior and predictions of successful outcomes generally infer both ability

(CAN) and effort (TRY) in addition to desire (WANT) as ingredients in purposeful action. As many subsequent writers in attribution research have noted (e.g., Schmidt & D'Addamio 1973), the negation of any of these elements will affect inferences about the probability of success. Thus, by negating ability (~ CAN), these proverbs imply that one will not TRY to change a problem situation:

$$\sim CAN \Longrightarrow \sim TRY$$

Informants' paraphrases of these two proverbs indicate that they do, in fact, rely on some such notion of inability. More than one-third of the informants (6 and 7, respectively) used the expression *cannot* in describing their meanings. In the case of "spilt milk," most informants point out that one cannot change something that is in the past; whereas "having one's cake and eating it too" is a matter of one choice's excluding another. By denying the possibility of attaining some desired end, both of these sayings discourage active striving.

Another significant subset of proverbs in Table 6.1 appears to rely on the same underlying belief that an active attempt (TRY) to do or change something presupposes belief in ability (CAN). However, rather than negating the possibility of changing a situation, sayings such as "God helps those who help themselves," "The squeaky wheel gets the grease," "Necessity is the mother of invention," and "Where there's a will there's a way" all assert that some goal *is* within reach, that a certain desired outcome *is* possible. By affirming the actor's ability (CAN), these sayings have the opposite effect of those just described. They lead to a recommendation for an active attempt (TRY) at goal attainment or problem resolution:

$$CAN \Longrightarrow TRY$$

Most paraphrases of these sayings refer to the possibility of doing or getting something, given some antecedent condition. In addition, a significant proportion of the paraphrases for several of the sayings include ethnopsychological inferences about the person. For example, in the case of "Necessity is the mother of invention," 5 informants made reference to either "ingenuity" or "creativity" in times of need. And, in explicating "God helps those who help themselves," 7 people mentioned variously "initiative," "self-reliance," "responsibility," or "independence." And, in the saying "Where there's a will there's a way," which makes overt reference to a psychological disposition ("will"), nearly all informants mentioned an internal state of desire ("desire" ($N = 4$), "want" ($N = 4$), "determination" ($N = 3$), "perseverance" ($N = 2$), "motivation" ($N = 2$), or "believe that you can" $N = 1$).

I have ordered this discussion of informants' paraphrases of the 11 sayings listed in Table 6.1 according to the sayings' implications for action. However, the paraphrases themselves do not make frequent reference to the recommendations for action implicit in all of them. The relevance of such implicit recommendations for proverb meanings is evident in the uses to which these sayings are put in everyday interaction. A brief examination of informants' judgments about similarities among the proverbs, and their reasons for them, indicates that these effects are recognized and can be articulated.

IMPLICATIONS FOR ACTION

After paraphrasing each proverb (written one to a card), the 17 students were asked to group them into piles of any size according to similarity in meaning. Informants were also asked to write brief reasons for the groupings they created.

The sorting data were analyzed by first computing an overall measure of similarity for all pairs of proverbs, taking into account the number of informants who placed each pair together in the same pile, and the size of the pile in each case (see Burton 1975). The resulting matrix of similarity scores among all pairs of proverbs can be represented in visual form using multidimensional scaling (MDS) (Kruskal et al. 1977). MDS depicts similarities among the proverbs in terms of spatial distance, such that sayings judged more similar to one another in meaning are placed closer to one another in the spatial mapping.[5] The MDS model of judged similarities among the 11 proverbs is depicted in Figure 6.1.

The configuration in Figure 6.1 aids in the interpretation of proverb meanings by directing attention to groups of proverbs that informants judged as similar. I do not assume that the horizontal and vertical axes underlying the MDS model will necessarily reflect dimensions of meaning common to all of the proverbs.[6] However, the most notable characteristic of the configuration is the overall right–left distribution of proverbs along the horizontal axis. Six sayings are arrayed vertically on the right and four along the left, with "Rome wasn't built in a day" occupying a more intermediate position. The diagram locates "The grass is always greener . . . ," "You can't have your cake . . . ," "Every cloud has . . . ," "Don't make a mountain . . . ," "There's no use crying . . . ," and "Time heals . . ." in opposition to "The squeaky wheel . . . ," "God helps . . . ," "Necessity is the mother of . . . ," and "Where there's a will . . . ." This arrangement indicates that in the sorting task few people grouped the proverbs on one side of the diagram together with those on the other and reflects the contrasting recommendations for action embedded in these proverbs. The proverbs on the left encourage some kind of goal-oriented action; those on the right recommend against such striving. Or, put another way, the proverbs on the right encourage adjustment of the person rather than the situation. If this interpretation is correct, the horizontal dimension captures the divergent inferences about whether to TRY to change a problem situation.

The reasons stated by informants who sorted the proverbs along these lines give some support to this interpretation. Consider first the kinds of

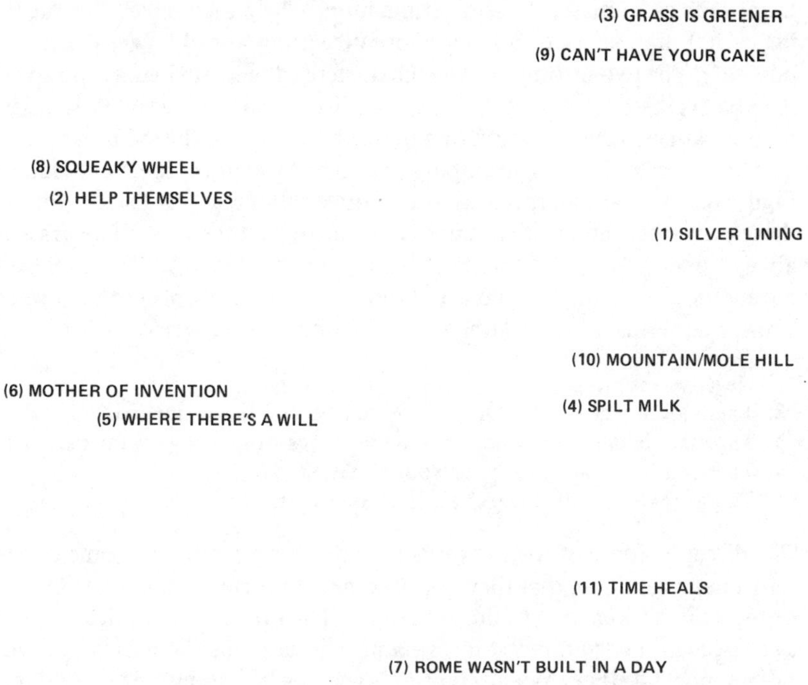

(3) GRASS IS GREENER

(9) CAN'T HAVE YOUR CAKE

(8) SQUEAKY WHEEL
(2) HELP THEMSELVES

(1) SILVER LINING

(10) MOUNTAIN/MOLE HILL
(6) MOTHER OF INVENTION
(5) WHERE THERE'S A WILL   (4) SPILT MILK

(11) TIME HEALS

(7) ROME WASN'T BUILT IN A DAY

Figure 6.1. Two-dimensional model of similarities among 11 American proverbs (Stress = .092)

rationale given by those who grouped together the proverbs "The squeaky wheel . . . ," "God helps . . . ," "Necessity is the mother . . . ," and "Where there's a will . . . ." Seven informants (out of the total of 17) placed these 4 proverbs together as a set or a subset of a larger group. The reasons given for their similarity are:

1. These give positive suggestions.
2. Positive reaction.
3. These tell you to go out and do something.
4. These are exhorting one to help themselves, they are motivators.
5. It's those people who initiate some solution that get it accomplished.
6. These imply the value of self-help, keeping at it, plugging away.
7. Concerned with self-determination and getting ahead.

Notice that a number of the informants articulate the rationale for their grouping by pointing to the proverbs' performative value. These sayings are said to be similar because they variously "suggest," "tell," or "exhort" one to take a particular course of action. In describing their meanings in this way, these informants are referring to the force of the inference about TRYING, analyzed above as an implicit recommendation. Other people simply describe the recommended goal-seeking behavior itself (in terms such as "initiate," "self-determination," "help themselves," or "keeping at it") and/or its positive outcome ("getting ahead," "get it accomplished"). The two informants who characterized these sayings as "positive" may be expressing the fact that their implied recommendation is an affirmation rather than a negation of a basic proposition in the cultural model.

The reasons given for grouping proverbs located on the right side of Figure 6.1 contrast sharply with the positive rationales just listed. Among these proverbs, the most commonly grouped together were "The grass is always greener . . . ," "You can't have your cake . . . ," "Don't make a mountain . . . ," and "It's no use crying . . . ." Five people grouped these four together as a set or subset. The reasons stated were:

1. Negative reaction.
2. These are no–nos. "Don't . . ." may not be said but is implied.
3. These are telling one to quit looking at things from a negative perspective.
4. These all imply acceptance of your situation.
5. Things take care of themselves; individuals must adapt to the situation.

The directive force of the proverbs is again made explicit by some of the informants who note that they take a command form by implying "Don't" or by "telling" someone to do something. The proverbial implication *not* to do something is noted by informants who describe them as "negative" or "no–nos." Rather than attempting to change the situation, individuals must variously "accept" or "adapt" and the like.

A number of informants made finer discriminations in their sortings of the proverbs located on the right side of Figure 6.1. Inspection of the diagram shows that the two proverbs "The grass is always greener . . ." and "You can't have your cake . . ." were judged quite similar to each other, as were "Don't make a mountain . . ." and "It's no use crying . . ." Five people grouped just the former two proverbs together and gave the following reasons for their judgments:

1. Sayings counsel one that he should be *happy* where he is.
2. These comment on the fact that people are not usually *content* with what they have.
3. Both for people who *want more* than they have.
4. Point out a human tendency toward *dissatisfaction*.
5. You'd say these to people who *moan and groan* too much.

It is apparent that, at this lower level of specificity, the reasons for placing just two similar proverbs together draw on ethnopsychological inferences about the state of the person, just as did the paraphrasings discussed earlier. Since "The grass is always greener . . ." is one of the two proverbs in this grouping, it is not surprising that informants refer to some of the same feelings or desires mentioned previously: "dissatisfaction," not "content" or "happy." These are emotions associated with desires that, for one reason or another, cannot be fulfilled.

The reasons given for grouping the two proverbs "The grass is always greener . . ." and "You can't have your cake . . ." indicate that some informants perform the sorting task more on the basis of an inference about the state of the person (e.g. the person is "not content") than on the basis of the specific proposition expressed metaphorically by the proverb (either that the goal is not realistic, in the case of the former, or that it cannot be reached, in the case of the latter). The ethnopsychological basis for judgments of similarity among the proverbs is also evident in the reasons given by the six informants who placed together the proverbs "Don't make a mountain . . ." and "It's no use crying . . . ," distinct from "The grass is always greener" and "You can't have your cake":

1. These would be said to complaining or *depressed* individuals.
2. Both directed toward someone who's *feeling sorry* for themselves in one way or another.
3. These remind us not to be too *concerned* with little problems as they will pass.
4. Advising getting things in perspective.
5. These are negative – tell you not to do something. Don't *make* something more *serious* than it is.
6. Negative proverbs with a reprimanding attitude used to *comfort*.

In addition to noting the directive force of these proverbs with terms like "advising," "telling," "reminding," or "reprimanding," and characterizing them as "negative," several reasons again refer to the emotional state of the person. However, these emotion attributions differ somewhat from those described earlier. Terms such as "depressed," "feeling sorry," and "too concerned" have a different tenor than do "dissatisfaction" or "discontent." The difference between these two sets of emotions follows from a distinction between seeking goals that cannot be had, on the one hand, and coping with present difficulties, on the other. Here again, the basis for informants' judgments of similarity among the proverbs rely more on inferences about emotional responses than on the specific propositions about perception of a problem ($\sim$ PROBLEM) or ability to change a situation or reach a goal ($\sim$ CAN).

The proverbs "Time heals all wounds" and "Rome wasn't built in a day" are also shown in Figure 6.1 to have been judged somewhat similar to one another. Insofar as they are generally aligned on the right side of the MDS diagram, they may be seen to advise adjustment of the person rather than an attempt to change the situation. The saying "Rome isn't built in a day" is more ambiguous in this respect since it advises patience in the short term, but persistence over the long term. Perhaps for this reason it is located in a more intermediate position on the horizontal dimension in Figure 6.1. Both sayings pertain to the perception of time. They seek to resolve a discrepancy between person and situation by adjusting the person's perspective on time: In the long run, things will get better; in the long run, goals will be attained. The reasons given by four informants who grouped these two sayings together refer to this perspective on time, as well as to the personal response (patience) that may be inferred from a lengthening of time perspective:

1. Both insinuate that things take time.
2. Things will be better, spirit inducers.
3. These are a reminder to be *patient,* things take time.
4. Counsel *patience.*

The reasons given for judging certain proverbs as similar are stated at different levels of inference, just as the paraphrases reflect different parts of the reasoning process used to interpret proverbs. This ability of informants to describe different aspects of the interpretive process may account for the considerable diversity found in the paraphrasing and sorting data. Because the task of grouping proverbs together requires a greater level of generality than simple paraphrasing, informants appear to have based their judgments more on the proverbs' implications for action than on the specific propositions that conceptualize a problem situation. Thus, some based their judgments of similarity on the basic opposition of an active attempt at change versus adjustment of the person. Others appear to have made judgments of similarity based on inferences about the specific emotional responses that mediate a certain kind of situation and the implied recommendation for adjustment. I have argued that both kinds of judgment are based on inferences about human psychology and action drawn from an underlying cultural model of the person. It is through a process of ethnopsychological reasoning that people link descriptions of a problem situation with recommendations for an appropriate response.

Conclusion

Proverbs appeal to reason. In particular, they appeal to common-sense reasoning based on cultural models of experience. Each proverb examined here represents a point of view, a way of looking at problems and persons that, because of our shared knowledge about such things, carries certain inevitable implications for action. By characterizing a problem situation in a certain way, as a matter of spilt milk or squeaky wheels, proverbs interpret that situation by identifying it as an instance of a more general model. Instantiation of part of an existing knowledge structure (such as the proposition that a certain event has been misperceived as a problem) then creates the basis for further inferences about emotion and action.

The inferential structure of proverb meanings – from problem description through psychological inference to implication for action – reflects the pragmatic work done by proverbs. Indeed, it seems likely that these peculiar bits of formulaic language are widely used precisely because they carry directive force.[7] As indirect directives, they are strategic linguistic devices for evaluating and shaping the course of social experience through appeals to common sense. The fact that proverbs are recognized as expressions of common sense or folk wisdom is indicative of their frequent use in attempting to clarify uncertainty.

An appeal to folk wisdom is a useful way of attempting to resolve personal conflict or ambivalence. The sayings examined here all attempt to lift a person out of a personal quandary or, in the terms of cognitive problem-solving, a "blocked condition," by suggesting a point of view that resolves a discrepancy between person and worldly circumstances (cf. Hutchins & Levin 1981). They introduce a new perspective by variously altering one's perception of time, of the problem, or of one's ability to do something about it. Once located in the framework of an underlying ethnopsychology, each type of assertion carries specific implications for emotion and action. Analysis of the processes of inference underlying proverb interpretation reveals the operation of specific cultural understandings about persons and action that have been identified previously by other students of American ethnopsychology (D'Andrade, this volume; Heider 1958; Hutchins n.d.; Schmidt & D'Addamio 1973).

It is a reassuring affirmation of the flexibility of language and culture that even this small corpus of proverbs represents contradictory ways of construing problem situations. The contrast between sayings such as "Where there's a will there's a way" and "You can't have your cake and eat it too" indicates that cultural models provide alternative (and sometimes mutually inconsistent) ways of interpreting experience. In this instance, these two sayings rely on the same ethnopsychology, which asserts that purposeful action typically presupposes belief in the ability to do or achieve something. One saying provides a way of affirming ability and recommending positive action; the other can be used to negate ability and discourage an active response. Such diverse, and even contradictory, devices for conceptualizing experience suggest that American proverbs and cultural models are readily adapted to a wide variety of purposes and occasions.

The attempt here to analyze proverbs through several types of interpretive data, including paraphrasing and similarity judgments, has been aimed at teasing out specific propositions and inferences that contribute to proverb meanings. This approach would be augmented by additional, complementary types of data, such as examples of discourse obtained through interviewing or natural observation. Alternatively, more structured, experimental elicitation could be devised to test the accuracy of the model sketched here. Both types of data would supplement, and probably correct, the account rendered here. But then, "You can't have your cake and eat it too." Or is it, "Where there's a will there's a way"?

Notes

1. This paper has profited from the contributions of a group of graduate students at the East-West Center who worked together with the author in collecting and analyzing the data discussed here. Jonathan Gurish, Joyce Kahane, and

Russell Young made especially important contributions but should not be held responsible for the arguments made here. I would also like to thank Paul Kay, and Lynn Thomas, as well as Willett Kempton and other participants in the Princeton Conference on Folk Models, especially the organizers, Dorothy Holland and Naomi Quinn, for helpful comments on an earlier version of this paper. The paper was first presented in a symposium organized by Holland and Quinn for the 80th Annual Meeting of the American Anthropological Association, entitled Folk Theories in Everyday Cognition.

2. In American English, proverbs appear to represent one end of a continuum of linguistic forms that vary in their degree of standardization and formalization, with no sharp distinction between them and other types of idiomatic or colloquial expressions. In contrast, Chinese language sayings form several distinct types, including two written forms, one of which is distinguishable by its four-character composition.

3. An important question for future research concerns the extent to which the relation between specific types of source domain and target domain are arbitrary, or sometimes associated with particular types of conceptualization. Thus, proverbs about human temperament frequently draw from the domain of animals (For example, "Curiosity killed the cat," "You can't teach an old dog new tricks," and "You can lead a horse to water, but you can't make him drink"), and those concerned with events beyond human control frequently use environmental imagery (such as "It never rains but it pours" and "The calm comes before the storm").

4. The fact that proverbs are difficult to recall from memory without an eliciting context or situation raises questions about the form in which they are stored in memory. It is clear that proverbs themselves are not stored in a distinct or bounded domain. There is no taxonomy of wise sayings. Rather, they are tied to cultural knowledge about types of situation or action–scenario. Such knowledge may be actively generated or assembled in the course of understanding specific events. Each proverb condenses a set of interlinked propositions that have general relevance for social life and can be used recurrently to intepret a range of events. This view of proverbs resembles Schank's (1980) reformulation of the notion of "script" as a reconstructive process that relies on various generalized sources of information called "Memory Organization Packets" (MOPs). These memory structures are the generalizations and abstractions from experience that are used to make predictions about future events, just as proverbs are used to make recommendations about a course of action.

5. MDS will represent a set of similarity scores in terms of any number of dimensions. In general, the investigator selects the MDS solution that most accurately displays the similarities while using the least number of dimensions. Analysis of our proverb-sorting data with MDS indicates that these data may be adequately represented in two dimensions ("stress" = .092).

6. Even in semantic domains where word meanings may be meaningfully scaled in relation to a few bipolar oppositions, such as adjectivelike terms used to describe personal traits (see White 1980), MDS will not provide much help in discovering the meanings of dimensions produced by complex inferential processes. For example, in their chapter for this volume, Holland and Skinner clearly show that a scaling model of terms for gender types gives few clues about informants' knowledge of male/female interactions that produced that model. In using MDS to represent relations among proverbs, there is even less reason to expect the dimensions of a scaling model to have specific semantic significance. The inferential processes that underlie proverb meanings are unlikely to map directly onto a few bipolar dimensions. There would have to be some components of meaning pertinent to all of the proverbs for the

MDS axes to have significance as dimensions of meaning. As seen in the fore-going discussion, most of the propositions and inferences that contribute to proverb meanings are relevant to only a subset of the sayings in Table 6.1. Except for the fundamental contrast in their implied recommendations for action (the opposition between sayings that encourage action and those that encourage adjustment, reflected in the horizontal dimension of Figure 6.1), there do not appear to be any components of meaning common to all sayings in the corpus.

7. The explanation for why proverbs are used rather than other kinds of ordinary language, or why they are used on certain occasions and not others, requires recourse to social and contextual information not discussed in this paper. The fact that proverbs are used at all may carry implicit social meaning concern-ing the nature of the relationship between speaker and listener. For example, some participants in the Folk Models conference argued that the use of prov-erbs such as those in Table 6.1 frequently indicates a bid for dominance in interaction.

References

Arewa, E. O. and A. Dundes
  1964. Proverbs and the ethnography of speaking folklore. American An-thropologist 66(6,2):70–85.
Briggs, C. L.
  1985. The pragmatics of proverb performances in New Mexican Spanish. American Anthropologist 87(4):793–810.
Brown, R. L.
  1970. A Book of Proverbs. New York: Taplinger Publishing Company.
Burton, M.
  1975. Dissimilarity measures for unconstrained sorting data. Multivariate Behavioral Research 10:409–423.
Carbonell, J. G. and S. Minton
  n.d. Metaphor and common-sense reasoning. Paper presented at conference, Folk Models, May, Institute for Advanced Study, Princeton, N.J.
Collins, V. H.
  1959. A Book of English Proverbs with Origins and Explanations. London: Longmans.
Dyer, M. G.
  1983. Understanding stories through morals and remindings. In Proceedings of the Eighth International Joint Conference on Artificial Intelligence. Pp. 75–77.
Heider, F.
  1958. The Psychology of Interpersonal Relations. New York: John Wiley and Sons.
Hutchins, E.
  n.d. An analysis of interpretations of on-going behavior. Unpublished Manu-script, Department of Anthropology, University of California, San Diego.
Hutchins, E. and J. Levin
  1981. Point of view in problem solving. Center for Human Information Pro-cessing Technical Report #105. San Diego: University of California.
Kirkpatrick, J. and G. M. White
  1985. Exploring ethnopsychologies. In Person, Self and Experience: Exploring Pacific Ethnopsychologies. G. M. White and J. Kirkpatrick, eds. Berkeley: University of California Press, Pp. 3–32.

Kruskal, J., F. Young and J. Seery
   1977. How to Use KYST–2, A Very Flexible Program to do Multidimensional
   Scaling and Unfolding. Murray Hill, N.J.: Bell Laboratories.
Lakoff, G. and M. Johnson
   1980. Metaphors We Live By. Chicago: University of Chicago Press.
Messenger, J. C.
   1959. The role of proverbs in a Nigerian judicial system. Southwestern Journal
   of Anthropology 15:64–73.
Newell, A. and H. Simon
   1972. Human Problem Solving. Englewood Cliffs, N.J.: Prentice-Hall.
Ridout, R. and C. Witting
   1967. English Proverbs Explained. London: Heinemann.
Salamone, F. A.
   1976. The arrow and the bird: Proverbs in the solution of Hausa conjugal-
   conflicts. Journal of Anthropological Research 32:358–371.
Schank, R. C.
   1980. Language and memory. Cognitive Science 4:243–284.
Schmidt, C. and J. D'Addamio
   1973. A model of the common-sense theory of intention and personal causation. In Proceedings of the Third International Conference on Artificial Intelligence. Stanford: Stanford University. Pp. 465–471.
Schultz, E.
   1980. Samoan Proverbial Expressions. Auckland: Polynesian Press. (First published in 1953.)
Simpson, J. A., ed.
   1982. The Concise Oxford Dictionary of Proverbs. London: Oxford University Press.
Stevenson, B.
   1948. The Home Book of Proverbs, Maxims and Familiar Phrases. New York:
   Macmillan Company.
White, G. M.
   1982. The role of cultural explanations in 'psychologization' and 'somatization.'
   Social Science and Medicine 16:1519–1530.
   1980. Conceptual universals in interpersonal language. American Anthropologist
   82(4):759–781.
Wilson, F. P., ed.
   1970. The Oxford Dictionary of English Proverbs. 3rd ed. Oxford: Clarendon
   Press.

7
Convergent evidence for a cultural model of American marriage[1]

Naomi Quinn

This paper analyzes two passages excerpted from a longer interview, illustrating the utility of a method of discourse analysis elsewhere (Quinn 1985a; 1985b; n.d.) applied to much more extensive interview material of the same sort. In the larger study from which these excerpts have been borrowed, husbands and wives in 11 marriages were interviewed, separately, over an average of 15 or 16 hours each, on the topic of their marriages.[2] Interpretation of the passages at hand draws on the more extended analysis of this entire body of material. The full analysis depends for its convincingness on its ability to account for features of discourse about marriage in many passages such as those examined here. Of course, the entire analysis cannot be presented in this brief paper, but the examples provided suggest its range. The two segments of discourse scrutinized here, one of which followed the other about midway through the first hour-long interview with a woman whom we call Nan, are reproduced below:[3]

3W-1: I think Tom and I both were *real* naïve about each other. I mean, I think that we got married on the strength of a lot of similar tastes and a lot of love and appreciation but not much real sense of who each other were. I really don't think that we, either of us, had examined each other and said – I mean, I don't think I had said, "Really, who is this Tom Harper, how can I describe him, what is he? What . . . ." You know, "Is that the kind of person I need to be married to?" I don't think I had ever consciously done that – examined my needs and to see if Tom'd fit them. I think it was an intuitive kind of thing and I look at it now and I don't think I necessarily could have done that. I mean, the things that have been strengths of our marriage are the same things that got us married – I think being comfortable with each other, the similar tastes, the same kind of – ways of dealing with a lot of things. And the things that have been difficult in the marriage I couldn't have foreseen; I don't think now but I have sometimes thought back, you know, "Gee, people really do go into marriage, with their eyes, closed." I just find it – how amazing that many marriages get to stay together, when you consider the way they do it.

3W-1: I think during some of Tom's and I – during some of the most difficult passages that we had when we have really despaired in a sense and thought, "This – we are going to be driven apart by all our problems," including, you know, our problems with each other, and one of the things we have both thought is that, "If I know Tom as well as I know him and love him as much as I love him and still have this much trouble being married to him, what in the world chance would I have of finding anybody else who would be any easier to be married to and I wouldn't know that person any better when I got - married him than I knew Tom."

I: Right, right and that would be the whole thing all over again.

3W-1:   Exactly and never having learned or worked through what actually you need to learn and work through to make the first marriage stick. And I think that's one of the things that - almost laziness in a sense or unwillingness to put out effort for nothing. Why in the world would you want to stop and not get the use out of all the years you've already spent together?

I: A sense of investment, ha?

3W-1:   Yeah, really, A sense of, well, through the good and the bad. We have learned a lot about each other. We've learned a lot of ways of working with each other. If it took seven more years before you learned that much with the next person. Where - you know, where would you go?

The object of the analysis to be demonstrated on these interview excerpts is reconstruction of the cultural understandings of marriage that must be assumed to underlie discourse about marriage in order to make such discourse comprehensible. The reader will find it useful, in following this demonstration, to refer to these interview passages.

Metaphors of marriage

An extremely helpful feature of the discourse, and hence a departure point for this analysis, is the metaphor in which talk of marriage is cast. Metaphors are rich clues partly because they are ubiquitous (Lakoff & Johnson 1980). It is possible to talk about marriage in the technical terms that American English provides - to speak of one's *spouse* rather than one's "partner" or the person to whom one is "hitched"; of being *married* rather than "getting tied down" or "jumping into marriage"; of getting *divorced* rather than "splitting up" or "bailing out" of a marriage that is "falling apart." As Nan's discourse illustrates, people sometimes use the nonmetaphorical alternatives. However, they do not sustain such nonmetaphorical language for long probably because the technical language is neutral toward the marital experience it describes. The range of available metaphorical language, by contrast, allows the speaker to make a variety of points about that experience.

The metaphors for marriage provide a first set of clues to the cultural model of marriage underlying discourse of the sort examined here. Superficially varied, these metaphors fall into a few classes. For example, Nan casts marriage in several different metaphors that have in common the expectation that it is to be enduring. In one metaphor, an extremely popular one in talk about marriage, MARRIAGE IS A MANUFACTURED PRODUCT. In Nan's words, such entities have "strengths" and "stay together," but they take work to produce – "And never having learned or worked through what actually you need to learn and work through to make the first marriage stick," she observes. She and other interviewees show a great deal of creativity in exploiting this metaphor. They speak of marriages that "last" and "work" as well-made products should, and they characterize a marriage that does so as a "good thing" and a "strong marriage," much as one would say of a manufactured product made to last that it was "good" and "strong." They pursue other entailments of the metaphor, recognizing, in comments such as the following, that the manufacture of such a product requires, not just work, but also craftsmanship, durable material, good components that have been put together well, and a whole that is structurally sound and substantially constructed:

2H-3: It's just that our relationship is extremely important to each of us and, you know, we want to work hard at making it so and making it better.

4H-4: When the marriage was strong, it was very strong because it was made as we went along – it was sort of a do-it-yourself project.

1H-2: I think that maybe I have an appreciation for the fact that a happy marriage is not entirely problem-free and that probably means that you really have to start out with something that's strong if it's going to last.

4H-4: And I suppose what that means is that we have both looked into the other person and found their best parts and used those parts to make the relationship gel.

9H-3: I guess stacking that up against what I saw in this other marriage, I guess that, you know, it seems like it was stuck together pretty good.

4H-2: They had a basic solid foundation in their marriages that could be shaped into something good.

2W-2: Each one [experience] is kind of like building on another, that our relationship just gets more solid all the time.

Moreover, this same metaphor of marriage as some kind of manufactured product can also characterize marriages that fail to endure: Such marriages may be "weakened" or "ruined" under a variety of circumstances; they are "broken" ones that are not "working" anymore; they are "shaky" or they have "strains" in them; or they may be only "the facade of a good marriage."

In another metaphor of enduringness that recurs in this discourse, MARRIAGE IS AN ONGOING JOURNEY. As Nan puts it, spouses go "through the good and the bad" together; and they make progress, as reflected in her objection to "stopping" one marriage and starting over with somebody new: "Where would you go?" As this last comment also suggests, a journey has a final destination, arrival at which provides another way of expressing the idea of marital enduringness. Another wife states this point more optimistically:

4W-1: That I have changed so much and that we have changed so much and that we have been able to work through so many basic struggles in our marriage and be at a place now where we trust each other, we love each other, we like each other. We appreciate each other. And feel pretty confident about being able to continue that way and continue working any other stuff that comes up. Just seems pretty amazing to me. It could have gone in so many different directions and that it didn't is incredible. But I think both of us take a whole lot of credit for the direction it went in, that we worked at this really hard.

This passage exploits a further entailment of the ongoing journey metaphor: the directionality of such a journey. Interviewees sometimes use this metaphor also to suggest how marriages fail to endure: not only do they "stop" or come to a point at which they are "unable to continue," but spouses also find themselves "in a place where they don't want to be," or they "split and start going in a different direction."

A third common metaphor of enduringness, MARRIAGE IS A DURABLE BOND BETWEEN TWO PEOPLE, also appears in one passage under analysis. The secureness of this bond is often reflected in metaphors picturing married couples as "cemented together," "bound together," "tied to each other," or, in the words of one husband quoted earlier, in a relationship that has "gelled." Here, Nan conveys the same notion obliquely, by the forceful means required to sever such a bond: "We are going to be driven apart by all our problems." Again, a marriage in danger of ending can be characterized in the same metaphorical terms as an enduring one.

These, then, are some metaphors in which Nan and other interviewees express their expectation that marriage is an enduring relationship. Another expectation about marriage reflected in metaphor is that it be beneficial. In the two passages from Nan's interview this expectation is reflected first in the metaphor of one spouse's "fit" to the other's "needs" – "I don't think I had ever consciously done that. Examined my needs and to see if Tom'd fit them." In this metaphor, A SPOUSE IS A FITTING PART. Again, this is not a lone example of such metaphorical usage; other interviewees make such comments about their spouses as, "I couldn't find a replacement. I couldn't find another woman to replace Beth"; "The best thing about Bill, for me, is that he fits me so well"; and "We've kind of meshed in a lot of ways."

In a second metaphor for marital benefit, Nan conceptualizes the years she has been married as time "spent" – "Why in the world would you want to stop and not get the use out of all the years you've already spent together?" she says. Here, MARRIAGE IS AN INVESTMENT. In American English, time is a resource, which, like money (Lakoff & Johnson 1980:7–9), can be invested. Other interviewees also regard the benefits of marriage as resources that spouses derive from the marriage, as reflected in such comments as, "And that was really something that we got out of marriage"; "We did a lot more talking about what we did or didn't want in our own marriage"; "I'm sure they must have something good in their marriage or they wouldn't still be together"; "I think she sort of felt that she would get those same things from marriage." Again, these metaphors of spouses as irreplaceable or well-fitting parts and of marriage as a container of resources illustrate but do not exhaust the metaphors interviewees use to express the idea that marriage is beneficial.

Nan's interview excerpt provides a good illustration of how interviewees frequently exploit the entailments of a given metaphor to make multiple points about marriage. Here, in the remark, "through the good and the bad," she makes the ongoing journey metaphor do double duty, characterizing marriage as something that is *both* enduring – a progression "through" successive experiences – and beneficial – some of these experiences are "good" ones. In her metaphor, marriage is also potentially costly, entailing encounters with bad as well as good. Other interviewees also make the point that marriage may entail costs as well as benefits. They talk, for instance, of "being short-changed in this relationship," or of the possibility of divorce "when the effort is more than the reward." Implicit in this last example is a folk social psychology[4] of voluntary relationships that, like its counterpart in academic exchange theory, assumes that the parties to such a relationship will not continue in it unless their benefits outweigh their costs, to render the relationship rewarding in net terms. Elsewhere in her interviews, Nan herself develops the implications of this assumption:

3W–12:   Because I think it costs me a lot and I don't think he's measuring that cost. And I'm scared it's going to cost me too much and leave me without being able to stay in the relationship.

A further implication of this exchange model of relationships such as marriage is that their continuation depends on *both* parties experiencing net benefit. Again, Nan makes this explicit when she says, at the beginning of the first passage, "Tom and I both were real naïve about each other. . . . I really don't think that we, either of us, had examined each other" for one's fit to the other's need. Such assertions about mutual needs to be met and mutual benefit to be realized are common in this discourse; interviewees frequently emphasize that they are speaking for "both of us," or add provisos such as "and I for her," or "and vice versa" to their descriptions of the benefits they derive or anticipate from marriage.

A third presupposition, that marriage is unknown at the outset, is vividly captured in Nan's metaphor of people who "go into marriage with their eyes closed." This is an instance of a general-purpose metaphor in American usage – KNOWING IS SEEING (Lakoff & Johnson 1980:48). In it, a lack of knowledge about marriage is cast as a failure to see, an equation reflected also in Nan's description of how she and her husband married without having examined each other, so that she did not know who he was, really. If initial ignorance of marriage can be captured in these metaphors of sightlessness, lack of observation, and nonrecognition, it is equally well reflected in another set of common metaphors picturing the manner of entry into marriage as precipitous and unprepared – "We had no idea what we were getting into"; "We sailed right into marriage"; "He jumped from one marriage into another"; or, in one particularly vivid example, people "falling into marriage like king pins at the bowling alley." These modes of entry contrast with the more considered ways people talk about leaving marriage – "walking away," "stopping and getting off," or "having to bail out," for example.

A fourth expectation reflected in the two passages with which we began is that, once experienced, marriage turns out to be difficult. Nan speaks directly of "the things that have been difficult in the marriage," and she also casts these things in a metaphor, commonly used to describe marital difficulties, of the "problems" that threaten to drive her and Tom apart. In their metaphorical characterizations of marriage, interviewees exploit the difficulty inherent not only in problems, but also in all kinds of mentally, psychically, and physically demanding situations: thus, marriage may involve struggle, trial, or conflict, for example. A favorite description of marital difficulties, probably because it is so conveniently conjoined with the notion of enduringness in the metaphor of marriage as an ongoing journey, speaks of the hardships endured in the course of that journey; this metaphor appears in Nan's interview excerpts as the "difficult passages that we had." Elsewhere, interviewees elaborate on this metaphor, speaking, for instance, of the uphill stretches or the rocky road to be traveled in a marriage. One husband uses a ship metaphor to capture, at once, the necessity for a marriage to be structurally sound in order to endure and the further understanding that it must be so built in order to withstand marital difficulties – the stormy weather through which it will sometimes be required to sail:

3H-6:   The self-righting concept that, you know, the marriage has enough soundness and equilibrium that it will take steps to right itself in any kind of stormy situation.

A final expectation about marriage revealed in Nan's remarks is that it takes effort. This expectation follows from the understanding that marriage is difficult: In our folk physics of difficult activities, with its basis in experience of the physical world, such activities require effort to perform. Nan alludes to this effort directly when she speaks of the "laziness" implicated in her "unwillingness to put out effort for nothing." She also describes effort in a metaphor of "working through" what "you need to learn and work through to make the first marriage stick." Here, the problem metaphor used earlier is extended by allusion to the kind of effort, "working through," required for problem solution. Other interviewees speak in terms of other kinds of effort: of the "searching" required to discover "where each of us were"; of the necessity, entailed by the journey metaphor, to "fight our way back almost to the beginning"; or that entailed by the manufactured product metaphor to "redo the whole thing." Frequently, also, by extension of this latter metaphor, interviewees allude to the "hard work" they have had to put in "for a good relationship." In the words of one husband quoted, "we want to work hard at . . . making it better."

These metaphors for marriage thus appear to be organized by five schemas for propositions about marriage, which can be glossed as follows:

MARRIAGE IS ENDURING
MARRIAGE IS MUTUALLY BENEFICIAL
MARRIAGE IS UNKNOWN AT THE OUTSET
MARRIAGE IS DIFFICULT
MARRIAGE IS EFFORTFUL

In the following section, we see how Nan draws on these proposition-schemas to construct a reasoned argument about marriage.

The variant of the schema notion adopted here is Hutchins's (1980:51), although what he calls simply a *schema* is here alluded to as a *proposition-schema* in recognition that mental schemas may organize other than propositional material (Lakoff 1984; see Quinn & Holland, in the Introduction to this volume). In Hutchins's terms, such a proposition–schema is a "template" from which any number of propositions can be constructed. The centrality of these five schemas to Americans' understanding of marriage is evidenced by the recurrence of propositions cast in metaphors of the enduringness of marriage, the mutual benefit to be derived from it, initial lack of knowledge about it, its difficulty, and the effort it requires, along with other propositions in which these same concepts are nonmetaphorically represented throughout the discourse under analysis in the present study. These five classes of metaphor, together with three others, virtually exhaust the metaphors people adopt in their talk about marriage.

The three additional categories of metaphor occurring in this talk delineate three further proposition–schemas that appear to play a role in the American cultural model of marriage:

MARRIAGE IS JOINT
MARRIAGE MAY SUCCEED OR FAIL
MARRIAGE IS RISKY

None of these three proposition–schemas figure in the two interview excerpts that are the focus of this analysis. Therefore, these schemas and the evidence, in metaphorical usage, for their role in Americans' understanding of marriage are sketched only briefly and partially here and treated no further (a full discussion of the metaphors for marriage appears in Quinn 1985a).

The notion that marriage is a joint arrangement is reflected in a rich variety of metaphors. The marital relationship, for instance, is described as a "unit" or a "pair," as being "together in this" or presenting a "united front." Some of these metaphors, for example, of marriage as a "partner-ship," or married life as "teaming up," convey at once the jointness of marriage and the effortfulness of this joint enterprise. Other metaphors bear the dual entailments of jointness and enduringness, when the meta-phorical link between spouses is, by its nature, an enduring one, as in the examples cited earlier in this section, of spouses "bound together" or "cemented together" or "tied to each other" or using the "best parts" of each "to make the relationship gel." Another metaphor already encoun-tered, that of a spouse as a fitting part, simultaneously carries the entail-ments of benefit and jointness.

The most frequent metaphors of success, and conversely of failure, ex-ploit an entailment of the manufactured product metaphor. They add another layer of meaning to that metaphor to characterize the successful marriage as one that "works" and the failed marriage, by contrast, as one that is no longer working. Another popular metaphor, this one building on that of marriage as an effortful activity, characterizes marital success in terms of some difficult task brought to completion – a marriage, like a problem, "worked out," or an unsuccessful one that perhaps "doesn't work out." Two of the varied metaphors of risk used to talk about mar-riage characterize it as a matter of chance, such as gambling – "there's so many odds against marriage," for instance – or as being in danger of survival – as in the comment, "the marriage may be in trouble." The jour-ney metaphor, which so aptly combines the concepts of enduringness, dif-ficulties encountered along the way, and the effort of overcoming those obstacles to progress, can also bear the additional entailment of risk to survival, as the danger inherent in an arduous journey. Like that for ef-fort, the schemas involving success (or failure) and risk derive not directly from our understanding of marriage but from our folk physics of dif-ficult activities, of which marriage is one. Not only do we recognize that such activities require effort for their execution, but we also know that in spite of such effort, they may or may not be successfully completed: The difficulties may be insurmountable, so that undertaking to overcome them carries the risk of failure. This folk physics of difficult activities, then, like the folk social psychology of voluntary relationships, is a cultural model within a cultural model. We can only understand why marriage should be cast in metaphors of effort, success or failure, and risk if we know about difficulty.

Reasoning about marriage

The demonstration that Nan's metaphors for marriage, and those of other interviewees, are organized by a small number of schemas for proposi-tions about marriage sets the stage for the next part of our analysis. This requires that we return to Nan's interview excerpts for a more fine-grained examination of her discourse. We now take advantage of another feature of such discourse: the reasoning people do in the course of their explanations of marriage. This reasoning lends convergent support for the five proposition-schemas identified on the basis of Nan's metaphors and supplies evidence for how these five schemas articulate with one another in Americans' cultural model of marriage. In this reasoning, propositions about marital enduringness, benefit, difficulty, and so on serve as building blocks for composite proposition-schemas. The more complex schema is created by conjoining two such propositions in a causal relation.

In order to uncover the logic of this reasoning, however, some preliminary decoding is required. It is necessary to decode the metaphors for marriage in which such reasoning is frequently couched to reveal the common schemas underlying these metaphors. It is also necessary to recognize regularity beneath another feature of the discourse – the varied syntax and semantics of causality in American English. A further syntactic feature of the discourse of particular relevance to this analytic task is the referencing of propositions developed earlier in a reasoning sequence in order to invoke these propositions again later in the same sequence. Making sense of such reasoning requires that these allusions be traced to their original referent so the concept reinvoked can be identified. One way speakers mark their references to earlier assertions is to repeat the metaphor in which the original proposition was cast. Thus, in the first of the two passages at hand, we see that Nan uses the metaphor KNOWING IS SEEING to talk about how married life begins. This metaphor is to tie together the argument of the entire passage, and its separate instantiations must be decoded and traced to their common referent.

Nan opens her argument in this passage by establishing that she and her husband were naïve about each other, not having "much sense of who each other were" at the time they got married. This is the first use of the KNOWING IS SEEING metaphor; Nan means not that they literally did not recognize each other but that she and her husband did not have much knowledge about each other at the outset. She plays out this use of the metaphor to dramatic effect when she goes on to note, "I really don't think that we, either of us, had examined each other" and ". . . I don't think I had said, 'Really, who is this Tom Harper, how can I describe him, what is he?' "

In the next sentence, Nan makes clear exactly what about her husband she did not notice at the beginning: Tom's fit to her needs. In this comment – "I don't think that I had ever consciously done that. Examined my needs and to see if Tom'd fit them" – "examining" and "seeing" are derived, once more, from the KNOWING IS SEEING metaphor and stand for the processes of understanding involved in evaluating and deciding about a situation. The analysis provided in the last section shows that the other metaphor introduced here, A SPOUSE IS A FITTING PART, is but one in a larger category of metaphors reflecting the proposition-schema, MARRIAGE IS MUTUALLY BENEFICIAL. In this latter meta-

phor, the fit of one spouse to the needs of the other allows each to fulfill
these needs and hence derive the expected benefit from the relationship.
Nan argues, more particularly, that some amount of misfit inevitably
results from failure to examine goodness of fit to needs before getting
married. As pointed out in the previous section, that Nan means this argument to hold mutually for herself and her husband is indicated by her
liberal use of reciprocals – "both," "either of us," "each other" – to talk
about their initial failure to examine the goodness of one's fit to the other's
needs.

That Nan means her assertions to be generalizations about marriage,
not something peculiar to her own marital experience, is brought home
by her summary, near the end of the passage: "Gee, people really do go
into marriage, with their eyes, closed." This comment can only be interpreted once the KNOWING IS SEEING metaphor is understood to refer
to its initial application to her own marriage: If your eyes are closed, you
cannot see and hence you will fail to observe any misfit of the person you
are marrying to the needs you have. Thus, that many people get married
in this manner bears the inference that not only her marriage to Tom but
also many other marriages result in a misfit of one spouse to the other's
needs.

Misfit to needs, then, represents mutual lack of marital benefit; having
one's eyes closed and not examining one another and not looking to see
who the other person is at the time one gets married all stand for lack
of knowledge about this important aspect of marriage at its inception.
Having made these two substitutions, we can see that the argument so
far, made explicit in the assertion, "I don't think I had ever done that.
Examined my needs and to see if Tom'd fit them," takes the form:

UNKNOWN AT THE OUTSET ======> ~MUTUALLY
                                                                BENEFICIAL

A homegrown notation has been adopted to depict the reasoning embedded
in passages of natural discourse such as this one. In this notation, the
proposition–schemas that constitute terms in longer reasoning sequences
continue to be represented in capital letters but in abbreviated form (i.e.,
ENDURING, MUTUALLY BENEFICIAL, UNKNOWN AT THE OUT-
SET, DIFFICULT, and EFFORTFUL). For ease of recognition, this ab-
breviation preserves the English sense of each proposition–schema rather
than converting that schema into arbitrary symbols. The negation of a
proposition is represented by a logical symbol commonly used for negation ($\sim$) at the front of that term. A right arrow represents a causal
link connecting a proposition derived from one of the five proposition-
schemas, or its negation, to another proposition or its negation to create
a complex schema. The direction of causality is from the left term to the
right term, with the direction of the arrow. In the remark at hand, "I don't

think I had ever consciously done that. Examined my needs and to see if Tom'd fit them," the direction of causality is revealed by the syntax, X (in order) *to Y,* one of many syntactic devices for expressing causality in English.

The next step in Nan's argument rests on a further extension of the KNOWING IS SEEING metaphor, in the identification of things "I couldn't have foreseen." Again, the metaphor marks this comment as an allusion to the unexamined needs described earlier. Thus, to interpret the statement, "The things that have been difficult in the marriage I couldn't have foreseen," we must recognize that the unforeseen things stand for the unexamined needs Nan and her husband Tom turned out not to fit. We have already identified this misfitting part metaphor as belonging to a class of metaphors that stands for the benefits of marriage. No decoding is required of "the things that have been difficult in the marriage," a phrase that introduces the proposition–schema MARRIAGE IS DIFFICULT in nonmetaphorical language. Substituting the referent of "things unforeseen" and decoding the misfitting part metaphor, we see that "The things that have been difficult in the marriage I couldn't have foreseen," bears the interpretation:

$$\sim\text{MUTUALLY BENEFICIAL} \Longrightarrow \text{DIFFICULT}$$

In this case, the direction of causality must be arrived at by inference. The sense of "foresee" requires that the difficulties in question were temporally preceded by the unexamined lack of fit to needs. Temporal order supports an inference of causal order; as Linde (this volume) observes, "the natural order of English is *post hoc, ergo propter hoc.*" Marital benefits that were not forthcoming at the outset of this marriage led to subsequent difficulties.

Finally, Nan concludes that it is "amazing that many marriages get to stay together, when you consider the way they do it." "The way they do it" is a clear reference to the assertion in the previous sentence, that people go into marriage with their eyes closed. As we have seen, the metaphor in this latter statement is one of marriage unknown at the outset. But "the way they do it" should lead to divorce; Nan uses a counterfactual construction to dramatize the seeming anomaly that so many marriages in fact do endure – as captured in the common metaphor of marriage as a well-made product that "stays together." Once the two metaphors in this conclusion are decoded to reveal it to be a statement about the relationship between initial ignorance of marriage and its ultimate enduringness, it remains only to reverse the counterfactual and specify the direction of causality. The logic of the assertion, "how amazing that many marriages get to stay together, when you consider the way they do it," is revealed to be:

$$\text{UNKNOWN AT THE OUTSET} \Longrightarrow \sim\text{ENDURING}$$

Here, causality is inferred from the syntax, *Y when X,* where *X* stands for the causal agent, and *Y* is what is caused.

What remains unexplained is the larger organization of the argument, which allows this speaker to go on from her first assertion concerning what people do not know about each other when they marry to a conclusion about marital enduringness. To make sense of this leap and to reconstruct the full sequence of reasoning that could account for the final conclusion she reaches, it is necessary to assume that Nan has in mind a further proposition she does not make explicit. This additional proposition derives from a schema in which marital difficulty is a proximate cause for the failure of marriages to endure:

$$\text{DIFFICULT} ===> \sim \text{ENDURING}$$

Inserting this proposition–schema into the chain of argument, we see, gives an account of how the speaker must have reasoned to have produced this discourse sequence. Another strong ground for granting Nan's implicit assumption of this causal schema is that propositions of this form are articulated in other reasoning in the discourse under study. Nan herself makes this relation between difficulty and enduringness explicit in the next passage, when she says, in metaphorical language we have analyzed earlier, "We are going to be driven apart by all our problems." Further illustrations appear in the discourse of other interviewees; for example:

7H-1: I don't know, we just reached a kind of crisis in the relationship. At this point, there were a lot of tears and that was either make or break at that point.

4W-1: I think it's amazing that anybody stays married. I really have – that for people to live together day in and day out is an amazing struggle.

The metaphors in which marital enduringness and difficulty are cast, in these two comments, are already familiar to the reader. These brief examples suggest that inserting an unstated assumption at this point in the analysis of Nan's reasoning is not arbitrary; there is plentiful evidence in the remainder of the discourse under study that speakers do make such a connection between marital difficulty and marital enduringness.

The full sequence of reasoning that must be assumed, then, in order to allow the conclusion Nan reaches, is as follows:

$$
\begin{array}{l}
\text{UNKNOWN AT THE OUTSET} ===> \sim \text{MUTUALLY BENEFICIAL} \\
\sim \text{MUTUALLY BENEFICIAL} ===> \text{DIFFICULT} \\
\underline{\qquad [\text{DIFFICULT} ===> \sim \text{ENDURING}]} \\
\text{UNKNOWN AT THE OUTSET} ===> \sim \text{ENDURING}
\end{array}
$$

Here, two final notational conventions are introduced. A line drawn below any set of proposition–schemas indicates that taken together, these schemas allow the further proposition–schema below the line. The proposition derived from this final schema, then, is the conclusion reasoned to: in this case, "How amazing that many marriages get to stay together when

you consider the way they do it." Square brackets around a proposition–schema indicate that it has not been made explicit in the argument
but that it must be assumed in order to arrive at the conclusion to which
the speaker has reasoned.

Thus, initial lack of knowledge about marriage leads to failure to experience marital benefit, which leads to marital difficulty, which leads to
divorce. The schematic structure allowing this longish causal chain is
readily available for reasoning about marriage. Moreover, chains of propositions violating this structure would not make sense to us. No one would
be likely to argue, for instance, that a marriage that was mutually beneficial
was therefore difficult, or that one in which mutual benefit was not forthcoming was therefore likely to endure. Such chains of reasoning do not, in
fact, occur in this discourse. The sequence of causally related proposition–
schemas displayed in the preceding paragraph seems to represent a widely
shared understanding of how American marriage works. That other interviewees invoke the same chain of reasoning, or segments of this chain,
in reasoning tasks similar to the one Nan has set herself, and that they,
like Nan, may reason through to their conclusions without explicitly stating
one or more of the propositions required to link together their argument
suggests that not only are the separate proposition–schemas for each causal
link in this chain available for reasoning about marriage but also that the
sequence of linked proposition–schemas is itself a stable composite schema,
available in its entirety.

As observed earlier, in the second excerpt the complex causal proposition–
schema linking propositions about marital enduringness and marital difficulty is explicitly stated. A further proposition–schema, MARRIAGE
IS EFFORTFUL, is introduced into Nan's argument in this passage. The
excerpt illustrates the articulation of this new schema with the rest of a
cultural model of marriage. Here, Nan sets about repairing the untenable
conclusion she was left with in the first passage: Given the way people
enter into it, how is any marriage to endure? Nan's dilemma stems from
a central contradiction in how she and other Americans think about
marriage.

The analysis of metaphors for marriage appearing in these passages
reveals that the statement "We are going to be driven apart by all our problems" contains two such metaphors: Marital difficulty is characterized as
problems that must be "worked through," and marital enduringness is captured in a metaphor of two people attached to each other so securely that
they must be "driven apart" to be separated. Causality is handled, in this
assertion, by the syntactic construction, *Y by X*. Thus decoded, the statement reads:

$$\text{DIFFICULT} \implies \sim \text{ENDURING}$$

Nan goes on to argue, however, that marital difficulties need not be
allowed to drive a couple apart. She proceeds by first disposing of one

possible solution: Leaving one marriage for another, she demonstrates, does *not* eliminate such difficulties. This is true because lack of knowledge about the person you are marrying inevitably leads to marital difficulties, so that one marriage is likely to be no easier than the other: "If I know Tom as well as I know him and love him as much as I love him and still have this much trouble being married to him, what in the world chance would I have of finding anybody else who would be any easier to be married to and I wouldn't know that person any better when I got – married him than I knew Tom." The schema underlying this assertion is:

UNKNOWN AT THE OUTSET ══════⟹ DIFFICULT

Causality is somewhat complex in this sentence, depending as it does on both the syntax of the sentence and the logical equivalence (her knowledge of a new husband would be the same as her knowledge of Tom when she married him) expressed at the end of it. Using upper-case letters to indicate logical relations and italics to indicate syntactic items, the causal structure of the argument can be seen to be:

IF [*if X, Y*] AND [$X' = X$] THEN [*if X', Y*]

The X in this argument, that she did not know Tom when she married him, was asserted in the earlier passage and does not need restating here.

This conclusion, that initial ignorance of marriage leads to subsequent marital difficulties, depends on a piece of reasoning also drawn from the preceding excerpt, which, once again, is not explicitly restated in this one: Since initial ignorance about each other leads to lack of one's fit to the other's needs, and thus to lack of mutual benefit, and since lack of benefit causes marital difficulty, then the consequence of this initial ignorance is subsequent difficulty. Represented in notation, the full sequence of reasoning on which Nan's assertion relies is:

[UNKNOWN AT THE OUTSET ══════⟹ ~MUTUALLY BENEFICIAL]
 [~MUTUALLY BENEFICIAL ══════⟹ DIFFICULT]
──
 UNKNOWN AT THE OUTSET ══════⟹ DIFFICULT

Because the notation that has been adopted is designed to represent causality as determinate, it is too crude to capture another feature of Nan's thinking that emerges at this point. A folk theory of probability, only hinted at here, enters into her argument by way of the likelihood assumption – ". . . what in the world chance would I have . . ." – that any new husband she finds will fit her needs (and she his) equally as imperfectly as Tom. The strategy of remarrying is rejected – one might as well stay in the first marriage.

The argument now goes on to establish how an enduring marriage *can* be achieved: through effort. You must, concludes Nan, learn or work through "what actually you need to learn and work through to make the first marriage stick." Here, effort is cast in the metaphor of problem solving, and enduringness is captured in another familiar metaphor of marriage as a well-made product – one that "sticks."

$$\text{EFFORTFUL} \implies \text{ENDURING}$$

In this statement, causality is made explicit in the syntax, X (in order) *to Y,* and rests on an entailment of the well-make product metaphor that specified processes are requisite to the manufacture of any such product: It is necessary to do X (in order) to make Y.

The last part of the passage restates this relation between effort and enduringness in the negative, with the purpose of clinching the argument against remarriage as an alternative strategy. To divorce and remarry someone new is to throw away the accumulated effort you have put into the first marriage. Moreover, an implication of the earlier assertion that one marriage is likely to be as mismatched and hence as difficult as another is that the effort required of any marriage is the same; no advantage is to be gained from starting over from the beginning. It follows that sufficient effort to make a marriage endure will never be accumulated: "If it took seven more years before you learned that much with the next person. Where – you know, where would you go?" (Nan has been married for seven years.) Learning "that much," in this remark, refers to "We have learned a lot," a reference, in turn, to "what actually you need to learn and work through" to make a marriage "stick," a few sentences earlier. This metaphor, as we saw in the previous section, invokes the effort entailed by learning and problem solving. Thus, the first term in Nan's conclusion, "if it took seven more years before you learned that much with the next person," stands for the lack of accumulated effort at the outset of a second marriage. As also shown in the last section, the second term, "Where would you go?" adopts a journey metaphor of indeterminate destination to suggest lack of marital enduringness. People who waste effort, we are cautioned, never get anywhere, a dictum as applicable to marriage as it is to problem solving or travel. The logic of this remark is:

$$\sim\text{EFFORTFUL} \implies \sim\text{ENDURING}$$

The syntax of causality here is *if X, Y.*

Again, we ask how the two propositions about marriage developed in this passage, the first asserting an inverse relation between marital difficulty and marital enduringness and the second asserting a relation between enduringness and effort, make sense as a whole. Why does one lead the speaker to assert the other? Again, a term in the argument has been left implicit. This is a schema for the relation between effort and difficulty. That difficulty cannot be overcome without effort is so well understood, we speculate, that Nan takes it for granted. By inserting this proposi-

tion–schema, we see how she must have reasoned to her final conclusion.
The overall pattern of her argument, then, is:

$$[\sim\text{EFFORTFUL} \Longrightarrow \text{DIFFICULT}]$$
$$\underline{\text{DIFFICULT} \Longrightarrow \sim\text{ENDURING}}$$
$$\sim\text{EFFORTFUL} \Longrightarrow \sim\text{ENDURING}$$

Reasoning in these passages tells a story about marriage that is con-
firmed by the reasoning sequences in the larger body of discourse under
analysis. A large part of this story has now emerged. Even though people
ordinarily do not know "what they are getting into" when they marry,
they do have certain powerful expectations. They expect marriage to be
an enduring relationship, but at the same time they view it as a voluntary
relationship, the continuance of which is contingent on its benefit. These
two assumptions, one about marriage and one drawn from our shared
understanding of voluntary relationships, pose a contradiction. The contradiction is realized when, as is typical, the expected benefits of marriage
do not automatically materialize. This problem is reconceptualized in the
manner Americans think about many things: Lack of marital benefit
becomes a difficulty to be overcome in the enterprise of making a marriage endure. Succeeding at this as at any task is largely a matter of effort. Taken together, the two reasoning sequences presented here reflect
a widely held set of expectations about how the prototypical American
marriage goes.

A notable feature of the reasoning embedded in this and other talk about
marriage is the emptiness of the causal connections posited between terms
of this cultural model of marriage. Effort is required for enduringness.
Difficulties result in a marriage that does not endure. Lack of mutual
benefits leads to marital difficulties. And so forth. However, the nature
of causality in each case goes unspecified. The simple arrow used in the
notation would seem to be an accurate representation of the causality of
reasoning. (An exception was the inability of the notation to handle Nan's
assertion about equal likelihood.) It is as if speakers invoke these causal
connections to reason with, abstracting for this purpose a kind of non-
specific causality out of a lot of more detailed knowledge about how the
world works. We may speculate that the speaker assumes the hearer to
share this latter knowledge of *why* lack of benefits might lead to marital
difficulty or *why* effort might overcome such difficulty, for example.

This "intersubjective sharing," in D'Andrade's term (this volume), would
explain how such knowledge can be dropped out of the argument under
construction without affecting its intelligibility or persuasiveness. However,
the analyst intent on reconstructing the full cultural model of marriage
may wish to fill in its details. To do so, we must pursue still a third trail
of evidence in this body of discourse: scattered commentary in which the
implicit assumptions nested within sequences of reasoning about marriage
are addressed more explicitly and spelled out more fully.

Nested cultural models

Some causal connections are so well understood that they rarely if ever bear comment. Such, for example, seems to be the nature of the connection between difficulty and effort. Understanding of this causal link is transported into the world of marriage from our understanding of the physical world. Perhaps because it is based on direct and repeated physical experience, the knowledge that performance of difficult activities requires effort seem perfectly obvious to us – as Whorf (1941:85) speculated about the more general idea on which this one rests: that the expenditure of energy produces effects. Other causal connections between the terms of the cultural model are not so taken-for-granted, however. Such, for example, is the nature of the link between MARITAL DIFFICULTY and MUTUAL BENEFIT. Why should difficulties arise over the attainment of such benefits?

The discourse at hand has already offered a clue. An important kind of benefit people expect out of marriage is need fulfillment. This expectation is reflected in Nan's observations, in the first passage, about examining her own needs and her husband's fit to them. In our folk psychology of human needs, certain needs, such as those for sex, love, companionship, support, understanding, can only be fulfilled by other people. Americans expect that the person one marries should fulfill most, if not all, of these kinds of needs. This expectation is sometimes stated explicitly, as in the comments these two husbands make about their wives:

7H-2:   I haven't met a single woman since Beth, at all, who would ever come close to matching her in terms of, what she can do for me. What another woman could – for how she could fulfill me. And I – and understand me, particularly. Beth understands me very well. She knows what makes me tick.

5H-9:   Maybe it's the combination that there is a – there's an intellectual stimulation with one another, there's an emotional stimulation with one another, there's a child-bearing stimulation with one another, or wrestling with great issues of the world, and so I think Eileen encapsulates for me an ongoing growth potential for me and all that gambit and vice versa, I believe so. And I think we have found parts of that in many other people many times, but no one who we felt could replace in that sense.

It is this expectation of need fulfillment that makes sense of the final theme in Americans' story about marriage – that it is to be jointly lived. Fulfillment of needs in marriage supposes a substantial amount of physical proximity, emotional intimacy, and coordination of daily activities. It becomes clear why dual metaphors of a spouse as a fitting or irreplaceable part – both joined to one and beneficial to one – are such apposite ones for characterizing the marital relationship.

By this folk psychology of needs and their fulfillment, people have different needs and are endowed with differential capabilities for fulfilling these needs in other people. Although such capabilities are, to a certain extent at least, learnable, individuals' differing natural endowments and divergent histories insure that at the outset of a marriage each spouse's needs and the other's capabilities will almost certainly be mismatched. This likelihood is heightened, as Nan explains, if people enter marriage, as they are apt to do, unobservantly or precipitously, without prior knowledge about each other's needs. Some interviewees say they began marriage ignorant even of the idea that it involves need fulfillment. Moreover, as other interviewees point out, individuals may change over the course of a marriage, often developing or discovering new needs that a spouse's capabilities cannot easily be stretched to meet. They speak of "growing out of touch with each other," "growing apart," or "going in a different direction," of "holding each other back," or a wife who is "holding me up," of coming to "a place where we have to separate," or being "at a point in growth and who we are that says, 'Okay, we need not and we probably should not perpetuate this.'" Some clear statements of the model of need fulfillment underlying such observations are:

4W-3: I think we are committed to making our marriage work. Making the effort to do the best we can until – unless at some point doing the best we can doesn't work, simply doesn't work. Doesn't meet our needs, doesn't make anybody happy and that kind of thing.

7H-1: I don't think – when a marriage gets to the point where you're really holding down the other person, you're really restricting them, it's not worth sticking together because life's too precious to waste your time, with another person. Unless they're really fulfilling you on an emotional level.

Thus, people expect marriage to be mutually beneficial, but, as we have seen, not automatically so. Some "misfit" of each spouse to the needs of the other, either at the outset of marriage, or later in its course, is to be anticipated.

What is difficult about marriage then, by this folk psychological theory, is fulfillment of a spouse's needs. The larger body of interviews from which these passages are drawn contains many other passages in which the difficulties of need fulfillment are elaborated. It is difficult, interviewees say, to communicate one's needs and to understand the needs one's spouse is communicating. It is difficult, sometimes impossible, to learn to fill these needs even when they have been comprehended. It is also difficult to sacrifice one's own desires, as the fulfillment of another's needs often necessitates. Because of these difficulties, deriving mutual benefit out of a marital relationship so the relationship will succeed is not an easy task.

Thus, only by deciphering certain American cultural understandings of the self can we fathom the connection in Americans' thinking about marriage between its benefits and its difficulties. The passages we analyze in this paper give only a sampling of that folk psychology; discussions of needs and their fulfillment arise naturally in the course of talk about marriage and are scattered throughout the entire body of discourse under study. This sporadic evidence must be drawn together to pemit reconstruction of the cultural model of needs and their fulfillment sketched here – so that the application of this folk psychology to marriage can be appreciated.

Americans' model of one piece of the world, marriage, contains within it assumptions drawn from models of other domains, some of which, like the folk physics of difficult activities, the folk social psychology of voluntary relationships, the folk theory of probability, and the folk psychology of human needs, are of wide applicability, available for recombination with more special-purpose models to structure not only the domain of marriage but also multiple domains of our experience. Because our cultural knowledge is organized in this hierarchical way (D'Andrade this volume), models nested within models, we must follow the explanatory trail left in discourse, which leads us from understandings about marriage to understandings about need fulfillment, for example. We must then retrace our steps to establish the implications of the nested cultural model for the cultural model under investigation.

Notes

1. An earlier version of this paper, under the title "What Discourse Can Tell about Culture: Convergent Evidence for a Cultural Model of American Marriage," was delivered at the 82nd Annual Meeting of the American Anthropological Association, November, 1983, in a symposium organized by Susal Gal entitled Making Conversation: Culture, Discourse Style, and Linguistic Structure. The revised version has benefited from the suggestions of Dorothy Holland. The research project on which this paper is based has been made possible by National Institute of Mental Health research grant No. 1 RO1 MH330370–01, National Science Foundation research grant No. BNS–8205739, and a stipend from the Institute for Advanced Study, Princeton, New Jersey. People who made the project successful are Rebecca Taylor, a talented research assistant who conducted a large portion of the interviews, and Laurie Moore, who also interviewed, as well as Phyllis Taylor, Donna Rubin and Georgia Hunter, who transcribed the interviews with skill. I am particularly indebted to Georgia, whose dedication to the enormous transcription task was heroic. I cannot adequately thank "Nan" and the other 21 anonymous wives and husbands who participated in the long interview process and left me with a lasting appreciation for their unique and creative ways of understanding their marriages.

2. All interviewees were native-born Americans who spoke English as a first language. All were married during the period of their interviews, all in their first marriages. Beyond these commonalities, they were selected to maximize diversity with regard to such obvious differences as their geographic and ethnic origins, their occupational and educational backgrounds, and the age of their marriages. No claim is made for the statistical representativeness of the people interviewed, nor would representativeness with respect to various sociological characteristics of the middle-sized southern town in which all interviewees resided even have been feasible for a sample so small. The study aimed to investigate how people organize knowledge rather than how any particular

feature of this knowledge varies across sociological categories such as gender, ethnicity, religion, or class.

3. This is a fictive name, of course. The code at the beginning of this and later interview segments contains, in order, an interviewee identification number, a *W* or an *H* to indicate a wife or a husband, and the number of the interview from which that segment was drawn in the sequence of interviews with that person. Husbands do not have the same identification numbers as their wives. As in the second segment from Nan's interview, comments or questions interjected by the interviewer are prefaced by an *I,* and resumption of the interviewee's part of the conversation is indicated by his or her identification number and letter. This and other interview segments reproduced in this paper have been regularized for stammers, stutters, elisions, slips of the tongue, and hesitations.

4. To characterize a given cultural model as "folk social psychology" or (later in this paper) "folk psychology," "folk physics," or "folk probability theory," is to invite the observation that our ordinary everyday ideas about a given phenomenon may not correspond, although they may be related, to their counterpart in current scientific theory. Although this relationship between folk and scientific models is not pursued in this paper, other papers in this volume discuss how widely shared cultural understandings may be "incorrect" from the stance of scientific explanation and evidence (Collins & Gentner, Kempton), may draw on existing social scientific models (Linde), and, as is likely the case with the folk social psychology of exchange in voluntary relationships discussed here, may contribute unanalyzed assumptions to those social scientific theories (Kay).

References

Hutchins, E.
  1980. Culture and Inference: A Trobriand Case Study. Cambridge, Mass.: Harvard University Press.
Lakoff, G.
  1984. Classifiers as a reflection of mind: A cognitive model approach to prototype theory. Berkeley Cognitive Science Report No. 19. Berkeley: University of California Institute of Human Learning.
Lakoff, G. and M. Johnson
  1980. Metaphors We Live By. Chicago: University of Chicago Press.
Quinn, N.
  1985a. American marriage through metaphors: A cultural analysis. North Carolina Working Papers in Culture and Cognition No. 1. Durham, NC: Duke University Department of Anthropology.
  1985b. American marriage and the folk social psychology of need fulfillment. North Carolina Working Papers in Culture and Cognition No. 2. Durham, NC: Duke University Department of Anthropology.
  n.d. American marriage: A cultural analysis. Unpublished manuscript in preparation, Department of Anthropology, Duke University, Durham, N.C.
Whorf, B. L.
  1941. The relation of habitual thought and behavior to language. *In* Language, Culture, and Personality: Essays in Memory of Edward Sapir, L. Spier, ed. Menasha, Wisc. Sapir Memorial Publication Fund. Pp. 75–93.

PART III
The role of metaphor and analogy in representing knowledge of presupposed worlds

8

The cognitive model of anger inherent in American English[1]

George Lakoff & Zoltán Kövecses

Emotions are often considered to be feelings alone, and as such they are viewed as being devoid of conceptual content. As a result, the study of emotions is usually not taken seriously by students of semantics and conceptual structure. A topic such as *The Logic of Emotions* would seem on this view to be a contradiction in terms, since emotions, being devoid of conceptual content, would give rise to no inferences at all, or at least none of any interest. We would like to argue that the opposite is true, that emotions have an extremely complex conceptual structure, which gives rise to wide variety of nontrivial inferences.

The conceptualization of anger

At first glance, the conventional expressions used to talk about anger seem so diverse that finding any coherent system would seem impossible. For example, if we look up *anger* in, say, *Roget's University Thesaurus*, we find about three hundred entries, most of which have something or other to do with anger, but the thesaurus does not tell us exactly what. Many of these are idioms, and they too seem too diverse to reflect any coherent cognitive model. Here are some example sentences using such idioms:

> He *lost his cool.*
> She was *looking daggers* at me.
> I almost *burst a blood vessel.*
> He was *foaming at the mouth.*
> You're beginning to *get to* me.
> You make my *blood boil.*
> He's *wrestling* with his anger.
> Watch out! He's *on a short fuse.*
> He's just *letting off steam.*
> Try to *keep a grip on yourself.*
> Don't *fly off the handle.*
> When I told him, he *blew up.*
> He *channeled* his anger into something constructive.
> He was *red with anger.*

He was *blue in the face.*
He *appeased* his anger.
He was *doing a slow burn.*
He *suppressed* his anger.
She kept *bugging* me.
When I told my mother, *she had a cow.*

What do these expressions have to do with anger, and what do they have to do with each other? We will be arguing that they are not random. When we look at inferences among these expressions, it becomes clear that there must be a systematic structure of some kind. We know, for example, that someone who is foaming at the mouth has lost his cool. We know that someone who is looking daggers at you is likely to be doing a slow burn or be on a short fuse. We know that someone whose blood is boiling has not had his anger appeased. We know that someone who has channeled his anger into something constructive has not had a cow. How do we know these things? Is it just that each idiom has a literal meaning and the inferences are based on the literal meanings? Or is there something more going on? What we will try to show is that there is a coherent conceptual organization underlying all these expressions, and that much of it is metaphorical and metonymical in nature.

METAPHOR AND METONYMY
The analysis we are proposing begins with the common cultural model of the physiological effects of anger:

> THE PHYSIOLOGICAL EFFECTS OF ANGER ARE IN-
> CREASED BODY HEAT, INCREASED INTERNAL
> PRESSURE (BLOOD PRESSURE, MUSCULAR PRESSURE),
> AGITATION, AND INTERFERENCE WITH ACCURATE
> PERCEPTION.

> AS ANGER INCREASES, ITS PHYSIOLOGICAL EFFECTS
> INCREASE.

> THERE IS A LIMIT BEYOND WHICH THE PHYSIO-
> LOGICAL EFFECTS OF ANGER IMPAIR NORMAL
> FUNCTIONING.

We use this cultural model in large measure to tell when someone is angry on the basis of their appearance – as well as to signal anger, or hide it. In doing this, we make use of a general metonymic principle:

> THE PHYSIOLOGICAL EFFECTS OF AN EMOTION STAND
> FOR THE EMOTION

Given this principle, the cultural model given above yields a system of metonymies for anger:

BODY HEAT:
Don't get *hot under the collar.*
Billy's a *hothead.*
They were having a *heated argument.*
When the cop gave her a ticket, she got all *hot and bothered* and started cursing.

INTERNAL PRESSURE:
Don't get a *hernia!*
When I found out, I almost *burst a blood vessel.*
He almost had a *hemorrhage.*

Increased body heat and/or blood pressure is assumed to cause redness in the face and neck area, and such redness can also metonymically indicate anger.

REDNESS IN FACE AND NECK AREA:
She was *scarlet with rage.*
He got *red with anger.*
He was *flushed with anger.*

AGITATION:
She was *shaking* with anger.
I was *hopping mad.*
He was *quivering with rage.*
He's *all worked up.*
She's *all wrought up.*

INTERFERENCE WITH ACCURATE PERCEPTION:
She was *blind with rage.*
I was beginning to *see red.*
I was so mad I *couldn't see straight.*

Each of these expressions indicate the presence of anger via its supposed physiological effects.

The cultural model of physiological effects, especially the part that emphasizes HEAT, forms the basis of the most general metaphor for anger: ANGER IS HEAT. There are two versions of this metaphor, one where the heat is applied to fluids, the other where it is applied to solids. When it is applied to fluids, we get: ANGER IS THE HEAT OF A FLUID IN A CONTAINER. The specific motivation for this consists of the HEAT, INTERNAL PRESSURE, and AGITATION parts of the cultural model. When ANGER IS HEAT is applied to solids, we get the version ANGER IS FIRE, which is motivated by the HEAT and REDNESS aspects of the cultural theory of physiological effects.

As we will see shortly, the fluid version is much more highly elaborated. The reason for this, we surmise, is that in our overall conceptual system we have the general metaphor:

THE BODY IS A CONTAINER FOR THE EMOTIONS

He was *filled* with anger.
She couldn't *contain* her joy.
She was *brimming* with rage.
Try to get your anger *out of your system.*

The ANGER IS HEAT metaphor, when applied to fluids, combines with the metaphor THE BODY IS A CONTAINER FOR THE EMOTIONS to yield the central metaphor of the system:

ANGER IS THE HEAT OF A FLUID IN A CONTAINER

You make my *blood boil.*
Simmer down!
I had reached the *boiling point.*
Let him *stew.*

A historically derived instance of this metaphor is:

She was *seething with rage.*

Although most speakers do not now use *seethe* to indicate physical boiling, the boiling image is still there when *seethe* is used to indicate anger. Similarly, *pissed off* is used only to refer to anger, not to the hot liquid under pressure in the bladder. Still, the effectiveness of the expression seems to depend on such an image.

When there is no heat the liquid is cool and calm. In the central metaphor, cool and calmness corresponds to lack of anger.

Keep *cool.*
Stay *calm.*

As we will see shortly, the central metaphor is an extremely productive one. There are two ways in which a conceptual metaphor can be productive. The first is lexical. The words and fixed expressions of a language can *code,* that is, be used to express aspects of, a given conceptual metaphor to a greater or lesser extent. The number of conventional linguistic expressions that code a given conceptual metaphor is one measure of the productivity of the metaphor. In addition, the words and fixed expressions of a language can *elaborate* the conceptual metaphor. For example, a stew is a special case in which there is a hot fluid in a container. It is something that continues at a given level of heat for a long time. This special case can be used to elaborate the central metaphor. "Stewing" indicates the continuance of anger over a long period. Another special case is "simmer," which indicates a low boil. This can be used to indicate a lowering of the intensity of anger. Although both of these are cooking terms, cooking plays no metaphorical role in these cases. It just happens to be a case where there is a hot fluid in a container. This is typical of lexical elaborations.

Let us refer to the HEAT OF FLUID IN A CONTAINER as the source domain of the central metaphor, and to ANGER as the target domain. We usually have extensive knowledge about source domains. A second way in which a conceptual metaphor can be productive is that it can carry over details of that knowledge from the source domain to the target domain. We will refer to such carryovers as metaphorical entailments. Such entailments are part of our conceptual system. They constitute elaborations of conceptual metaphors. The central metaphor has a rich system of metaphorical entailments. For example, one thing we know about hot fluids is that, when they start to boil, the fluid goes upward. This gives rise to the entailment:

> WHEN THE INTENSITY OF ANGER INCREASES, THE FLUID RISES
> His pent-up anger *welled up* inside him.
> She could feel her *gorge rising*.
> We got a *rise* out of him.
> My anger kept *building up* inside me.
> Pretty soon I was in a *towering rage*.

We also know that intense heat produces steam and creates pressure on the container. This yields the metaphorical entailments:

> INTENSE ANGER PRODUCES STEAM
> She got *all steamed up*.
> Billy's just *blowing off steam*.
> I was *fuming*.

> INTENSE ANGER PRODUCES PRESSURE ON THE CONTAINER
> He was *bursting with anger*.
> I could barely *contain* my rage.
> I could barely *keep it in* anymore.

A variant of this involves keeping the pressure back:

> I *suppressed* my anger.
> He *turned his anger inward*.
> He managed to keep his anger *bottled up* inside him.
> He was *blue in the face*.

When the pressure on the container becomes too high, the container explodes. This yields the entailment:

> WHEN ANGER BECOMES TOO INTENSE, THE PERSON EXPLODES
> When I told him, he just *exploded*.
> She *blew up* at me.
> We won't tolerate any more of your *outbursts*.

This can be elaborated, using special cases:

> Pistons: He *blew a gasket.*
> Volcanos: She *erupted.*
> Electricity: I *blew a fuse.*
> Explosives: She's *on a short fuse.*
> Bombs: That really *set me off.*

In an explosion, parts of the container go up in the air.

> WHEN A PERSON EXPLODES, PARTS OF HIM GO UP IN
> THE AIR.
> I *blew my stack.*
> I *blew my top.*
> She *flipped her lid.*
> He *hit the ceiling.*
> I *went through the roof.*

When something explodes, what was inside it comes out.

> WHEN A PERSON EXPLODES, WHAT WAS INSIDE HIM
> COMES OUT
> His anger finally *came out.*
> Smoke was *pouring out of his ears.*

This can be elaborated in terms of animals giving birth, where something
that was inside causing pressure bursts out:

> WHEN A PERSON EXPLODES, WHAT WAS INSIDE HIM
> COMES OUT
> She was *having kittens.*
> My mother will *have a cow* when I tell her.

Let us now turn to the question of what issues the central metaphor
addresses and what kind of ontology of anger it reveals. The central
metaphor focuses on the fact that anger can be intense, that it can lead
to a loss of control, and that a loss of control can be dangerous. Let us
begin with intensity. Anger is conceptualized as a mass, and takes the grammar of mass nouns, as opposed to count nouns. Thus, you can say:

> How much anger has he got in him?

but not:

> *How many angers does he have in him?

Anger thus has the ontology of a mass entity, that is, it has a scale indicating its amount, it exists when the amount is greater than zero and
goes out of existence when the amount falls to zero. In the central
metaphor, the scale indicating the amount of anger is the heat scale. But,
as the central metaphor indicates, the anger scale is not open-ended; it

has a limit. Just as a hot fluid in a closed container can only take so much heat before it explodes, so we conceptualize the anger scale as having a limit point. We can only bear so much anger, before we explode, that is, lose control. This has its correlates in our cultural theory of physiological effects. As anger gets more intense the physiological effects increase and those increases interfere with our normal functioning. Body heat, blood pressure, agitation, and interference with perception cannot increase without limit before our ability to function normally becomes seriously impaired and we lose control over our functioning. In the cultural model of anger, loss of control is dangerous, both to the angry person and to those around him. In the central metaphor, the danger of loss of control is understood as the danger of explosion.

The structural aspect of a conceptual metaphor consists of a set of correspondences between a source domain and a target domain. These correspondences can be factored into two types: ontological and epistemic. Ontological correspondences are correspondences between the entities in the source domain and the corresponding entities in the target domain. For example, the container in the source domain corresponds to the body in the target domain. Epistemic correspondences are correspondences between knowledge about the source domain and corresponding knowledge about the target domain. We can schematize these correspondences between the FLUID domain and the ANGER domain as follows:

Source: HEAT OF FLUID IN CONTAINER
Target: ANGER

Ontological Correspondences:

> The container is the body.
> The heat of fluid is the anger.
> The heat scale is the anger scale, with end points zero and limit.
> Container heat is body heat.
> Pressure in container is internal pressure in the body.
> Agitation of fluid and container is physical agitation.
> The limit of the container's capacity to withstand pressure caused by heat is the limit on the anger scale.
> Explosion is loss of control.
> Danger of explosion is danger of loss of control.
> Coolness in the fluid is lack of anger.
> Calmness of the fluid is lack of agitation.

Epistemic correspondences:

Source: The effect of intense fluid heat is container heat, internal pressure, and agitation.
Target: The effect of intense anger is body heat, internal pressure, and agitation.

Source: When the fluid is heated past a certain limit, pressure increases to the point at which the container explodes.
Target: When anger increases past a certain limit, pressure increases to the point at which the person loses control.

Source: An explosion is damaging to the container and dangerous to bystanders.
Target: A loss of control is damaging to an angry person and dangerous to other people.

Source: An explosion may be prevented by the application of sufficient force and energy to keep the fluid in.
Target: A loss of control may be prevented by the application of sufficient force and energy to keep the anger in.

Source: It is sometimes possible to control the release of heated fluid for either destructive or constructive purposes; this has the effect of lowering the level of heat and pressure.
Target: It is sometimes possible to control the release of anger for either destructive or constructive purposes; this has the effect of lowering the level of anger and internal pressure.

The latter case defines an elaboration of the entailment WHEN A PERSON EXPLODES, WHAT WAS INSIDE HIM COMES OUT:

> ANGER CAN BE LET OUT UNDER CONTROL
> He *let out* his anger.
> I *gave vent* to my anger.
> *Channel* your anger into something constructive.
> He *took out* his anger on me.

So far, we have seen that the cultural theory of physiological reactions provides the basis for the central metaphor, and that the central metaphor characterizes detailed correspondences between the source domain and the target domain – correspondences concerning both ontology and knowledge.

At this point, our analysis enables us to see why various relationships among idioms hold. We can see why someone who is in a towering rage has not kept cool, why someone who is stewing may have contained his anger but has not gotten it out of his system, why someone who has suppressed his anger has not yet erupted, and why someone who has channeled his anger into something constructive has not had a cow.

Let us now turn to the case where the general ANGER IS HEAT metaphor is applied to solids:

> ANGER IS FIRE
> Those are *inflammatory* remarks.
> She was *doing a slow burn.*
> He was *breathing fire.*
> Your insincere apology just *added fuel to the fire.*

> After the argument, Dave was *smoldering* for days.
> That *kindled my ire.*
> Boy, am I *burned up!*
> He was *consumed* by his anger.

This metaphor highlights the cause of anger (kindle, inflame), the intensity and duration (smoldering, slow burn, burned up), the danger to others (breathing fire), and the damage to the angry person (consumed). The correspondences in ontology are as follows:

Source: FIRE
Target: ANGER

> The fire is anger.
> The thing burning is the angry person.
> The cause of the fire is the cause of the anger.
> The intensity of the fire is the intensity of the anger.
> The physical damage to the thing burning is mental damage to the angry person.
> The capacity of the thing buring to serve its normal function is the capacity of the angry person to function normally.
> An object at the point of being consumed by fire corresponds to a person whose anger is at the limit.
> The danger of the fire to things nearby is danger of the anger to other people.

The correspondences in knowlege are:

Source: Things can burn at low intensity for a long time and then burst into flame.
Target: People can be angry at a low intensity for a long time and then suddenly become extremely angry.

Source: Fires are dangerous to things nearby.
Target: Angry people are dangerous to other people.

Source: Things consumed by fire cannot serve their normal function.
Target: At the limit of the anger scale, people cannot function normally.

Putting together what we have done so far, we can see why someone who is doing a slow burn has not hit the ceiling yet, why someone whose anger is bottled up is not breathing fire, why someone who is consumed by anger probably cannot see straight, and why adding fuel to the fire might just cause the person you are talking to to have kittens.

THE OTHER PRINCIPAL METAPHORS

As we have seen, the ANGER IS HEAT metaphor is based on the cultural model of the physiological effects of anger, according to which increased body heat is a major effect of anger. That cultural model also maintains that agitation is an important effect. Agitation is also an important part of our cultural model of insanity. According to this view, people who are insane are unduly agitated – they go wild, start raving, flail their arms, foam at the mouth, and so on. Correspondingly, these physiological effects can stand, metonymically, for insanity. One can indicate that someone is insane by describing him as foaming at the mouth, raving, going wild, for example.

The overlap between the cultural models of the effects of anger and the effects of insanity provides a basis for the metaphor:

> ANGER IS INSANITY
> I just touched him, and he *went crazy.*
> You're *driving me nuts!*
> When the umpire called him out on strikes, he *went bananas.*
> One more complaint and I'll *go berserk.*
> He got so angry, he *went out of his mind.*
> When he gets angry, he *goes bonkers.*
> She went into an *insane rage.*
> If anything else goes wrong, I'll *get hysterical.*

Perhaps the most common conventional expression for anger came into English historically as a result of this metaphor:

> I'm *mad!*

Because of this metaphorical link between insanity and anger, expressions that indicate insane behavior can also indicate angry behavior. Given the metonymy INSANE BEHAVIOR STANDS FOR INSANITY and the metaphor ANGER IS INSANITY, we get the metaphorical metonymy:

> INSANE BEHAVIOR STANDS FOR ANGER
> When my mother finds out, she'll *have a fit.*
> When the ump threw him out of the game, Billy started *foaming at the mouth.*
> He's *fit to be tied.*
> He's about to *throw a tantrum.*

Violent behavior indicative of frustration is viewed as a form of insane behavior. According to our cultural model of anger, people who can neither control nor relieve the pressure of anger engage in violent frustrated behavior. This cultural model is the basis for the metonymy:

> VIOLENT FRUSTRATED BEHAVIOR STANDS FOR ANGER
> He's *tearing his hair out!*
> If one more thing goes wrong, I'll start *banging my head against the wall.*
> The loud music next door has got him *climbing the walls!*
> She's been *slamming doors all morning.*

The ANGER IS INSANITY metaphor has the following correspondences:

Source: INSANITY
Target: ANGER

> The cause of insanity is the cause of anger.
> Becoming insane is passing the limit point on the anger scale.
> Insane behavior is angry behavior.

Source: An insane person cannot function normally.
Target: A person who is angry beyond the limit point cannot function normally.
Source: An insane person is dangerous to others.
Target: A person who is angry beyond the limit point is dangerous to others.

At this point, we can see a generalization. Emotional effects are understood as physical effects. Anger is understood as a form of energy. According to our cultural understanding of physics, when enough input energy is applied to a body, the body begins to produce output energy. Thus, the cause of anger is viewed as input energy that produces internal heat (output energy). Moreover, the internal heat can function as input energy, producing various forms of output energy: steam, pressure, externally radiating heat, and agitation. Such output energy (the angry behavior) is viewed as dangerous to others. In the insanity metaphor, insanity is understood as a highly energized state, with insane behavior as a form of energy output.

All in all, anger is understood in our cultural model as a negative emotion. It produces undesirable physiological reactions, leads to an inability to function normally, and is dangerous to others. The angry person, recognizing this danger, views his anger as an opponent.

ANGER IS AN OPPONENT (IN A STRUGGLE)
I'm *struggling* with my anger.
He was *battling* his anger.
She *fought back* her anger.
I've been *wrestling* with my anger all day.
I was *seized* by anger.
I'm finally *coming to grips with* my anger.
He *lost control over* his anger.
Anger *took control* of him.
He *surrendered* to his anger.
He *yielded* to his anger.
I was *overcome* by anger.
Her anger has been *appeased.*

The ANGER IS AN OPPONENT metaphor is constituted by the following correspondences:

Source: STRUGGLE
Target: ANGER

> The opponent is anger.
> Winning is controlling anger.
> Losing is having anger control you.
> Surrender is allowing anger to take control of you.
> The pool of resources needed for winning is the energy needed to control anger.

One thing that is left out of this account so far is what constitutes "appeasement." To appease an opponent is to give in to his demands. This suggests that anger has demands. We will address the question of what these demands are below.

The OPPONENT metaphor focuses on the issue of control and the danger of loss of control to the angry person himself. There is another metaphor that focuses on the issue of control, but whose main focus is the danger to others. It is a very widespread metaphor in Western culture, namely, PASSIONS ARE BEASTS INSIDE A PERSON. According to this metaphor, there is a part of each person that is a wild animal. Civilized people are supposed to keep that part of them private, that is, they are supposed to keep the animal inside them. In the metaphor, loss of control is equivalent to the animal getting loose. And the behavior of a person who has lost control is the behavior of a wild animal. There are versions of this metaphor for the various passions – desire, anger, and so forth. In the case of anger, the beast presents a danger to other people.

> ANGER IS A DANGEROUS ANIMAL
> He has a *ferocious* temper.
> He has a *fierce* temper.
> It's dangerous to *arouse* his anger.
> That *awakened* my ire.
> His anger *grew.*
> He has a *monstrous* temper.
> He *unleashed* his anger.
> Don't let your anger *get out of hand.*
> He *lost his grip* on his anger.
> His anger is *insatiable.*

An example that draws on both the FIRE and DANGEROUS ANIMAL metaphors is:

> He was *breathing fire.*

The image here is of a dragon, a dangerous animal that can devour you with fire.

The DANGEROUS ANIMAL metaphor portrays anger as a sleeping animal that is dangerous to awaken; as something that can grow and thereby become dangerous; as something that has to be held back; and as something with a dangerous appetite. Here are the correspondences that constitute the metaphor.

Source: DANGEROUS ANIMAL
Target: ANGER

> The dangerous animal is the anger.
> The animal's getting loose is loss of control of anger.
> The owner of the dangerous animal is the angry person.
> Sleeping for the animal is anger near the zero level.
> Being awake for the animal is anger near the limit.

Source: It is dangerous for a dangerous animal to be loose.
Target: It is dangerous for a person's anger to be out of control.

Source: A dangerous animal is safe when it is sleeping and dangerous when it is awake.
Target: Anger is safe near the zero level and dangerous near the limit.

Source: A dangerous animal is safe when it is very small and dangerous when it is grown.
Target: Anger is safe near the zero level and dangerous near the limit.

Source: It is the responsibility of a dangerous animal's owner to keep it under control.
Target: It is the responsibility of an angry person to keep his anger under control.

Source: It requires a lot of energy to control a dangerous animal.
Target: It requires a lot of energy to control one's anger.

There is another class of expressions that, as far as we can tell, are instances of the same metaphor. These are cases in which angry behavior is described in terms of aggressive animal behavior.

> ANGRY BEHAVIOR IS AGGRESSIVE ANIMAL BEHAVIOR
> He was *bristling* with anger.
> That *got my hackles up.*
> He began to *bare his teeth.*
> That *ruffled her feathers.*
> She was *bridling with anger.*
> Don't *snap* at me!
> He started *snarling.*
> Don't *bite my head off!*
> Why did you *jump down my throat?*

Perhaps the best way to account for these cases would be to extend the ontological correspondences of the ANGER IS A DANGEROUS ANIMAL metaphor to include:

The aggressive behavior of the dangerous animal is angry behavior.

If we do this, we can account naturally for the fact that these expressions indicate anger. They would do so via a combination of metaphor and metonymy, in which the aggressive behavior metaphorically corresponds to angry behavior, which in turn metonymically stands for anger. For example, the snarling of the animal corresponds to the angry verbal behavior of the person, which in turn indicates the presence of anger.

Aggressive verbal behavior is a common form of angry behavior, as *snap, growl, snarl,* and so forth indicate. We can see this in a number of cases outside of the animal domain:

AGGRESSIVE VERBAL BEHAVIOR STANDS FOR ANGER
She gave him a *tongue-lashing.*
I really *chewed* him *out* good!

Other forms of aggressive behavior can also stand metonymically for anger, especially aggressive visual behavior:

AGGRESSIVE VISUAL BEHAVIOR STANDS FOR ANGER
She was *looking daggers* at me.
He *gave me a dirty look.*
If *looks could kill,* . . . .
He was *glowering* at me.

All these metonymic expressions can be used to indicate anger.

As in the case of the OPPONENT metaphor, our analysis of the DANGEROUS ANIMAL metaphor leaves an expression unaccounted for – "insatiable." This expression indicates that the animal has an appetite. This "appetite" seems to correspond to the "demands" in the OPPONENT metaphor, as can be seen from the fact that the following sentences entail each other:

Harry's anger is *insatiable.*
Harry's anger cannot be *appeased.*

To see what it is that anger demands and has an appetite for, let us turn to expressions that indicate causes of anger. Perhaps the most common group of expressions that indicate anger consists of conventionalized forms of annoyance: minor pains, burdens placed on domestic animals, and so forth. Thus we have the metaphor:

THE CAUSE OF ANGER IS A PHYSICAL ANNOYANCE
Don't be *a pain in the ass.*
Get *off my back!*
You don't have to *ride me so hard.*
You're *getting under my skin.*
He's *a pain in the neck.*
Don't *be a pest!*

These forms of annoyance involve an offender and a victim. The offender is at fault. The victim, who is innocent, is the one who gets angry.

There is another set of conventionalized expressions used to speak of, or to, people who are in the process of making someone angry. These are expressions of territoriality, in which the cause of anger is viewed as a trespasser.

CAUSING ANGER IS TRESPASSING
You're beginning to *get to* me.
This is where I *draw the line!*
Don't *step on my toes!*

Again, there is an offender (the cause of anger) and a victim (the person who is getting angry). In general, the cause of anger seems to be an offense, in which there is an offender who is at fault and an innocent victim, who is the person who gets angry. The offense seems to constitute some sort of injustice. This is reflected in the conventional wisdom:

Don't get *mad,* get *even!*

In order for this saying to make sense, there has to be some connection between anger and retribution. Getting even is equivalent to balancing the scales of justice. The saying assumes a model in which injustice leads to anger and retribution can alleviate or prevent anger. In short, what anger "demands" and has an "appetite" for is revenge. This is why warnings and threats can count as angry behavior:

If I get mad, watch out!
Don't get me angry, or you'll be sorry.

The angry behavior is, in itself, viewed as a form of retribution.

We are now in a position to make sense of another metaphor for anger:

ANGER IS A BURDEN
Unburdening himself of his anger gave him a sense of *relief.*
After I lost my temper, I felt *lighter.*
He *carries* his anger around with him.
He *has a chip on his shoulder.*
You'll feel better if you *get it off your chest.*

In English, it is common for responsibilities to be metaphorized as burdens. There are two kinds of responsibilities involved in the cultural model of anger that has emerged so far. The first is a responsibility to control one's anger. In cases of extreme anger, this may place a considerable burden on one's "inner resources." The second comes from the model of retributive justice that is built into our concept of anger; it is the responsibility to seek vengeance. What is particularly interesting is that these two responsibilities are in conflict in the case of angry retribution: If you take out your anger on someone, you are not meeting your responsibility to control your anger, and if you do not take out your anger on someone, you are not meeting your responsibility to provide retribution. The slogan "Don't get mad, get even!" offers one way out: retribution without anger. The human potential movement provides another way out by suggesting that letting your anger out is okay. But the fact is that neither of these solutions is the cultural norm. It should also be mentioned in passing that the human potential movement's way of dealing with anger by sanctioning its release is not all that revolutionary. It assumes almost all of our standard cultural model and metaphorical understanding, and makes one change: sanctioning the "release."

SOME MINOR METAPHORS

There are a few very general metaphors that apply to anger as well as to many other things, and are commonly used in comprehending and speaking about anger. The first we will discuss has to do with existence. Existence is commonly understood in terms of physical presence. You are typically aware of something's presence if it is nearby and you can see it. This is the basis for the metaphor:

> EXISTENCE IS PRESENCE
> His anger *went away*.
> His anger eventually *came back*.
> My anger *lingered on* for days.
> She couldn't *get rid of* her anger.
> After a while, her anger just *vanished*.
> My anger slowly began to *dissipate*.
> When he saw her smile, his anger *disappeared*.

In the case of emotions, existence is often conceived of as location in a bounded space. Here the emotion is the bounded space and it exists when the person is in that space:

> EMOTIONS ARE BOUNDED SPACES
> She flew *into* a rage.
> She was *in* an angry mood.
> He was *in* a state of anger.
> I am not easily roused *to* anger.

These cases are relatively independent of the rest of the anger system, and are included here more for completeness than for profundity.

THE PROTOTYPE SCENARIO

The metaphors and metonymies that we have investigated so far converge on a certain prototypical cognitive model of anger. It is not the only model of anger we have; in fact, there are quite a few. But as we shall see, all of the others can be characterized as minimal variants of the model that the metaphors converge on. The model has a temporal dimension, and can be conceived of as a scenario with a number of stages. We will call this the "prototype scenario"; it is similar to what De Sousa (1980) calls the "paradigm scenario." We will be referring to the person who gets angry as *S*, short for the Self.

Stage 1: offending event
> There is an offending event that displeases *S*. There is a wrongdoer who intentionally does something directly to *S*. The wrongdoer is at fault and Self is innocent. The offending event constitutes an injustice and produces anger in *S*. The scales of justice can only be balanced by some act of retribution. That is, the intensity of retribution must be roughly equal to the intensity of offense. *S* has the responsibility to perform such an act of retribution.

Stage 2: anger
> Associated with the entity anger is a scale that measures its intensity. As the intensity of anger increases, *S* experiences physiological effects: increase in body heat, internal pressure, and physical agitation. As the anger gets very intense, it exerts a force upon *S* to perform an act of retribution. Because acts of retribution are dangerous and/or socially unacceptable, *S* has a responsibility to control his anger. Moreover, loss of control is damaging to *S*'s own well-being, which is another motivation for controlling anger.

Stage 3: attempt at control
> *S* attempts to control his anger.

Stage 4: loss of control
> Each person has a certain tolerance for controlling anger. That tolerance can be viewed as the limit point on the anger scale. When the intensity of anger goes beyond that limit, *S* can no longer control his anger. *S* exhibits angry behavior and his anger forces him to attempt an act of retribution. Since *S* is out of control and acting under coercion, he is not responsible for his actions.

Stage 5: act of retribution
> *S* performs the act of retribution. The wrongdoer is the target of the act. The intensity of retribution roughly equals the intensity of the offense and the scales are balanced again. The intensity of anger drops to zero.

At this point, we can see how the various conceptual metaphors we have discussed all map onto a part of the prototypical scenario, and how they jointly converge on that scenario. This enables us to show exactly how the various metaphors are related to one another, and how they function together to help characterize a single concept. This is something that Lakoff and Johnson (1980) were unable to do.

The course of anger depicted in the prototype scenario is by no means the only course anger can take. In claiming that the scenario is prototypical we are claiming that according to our cultural theory of anger, this is a normal course for anger to take. Deviations of many kinds are both recognized as existing and recognized as being noteworthy and not the norm. Let us take some examples:

Someone who "turns the other cheek," that is, who does not get angry or seek retribution. In this culture, such a person is considered virtually saintly.

Someone who has no difficulty controlling his anger is especially praiseworthy.

A "hothead" is someone who considers more events offensive than most people, who has a lower threshold for anger than the norm, who cannot control his anger, and whose acts of retribution are considered out of proportion to the offense. Someone who is extremely hotheaded is considered emotionally "unbalanced."

On the other hand, someone who acts in the manner described in the prototypical scenario would not be considered abnormal at all.

Before turning to the nonprototypical cases, it will be useful for us to make a rough sketch of the ontology of anger: the entities, predicates, and events required. This will serve two purposes. First, it will allow us to show in detail how the nonprototypical cases are related to the prototypical model. Second, it will allow us to investigate the nature of this ontology. We will include only the detail required for our purposes.

It is part of our cultural model of a person that he can temporarily lose control of his body or his emotions. Implicit in this concept is a separation of the body and the emotions from the S. This separation is especially important in the ontology of anger. Anger, as a separable entity, can overcome someone, take control, and cause him to act in ways he would not normally act. In such cases, the S is no longer in control of the body. Thus, the ontology of anger must include an S, anger, and the body. A fuller treatment would probably also require viewing the mind as a separate entity, but that is beyond our present purposes.

Since anger has a quantitative aspect, the ontology must include a scale of anger, including an intensity, a zero point, and a limit point. The basic anger scenario also includes an offending event and a retributive act. Each of these has a quantitative aspect, and must also include an intensity, a zero point, and a limit. In the prototypical case, the offending event is an action on the part of a wrongdoer against a victim. The retribution takes the form of an act by an agent against some target.

The ontology of anger also includes a number of predicates: *displeasing, at fault, exert force on, cause, exist, control, dangerous, damaging, balance,* and *outweigh.* There are also some other kinds of events: the physiological effects; the angry behaviors; and the immediate cause of anger, in case it is not the same as the offending event.

SUMMARY OF THE ONTOLOGY OF ANGER

Aspects of the person: S
                                  Body
                                  Anger

Offense and retribution: Offending Event
                                  Retributive Act

Scales of intensity: Intensity of Anger
                                  Intensity of Offense
                                  Intensity of Retribution

End points: Zero
                                  Limit

Predicates: Displease
                                  At Fault
                                  Cause
                                  Exist
                                  Exert Force on
                                  Control
                                  Dangerous
                                  Damaging
                                  Balance
                                  Outweigh

Other events: Physiological Reactions
                                  Angry Behaviors
                                  Immediate Cause

RESTATEMENT OF THE PROTOTYPICAL SCENARIO

Given the preceding ontology and principles of the cultural model, we can restate the prototypical anger scenario in terms that will facilitate showing the relationships among the wide variety of anger scenarios. We will first restate the prototypical scenario and then go on to the nonprototypical scenarios.

PROTOTYPICAL ANGER SCENARIO

Constraints:
     Victim = S
     Agent of Retribution = S
     Target of Anger = Wrongdoer
     Immediate Cause of Anger = Offending Event
     Angry Behavior = Retribution

Stage 1: Offending Event
     Wrongdoer offends S
     Wrongdoer is at fault
     The offending event displeases S

The intensity of the offense outweighs the intensity of the retribution (which equals zero at this point), thus creating an imbalance. The offense causes anger to come into existence.

Stage 2: Anger
Anger exists.
S experiences physiological effects (heat, pressure, agitation).
Anger exerts force on the S to attempt an act of retribution.

Stage 3: Attempt to control anger
S exerts a counterforce in an attempt to control anger.

Stage 4: Loss of control
The intensity of anger goes above the limit.
Anger takes control of S.
S exhibits angry behavior (loss of judgment, aggressive actions).
There is damage to S.
There is a danger to the target of anger, in this case, the wrongdoer.

Stage 5: Retribution
S performs retributive act against W (this is usually angry behavior directed at W).
The intensity of retribution balances the intensity of offense.
The intensity of anger drops to zero.
Anger ceases to exist.

THE NONPROTOTYPICAL CASES

We are now in a position to show how a large range of instances of anger cluster about the above prototype. The examples are in the following form: a nonprototypical anger scenario with its name in **boldface**, followed by an informal description; an account of the minimal difference between the given scenario and the prototype scenario; finally, an example sentence.

Insatiable anger: You perform the act of retribution and the anger just does not go away.
In Stage 5, the intensity of anger stays above zero and the anger continues to exist.
Example: His anger lingered on.

Frustrated anger: You just cannot get back at the wrongdoer and you get frustrated.
It is not possible to gain retribution for the offensive act. S engages in frustrated behavior.
Option: S directs his anger at himself.
Examples: He was climbing the walls. She was tearing her hair out. He was banging his head against the wall. He's taking it out on himself.

Redirected anger: Instead of directing your anger at the person who made you angry, you direct it at someone or something else.

The target of anger is not the wrongdoer.
Examples: When I lose my temper, I kick the cat. When you get angry, punch a pillow until your anger goes away. When something bad happened at the office, he would take it out on his wife.

Exaggerated response: Your reaction is way out of proportion to the offense.
The intensity of retribution outweighs the intensity of offense.
Examples: Why jump down my throat? You have a right to get angry, but not to go *that* far.

Controlled response: You get angry, but retain control and consciously direct your anger at the wrongdoer.
S remains in control. Everything else remains the same.
Example: He vented his anger on her.

Constructive use: Instead of attempting an act of retribution, you put your anger to a constructive use.
S remains in control and performs a constructive act instead of a retributive act. The scales remain unbalanced, but the anger disappears.
Example: Try to channel your anger into something constructive.

Terminating event: Before you have a chance to lose control, some unrelated event happens to make your anger disappear.
Anger doesn't take control of *S*. Some event causes the anger to go out of existence.
Example: When his daughter smiled at him, his anger disappeared.

Spontaneous cessation: Before you lose control, your anger just goes away.
Anger doesn't take control of *S* and the intensity of anger goes to zero.
Example: His anger just went away by itself.

Successful suppression: You successfully suppress your anger.
S keeps control and the intensity of anger is not near the limit.
Example: He suppressed his anger.

Controlled reduction: Before you lose control, you engage in angry behavior and the intensity of anger goes down.
S does not lose control, *S* engages in angry behavior and the intensity of anger goes down.
Example: He's just letting off steam.

Immediate explosion: You get angry and lose control all at once.
No Stage 3. Stages 2 and 4 combine into a single event.
Example: I said "Hi Roundeyes!" and he blew up.

Slow burn: Anger continues for a long time.
Stage 2 lasts a long time.
Example: He was doing a slow burn.

Nursing a grudge: *S* maintains his anger for a long period waiting for a chance at a retributive act. Maintaining that level of anger takes special effort.

Stage 2 lasts a long time and requires effort. The retributive act does not equal angry behavior.

Don't get mad, get even: This is advice (rarely followed) about the pointlessness of getting angry. It suggests avoiding Stages 2, 3, and 4, and instead going directly to Stage 5. This advice is defined as an alternative to the prototypical scenario.

Indirect cause: It is some result of the wrongdoer's action, not the action itself, that causes anger.

The offense is not the immediate cause of anger, but rather is more indirect - the cause of the immediate cause.

Consider the following case: Your secretary forgets to fill out a form that results in your not getting a deserved promotion. Offending event = secretary forgets to fill out form. Immediate cause = you do not get promotion. You are angry *about* not getting the promotion. You are angry *at* the secretary *for* not filling out the form. In general, *about* marks the immediate cause, *at* marks the target, and *for* marks the offense.

Cool anger: There are no physiological effects and S remains in control.

Cold anger: S puts so much effort into suppressing the anger that temperature goes down, while internal pressure increases. There are neither signs of heat nor agitation, and there is no danger that S will lose control and display his anger. In the prototypical case, a display of anger constitutes retribution. But since there is no such display, and since there is internal pressure, release from that pressure can only come through retribution of some other kind, one that is more severe than the display of emotion. It is for this reason that cold anger is viewed as being much more dangerous than anger of the usual kind. Expressions like *Sally gave me an icy stare* are instances of cold anger. This expression implies that Sally is angry at me, is controlling her anger with effort, and is not about to lose control; it suggests the possibility that she may take retributive action against me of some sort other than losing her temper.

Anger with: To be angry with someone, S has to have a positive relationship with the wrongdoer, the wrongdoer must be answerable to S, the intensity is above the threshold, but not near the limit. Perhaps the best example is a parent–child relationship, where the parent is angry with the child.

Righteous indignation: The offending event is a moral offense and the victim is not the S. The intensity of anger is not near the limit.

Wrath: The intensity of the offense is very great and many acts of retribution are required in order to create a balance. The intensity of the anger is well above the limit and the anger lasts a long time.

There appears to be a recognizable form of anger for which there are no conventional linguistic expressions, so far as we can tell. We will call this a manipulative use of anger. It is a case where a person cultivates his anger and does not attempt to control it, with the effect that he intimidates those around him into following his wishes in order to keep him from getting angry. This can work either by fear or by guilt. The people manipulated can either be afraid of his anger or may feel guilty about what the anger does to him. This form of anger is fairly distant from the prototype and it is no surprise that we have no name for it.

Interestingly enough, there is a linguistic test that can be used to verify that what we have called the prototypical scenario is indeed prototypical. It involves the use of the word *but*. Consider the following examples (where the asterisk indicates a semantic aberration):

> Max got angry, but he didn't blow his top.
> *Max got angry, but he blew his top.
> Max blew up at his boss, but the anger didn't go away.
> *Max blew up at his boss, but the anger went away.
> Sam got me angry, but it wasn't him that I took my anger out on.
> *Sam got me angry, but it was him that I took my anger out on.

The word *but* marks a situation counter to expectation. In these examples, the prototypical scenario defines what is to be expected. The acceptable sentences with *but* run counter to the prototypical scenario, and thus fit the conditions for the use of *but*. The unacceptable sentences fit the prototypical scenario, and define expected situations. This is incompatible with the use of *but*. Thus we have a linguistic test that accords with our intuitions about what is or isn't prototypical.

Each of the nonprototypical cases just cited is a case involving anger. There appear to be no necessary and sufficient conditions that will fit all these cases. However, they can all be seen as variants of the prototypical anger scenario. Prototypes often involve clusters of conditions and the prototypical anger scenario is no exception. The clustering can be seen explicitly in identity conditions such as: Victim = Self, Target = Wrongdoer, Offending Event = Immediate Cause, and so forth. When these identities do not hold, we get nonprototypical cases. For example, with righteous indignation, Victim does not have to equal Self. In the case of an indirect cause, Offending Event does not equal Immediate Cause. In the case of redirected anger, Target does not equal Wrongdoer. Usually the act of retribution and the disappearance of anger go together, but in the case of spontaneous cessation and insatiable anger, that is not the case. And in the Don't-get-mad-get-even case, angry behavior is avoided, and is therefore not identical to the act of retribution. Part of what makes the prototypical scenario prototypical is that it is sufficiently rich so that variations on it can account for nonprototypical cases, and it also has a conflation of conditions that are not conflated in nonprototypical cases.

The point is that there is no single unified cognitive model of anger. Instead there is a category of cognitive models with a prototypical model in the center. This suggests that it is a mistake to try to find a single cognitive model for all instances of a concept. Kinds of anger are not all instances of the same model; instead they are *variants* on a prototypical model. There is no common core that all kinds of anger have in common. Instead, the kinds of anger bear family resemblances to one another.

METAPHORICAL ASPECTS OF THE PROTOTYPE SCENARIO

The analysis we have done so far is consistent with a certain traditional view of metaphor, namely:

> The concept of anger exists and is understood independently of any metaphors.
> The anger ontology and the category of scenarios represent the literal meaning of the concept of anger.
> Metaphors do no more than provide ways of talking about the ontology of anger.

This view entails the following:

> The elements of the anger ontology really, literally exist, independent of any metaphors.

A brief examination of the anger ontology reveals that this is simply not the case. In the ontology, anger exists as an independent entity, capable of exterting force and controlling a person. This is what Lakoff and Johnson (1980) refer to as an "ontological metaphor." In this case, it would be the ANGER IS AN ENTITY metaphor. A person's anger does not really, literally exist as an independent entity, though we do comprehend it metaphorically as such. In the ontology, there is an intensity scale for anger, which is understood as being oriented UP, by virtue of the MORE IS UP metaphor. The intensity scale has a limit associated with it – another ontological metaphor. Anger is understood as being capable of exerting force and taking control of a person. The FORCE and CONTROL here are also metaphorical, based on physical force and physical control. The anger ontology also borrows certain elements from the ontology of retributive justice: offense and retribution, with their scales of intensity and the concept of balance. These are also metaphorical, with metaphorical BALANCE based on physical balance. In short, the anger ontology is largely constituted by metaphor.

Let us now examine these constitutive metaphors. Their source domains – ENTITY, INTENSITY, LIMIT, FORCE, and CONTROL – all seem to be superordinate concepts, that is concepts that are fairly abstract. By contrast, the principal metaphors that map onto the anger ontology – HOT FLUID, INSANITY, FIRE, BURDEN, STRUGGLE – appear to be basic-level concepts, that is, concepts that are linked more directly to experience, concepts that are information-rich and rich in conventional mental imagery. Let us call the metaphors based on such concepts "basic-level metaphors." We would like to suggest that most of our understanding of anger comes via these basic-level metaphors. The HOT FLUID and FIRE metaphors give us an understanding of what kind of entity anger is. And the STRUGGLE metaphor gives us a sense of what is involved in controlling it. Without these metaphors, our understanding of anger would be extremely impoverished, to say the least. One is tempted to ask which is more primary: the constitutive metaphors or the basic-level ones. We do not know if that is a meaningful question. All we know is that both exist, and have their separate functions: The basic-level metaphors allow us to comprehend and draw inferences about anger, using our knowledge of familiar, well-structured domains. The constitutive metaphors provide the bulk of the anger ontology.

The embodiment of anger

We have seen that the concept of anger has a rich conceptual structure and that those who view it as just a feeling devoid of conceptual content are mistaken. But the opposite view also exists. Schachter and Singer (1962) have claimed that emotions are *purely cognitive,* and that there are no physiological differences among the emotions. They claim that the feeling of an emotion is simply a state of generalized arousal, and that *which* emotion one feels is simply a matter of what frame of mind one is in. The results of Ekman, Levenson, and Friesen (1983) contradict the Schacter–Singer claims with evidence showing that pulse rate and skin termperature do correlate with particular emotions.

Although the kind of analysis we have offered does not tell us anything direct about what the physiology of emotions might be, it does correlate positively with the Ekman group's results. As we saw, the conceptual metaphors and metonymies used in the comprehension of anger are based on a cultural theory of the physiology of anger, the major part of which involves heat and internal pressure. The Ekman group's results (which are entirely independent of the analysis given here) suggest that our cultural theory of the physiology of anger corresponds remarkably well with the actual physiology: when people experience anger their skin temperature and pulse rate rises.

Although the cultural theory is only a "folk" theory, it has stood the test of time. It has made sense to hundreds of millions of English speakers over a period of roughly a thousand years. The Ekman group's results suggest that ordinary speakers of English by the million have had very subtle insight into their own physiology. Those results suggest that many of the details of the way we conceptualize anger arise from the autonomic nervous system, and that the conceptual metaphors and metonymies used in understanding anger are by no means arbitrary; instead they are motivated by our physiology.

The Ekman group's results, together with our hypothesis concerning conceptual embodiment, make an interesting prediction. It predicts that if we look at metaphors and metonymies for anger in the languages of the world, we will not find any that contradict the physiological results that they found. In short, we should not find languages where the basic emotion of anger is understood in terms of both cold and freedom from pressure. The nonbasic case of *cold anger* discussed above is irrelevant, since it is a special form of anger and not an instance of the normal basic-anger emotion, and since it does involve internal pressure.

If Schachter and Singer are right and the Ekman group has made a mistake, then the English metaphors and metonymies for anger are arbitrary, that is, they are not embodied, not motivated by any physiological reality. The heat and internal pressure metaphors should thus be completely accidental. If there is no physiological basis for anger at all, as Schachter and Singer suggest, we would then expect metaphors for anger to be randomly distributed in the languages of the world. We would expect metaphors for cold and freedom from pressure to be just as common as metaphors for heat and pressure; in fact, on the Schacter–Singer account, we would expect that metaphors based on shape, darkness, trees, water – anything at all – would be just as common as metaphors based on heat and pressure. The research has not been done, but our guess is that the facts will match the predictions of the Ekman group. If those predictions hold up, it will show that the match between the Ekman group's results and ours is no fluke, and it will give even more substance to our claim that concepts are embodied.

Review

We have shown that the expressions that indicate anger in American English are not a random collection, but rather are structured in terms of an elaborate cognitive model that is implicit in the semantics of the language. This indicates that anger is not just an amorphous feeling, but rather that it has an elaborate cognitive structure.

However, very significant problems and questions remain.

First, there are aspects of our understanding of anger that our methodology cannot shed any light on. Take, for example, the range of offenses that cause anger and the corresponding range of appropriate responses. Our methodology reveals nothing in this area.

Second, the study of the language as a whole gives us no guide to individual variation. We have no idea how close any individual comes to the model we have uncovered, and we have no idea how people differ from one another.

Third, our methodology does not enable us to say much about the exact psychological status of the model we have uncovered. How much of it do people really use in comprehending anger? Do people base their actions on this model? Are people aware of the model? How much of it, if any, do people consciously believe? And most intriguingly, does the model have any effect on what people *feel?*

Certain things, however, do seem to be clear. Most speakers of American English seem to use consistently the expressions we have described and make inferences that appear, so far as we can tell, to be consistent with our model. We make this claim on the basis of our own intuitive observations, though to really establish it, one would have to do thorough empirical studies. If we are right, our model has considerable psychological reality, but how much and what kind remains to be determined. The fact that our analysis meshes so closely with the physiological study done by the Ekman group suggests that emotional concepts are embodied, that is, that the actual content of the concepts are correlated with bodily experience.

This is especially interesting in the case of metaphorical concepts, since the correlation is between the metaphors and the physiology, rather than directly between the literal sense and the physiology. It provides confirmation of the claim by Lakoff and Johnson (1980) that conceptual metaphors are not mere flights of fancy, but can even have a basis in bodily experience.

What does all this say about cultural models? First, they make use of imaginative mechanisms – metaphor, metonymy, and abstract scenarios. Second, they are not purely imaginative; they can be motivated by the most concrete of things, bodily experience. Third, linguistic evidence is an extraordinarily precise guide to the structure of such models.

Note

1. This is a shortened, slightly revised version of the chapter entitled "Anger" that appears as Case Study 1 in Women, Fire, and Dangerous Things: What Categories Reveal about the Mind, by George Lakoff, University of Chicago Press, 1987.

References

DeSousa, R.
    1980. The rationality of emotions. *In* Explaining Emotions, A. O. Rorty, ed. Berkeley: University of California Press. Pp. 127–151.
Ekman, P., R. W. Levenson, and W. V. Friesen
    1983. Autonomic nervous system activity distinguishes among emotions. Science 221(4616):1208–1210.
Lakoff, G. and M. Johnson
    1980. Metaphors We Live By. Chicago: University of Chicago Press.
Schachter, S. and J. Singer
    1962. Cognitive, social and physiological determinants of emotional states. Psychological Review 69:379–399.

9
Two theories of home heat control[1]

Willett Kempton

Human beings strive to connect related phenomena and make sense of the world. In so doing, they create what I call folk theory. The word *folk* signifies both that these theories are shared by a social group and that they are acquired from everyday experience or social interaction. To call them *theories* is to assert that they use abstractions that apply to many analogous situations, enable predictions, and guide behavior. I contrast folk theories with institutionalized theories, which are used by specialists and acquired from scientific literature or controlled experiments. Thus, a folk theory is one type of cultural model.

This chapter analyzes folk theories for home heating control, particularly thermostat control. From interviews with Michigan residents, folk theories were inferred using methods developed by Lakoff and Johnson (1980; also see Lakoff & Kövecses this volume) and Quinn (1982; this volume). The inferred folk theories were compared with behavior guided by the theory, using both observed behavior and self-reported behavior. The interviews also elicited lists of devices analogous to thermostats and a history of use in present and past residences.

The concept of folk theory

Anthropological interest in folk theory has germinated over the past few years in the form of two recent volumes (Dougherty 1985; Marsella & White 1982) and the conference leading to the present volume. Present work on folk models and folk theory continues the expansion of cognitive anthropology from folk categories to more complex structures, such as sets of propositions (D'Andrade 1981; Kay 1966), inference rules (Cole & Scribner 1974; Hutchins 1980), cognition in everyday activities (Holland 1985; Lave & Rogoff 1983; Murtaugh, Faust, & de la Rocha unpublished), and connections in discourse (Agar 1980; Rice 1980).

Recent discoveries by psychologists and educators provide the most precisely defined example of folk theory to date. Related cognitive structures have been called "naïve theory" (DiSessa 1982; McCloskey 1983a; McCloskey, Caramazza & Green 1980), "mental models" (de Kleer &

Brown 1983; Gentner & Stevens 1983; Johnson-Laird 1981), "naïve problem representation" (Larkin 1983; Larkin et al. 1980), or "intuitive theory" (McCloskey 1983b; see DiSessa 1985 for a contrasting view).[2] I describe one study to provide an example of folk theory and to show how my perspective differs. The study compared folk theories of motion with physicists' theories of motion:

> . . . People develop on the basis of their everyday experience remarkably
> well-articulated naïve theories of motion . . . theories developed by dif-
> ferent individuals are best described as different forms of the same basic
> theory. Although this basic theory appears to be a reasonable outcome of
> experience with real-world motion, it is strikingly inconsistent with the
> fundamental principles of classical physics. In fact, the naïve theory is
> remarkably similar to a pre-Newtonian physical theory popular in the
> fourteenth through sixteenth centuries. (McCloskey 1983a:299)

To paraphrase this quotation, the folk theory of motion (1) is based on everyday experience; (2) varies among individuals, although important elements are shared; and (3) is inconsistent with principles of institutionalized physics. McCloskey makes a fourth finding, that the folk theory persists in the face of formal physics training. Students simply reinterpret classroom material to fit their preexisting folk theory (McCloskey 1983a:318). The physics instructors would not usually even be aware their students had a preexisting folk theory.[3]

To an anthropologist, the nonrecognition of conflicting systems and the persistence of the folk system both resemble phenomena at a cultural boundary. Isolated elements and terms diffuse across the cultural boundary, but they are incorporated into the prior folk theory rather than inducing change. There is also a parallel in that one culture seems dominant: When the folk and institutional theories differ, the folk theory is considered wrong. The research just cited does not question the correctness of the institutional theory, since a major objective of the classroom studies has been to improve teaching.

Wiser and Carey caution that we cannot understand folk theory by simply diagnosing its failure to solve problems in the domain of the expert. We must find the problems it does solve correctly and examine the explanatory mechanisms it uses to do so (Wiser & Carey 1983:295). Anthropologists' naturalistic proclivities have led them away from folk theory in the classroom and toward the environments in which folk theory earns its keep in everyday use; many examples are found in this volume.

Residential thermostats

This study deals with home heating thermostats for several reasons. Home heating systems are fairly simple and well understood (at least in comparison with marriage, disease etiology, gender roles, divination, the mind, and other topics of this volume). Information about them is communicated almost entirely through folk channels – no one must study thermostats in high school or pass examinations; there is no widespread institutionalized dogma. Yet, many people adjust their thermostats, typically more than once per day, so they must have some principles or theories guiding this behavior. Also, since the range of behavior affected by the theory is restricted – turning a single dial – behavioral records can be collected automatically. By comparing behavior patterns with interviews, we can better infer how folk theory guides the behavior we observe. Finally, this domain was selected because an improved understanding of what people do with thermostats would have significant practical consequence for national energy programs.

The following discussion draws from two sets of interviews and one set of behavioral data. The first set of interviews, with people in 30 Michigan households, elicited general information about energy management. Since these interviews were exploratory, they often did not go into much detail on thermostats. The second is a set of 8 interviews, with 12 Michigan informants, that focused on thermal comfort and especially dealt with thermostat control. I use the interview data to infer folk theory, which in turn is compared with behavioral patterns. The data on behavior derive from automatic recordings of thermostat settings in 26 houses in New Jersey. In addition, my analysis draws from discussions with heating specialists and energy conservation analysts and from technical energy articles.

This study reports the first phase of our research on this topic. The second phase, now being analyzed, combines both interview and behavioral data from the same households. Although the combined method is conceptually appealing, the expense of combined data – particularly when using automatic recorders – has necessitated smaller samples than we are able to draw on here.

I hypothesize that two theories of thermostats exist in the United States (and perhaps throughout the industrialized world). One, the feedback theory, holds that the thermostat senses temperature and turns the furnace on and off to maintain an even temperature. The other, which I call the valve theory, holds that the thermostat controls the amount of heat. That is, like a gas burner or a water valve, a higher setting causes a higher rate of flow. Technically knowledgeable readers of this paper have commented that the feedback theory is correct and the valve theory is wrong. However, as I will demonstrate, both folk theories simplify and distort as compared to a full physical description, each causes its own types of operational errors and inefficiencies, and each has certain advantages.

Records of thermostat use

Behavioral records of thermostat settings have been collected by Princeton University's Center for Energy and Environmental Studies (Dutt,

Eichenberger, & Socolow 1979; Socolow 1978). During a 2-year period, automatic devices recorded hourly thermostat settings (and many other energy variables) of 26 upper middle-class families in identical townhouses. Here, I examine 2 of those homes to illustrate 2 patterns of thermostat adjustment, which I link to the 2 folk theories.

Figure 9.1 shows hourly measurements of thermostat settings in one house over a 3-day period in the winter of 1976. The solid line shows the hourly thermostat setting, and the dotted line shows the room temperature. We see that the thermostat usually is changed at times when occupants and activities change: 8 A.M., noon, and 5 to 8 P.M. During other periods, not shown in Figure 9.1, the thermostat may be left at the same setting for several days. I conclude that the thermostat setting is changed when the desired temperature changes: when waking or going to sleep, when entering or exiting the house, and around mealtimes.

Figure 9.2 shows hourly thermostat settings for a second house, also during the winter of 1976. In this house, the thermostat is often changed between each hourly datum. In fact, the only times on the figure when the thermostat is not changed are probable sleeping times, for example, from 1 A.M. to 7 A.M. Monday, and from 10 P.M. Monday to 8 A.M. Tuesday. It appears that whenever someone is awake in this house, the thermostat is adjusted at least hourly. Examination of the full 2 years of data (not shown here) also shows many thermostat adjustments, not at regular times, and a wide range of settings (from 61° to 85° F; 16° to 29°C).

I hypothesize that the frequent thermostat settings of this second household result from the residents' having a valve theory of their thermostat.[4] Although I could not interview the people in the households shown in Figures 9.1 and 9.2, informants in my interviews do report following similar patterns (though rarely as extreme as Figure 9.2). The next two sections discuss interview evidence for the two theories.

The feedback theory

According to the feedback theory, the thermostat turns the furnace on or off according to room temperature. When the room is colder than the setting on the thermostat dial, the thermostat turns the furnace on. Then, when the room is as warm as the setting, it turns the furnace off. Since the theory posits that the furnace runs at a single constant speed, the thermostat can control the amount of heating only by the length of time the furnace is on. Thus, if the dial is adjusted upward only a little, the furnace will run a short time and turn off; if it is adjusted upward a large amount, the furnace must run longer to bring the house to that temperature. Left at one setting, the thermostat will switch the furnace on and off as necessary to maintain approximately that temperature.

Heating engineers are fairly comfortable with the folk theory described

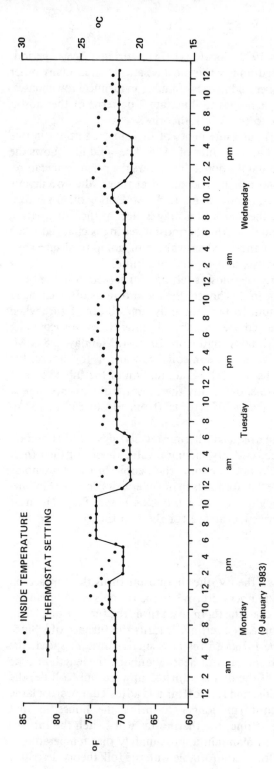

Figure 9.1. Pattern of thermostat adjustments consistent with the feedback theory

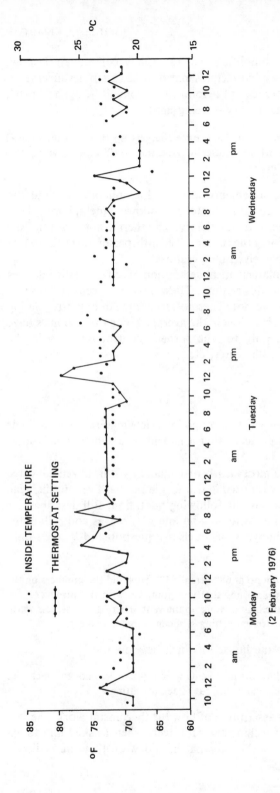

Figure 9.2. Pattern of thermostat adjustments consistent with the valve theory

227

here – they consider it simplified, but essentially correct. As I show, however, their evaluation of correctness may be based on irrelevant criteria.

In interview segments such as the following (from a Michigan farmer), I infer that the feedback theory is being used:

> You just turn the thermostat up, and once she gets up there [to the desired temperature] she'll kick off automatically. And then she'll kick on and off to keep it at that temperature.

From anthropomorphic statements such as this and others about the thermostat "feeling it is too cold," I infer the following metaphor (Lakoff & Johnson 1980) for the feedback theory: The thermostat is a little person with a switch controlling the furnace. The little person turns the switch on and off, based on perceived temperature.

Thermostats and the mathematical description of self-regulating devices (Wiener 1948) are new to this century. These devices trace their ancestry to Watt's steam engine governor. Thermostats are the only self-regulating devices whose operation is visible in the average home (most homes have visible thermostats not only for the furnace control but also in the refrigerator, oven, portable heater, etc.).

The valve theory

I elucidate the valve theory first through interview material from a single informant then present evidence that it is held by a substantial proportion of Americans.

The valve theory was most clearly articulated by Bill, a well-educated man in his thirties. Bill was raised in California but has lived in Michigan for three years. As shown in the following quotation, Bill described the thermostat dial as not just switching on and off, but as controlling the rate of heat flow. (In dialogues, *W* labels my question and *B* labels Bill's response.)

W: What would the system do at 68° versus 85°? How did the numbers on the thermostat dial relate to anything that was going on with the furnace?

B: Well, you could feel the heat coming up the vent. There'd be less, less warm air, less hot air at the different setting. I mean – that was clear.

Similarly, in describing the house in which he grew up:

B: I do remember, as a kid, the heat vents were more or less hot to touch – to the hand as a sensor near the vent – at different settings. . . .

When I asked Bill for a description of how the thermostat works, he said he could not describe it technically. However, when I asked him to explain how it works in relation to what he did with it, he immediately explained:

B: I think it's pretty simple really. Um, I assume, um, that there is some kind of linear relationship between where the lever is and the way some kind of heat generating system functions. And, um, that it's like stepping on the gas pedal; that there I have a notion of hydraulics, you know, the harder you push there is, the more fluid gets pushed into the engine, and the more explosions there are, and the faster it goes. And so here, the, the harder or the more you push the lever or twist the lever in – there is a scale which indicates, you know, regular units – the . . . more power the system puts out to generate heat. . . .

Bill's analogy of an automobile gas pedal describes the continuously varying flow of heat he believes he is regulating.

To elicit operational practices, I posed hypothetical situations. Bill's practices were consistent with his theory and his metaphor:

W: Let's say you're in the house and you're cold. . . . Let's say it's a cold day, you feel cold, you want to do something about it.
B: Oh, what I might do is, I might turn the thing up high to get out, a lot of air out fast, then after a little while turn it off or turn it down.
W: Un-huh
B: So there are also, you know, these issues about, um, the rate at which the thing produces heat, the higher the setting is, the more heat that's produced per unit of time, so if you're cold, you want to get warm fast, um, so you turn it up high. Um, my feeling is, my, my kind of Calvinist or Puritan feeling is that that's sinful. That, that really ought to turn it to the setting, the warmth setting which you think you'll eventually be comfortable and just bear the cold until the thing slowly heats up the house to that level.

Although Bill believes that a higher setting would cause the house to heat up faster, he may refrain from doing this because he considers it wanton. Thus, for reasons other than the theory of the thermostat itself, he sometimes operates the device in the same way as someone who holds the feedback theory.

His conceptualization of why the house maintains a steady temperature is radically different from that predicted by the feedback theory.

W: OK, so how would you use the thermostat and, and how would it be different from the way you used that oven?
B: Um, well, I guess you'd find some kind of moderate, steady, steady setting, setting for the thermostat to maintain a comfortable temperature in a steady state.
W: OK, and that would be something intermediate between having it cranked all the way up for heating up quickly, which would be too much, and having it all the way down, which would not be enough?
B: Right, yea.
W: So what, what's this, what's steady state about? You're trying to balance off what against what?
B: Humm. Uh, well I guess basically, the amount of heat that comes into the system has to equal the amount that's somehow disappearing.

In this passage, Bill states that an even temperature is not maintained by the thermostat itself; rather, it is a balance set by the human operator.

The operator adjusts the rate of heat entering the system to equal the amount leaving or dissipating. The operator's balance of energy input against dissipation is also captured by the gas pedal analogy to which Bill referred frequently. When Bill says the thermostat is like a gas pedal, he is using what Gentner (1983) calls analogy or structure mapping – the gas pedal is analogous to the thermostat because they both have the same relations between objects and actions, not because they have similar attributes or appearance.

A person who is attempting to balance heat against dissipation would reasonably change the thermostat setting frequently. The result would be a pattern of many adjustments like that seen in Figure 9.2.

Since our environment contains many more valves than feedback devices, everyone is likely to have a valve theory (applied to water faucets, etc.). People who have a feedback theory will also have a valve theory and will apply the feedback theory to only a small set of devices. To elicit devices Bill saw as similar to thermostats, I suggested that the burner on a gas stove operates like Bill's description of the thermostat; the higher you turn it, the more heat you get. He agreed, so I asked which other devices would be similar:

B: I just flashed to electric mixers. The higher you turn them, the faster they go . . . the harder you push on the gas, the faster the car moves . . . turning on the faucet . . . you can see the water squirting out in greater volume at a greater rate, you know, as the lever is increased to turn it up.

By contrast, he discards on–off controls as different:

B: What other analogies might I think of? Uh, turning on and off the lights just, uh, that's a more binary kind of process.

Bill's device analogies are consistent with his abstract description, his reported operational practices, and the metaphors he uses to describe the thermostat.

Bill recognized that his model of thermostat operation may be different from that of specialists. In fact, early in the interview he described himself as not having any knowledge about thermostats. He thought someone had given him a formal explanation, but he could not remember it. Since he could not reproduce the institutionally sanctioned explanation, he describes himself as "ignorant":

B: Now um, I really am ignorant about the functioning of these devices . . . once or twice, somebody might have described to me how the thermostat operated, but, my reaction at the time was maybe comprehension, but the sense of feeling out of control. And, maybe partly because of anxiety or lack of familiarity with the device, I've since forgotten what I was told.
W: That's fine.
B: Yea, so, this really would be, if I tried speculating on how they worked, it would really be just that.

W: Speculation.
B: Sort of *de novo*.

Bill's denial of a solid understanding here is belied by the other quotations, which show a detailed and complete theory of thermostat operation, including a set of predictions, past perceptions, and operating rules consistent with his theory. Further, his theory is stable enough to resist change. Later in the interview, he hypothesizes a possible second "level of sophistication" that some thermostats might have, in order to explain why his parents' furnace seemed to turn on and off without human intervention:

B: . . . I can imagine the devices at varying levels of sophistication and you'd have this, uh, kind of, feedback arrangement on, that exists for my parents'.
W: Un-huh.
B: Uh, where, uh, you know, it's not the human, the human operator isn't the only person that – the only agent that – turns the system on and off. The system itself is self-regulating. So, hm, in the course of the night, you know, it could turn on and, and off according to some measurement that it's making of the temperature, in the room. And um, um, you know, in my parents' house you could hear that thing going on and off in the course of the night making those irritating, windy sounds.
W: Irritating, windy sounds. This is the drafts you were talking about before.
B: Right. Um, now, I can't remember whether the thermostat in this other house had that self-control, kind of procedure. I don't think it did and I think that might have been one of the reasons why we couldn't leave it on all night.

Bill proposed this partial feedback theory to explain what he could not explain with his valve theory, but he seemed to consider the feedback thermostat (in his parents' house) to be a special case. In discussing my analysis with Bill 7 months later, he described this partial feedback theory as transitory:

B: I didn't have the feedback theory until your questioning forced it upon me . . . I discovered it for the moment, but later forgot it. When I went back to using the thermostat, I probably went back to doing it the same way.

Bill's reported return to the valve theory suggests that folk theory is resistant to change.

Informal data suggest even more that the valve theory is resistant to change. In casual discussions of this material with proponents of the feedback theory, three individuals told me that their spouse turned up the thermostat to heat the house faster, that this practice was ineffective, and that their repeated attempts to convince their spouse of this had failed. Their failures may be attributed to the proselytizers' working to convey an individual belief when they needed to convey an entire theory. Worse, they had to supplant a theory that was already working satisfactorily and that was not explicitly acknowledged as existing.

To summarize the valve theory as described by Bill, the thermostat controls the rate at which the furnace generates heat. People maintain a constant temperature in their houses by adjusting the setting so that the amount of heat coming in just balances the amount being dissipated. Devices that operate similarly include the water faucet and the gas pedal on an automobile. Bill allows that some sophisticated systems may consider temperature and automatically adjust the heat from the furnace. Even though Bill's theory resists change, he devalues his own theory relative to the institutionally sanctioned one. Despite having a fully elaborated conceptualization and complex operating rules, he describes himself as "ignorant about the functioning of these devices."

Is Bill's valve theory unusual? No national survey data exist on this issue, but estimates can be made. Of the 12 informants in my focused interviews, the valve theory was given in full form by 2, and in partial form by at least 3 more; data were indeterminate in some of the more brief interviews. Another study, in Wales, interviewed residents of 38 new thermostatically controlled rural houses. When asked whether a cold house would warm up quicker to the desired level if the thermostat were turned up full, past its normal setting, 62% said it would (O'Sullivan & McGeevor 1982:104). A third study asked 43 college students in Cambridge, Massachusetts, to assume they entered a cold house and wanted it to heat up as quickly as possible. Those who would turn it above the desired temperature for faster heating ranged from 24% to 46%, the percentage varying with previous questions about analogous situations (Gentner & Tenney, unpublished 1983 data). Therefore, from those limited studies I estimate that 25% to 50% of the population of the United States uses at least part of the valve theory. My sense, which I do not yet have formal data to support, is that the majority of the population holds a combination of these two theories.

Functionality of the two theories

In many anthropological studies, it would be nonsensical or impractical to evaluate the functionality of a folk theory. In this study, the domain and the goals of the folk are fairly straightforward. Known scientific theories describe home heating systems, and the major goals of using them are presumably to be comfortable without spending too much money. Thus, the functionality question can be addressed by asking how well each folk theory meets the goals of its users (this approach is advocated in more detail by Rappaport 1979:98; and by Kempton & Lave 1983).

MANAGEMENT EFFORT AND THERMAL COMFORT

The valve theory does rather well in many situations. For example, if one assumes that thermostats do not have feedback mechanisms, a house would become colder when the weather is colder. The corresponding management rule is: When it is colder outside, you must turn up the heat. This practice is rationalized by the device model itself. Conversely, with a feedback device model, this adjustment would not seem necessary. In fact, the valve theory leads to correct management, since in many houses infiltration and distribution asymmetries will cool marginal rooms more in cold weather.

A second issue is whether a higher setting provides faster warmup. The feedback theory denies faster warmup because the furnace runs at a constant rate. However, due to human comfort factors and characteristics of interacting systems, a person entering a cold house from outside will not feel warm when the air first reaches the correct temperature.[5] Thus, greater comfort would be realized if the thermostat were set high, to raise the air temperature above normal initially, then returned to the normal setting. Again, the correct action would logically follow from the valve model, but not from the feedback model.

ENERGY USE

The valve theory correctly predicts a third fact of considerable importance to the user: More fuel is consumed at higher settings than at lower ones. The prediction is correct, even if the explanation is wrong (higher fuel use does not occur not because of a valve opening wider but because higher inside temperatures cause more heat loss through the shell of the house). Nevertheless, higher use is a direct prediction of the valve theory, not of the feedback theory. Consequently, some interviews suggest that valve theorists are more likely to believe correctly that night setback saves energy. The following quote illustrates how the informant's husband follows the logic of the feedback theory to an erroneous conclusion:

I: Now, my husband disagrees with me. He, he feels, and he will argue with me long enough, that we do not save any fuel by turning the thermostat up and down. . . . Because he, he feels that by the time you turn it down to 55 and all the objects in the house drops to 55°, and in order to get all the objects in the house back up to 65°, you're going to use more fuel than if you would have left it at 65 and it just kicks in now and then.

This error is due to having the feedback theory without having additional theories of the interacting systems, particularly a theory of heat loss at different indoor temperatures. The feedback theory would work if it were augmented. But the necessary augmentations would complicate the model considerably – perhaps beyond the level of complexity most people are willing to bother learning about home heating. By contrast, if one considers the thermostat to be like a valve, these problems are solved with little effort.

These points favor the valve theory. However, it seems to encourage frequent unneeded adjustments of the thermostat. These adjustments may induce considerable waste of time and human effort. Frequent adjustments will not necessarily increase energy consumption as long as the thermostat is turned back down as soon as the house becomes warm. If the occupant forgets, energy will be wasted.

THE EXPERT'S PERSPECTIVE

Another problem with the valve theory is that it does not correspond to the mechanism inside the device. Inside, one sees a temperature-activated switch that can be on or off but cannot control the amount of heat from the furnace. This fact will seem a decisive failure to the few technically minded people who might actually look inside, but it is of little consequence for normal use of the thermostat.

Why do heating experts consider the valve theory incorrect when it provides its users with about the same number of useful predictions as the feedback theory? After their training, experts possess a full, institutionally sanctioned theory. This full theory can be arrived at from the feedback theory by simply adding details and adjacent systems. By contrast, arriving from the valve theory requires a conversion – at some point, the learner will say something like, "Oh, I see, it's not a valve, it's an automatic switch." The technical experts will evaluate folk theory from this perspective – not by asking whether it fulfills the need of the folk. But it is the latter criterion on which the anthropologist will rely due to her methodological training, and on which sound public policy must be based.

Change in folk theory

By examining folk theory as it changes, further clues are provided about the consistency between the theory's metaphor and the inferences and practices derived from it. Such data were fortuitously provided in one interview, in which the informant initially held parts of each theory and later shifted predominately to the feedback theory. This is shown in the following series of quotes, which also illustrate the difficulties in definitively identifying a person's theory without an extensive interview.

This informant, Peggy, is a language teacher who grew up in Michigan. In the beginning of the interview, she described the thermostat as sensitive to temperature:

P: I guess, what I always thought was when you turn the, the temperature, you turn the thermostat to 65, the furnace works to keep the room at 65 and then as soon as it's 65, the furnace stops working and then when it starts to get a little bit cold again the furnace will work again. And I think, that the, the temperature on the thermos – I think it keeps it at that temperature in that area. So maybe on the other side of the room, there might be window or a door and it could be draftier over there. But where the thermostat is, it will always be 65.

Peggy is clearly aware of the feedback nature of the thermostat. Correspondingly, when I elicited the list of similar devices, Peggy choose a different set from Bill's:

P: I guess it might be like an oven. You know, when you want to cook something at 350? You turn the oven on to 350 and it, a, the, fire or the electricity or whatever, or the gas, works to keep the temperature at 350 and to not get hotter and to not get colder.

She also mentioned the refrigerator, saying that it has a number or letter for coldness, and the refrigerator is "working to maintain an even temperature"; another example was the dial on the toaster, which selects "lighter or darker."

After these portions of the interview, I was certain that Peggy had a feedback theory. It was thus a surprise when I asked for her operating rules:

W: Let's say it's very cold . . . you come into the house and it's *very* cold, and you want to heat the house up. Let's say you want to heat the house up to 65. What would you do . . .
P: If it's very, very cold?
W: Un-huh.
P: I might turn it up to 70, for maybe 20 minutes, half an hour and then turn it back down to 65 to see if I can get it warmer faster.
W: Uhh [*trying to maintain composure*] You wouldn't turn it to 80 or something, 85?
P: I wouldn't feel comfortable doing that, no.
W: Because of danger, or because of just cost, it would be wasteful, or?
P: Yeah, I think it would be wasteful. I don't know, I just, I, even 70 seems immoral, somehow, you know.
W: Yeah [*laugh*]. Well, I don't consider [it] a moral issue, I don't inject that, I just try to get an idea of what you think would work best for you. Let's, you could take two cases, maybe. In one case, there's no more energy crisis and you don't have to worry about it any more.
P: Yeah, maybe 80.

Of the 12 informants interviewed in depth about the thermostat, Peggy was one of 3 who described the thermostat with feedback theory but nevertheless in practice turned it higher to heat faster. Such complications make it difficult to determine which theory is being used from the answer to a single fixed question (as we might like to do in a survey to estimate national rates of these theories).

In elaborating on this practice, Peggy compares the house thermostat with the oven:

P: But I think people have the general idea, and I guess I do too, that the higher you put it [the house thermostat], the faster and harder it's going to work.
W: Right, the harder it will work.
P: . . . I know the oven, when you turn it on 450, well we have a gas oven, the flame is higher than it is if you turn it on at 200.

During this description of the oven, she hesitates and says "But it might not work that way at all," meaning perhaps turning the house thermostat up further does not make it run faster; she says "It could be either way."

In thinking over the issue, she notes that her immediately previous description of turning the thermostat up to heat the house faster . . .

P: . . . contradicts what I said at the beginning. That a thermos – how a thermostat works, that it works up to a certain point and then when it gets to that point it turns off until, or it goes down until it needs to go on again. So I thought, well if it does that, then if I turn it at 80, it's going to get to 65 after ten minutes. If I turn it on 65, it's going to get to 65 . . . after ten minutes. And if I forget about it [at 80], it's going to keep going up to 80 unless I turn it back.

P: So, . . . I thought that it probably contradicted what I said before, but then I kept thinking about the oven and how I know [*unintelligible*] it gets hotter faster.

W: Un-huh.

P: So I thought, well maybe some furnaces are different.

W: Yeah, yeah.

P: Maybe some are very well regulated and maybe some do just produce a little more heat.

The concrete, observable case of the oven brings Peggy to use the valve theory in practice (whether she is correct about the oven is irrelevant here), but some internal reason seems to draw her to the feedback theory in her abstract description. I asked her how she arrived at her initial description of the thermostat.

P: I don't know. I don't think I learned it from my parents because I never paid much attention to the thermostat. . . . [*later*] Oh, I know, one time when I was living in the same house [with friends] and I lived in one of the bedrooms that didn't have a register. It was an added-on, it was an addition to the house and they, they didn't bother to put, you know, to connect the furnace . . . there was no register or, yeah, so there was a little space heater in there and I know you turned the knob on that space heater, to a certain temperature and then the little, you know, the coils would light up and make a lot of noise, and then when it got to be that temperature, the whole thing would just turn off. And then a few minutes later it came back on.

W: So you could see that happening.

P: I – you could see that happening and feel that happening. And I may have thought, yea, that must be how the furnace, the regular furnace works too. And then maybe from things people said.

This striking example shows how an immediately visible device can display its operation and thus influence folk theory. This experiential background, as Peggy points out, may also have dovetailed with someone's explanation, thereby reinforcing her recollection of both. As a result of integrating this information during the interview, Peggy said that the interview made her realize that turning the setting above the desired temperature was not effective.

Another event that makes system operation highly salient is a change in the type of system. A rural couple who switched from nonthermostatic space heaters to a furnace describe the change:

I: With the other ones, the space heaters, there was just no regulating to it. You know, if the temperature dropped outside, if you didn't wake up and go out and turn it up, it drops, you know, it would cool down. But with, naturally with the thermostatically controlled fuel oil furnace, it would kick on automatically by itself when it got down below that temperature.

The amount of adjustment needed for a true value-controlled system is highly salient. Accordingly, this couple, and another who had grown up with wood heat, had a fully elaborated and consistent feedback theory.

Conclusions

In studying residential heat control, I found that two folk theories were applied to thermostats. Of the two, the feedback theory is more closely related to expert theory.

Home heating, like many other areas of knowledge in our society, has a "correct" set of theories defined by experts and their institutions. Informants who held the valve theory were insecure about it – they denied understanding the device, even when they had complete descriptive models and elaborate procedures for using it. This insecurity has also been manifested on several occasions of giving this paper as a talk. Some questioners seem to be inhibited by feeling that they may have a "wrong" theory and they do not want to be embarrassed by their questions. One might suppose that choice of the correct theory for thermostats concerns straightforward technical facts and presume that the experts must know how thermostats really work – after all, they design them! We have seen, however, that the folk theory endorsed by the experts may not work as well in practical day-to-day application. A theory that is useful for designing thermostats is not guaranteed to be a good theory for using them.

More needs to be known before this research can have practical applications. In earlier work on household methods for measuring energy, my colleagues and I argued that many folk measurement methods are counterproductive and that individuals would benefit if folk methods were made more similar to expert ones (Kempton et al. 1982; Kempton & Montgomery 1982). In the case of folk theory for thermostats, the jury is still out. If people converted from the valve to the feedback model, they would save management effort by not having to adjust the thermostat so often and they would occasionally save energy by not forgetfully leaving it set high. However, widespread conversion to feedback theory would risk eliminating the theoretical rationale for night setback – an immensely larger penalty. A simple valve theory always directly predicts less use from lower settings since the valve is partially shut at lower settings. This prediction of lower use is not made by a simple feedback theory alone, but requires an accompanying theory of heat loss. The problem is seen by the quote on page 233, in which a feedback theorist argued that savings from night setback of the thermostat would be cancelled by subsequent turning up of the thermostat.

More research is needed, since two problems with the valve theory do argue for conversion. First, the problems with the first order feedback theory can be solved by simply adding on components, whereas problems with the valve model require ad hoc repairs (as in Bill's Calvinism) or replacement of the entire model. A second argument is that when the operation of the system is made visible (either by a miniature model – the space heater – or by system conversion), the folk, on their own, choose feedback theory.

Postscript: thermostat management as an industry

I close with a down-to-earth question: What is thermostat management worth? Although no national data exist on thermostat energy savings, rough estimates can be made. During the 1982 heating year, households in the United States spent $85 billion on direct energy purchases, averaging $1,022 per household (DOE, EIA 1983). Since the 1973 oil embargo, households have decreased their energy use by about 15% (Crane 1984; Williams, Dutt, & Geller 1983), which represents a current savings of $15 billion per year. Heating accounts for roughly half of residential energy cost; since consumers know more conservation methods for heating than for appliances, I estimate that heating accounts for two-thirds of the savings, or $10 billion annually. The only reliable estimate of actual thermostat savings has been made by Fels and Goldberg (1984), who analyzed New Jersey residential gas consumption. By a statistical procedure that compared monthly gas use with weather fluctuations, they were able to separate the effects of thermostat setting from other factors, such as home improvement (e.g., insulation) or more efficient appliances. They estimate that more than half of the natural gas savings were due to lower thermostat settings. If we assume the same proportion applies generally to heating fuels,[6] $5 billion is saved annually due to changes in home thermostat use since the oil embargo. To put this number in perspective, Socal's recent agreement to purchase Gulf for $13 billion was the largest corporate acquisition in history (Cole 1984). With three years of thermostat savings, American households could have outbid Socal and purchased Gulf Oil for themselves.

Although the dollar figure is an approximation, one can safely conclude that thermostat management provides American households with annual savings in the billions. Yet little reliable data link my aggregate national estimate to specific behavioral changes (e.g., nighttime setback versus constant lower settings), or to the cognitive and social systems that generate the behavior. Whatever the cause, increased household thermostat management now provides disposable income for other spending. Thus, thermostat management can be considered a multibillion dollar cottage industry. Further study of this industry's production methods would seem warranted.

Notes

1. For comments on this paper, I am grateful to Dan Bobrow, Roy D'Andrade, Gautam Dutt, Peter Gladhart, Dedre Gentner, Dorothy Holland, Charlotte Linde, Ann Millard, Bonnie Morrison, William Rittenberg, Jeff Weihl, and an anonymous reviewer for *Cognitive Science*. Other helpful questions were raised following my presentations of this material at University of California, Irvine, the Princeton Conference on Folk Models, Xerox PARC, the MSU Families and Energy Conference, and at Bolt Beranek and Newman, Inc. Unpublished data were kindly provided by Gautam Dutt at Princeton University and Jim Barnett at the National Bureau of Standards (thermostat behavior records); and by Dedre Gentner and Yevette Tenney at BBN (Cambridge survey of college students). This work is supported by the National Science Foundation, under grant BNS–82 10088, and by the Michigan State University Agricultural Experiment Station, as project 3152. This paper is Michigan Agricultural Experiment Station Journal Article No. 11141, and also appears in *Cognitive Science* 10(1):75–90 (1986).
2. DiSessa (1985) argues that the things McCloskey calls single coherent theories are in fact data-driven collections of heterogeneous "phenomenological primitives." These primitives originate in superficial interpretations of reality applied to common situations via recognition. The data in this paper argue for more connectedness than DiSessa sees, although I acknowledge the possibility that the word *theory* conveys more consistency and coherence than is appropriate.
3. Nonrecognition of cognitive variation within a culture, and even within a single family, seems common (Kempton 1981).
4. Although I propose folk theory as an explanation of the pattern in Figure 9.1, many factors contribute to thermostat setting, and frequent shifts could be due to non-folk-theoretical causes such as domestic conflict over desirable setting.
5. This can be demonstrated by a simple thought experiment. On entering a warm building with a point-source of heat (say, a wood stove), a person feels cold although the building is warm. That person will choose to stand near the point source, despite the higher-than-normal temperature. After the person has "warmed up," he or she will choose a normal temperature. In the case of turning the thermostat up on entering a cold house, there appear to be two physical causes: (1) The cold near-body masses – clothing, skin surface, and trapped surface air – are heated more rapidly by warmer ambient temperature; and (2) When air temperature rises but (slower-heating) wall and furniture surfaces are still cold, a person will feel colder than air temperature because of infrared radiation losses. A more complete analysis of these effects would require quantitative analysis of their relative magnitudes and time constants.
6. This figure probably underestimates the thermostat's proportion, since Fels and Goldberg calculated it to be 50% of all gas conservation, whereas I consider it only 50% of heating conservation.

References

Agar, M.
  1980. Stores, background knowledge and themes: Problems in the analysis of life history narrative. American Ethnologist 7(2):223–240.
Cole, M. and S. Scribner
  1974. Culture and Thought: A Psychological Introduction. New York: John Wiley and Sons.
Cole, R. J.
  1984. Socal Agrees to Buy Gulf in Record Deal. *New York Times,* 6 March 1984, p. 1.
Crane, L. T.
  1984. Residential energy conservation: How far have we progressed and how much farther can we go? Committee print 98-R, Committee on Energy and Commerce, U.S. House of Representatives. Washington, D.C.: U.S. Government Printing Office.
D'Andrade, R. G.
  1981. The cultural part of cognition. Cognitive Science 5(3):179–195.
de Kleer, J. and J. S. Brown
  1983. Assumptions and ambiguities in mechanistic mental models. *In* Mental Models, D. Gentner and A. L. Stevens, eds. Hillsdale, N.J.: Lawrence Erlbaum Associates. Pp. 155–190.
DiSessa, A. A.
  1982. Unlearning Aristotelian physics: A study of knowledge-based learning. Cognitive Science 6:37–75.
  1985. Final report on intuition as knowledge. Unpublished manuscript, M.I.T. Laboratory for Computer Science, M.I.T., Cambridge, Mass.
Dougherty, J. W. D., ed.
  1985. Directions in Cognitive Anthropology. Urbana: University of Illinois Press.
Dutt, G. S., A. Eichenberger, and R. H. Socolow
  1979. Twin Rivers Project, public data set documentation. Report PU/CEES No. 78, Princeton, N.J.: Princeton University Center for Energy and Environmental Studies.
Department of Energy, Energy Information Administration
  1983. Residential energy consumption survey: Consumption and expenditures April 1981 through March 1982, Part 1: National Data. DOE/EIA-0321/1(81). Washington, D.C.: U.S. Government Printing Office.
Fels, M. F. and M. L. Goldberg
  1984. With just billing and weather data, can one separate lower thermostat settings from extra insulation? *In* Families and Energy: Coping with Uncertainty, B. M. Morrison and W. Kempton, eds. East Lansing: Institute for Family and Child Study, Michigan State University. Pp. 195–206.
Gentner, D.
  1983. Structure-mapping: A framework for analogy. Cognitive Science 7:155–170.
Gentner, D. and A. L. Stevens, eds.
  1983. Mental Models. Hillsdale, N.J.: Lawrence Erlbaum Associates.
Holland, D.
  1985. From situation to impression: How Americans use cultural knowledge to get to know themselves and one another. *In* Directions in Cognitive Anthropology, J. W. D. Dougherty, ed. Urbana: University of Illinois Press. Pp. 389–411.
Hutchins, E.
  1980. Culture and Inference: A Trobriand Case Study. Cambridge, Mass.: Harvard University Press.

Johnson-Laird, P. N.
  1981. The form and function of mental models. *In* Proceedings of Third Annual Conference of the Cognitive Science Society. Berkeley: University of California. Pp. 103-105.
Kay, P.
  1966. Ethnography and theory of culture. Bucknell Review 14:106-113.
Kempton, W.
  1981. The Folk Classification of Ceramics: A Study of Cognitive Prototypes. New York: Academic Press.
Kempton, W., P. Gladhart, D. Keefe, and L. Montgomery
  1982. Willett Kempton, letter and papers. *In* Fiscal Year 1983 Dept. of Energy Budget Review (Conservation and Renewable Energy). Hearings before the Committee on Science and Technology, U.S. House of Representatives, No. 112, Vol. 2. Pp. 1015-1068. Washington, D.C.: U.S. Government Printing Office.
Kempton, W. and J. Lave
  1983. Review of Mental Models, D. Gentner and A. L. Stevens, eds. American Anthropologist 85(4):1002-1004.
Kempton, W. and L. Montgomery
  1982. Folk quantification of energy. Energy – The International Journal 7(10): 817-827.
Lakoff, G. and M. Johnson
  1980. Metaphors We Live By. Chicago: University of Chicago Press.
Larkin, J. H.
  1983. The role of problem representation in physics. *In* Mental Models, D. Gentner and A. L. Stevens, eds. Hillsdale, N.J.: Lawrence Erlbaum Associates. Pp. 75-98.
Larkin, J., J. McDermott, D. P. Simon, and H. A. Simon
  1980. Expert and novice performance in solving physics problems. Science 208:1335-1342.
Lave, J. and B. Rogoff, eds.
  1983. Everyday Cognition: Its Development in Social Context. Cambridge, Mass.: Harvard University Press.
Marsella, A. J. and G. M. White, eds.
  1982. Cultural Conceptions of Mental Health and Therapy. Dordrecht, Holland: D. Reidel Publishing Company.
McCloskey, M.
  1983a. Naïve Theories of Motion. *In* Mental Models, D. Gentner and A. L. Stevens, eds. Hillsdale, N.J.: Lawrence Erlbaum Associates. Pp. 299-324.
  1983b. Intuitive physics. Scientific American 248(4):122-130.
McCloskey, M., A. Caramazza, and B. Green
  1980. Curvilinear motion in the absence of external forces: Naïve beliefs about the motion of objects. Science 210:1139-1141.
O'Sullivan, P., and P. A. McGeevor
  1982. The effects of occupants on energy use in housing. *In* Energy Conservation in the Built Environment. Proceedings of CIB W67 Third International Symposium, Vol. 5. Dublin: An Foras Forbartha. Pp. 5.96-5.107.
Quinn, N.
  1982. "Commitment" in American marriage: A cultural analysis. American Ethnologist 9(4):775-798.
Rappaport, R. A.
  1979. On cognized models. *In* Ecology, Meaning, and Religion. Richmond, Calif.: North Atlantic Books. Pp. 97-144.
Rice, G.
  1980. On cultural schemata. American Ethnologist 7(1):152-171.

Socolow, R. H., ed.
  1978. Saving Energy in the Home: Princeton's Experiments at Twin Rivers. Cam-
    bridge, Mass.: Ballinger.
Wiener, N.
  1948. Cybernetics, or Control and Communication in the Animal and the
    Machine. New York: M.I.T. Press and John Wiley and Sons. (2nd ed. 1961)
Williams, R. H., G. S. Dutt, and H. S. Geller
  1983. Future energy savings in U.S. housing. Annual Review of Energy
    8:269–332.
Wiser, M. and S. Carey
  1983. When heat and temperature were one. *In* Mental Models, D. Gentner and
    A. L. Stevens, eds. Hillsdale, N.J.: Lawrence Erlbaum Associates. Pp.
    267–297.

10
How people construct mental models[1]

Allan Collins & Dedre Gentner

Analogies are powerful ways to understand how things work in a new domain. We think this is because analogies enable people to construct a structure–mapping that carries across the way the components in a system interact. This allows people to create new mental models that they can then run to generate predictions about what should happen in various situations in the real world. This paper shows how analogies can be used to construct models of evaporation and how two subjects used such models to reason about evaporation.

As Lakoff and Johnson (1980) have documented, our language is full of metaphor and analogy. People discuss conversation as a physical transfer: (e.g., "Let's see if I can get this across to you" (Reddy 1979). They analogize marriage to a manufactured object: (e.g., "They had a basic solid foundation in their marriages that could be shaped into something good" (Quinn this volume). They speak of anger as a hot liquid in a container (Lakoff & Kövecses this volume); and they describe their home thermostat as analogous to the accelerator on a car (Kempton this volume).

Why are analogies so common? What exactly are they doing for us? We believe people use them to create generative mental models, models they can use to arrive at new inferences. In this paper, we first discuss the general notion of a generative mental model, using three examples of artificial intelligence models of qualitative physics; second, we lay out the analogy hypothesis of the paper, which we illustrate in terms of the component analogies that enter into mental models of evaporation; and finally, we describe how two subjects used these analogies in reasoning about evaporation.

The notion of running a generative model can be illustrated by an example from Waltz (1981). People hearing "The dachshund bit the mailman on the nose" spontaneously imagine scenarios such as the dachshund standing on a ledge, or the mailman bending down to pet the dachshund. Similarly, if you try to answer the question, "How far can you throw a potato chip?" your thought processes may have the feel of a mental simulation. Examples such as these suggest that simulation and generative inference are integral to language understanding (Waltz 1981). However, such

Table 10.1. *Examples of liquids in different states (after Hayes 1985)*

	Supported on surface	Supported in space	Unsupported
Still, in Bulk	Liquid on a wet surface	Liquid in a container	–
Moving, in Bulk	Liquid flowing on a surface, e.g., a roof	Liquid pumped in pipe	Liquid pouring from a container
Still, Divided	Dew drops on a surface	Mist filling a valley?	Cloud
Moving, Divided	Raindrops on a window	Mist rolling down a valley?	Rain

imagistic descriptions have a magical quality, which we try to resolve in terms of the formalisms of mental models research.

Inference and qualitative simulation become possible when the internal structure of a model is specified in terms of connections between components whose input–output functions are known. Hayes (1985) and de Kleer (1977) have independently tried to characterize how people decompose different systems in order to reason about the world. Both came up with tacit partitions of the world in order to simulate what will happen in a particular situation. Hayes attacked the problem of how people reason about liquids and de Kleer how they reason about sliding objects. Forbus (1981) later extended the de Kleer analysis to bouncing balls moving through two dimensions. Understanding these ideas is central to our argument about the role of analogies in constructing mental models, so we briefly review the way these three authors partition the world in order to construct qualitative simulations.

Hayes (1985) partitions the possible states of liquids into a space with three dimensions: (1) whether the liquid is moving or still; (2) whether it is in bulk or divided (e.g., a lake vs. mist); and (3) whether it is on a surface, supported in space, or unsupported. For example, rain is liquid that is moving, divided, and unsupported, whereas pouring liquid is moving, in bulk, and unsupported. Spilled liquid is still, in bulk, and on a surface except when it is first moving on the surface. Hayes gives examples for most of the possible states in these three dimensions (see Table 10.1), except some that are impossible (e.g., bulk liquid that is both still and unsupported).

Hayes shows how one can construct transitions between different liquid states using a small number of possible transition types in order to construct "a history" of some event. He illustrates this with the example of pouring milk from a cup onto a table. Initially, the milk is contained in

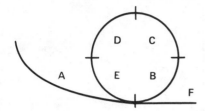

Figure 10.1. Partitioning of loop-the-loop track (after de Kleer 1977)

bulk in the cup as it is tipped. When the surface reaches the lip of the cup, there begins a falling from the cup to the table, which extends through time until the cup is empty, except for the wetness on its surface. Beginning at the point when the falling liquid hits the table, there is a spreading of the liquid on the table top until the pool of liquid reaches the table edge. At that point, another falling starts along the length of the edge that the spreading reaches. This falling continues until there is only a wetness on the table top. The falling also initiates a spreading on the floor, which lasts until there is a nonmoving wetness covering an area of the floor. Because people can construct this kind of history out of their knowledge of liquid states and the transitions between them, they can simulate what will happen if you pour a cup of milk on a table. Alternatively, if they find liquid on the floor and table, they can imagine how it got there.

In the roller coaster world that de Kleer (1977) has analyzed, he partitions the kinds of track a ball might roll along into concave, convex, and straight tracks. de Kleer uses a small number of allowable transitions – for example, slide forward, slide back, and fall – to construct a simulation of the behavior of a ball on a loop-the-loop track such as shown in Figure 10.1. In the figure, the track starts in segment *A* and continues up and around through segments *B, C, D, E,* and *F.*

By constructing all possible continuations for a given input, one forms a directed graph, which de Kleer calls the *envisionment.* Each alternative transition is a branch that can be followed out. Suppose one starts a ball rolling at the end of segment *A.* It will slide forward to segment *B.* From *B*, it can slide forward into *C* or slide back to *A.* If a slide forward occurs, then the ball can either slide forward into *D* or fall. Sliding backward from *B* into *A* leads to oscillation.

The same sort of branching of possible states occurs in Hayes's physics of liquids. For example, in the milk-pouring episode, the spread of milk on the table may never reach the edge, in which case the episode ends with wetness on the table and in the cup. Thus, using qualitative models can allow a person to generate all the different possible events that might happen.

Forbus (1981) has made a similar analysis of bouncing balls in two-dimensional space. To do this, he developed a vocabulary for partition-

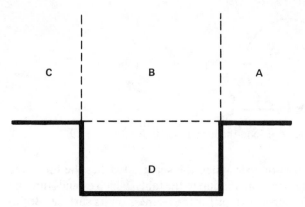

Figure 10.2. Partitioning of two-dimensional space above a well (after Forbus)

ing space into places in which significantly different behaviors can occur. In this model, the qualitative state of an object at a given moment consists of a place, an activity (e.g.: *fly* or *collide*), and a direction (e.g., *left and up*). As in the other two models discussed, simulation rules specify the allowable transitions between qualitative states. Figure 10.2 shows his example of how a space above a well would be partitioned into regions.

Table 10.2 shows the allowable state transitions for a ball moving in a region. The table shows the region in which the ball will be next (including "same") and its next direction. What the ball will do next – its next activity – depends on the kind of place it enters next. If the next place is a surface, the next activity is a collision; otherwise, the next activity will be a continuation of its present motion. If we begin with a ball in region *A* that is headed left and down, it can either go downward and collide with the surface below *A,* or go into the middle region *B,* where its direction will also be left and down. From *B,* going left and down, it can either go into the lower region *D* or into the left region *C,* still heading left and down. If it goes into *D,* it can collide either with the left side wall or with the bottom. Collisions with vertical walls reverse the left–right direction; collisions with horizontal walls reverse the up–down direction. As should be evident, it is possible to imagine a number of different paths for the ball to travel, only some of which end up with the ball caught in the well.

The point of these examples is that they illustrate how people might be able to construct mental models that have the introspective feel of manipulating images (Kosslyn 1980). Put in the terms of Hayes, de Kleer, and Forbus, there is no magic to starting a ball moving or a liquid flowing mentally and seeing what happens. You do not have to know in advance what happens, and you do not have to store a mental moving picture of the events. Indeed, you may decide that a particular candidate event

Table 10.2. *Transition rules for a ball moving from region to region in For-bus's (1981) bouncing ball world showing next place and next direction for the case of a ball moving in some region of space*

Direction	Next Place	Next Direction
none	same	D
D	down	D
LD	down	LD
	left	LD
L	same	LD
LU	same	L
	left	L
	left	LU
	up	LU
U	same	D
	up	U
RU	same	R
	right	R
	right	RU
	up	RU
R	same	RD
RD	right	RD
	down	RD

Note: Regions are represented by words and directions by capital letters. Each line represents a next-place, next-direction pair.

could not ever have occurred. All you have to know is what inputs lead to what outputs for each state transition and how those kinds of states are connected together.

The analogy hypothesis

It should by now be clear that qualitative-state models provide a power-ful, versatile way for people to reason about familiar domains in which the states and transitions are known. But what happens when people want to go beyond familiar physical situations and reason about domains, such as evaporation, in which the states and transitions may be unfamiliar or even invisible? Here, we come to the central proposal of this paper, the analogy hypothesis. According to this hypothesis, a major way in which people reason about unfamiliar domains is through analogical mappings. They use analogies to map the set of transition rules from a known domain (the base) into the new domain (the target), thereby constructing a mental model that can generate inferences in the target domain. Any system whose transition rules are reasonably well specified can serve as an analogical model for understanding a new system (Collins & Gentner, 1982; Gentner 1982).

So far, this analogy hypothesis is a special case of Gentner's (1982; 1983; Gentner & Gentner 1983) more general claim that analogy is a mapping of structural relations from a base domain to a target domain that allows people to carry across inferences from the base to the target. To construct a mental model in a new domain, a particularly powerful set of relations to map across is the transition rules between states. These rules allow one to generate inferences and create simulations in the target domain analogous to the ones that can be performed in the base domain.

However, the situation is often more complicated. Often, no one base domain seems to provide an adequate analogy for all the phenomena in the target domain. In these cases, we find that people partition the target system into a set of component models, each mapped analogically from a different base system. As we demonstrate, people vary greatly in the degree to which they connect these component models into a consistent whole. An extreme case of inconsistency is the *pastiche model,* in which a target domain model is given by a large number of minianalogies, each covering only a small part of the domain and each somewhat inconsistent with the others. At the other extreme, some people connect together their component models into a consistent overall model. Thus, they can combine the results of their mappings to make predictions about how the overall target system will behave.

The remainder of this paper illustrates the analogy hypothesis by showing how analogies can be used to construct different versions of a molecular model of evaporation (see Stevens & Collins 1980). We then show how two subjects used these analogies to reason about evaporation.

A molecular model of evaporation involves a set of component subprocesses:

1. How molecules behave in the water
2. How molecules escape from the water to the air
3. How molecules behave in the air
4. How molecules return to the water from the air
5. How molecules go from liquid to vapor, and vice versa

Notice that this analysis bears some similarity to the Forbus analysis of bouncing balls. There are two regions, the water and the air, and the transitions (i.e., escape and return) between them. The behavior of the molecules in the water and air describes the transitions that keep the molecules in the same region. There is also a second kind of transition, from liquid to vapor and vice versa. Thus, there are two types of state transi-

SAND-GRAIN MODEL

EQUAL SPEED MODEL

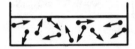

RANDOM SPEED MODEL

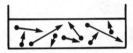

MOLECULAR ATTRACTION MODEL

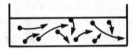

Figure 10.3. Component models of the behavior of molecules in water

tions that occur for evaporation processes: from one region to another, and from one phase to another.

We contrast different possible views of each of these component processes. Some of these views we have clearly identified in subjects' protocols; others are only alluded to. Where the protocols were unclear as to which of two alternative models was implied, we have generally included both models. This is not an exhaustive set of all possible component models but only of those that were suggested in subjects' protocols. However, they do show how people can derive their views from different analogies.

BEHAVIOR IN WATER

Figure 10.3 shows four different analogical models that subjects might have of how molecules behave in water. The first view we call the *sand-grain model* – the molecules just sit there like grains of sand, moving and slipping when something pushes on them. The temperature of the water

HEAT THRESHOLD MODEL

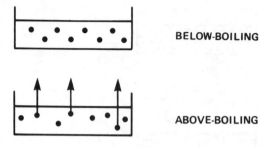

BELOW-BOILING

ABOVE-BOILING

ROCKETSHIP and MOLECULAR ESCAPE MODELS

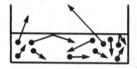

Figure 10.4. Component models of how water molecules escape from water to air

is the average temperature of the individual molecules. This is a very primitive model. The next two views assume that the molecules are bouncing around in the water like billiard balls in random directions (Collins & Gentner 1983). In both views, the speed of the molecules reflects the temperature of the water. The difference is that in one version – the *equal speed model* – all the molecules are moving at the same speed. The other version is a *random speed model,* which allows for differences in speed for different particles. On this view, temperature reflects the average speed of a collection of molecules. The fourth view, called the *molecular attraction model,* incorporates attraction between molecules into the random speed model. In it, molecules move around randomly, but their paths are highly constrained by the attractive (or repulsive) electrical forces between molecules. This view is essentially correct.

ESCAPE FROM THE WATER

Figure 10.4 shows three possible component models for escape (pictorially, two are the same). What we labeled the *heat-threshold* model is a threshold view of escape: The molecules have to reach some temperature, such as the boiling point of the liquid, and then they pop out of the liquid, the way popcorn pops out of the pan when it is heated. The remaining two models focus on molecular velocity, rather than on the incorrect notion of molecular temperature. The *rocketship model* is based on the assumption that the molecules in the water are moving in random direc-

CONTAINER MODEL

VARIABLE-SIZE-ROOM MODEL

COLD AIR   WARM AIR

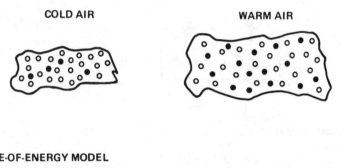

EXCHANGE-OF-ENERGY MODEL

COLD AIR   WARM AIR

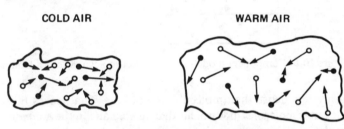

Figure 10.5. Component models of the behavior of water molecules in air (water molecules are filled circles, air molecules are open circles)

tions. To escape from the water (like a rocketship from the earth), a molecule must have an initial velocity in the vertical direction sufficient to escape from gravity. The third view, the *molecular escape model,* posits that the initial velocity must be great enough to escape from the molecular attraction of the other molecules. Both latter models are in part correct, but the major effect is due to the molecular attraction of the water.

BEHAVIOR IN THE AIR

Three component models of how the water molecules behave in the air are depicted in Figure 10.5. The *container model* posits that the air holds water molecules and air molecules mixed together until it is filled up (at 100% humidity). The *variable-size-room model* is a refinement of the container model to account for the fact that warm air holds more moisture than cold air. In this model, molecules in warm air are further apart and

CROWDED ROOM MODEL

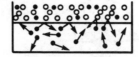

AGGREGATION MODEL

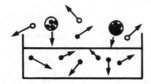

RECAPTURE MODEL

Figure 10.6. Component models of how water molecules return from air to water

so are less dense than molecules in cold air. That leaves more space to put water molecules in warm air than in cold air. In the *exchange-of-energy model,* the chief reason that cold air holds less moisture than warm air is that its air molecules are less energetic. When water molecules in the air collide with air molecules, they are more likely to give up energy if the air is cold (and hence less energetic) than if it is warm. If the water molecules become less energetic, they are more easily captured by the molecular attraction of other water molecules (or a nucleus particle) in the air. When enough water molecules aggregate, they will precipitate. This latter view is essentially correct.[2]

RETURN TO THE WATER

Figure 10.6 shows three models of how water molecules return to the water. The *crowded room model* assumes that when all the space in the air is filled, no more water molecules can get in. This is more a prevention-of-escape model than a return model. The *aggregation model* assumes that water molecules move around in the air until they encounter a nucleus or particle (which could be another water molecule) around which water accumulates. The less energetic the molecule, the more likely it is to be caught by the molecular attraction of the particle. As these particles ac-cumulate water, gravitational forces overcome the random movement of the particles and they precipitate. The *recapture model* assumes that particles are attracted by the surface of the water (or other surfaces). The less energy they have, the more likely they are to be recaptured. The action in this view takes place near the surface, unlike the aggregation view. A fourth possibility is to ignore return processes altogether. Some of our subjects described evaporation solely in terms of water leaving the liquid state and appeared unaware of any need to consider the other direction, of water vapor returning to the liquid state. Both the aggregation and the recapture models are essentially correct, but the aggregation model takes place over a long time period with relatively high humidities, whereas the recapture model is applicable in any situation in which evaporation is occurring.

LIQUID-VAPOR TRANSITION
Figure 10.7 shows four different views we have identified for the transition from liquid to vapor and from vapor to liquid. One view, *the coterminus model,* is that the transition occurs when the molecules leave the

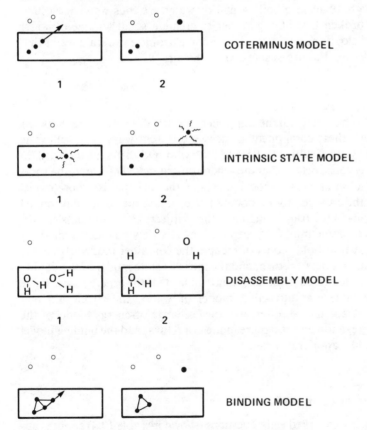

Figure 10.7. Component models of the liquid–vapor transition

water and escape to the air, and vice versa. In this view, the two transitions, between water and air, and between liquid and vapor, are the same transition. In other words, whether a molecule is in the vapor or liquid state depends solely on the location: All molecules beneath the surface of the water are liquid, and all molecules above the surface of the water are vapor. A second view, *the intrinsic state model,* treats the liquid or gas state as an intrinsic property of the molecule. If the molecule becomes hot enough, it changes from liquid to vapor, and if it becomes cold enough, it changes from vapor to liquid. Location is correlated with state in that molecules in the vapor state tend to move into the air, whereas molecules in the liquid state remain in the water. A third view, *the disassembly model,* is based on a little chemistry: In it, liquid water is thought of as made up of molecules of H_2O, whereas the hydrogen and oxygen are thought to be separated in water vapor. The expert view, which we call the *binding model,* is based on molecular attraction: Water molecules in the liquid state are partially bound together by electrical attraction of the neighboring molecules, whereas molecules in the gaseous state bounce around rather freely. The bubbles in a boiling pan of water are thus water molecules that have broken free of each other to create a small volume of water vapor, and clouds and mist are microscopic droplets of liquid water that have condensed but are suspended in the air.

COMBINING COMPONENT MODELS

Table 10.3 summarizes all the component models described here. Subjects can combine these component models in different ways. The following section shows two subjects, *RS* and *PC,* who had different models. *RS* had a model constructed from the random speed model of water, the rocketship or molecular escape model of escape, the variable-size-room-model of the air, the crowded room model of return, and the coterminus model of the liquid–vapor transition. The other subject, *PC,* had a less consistent and less stable model of evaporation. His view included something like the heat-threshold model of escape, the container model of the air, the recapture model of return, and the intrinsic state model of the liquid–vapor transition. In contrast, as we have indicated, the expert view is made up of the molecular attraction model of water, the rocketship and molecular escape models of escape, the exchange-of-energy model of the air, the aggregation and recapture models of return, and the binding model of the liquid–vapor transition.

An experiment on mental models

Four subjects were asked eight questions (shown in Table 10.4) about evaporation. They were asked to explain their reasoning on each question. The

Table 10.3. *Component models of evaporation*

Models of Water
  Sand–Grain Model
  Equal Speed Model
  Random Speed Model
  Molecular Attraction Model

Models of Escape
  Heat-Threshold Model
  Rocketship Model
  Molecular Escape Model

Models of Air
  Container Model
  Variable-Size-Room Model
  Exchange-Of-Energy Model

Models of Return
  Crowded Room Model
  Aggregation Model
  Recapture Model

Models of Liquid–Vapor Transition
  Coterminus Model
  Intrinsic State Model
  Disassembly Model
  Binding Model

Table 10.4. *Evaporation questions*

Question 1. Which is heavier, a quart container full of water or a quart container full of steam?

Question 2. Why can you see your breath on a cold day?

Question 3. If you put a thin layer of oil on a lake, would you increase, decrease, or cause no change in the rate of evaporation from the lake?

Question 4. Which will evaporate faster, a pan of hot water placed in the refrigerator or the same pan left at room temperature and why?

Question 5. Does evaporation affect water temperature, and if so how? Why or why not?

Question 6. If you wanted to compress some water vapor into a smaller space but keep the pressure constant, what would you do? Why?

Question 7. On a hot humid day, you must sweat *more* or *less* or *the same amount* as on a hot dry day at the same temperature. Why?

Question 8. If you had two glasses of water sealed in an air-tight container, and one was half filled with pure water, while the other half was filled with salt water, what would you expect to happen after a long period of time (say about a month)? Why?

subjects were two male Harvard undergraduates, one female secretary with a college degree, and one female doctoral student in history. All were reasonably intelligent but were novices about evaporation processes. Our analysis centers on the first two subjects because they best illustrate the kind of reasoning we see in novice subjects.

ANALYSIS OF SUBJECT *RS*'S MODEL OF
EVAPORATION PROCESSES

The first subject (*RS*) has a model of evaporation processes based on (1) the random speed model of water, (2) some variation of either the rocketship or the molecular escape model of escape, (3) the variable-size-room model of the air, (4) the crowded room model of return, and (5) the coterminus model of the liquid–vapor transition. His view includes notions of the energy needed for molecules to escape from a body of water and the difficulty water molecules have in entering a cold air mass because of the higher density. He seems to share a common misconception with the second subject: namely, that visible clouds (such as one sees coming out of a boiling kettle) are made up of water vapor rather than recondensed liquid water. This misconception forced him into several wrong explanations, even though his reasoning powers are impressive. As we show, he seems to check out his reasoning by running different models of evaporation processes (Stevens & Collins 1980) and to try to account for any differences in results when he finds them.

We present the most relevant portions of his responses to three of the questions and our analysis of his reasoning processes (omitted portions of his response are indicated by dots).

Q2: On a cold day you can see your breath. Why?
RS: I think again this is a function of the water content of your breath that you are breathing out. On a colder day it makes what would normally be an invisible gaseous expansion of your breath (or whatever), it makes it more dense. The cold temperature causes the water molecules to be more dense and that in turn makes it visible relative to the surrounding gases or relative to what your breath would be on a warmer day, when you don't get that cold effect causing the water content to be more dense. . . . So I guess I will stick with that original thinking process that it is the surrounding cold air – that the cold air surrounding your expired breath causes the breath itself (which has a high water content and well I guess carbon dioxide and whatever else a human being expels when you breathe out), causes the entire gaseous matter to become more dense and as a consequence become visible relative to the surrounding air.

What in fact happens on a cold day is that the invisible water vapor in one's breath condenses, because it is rapidly cooled. This condensed liquid water is visible as clouds or mist. However, the subject did not know that the clouds were liquid rather than water vapor, since he seems to think of water molecules in the air as vapor by definition (i.e., the coterminus model), so he needed to find some other account of what happens. For

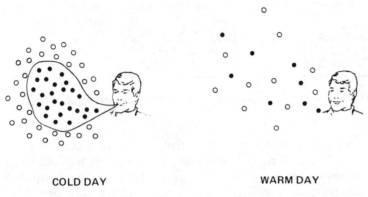

COLD DAY   WARM DAY

Figure 10.8. *RS*'s model of why you see your breath on a cold day

that, he turned to his knowledge that cold air masses are more dense than warm air masses – his protocol includes a clear statement of the variable-size-room model of the air. Our depiction of the process he imagined is shown in Figure 10.8.

What his view seems to involve is a vapor-filled gas cloud being emitted from a person's mouth. On a cold day, the surrounding air cools the emitted breath, causing it to compact into a small visible cloud. The denser the breath, the more visible it is. This latter inference has its analogue with smoke or mist: The more densely packed they are, the more visible they are. In fact, as the breath disperses, the particles become less visible. This suggests that the subject may be invoking an analogy, not explicitly mentioned, to the behavior of smoke or mist in constructing his model.

The next protocol segment clearly illustrates his belief in the variable-size-room model of the air and the crowded room model of return.

Q4: Which will evaporate faster, a pan of hot water placed in the refrigerator or the same pan left at room temperature? Why?

RS: When I first read that question, my initial impression, that putting a pan of hot water in the refrigerator you suddenly have these clouds of vapor in it, threw me off for a second. I was thinking in terms of there is a lot of evaporation. Well I guess, as I thought through it more, I was thinking that it was not an indication of more evaporation, but it was just (let us say) the same evaporation. Immediately when you put it in anyway, it was more visible. Ahmm, as I think through it now, my belief is that it would evaporate less than the same pan left standing at room temperature and my reasoning there is that the air in the refrigerator is going to be relatively dense relative to the room temperature air, because at a colder temperature again its molecules are closer together and that in effect leaves less room to allow the molecules from the hot water to join the air. . . .

Here, the subject first simulates what happens at the macroscopic level when you put a pan of hot water in the refrigerator. He imagines clouds

COOL AIR MASS   WARM AIR MASS

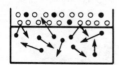 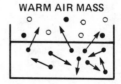

Figure 10.9. *RS*'s model of evaporation from a hot pan of water in the refrigerator

of steam coming out of the pan and initially thinks there must be more evaporation. It is unlikely he would ever have seen what happens when you put a pan of hot water in a refrigerator. He probably constructed this process from some analogous situation(s), such as warm breath on a cold day, running hot water in a cold room, or mist rising off a lake, for example. He is correct about the visible clouds of vapor, but as he concluded later, these clouds do not represent more evaporation. In fact, they represent condensation of the evaporated moisture (which he did not know).

This subject frequently considers different perspectives on a question. Thus, he did not stop with his macroscopic analysis; he also simulated what would happen at a microscopic level. Figure 10.9 shows his view of why cold air leads to less evaporation. It is a clear statement of what we have called the crowded room model. There is not enough space, so some of the water molecules bounce back into the water, as shown in the picture, whereas they do not when the air is warm. This is an incorrect model that *RS* probably constructed on his own. However, it leads to a correct prediction in this case.

The last protocol segment shows *RS* following three different lines of reasoning:

Q5:   Does evaporation affect water temperature? If so, in what way, and why?
RS: . . . My initial impression is that it doesn't. It does not affect the water temperature. The surfaces of that water, the exterior surfaces of that water are in
contact with air or some other gaseous state, which allow molecules from the
water to evaporate into that other gaseous substance. So I guess I don't see where
the loss of water molecules would affect the water temperature.

In a way, however, I guess those water molecules that do leave the surface
of the water are those that have the highest amounts of energy. I mean, they
can actually break free of the rest of the water molecules and go out into the
air. Now if they have a, if they are the ones with the most energy, I guess generally heat is what will energize molecules, then that would lead me to believe
that maybe, although it may not be measurable, maybe with sophisticated instruments it is, but maybe it would be measurable after your most energetic molecules have left the greater body of water. Those that remain are less energetic
and therefore their temperature perhaps is less than when all of the molecules
that have already left or were a part of the whole. So I guess that has led me
into a circle to perhaps change my initial response – maybe now I could im-

agine where even if not measurable because of a lack of a sensitive enough instrument, maybe my logic or nonlogic (whichever the case may be) has allowed me to believe that maybe there is an effect on the water temperature. So I feel pretty good about it . . . . I guess even the original model with the sun striking the surface of water, that I thought initially, threw me off. Maybe that is accurate too, because the sun's rays certainly don't go down to the bottom. So I guess it depends how deep we are talking, of course. But it would penetrate only so far into the surface of the lake and energize those layers that are at the top surface of the lake or water, whatever the body of water is. So those top layers would then be more energized than deeper layers, and it would obviously be more able to evaporate off. As they evaporate off, assuming conditions are constant and you have got a situation where the succeeding layers get struck by the same heat energy, in this case the sun, from the sun. And they become as the preceding layers were, they become energized and then go off. You are left with less and less water, where a surface is at a given temperature and the rest is at a lower temperature, but your volume is less. So therefore it sounds like again, I am getting to the point where the average temperature would increase, ahmn, because you have less volume, but the surface is at a higher energy level then as a percentage of the whole.

Initially, he cannot think of any way in which evaporation affects the temperature of the water and starts to conclude that there is no effect. This is a lack-of-knowledge inference, that we discuss elsewhere (Collins 1978; Gentner & Collins 1981).

Then, based on the random speed model of water and either the rocketship or molecular escape model of escape (which make the same prediction here), he infers that the higher energy molecules are the ones that will escape, leaving behind molecules with less energy. This, he infers correctly, will cool the water. Said in another way, molecules headed up from the surface with less energy will not escape, whereas those with more energy will escape. This is a subtle inference that follows directly from the rocketship and molecular escape models. Notice he does not have the misconception that all molecules in the water are moving at the same speed (i.e., the equal speed model). His reasoning depends crucially on variation in speed (i.e., the random speed model).

Later in his response, however, he comes up with an argument that leads to a conclusion opposite to the one above. He realizes that as water evaporates away, there is less water left for the sun to heat. Thus, given a fixed input of energy, the temperature of the water will rise. Why does he adopt this line of reasoning, given that nothing in the question supposed there was any further input of energy? *RS* seems here to be considering a canonical example of evaporation: the sun's warming a lake. Under these conditions, the temperature of the remaining water will indeed rise.

Here, two generative models come into conflict. The first view is based on a microscopic model of molecules escaping. The second view is based on layers of water evaporating, leaving behind less water to be heated by the sun. As in the previous protocol, the subject worked on the problem from different viewpoints; but in this case, two opposing conclusions seemed correct and he did not know how to choose between them.

We have tried to show how RS drew on a set of underlying component models to construct his molecular model of evaporation and how he used his model to find answers to novel questions. Based on this model, RS was able to deal quite successfully with the eight questions (he gave essentially correct answers on seven of eight questions). Nevertheless, his model was incorrect in the ways we have described.

ANALYSIS OF SUBJECT PC'S MODEL OF
EVAPORATION PROCESSES

The second subject, PC had many more difficulties in dealing with these questions. His view was much less coherent. He relied frequently on local analogies to phenomena he had observed or things he had heard about, shifting among them without checking their consistency. This shifting made it difficult to ascertain his models, especially his model of water itself. However, most of his responses suggest that he combined (1) the sand-grain model of water, (2) the heat-threshold model of escape, (3) the container model of the air, (4) the recapture model of return, and (5) the intrinsic state model of the liquid–vapor transition. What is most striking about his view is how he treats heat as an intrinsic property of individual molecules rather than as a property of aggregates of molecules, as experts do.

The first protocol shows PC's response to question two:

Q2: On a cold day you can see your breath; why?
PC: The reason is because the air that you breathe, or rather the air that you should breathe out, comes from your body and is hot air. The air which surrounds your body, because it is a cold day, will be cold air. When the hot air that you breathe meets with the cold air of the atmosphere, it will tend to vaporize almost like steam from a kettle, which of course, can be seen. Thus unlike on a hot day, when there is hot air around you and the hot air that you breathe are the same temperature, roughly, you cannot see your breath because the steam will not be formed, but on a cold day because of the variation in the temperatures and the vaporization of your breath, you can see when you are breathing. This phenomenon would not occur on a hot day because of the similarity in temperature.

This response would be correct as far as it goes if the words *vaporize* and *vaporization* were replaced by the words *condense* and *condensation*. This could be a simple lexical confusion, but other answers suggest it is a conceptual confusion (i.e., he really does think that the visible cloud formed is vapor). One piece of evidence for this belief occurs in answer to question four, where he refers to "the water which has already condensed in the refrigerator" (see below), suggesting he does understand the distinction between vaporizing and condensing. Furthermore, it is a common misconception to think of a cloud of steam as water vapor, rather than recondensed liquid water. His response suggests he does not have a coterminus model of the liquid–vapor transition, as *RS* had, since he sees the transition occurring in the air. Rather, he appears to have constructed a version of the intrinsic state model, where the transition depends on a temperature difference between the air and the liquid water.

His analysis relies on an analogy to a core observation he has seen many times – steam from a kettle. To solve the problem, he has to find some factor in common between one's breath on a cold day and steam from the kettle that is different from one's breath on a warm day. The factor he comes up with is the temperature difference. Boiling water from a kettle is much warmer than room air. Likewise, warm breath is much warmer than air on a cold day. But warm breath is about the same temperature as air on a warm day. Since he believes that steam is vaporized water, he therefore concludes that the temperature difference must somehow cause vaporization of water. He does not push his analysis down to a microscopic level, as did *RS,* to account for how this might be. Instead, he stops with identifying the analogous factor in the two situations.

PC's response to the fourth question shows some of the conceptual problems he has:

Q4:   Does a pan of hot water in the refrigerator evaporate more, less, or the same amount as the same pan left standing at room temperature? Why?

PC: Hmmmm. Hot water, when it meets with – wait a second. Hot water will only evaporate if it is sufficiently heated. By placing the hot water in a refrigerator you are not heating it, you are cooling it, and in fact the reverse process will occur. That is, the water will decrease in temperature and the refrigerator's temperature itself will also decrease. Not only that, but also the water which has already condensed in the refrigerator, because of the heat from the hot water when you put it in the refrigerator, will go into water itself because of the difference in the temperatures. To sum up, the pan of water in the refrigerator will not evaporate at the same rate, but will evaporate at a lesser rate than the same pan left standing at room temperature for the above reason.

This question came soon after the question about breath on a cold day, and *PC* starts out answering the same way, "Hot water, when it meets with – ." This line of reasoning would conclude "the cold air, vaporizes to produce clouds of steam, and so there is more evaporation" just as *RS* has at first imagined and *PC* had argued in response to question two. But *PC* aborted that line of reasoning, whereas *RS* pursued it and ruled it out as incorrect.

The next sentence reveals *PC*'s heat-threshold model of escape: that the temperature of the water has to be sufficiently high (presumably boiling) for evaporation to occur. Sometimes in his answers, *PC* invoked this heat-threshold notion, and other times he violated it.

In answer to the question, *PC* concludes that evaporation will decrease for two reasons. First, the water in the pan will cool, and hence evaporate less or not at all. Second, the water that has condensed in the refrigerator will tend to "return to the pan of water." Both ideas are essentially correct, but there are several incorrect statements associated with the latter argument. One is that the refrigerator's temperature will decrease (just like the water's temperature) because a warm pan of water is put in it – the opposite is in fact true. Then he seems to conclude that the warm temperature of the water will cause condensation because of the temperature difference with the air: a kind of inverse process from the one he argued for in response to question two. In fact, the warmth from the pan of water will tend to reduce condensation.

Nowhere in this or other answers does he regard the air as anything other than a passive container for water and air molecules – he does not mention anything like the variable-room-size model that *RS* described, or the exchange-of-energy model that experts hold. In fact, he seems unaware that cooler air holds less moisture than warm air. However, he does seem to have a notion in this and other answers that molecules from the air will return to the water. This notion seems to depend on what he calls "condensation" in this answer, but not so clearly in other statements he makes. We have characterized this as a recapture model of return, rather than an aggregation model. Even though he seems to say that recapture must be preceded by "condensation," it is not clear that his "condensation" involves aggregation of molecules, as in the expert model. Rather, in keeping with his intrinsic state model of the vapor–liquid transition, "condensation" may be a change in state that occurs individually to each molecule.

PC's answer to the sixth question provides the clearest example of his view of heat as an intrinsic property:

Q6: What would you do if you want to compress some water vapor into a smalller space but keep the pressure constant?
PC: Hot air rises. Vapor is air, ok. Therefore, if you have a greater amount of vapor and you want to compress it, all you do is you heat the vapor so that by heating it, one will be causing the molecules to react faster which would increase the temperature of initially some molecules of steam, which will then go to the top and which will eventually increase the temperature overall, which will all – *all* the molecules will want to go to the top of the container, and as a result one will have a level of steam at the very top of the container and a vacuum at the end of the container – now I have got to get that down. Initially, the temperature of some of the molecules of steam, which because hot air, in this case steam, will always rise above in the colder air, the hotter steam will rise to the top of the container. Eventually, all the molecules of steam will be all trying to get to the top of the container, which will cause a greater density of the gas, i.e., steam, leaving a vacuum at the bottom of the container.

Figure 10.10 represents the microscopic model *PC* constructed to answer this question. He makes a classic error: He applies a correct macroscopic rule incorrectly at the microscopic level (Stevens & Collins 1980). He has

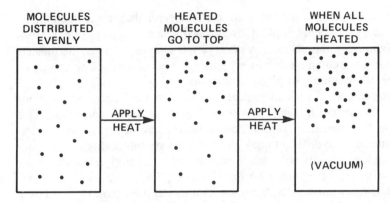

Figure 10.10. *PC*'s model of how to compress water by heating it

learned somewhere that hot air rises. The reason for this is that hot air particles have more energy, on the average, than cold air particles. This causes hot air to be less dense than cool air, and so it rises above cool air. But *PC* applies this aggregate property to individual molecules, where it does not apply. Thus, he imagines that each molecule, if it receives heat energy, will tend to rise to the top. Here, he reveals his view of temperature as intrinsic to individual molecules that underlies his heat-threshold model of escape and his intrinsic state model of the liquid–vapor transition. Eventually, in his view, each molecule will receive heat energy, and so they will all collect at the top, leaving a vacuum at the bottom. The correct answer is just the opposite. Cooling the vapor will cause each molecule to have less energy on the average, and so the same number of molecules will take up less space with no increase in pressure on the side of the container.

PC's reasoning about evaporation is much less consistent than *RS*'s. He shifts around among a variety of principles and models to reason about these questions. Not surprisingly, he is less accurate than *RS*: only three out of eight of his answers were correct, as compared to seven out of eight for *RS*.

Conclusion

This paper traces the way people construct models of evaporation processes by using analogies from other domains. Our thesis is that people construct generative models by using analogy to map the rules of transition and interaction from known domains into unfamiliar domains.

Analogy is a major way in which people derive models of new domains (Gentner 1982; 1983; Gentner & Gentner 1983; Lakoff & Johnson 1980; Rumelhart & Norman 1981; Winston 1980). Analogy can serve to transfer knowledge from a familiar concrete domain to an abstract domain, such as emotions or marriage (cf. Lakoff & Kövecses this volume; Quinn this volume). But even when there are many observable surface phenomena in the target domain, people still rely heavily on analogies in their reasoning. Kempton's (this volume) work on people's models of home thermostats and our research on models of evaporation both show the importance of analogical reasoning in physical domains.

The existence of such analogical models raises two important questions for further research. First, how are different analogies combined? One goal of this paper is to examine how subjects combine component models constructed from different analogies. People vary substantially in the consistency and stability with which they coordinate multiple analogies for a domain. We have shown how one subject, *RS*, combined his component analogies into a relatively consistent model of evaporation and used it to reason fairly correctly about novel questions relating to evaporation processes. His model contrasts with that of another subject, *PC*, with a less coherent understanding of evaporation. *PC* invokes different principles or models for every answer. He aborts one line of reasoning when it contradicts another line of reasoning, without trying to trace the reason for the inconsistency. He uses principles that apply at one level of analysis in reasoning at another level of analysis.

A second, more basic question is, where do these models come from? Although they are partly idiosyncratic, they must be heavily influenced by cultural transmission. If these models were purely experiential, derived independently by each individual, it is unlikely that notions of molecules and temperature would figure so prominently. On the other hand, our subjects' models of such concepts as molecules differ in some rather striking ways from expert models. The interplay between scientific models and the idiosyncratic interpretations that individuals place on them is a topic ripe for serious study.

Notes

1. This research was supported by the Personnel and Training Programs, Psychological Sciences Division, Office of Naval Research, under contract number N00014-79-C-0338, Contract Authority Identification Number NR 154-428. We thank Michael Williams for an engaging conversation on the analogy hypothesis of this paper and Ken Forbus for his comments on a draft of the paper.
2. It is true that, in normal outdoor conditions, warm air tends to be less dense than cool air, as in the variable-size-room model; but the difference in evaporation rate does not require this density difference. Even in a sealed container, warming the air will enable it to hold more water.

References

Collins, A.
    1978. Fragments of a theory of plausible reasoning. *In* Proceedings of Conference on Theoretical Issues in Natural Language Processing, Vol. 2. Urbana: University of Illinois. Pp. 194–201.

Collins, A. and D. Gentner
1982. Constructing runnable mental models. *In* Proceedings of the Fourth Annual Conference of the Cognitive Science Society. Ann Arbor: University of Michigan. Pp. 86–89.
1983. Multiple models of evaporation processes. *In* Proceedings of the Fifth Annual Conference of the Cognitive Science Society. Rochester, N.Y.: University of Rochester.
de Kleer, J.
1977. Multiple representations of knowledge in a mechanics problem solver. *In* Proceedings of the Fifth International Joint Conference on Artificial Intelligence. Cambridge, Mass.: M.I.T. Pp. 299–304.
Forbus, K. D.
1981. A study of qualitative and geometric knowledge in reasoning about motion. M.I.T. AI Technical Report 615. Cambridge, Mass.: M.I.T.
Gentner, D.
1982. Are scientific analogies metaphors? *In* Metaphor: Problems and Perspectives, D. S. Miall, ed. Brighton, England: Harvester Press. Pp. 106–132.
1983. Structure-mapping: A theoretical framework for analogy. Cognitive Science 7(2):155–170.
Gentner, D. and A. Collins
1981. Inference from lack of knowledge. Memory and Cognition 9:434–443.
Gentner, D. and D. R. Gentner
1983. Flowing waters or teeming crowds: Mental models of electricity. *In* Mental Models, D. Gentner and A. L. Stevens, eds. Hillsdale, N.J.: Lawrence Erlbaum Associates. Pp. 99–129.
Hayes, P.
1985. Ontology for liquids. *In* Formal Theories of the Commonsense World, J. Hobbs and R. Moore, eds. Norwood, N.J.: Ablex. Pp. 71–108.
Kosslyn, S.
1980. Image and Mind. Cambridge, Mass.: Harvard University Press.
Lakoff, G. and M. Johnson
1980. Metaphors We Live By. Chicago: University of Chicago Press.
Reddy, M.
1979. The conduit metaphor. *In* Metaphor and Thought, A. Ortony, ed. Cambridge, England: Cambridge University Press. Pp. 284–324.
Rumelhart, D. E. and D. A. Norman
1981. Analogical processes in learning. *In* Cognitive Skills and Their Acquisition, J. R. Anderson, ed. Hillside, N.J.: Lawrence Erlbaum Associates. Pp. 335–359.
Stevens, A. L. and A. Collins
1980. Multiple conceptual models of a complex system. *In* Aptitude, Learning and Instruction, Vol. 2, R. E. Snow, P. Federico, and W. E. Montague, eds. Hillsdale, N.J.: Lawrence Erlbaum Associates. Pp. 177–197.
Waltz, D. L.
1981. Toward a detailed model of processing for language describing the physical world. *In* Proceedings of the Seventh International Joint Conference on Artificial Intelligence, Ann Drinan, ed. Vancouver: University of British Columbia. Pp. 1–6.
Winston, P. H.
1980. Learning and reasoning by analogy. Communications of the ACM 23:689–703.

PART IV
Negotiating social and psychological realities

11
Myth and experience in the Trobriand Islands[1]

Edwin Hutchins

This chapter examines how the knowledge of a myth is brought to bear on the interpretation of experience. This topic requires an eclectic approach since the issues it raises are simultaneously part of a venerable tradition in anthropology concerning the role of myth in society and part of a new research area in cognitive science concerning the nature of the processes by which people interpret and understand their world.

The experiences to be interpreted are those surrounding an encounter between a Trobriand Island village and the spirit of one of its recently deceased members. I begin with a brief ethnographic sketch of the nature of spirits of the dead in the Trobriand Islands, which will enable the reader to make sense of the events reported. The next section describes an actual case of a spirit haunting a village. This haunting set the stage for the phenomenon we wish to understand – that is, an old woman's account of how she saw a cosmological question in these events and how a sacred myth provided her with an answer to her question. The heart of the paper is an examination of the relationship between the myth itself and the phenomena it is marshaled to explain. I argue that the myth has two kinds of connections to experience. One is an explicit link based on a belief in the power of mythic events as historical precedents. The events in the myth are seen as causes of important aspects of the experience. The second kind of connection is an implicit and unadmitted link based on a similarity of organization between the events of the myth and the experience of events of life. Although the historical link is emphasized by Trobrianders, an examination of the implicit link based on shared structure shows the myth to be a transformed description of repressed thoughts about contemporary relations between the living and spirits of the dead. That is, the myth is shown to be a cultural defence mechanism. I conclude with a discussion of how this role of myth bears on two otherwise anomalous properties of myths: the tenacity of native belief and the radical disjunction between historical time and mythic time.

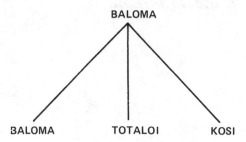

Figure 11.1. Classes of spirits of the dead

The ways of the spirits

The class of beings that are spirits of the dead in the Trobriands all fall under the generic term *baloma*. In some contexts, including the recitation of myth, the archaic term *yaluwa* may be used instead. Within the category of spirits of the dead are several subcategories that partition the world of spirits on the basis of some of their salient attributes (see Figure 11.1). Each category has a specific term associated with it. It is important to note that *baloma* occurs both as a generic term for all spirits of the dead and as an unmarked specific term that can stand in contrast to other specific types of spirits.

BALOMA

Before the marked terms can be discussed, more needs to be said about the nature of the unmarked specific category of *baloma*.[2] When a person dies, his or her *baloma* leaves the body and goes to reside on the island of Tuma, a real island located about 10 miles northwest of the main island in the Trobriand group. Arriving at Tuma, the *baloma* meets a spirit named Topileta, who "acts as a kind of Cerebus or St. Peter in so far as he admits the spirit into the nether world, and is even supposed to be able to refuse admission" (Malinowski 1954:156).

The *baloma* "live" normal lives on Tuma and return to their natal villages during the harvest season each year to partake of the spiritual goodness of harvested yams and valuables placed for them on special platforms out of doors. While they are in the village, the *baloma* sometimes indulge in mildly annoying pranks, such as making noises and moving things, but people do not find them eerie nor do they fear them the way Europeans fear ghosts. At the end of the harvest feast, the *baloma* are unceremoniously driven from the village by gangs of children who shout and swing sticks. This driving-out is called *yoba*. The *baloma* then return to Tuma, where they remain until the next year's harvest feast.

At any time of the year, *baloma* may intercede invisibly in human affairs by bringing bad luck to people who have behaved badly. For example, a village that is constantly embroiled in petty squabbles may find a poor harvest because the *baloma* of the village feel that the people have not comported themselves with dignity.

Baloma frequently appear in dreams or even to people who are awake to announce to a woman that she will become pregnant or to suggest a course of action to an important person. In such cases, the *baloma* is seen and recognized as a person who once lived. The only other circumstances in which *baloma* are visible to the living are those near the boundary of life and death. A person on a deathbed may see into the spirit world while speaking to those in the world of the living who are keeping the death vigil. Also, the spirits of the recently deceased may appear to the living. In the latter case, the terminology of spirits of the dead is elaborated in reference to the behavior of the spirits.

TOTALOI

The spirits of the recently dead sometimes linger for a day or two after death to say good-bye to loved-ones. They may present themselves to persons either in dream or awake. These spirits are called *totaloi,* from the root *-taloi,* referring to the minor rituals of leave-taking performed by socially engaged persons when they part company. Such encounters are sad, but not at all frightening. For example, the spirit of a young girl appeared to her mother the day after her death to request that her favorite hymn be sung in church.

KOSI

Other spirits called *kosi* stay around the village longer and frighten people. They are much more malevolent than *baloma*. When a *kosi* is in a village at night, villagers say that it "rounds the village." The verb "round" describes the movement of the spirit from house to house through the roughly circular layout of the village. The literalness of this usage was not apparent to me until, on the nights of the encounter described below, I could actually follow the progress of the *kosi* as the screams of those visited emanated first from one part of the village, then from another.

The unpleasantness and the duration of visits from *kosi* are said to be related to the social character of the deceased while he or she was alive. If the deceased was a sorcerer, an adulterer, or a thief, for example, the *kosi* is expected to be malicious and will remain in the village for a long time. Some of my informants speculated, in contradiction to Malinowski (1954:156), that the reason the *kosi* of evil people stay in the village for a long time is that Topileta refuses them entry at Tuma and they then have no place to go.[3]

According to Malinowski (1954:154), *kosi* are only encountered out of doors. In the days following the death of a villager, the sound of footfall in darkness on a jungle path at night or the otherwise unexplained rustling of vegetation in the deceased's garden enclosure may be taken as evidence of the presence of a *kosi*. In the village, a *kosi* might call out a person's name or throw a stone or slap the thatched wall of a house much as a *baloma* might do during the harvest season. Summing up the reaction of Trobrianders in his times, Malinowski called *kosi,* "the frivolous and meek ghost of the deceased who vanishes after a few days of irrelevant existence" (1954:154). Modern-day Trobrianders agree that Malinowski's description is an accurate depiction of the behavior of *kosi* in the past, but times have changed. In more recent times, in addition to frightening people with their poltergeistlike activities out of doors, *kosi* have taken to confronting people in a visible form in their homes as they lie in what we would call hypnagogic sleep. The Trobrianders call this state *kilisala* and describe it as resting with the eyes closed, but with the ears open and the mind awake. They are adamant that it is not sleep, and the events experienced in that state are real events of this world, not dreams or hallucinations. The assertion that these events are real is supported by items of evidence such as the fact that *kosi* knock things off of shelves and throw stones on the roof when everyone is wide awake. In those contexts though, the *kosi* is not seen.

Encounter with a kosi

In March 1976, Toigisasopa (a pseudonym), a prominent and feared citizen of a large Trobriand village, died. For more than a month following his death, the village was plagued by almost nightly visits from his *kosi*. Occasionally, the *kosi* appeared as the ghoulish figure of the rotting corpse of the deceased. As time went on, his reported appearance became increasingly revolting.

The following is a translation of an excerpt of an interview with a woman who had twice been visited by this *kosi*.

He was out walking about and he came to our place. I woke and saw him come in. His face was awful – completely black, his arms and legs were like those of an undernourished child and his belly was bloated. He just came in and grabbed my legs. I lay there. My body was completely numb and paralysed. Then I kicked and the old man [her husband] felt me kicking. He roused me and I grabbed him and cried out. He asked, "What was it?" "Toigisasopa's ghost!" By then my body was recovering from numbness a bit. The stench was awful. The first time he just looked black, but this second time, you know, it was as if there were holes in his body as well. It gave the house a terrible odor.

Myth interprets life

For nearly a month, I heard reports of the activities of the ghost. Many villagers reported evidence of the *kosi*'s presence, and the village as a whole was quite disturbed by the length of the stay of the *kosi*.[4] Near the end of Toigisasopa's stay in the village, an old woman came to me with the following account.

One night as she lay in her house, she heard banging on the side of her neighbor's house and heard her neighbors yelling to drive the *kosi* away. She later reported:

I had gotten up and was sitting there. I thought, "perhaps that was a *kosi*." This one will not soon disappear because when he went to Tuma, Topileta closed [the way in]. Because he was a thief. He stole seed yams in the garden, and whatever he saw unattended in the village he would put in his basket as well. Everyone saw him do it. You see, this was his one bad habit. It was nothing of consequence; he seemed a good man except for this. Now he has died. Who knows, perhaps he was a sorcerer, perhaps . . . . Anyway, I thought to myself, "Why is it that the *kosi* and *baloma* see us, but we do not see them?"

She said that in considering this question, she remembered that it had not always been so. Long ago, the *baloma* would come into the village and sit with their kin, chewing betel nut and conversing in a pleasant way. They were generally amicable and even helpful. This old woman remembered the myth of Baroweni, and it, she claimed, provided the answers to her questions.

Myths form one of several classes of oral tradition in the Trobriands. The major distinction of importance here is between sacred myths, called *liliu* or *libogwa*, and folk tales, *kukwanebu*. Both *liliu* and *kukwanebu* are sometimes performed in the story-telling sessions that occupy many idle hours in the rainy season. The events that are depicted in both genres are placed in time long, long ago beyond the stretch of ordinary historical time. *Kukwanebu* are told largely for their entertainment value, and tend to be a bit bawdy, whereas *liliu* are thought to have a message and the events they describe are often taken as historical precedents for the states of affairs in the contemporary world. Some myths establish sociocultural precedents concerning the ownership of land and the ranking of descent groups. Others concern fundamental states of existence, such as the inevitability of aging and death or, in the myth of Baroweni, the invisibility of the spirits of the dead.

THE MYTH OF BAROWENI

A full translation of the telling of the myth as I recorded it is given below. I have included some additional commentary on a paragraph-by-paragraph basis where the telling of the myth assumes listener knowledge that is particular to Trobriand culture. By and large, these are things that from the Trobriand perspective go without saying.

Hey, Baroweni's mother had died. She had died and Baroweni was already pregnant. When she was due to give birth, another woman in the village was dying. She was on the verge of death – they had already made the mortuary preparations for her. Baroweni went to her and said, "Go to my mother. Tell my mother, 'Hey, your child is pregnant and will soon give birth. Take food to her.'"

This section establishes the relationships of the major actors in the myth to each other. The mother/daughter relationship cited is important because

Trobriand mothers have a special obligation to care for their pregnant daughters. In fact, the female matrilineal kin of the pregnant woman are responsible for feeding and caring for both the new mother and the infant for several months after birth. Asking a dying person to take messages to Tuma is a common occurrence. Trobrianders make no effort to conceal their assessment of an ailing person's chances of survival from that person, and those who are about to die provide an obvious communications link between the world of the living and the world of the dead.

So the dying woman died and went [to Tuma]. She told her companion there [Baroweni's mother], "Your child is pregnant and close to giving birth, but what shall she eat?" She said, "She told me to come and tell you, 'You should take food to her.'"
So the spirit [Baroweni's mother] got up and began cutting taro shoots. She raised the taro shoots onto her head and rose up [as a spirit rises when it leaves the corporal body]. She came. She continued on, what's it, at Tuma on the main beach at Kuruvitu, on their beach at Tuma. She came ashore and continued on there to Libutuma.

There is an interesting mixing of attributes here. The spirit carries her load on her head as all Trobriand women do, yet the verb used to describe her rising is not one used for a woman, but one used to describe the rising of a spirit from a corporeal body.

[directed to me] Shall I sing the song that you might hear it?
"Baroweni, Baroweni, Baroweniweni. I will set it down, I will set it down. Oh, my neck. Oh, my neck . . . Oh, my neck. We [inclusive dual] suppose a girl is standing with us whose name is *yaluwa*."

As we shall see, variants of this ditty are sung at several points in the story. Baroweni's mother whines her daughter's name and complains of her desire to set down her load and the pain it causes in her weak spirit neck. The last phrase in the ditty suggests a dual persona for the mother. She supposes or assumes a girl is standing with her, but her name is just *yaluwa* or spirit.

So she walked and cried, and in that way she entered a village. She just cried, she was crying for her child. Because she was a spirit she couldn't touch anything or hold it. She had already died, and there was nothing she could hold.

This makes clear the source of the mother's discomfort. She is carrying real taro, but as a spirit, she is known to be unable to carry anything. The explanation of this comes in the next sentence of the telling of the myth.

However, this is a *liliu*. This happened long long ago and for that reason [it is as it is].

Here is the first of several indications that inferences based on present-day understandings of the world are not always applicable to myth. That it happened long, long ago is sufficient explanation of events that violate common-sense knowledge. I return to this point later.

She just continued on to – what's its name – Yalaka . . . Buduwelaka. Yes at Buduwelaka she was just the same, crying, crying for her child.
  "Baroweni, Baroweni, Baroweniweni. I will set it down, I will set it down. Oh, my neck Ya! Oh, my neck. She just scoops it up the girl that stands with us [inclusive dual]. Her name is *yaluwa*. We are surely overloaded."
  This because she had already died.

The ditty Baroweni's mother sings is a magic spell she uses to cause the taro to be carried. Since she is dead, she cannot carry things in a normal fashion. Notice that the mother's persona is completely confounded with that of the spirit girl whose presence she invokes. She says she herself would like to put the basket down, it is her neck that hurts, yet she refers to herself and the spirit girl using the inclusive dual form of the first person pronoun.

She just brought it and continued on to Okupukopu. At Okupukopu she chanted just the same as she was crying, crying for her child.
  "Baroweni, Baroweni, Baroweniweni. I will set it down, I will set it down. Oh, my neck. Oh, my neck. Oh, my neck Ya! Oh, my neck. What is her name? What is she? Girl or person? But her name is *yaluwa*."
  Because she was already dead there was nothing she could touch or carry on her head. And this: she was of the time long ago, our [exclusive plural] ancestor's time. [*then, directed to me*] I shall take it to its conclusion that you should grasp it?

The use of the exclusive plural possessive form here in referring to the ancestors makes it clear that these asides about the time of the ancestors and the special nature of events that happened then are directed at me as an outsider to the culture. I suspect she uses this form in order to say, "This is how it was with Trobriand ancestors. How it was with your European ancestors is irrelevant."

She continued on from Okupukopu to Ilalima. At Ilalima it was just the same. She went then to Osapoula.
  It was night when she arrived and everyone was sleeping. She knocked on the coconut fronds [the wall of the house]. Her child woke up and said, "Who are you?"

Having the spirit mother arrive in the village at night is plausible since spirits are most active at night. It also simplifies the story because even though the mother is at this point in time a visible spirit, it is possible for her to go unseen in the darkness while the village sleeps.

She said, "I am your mother. I have brought your food. Open the house."
  Her child opened up her house. She went to her and saw her mother putting down the food basket she had been carrying on her head. In the night there she [mother] told her, she said, "Hey, go prepare the area behind the house as if, wa, as if you were to plant flowers there."
  She said, "Take these [the taro stalks] and bury them. They will be yours to

eat with your child. When the seed root has sprouted, cut off the side roots. Cut off the side roots and replant the seed. The side roots alone you shall eat with your son. You prepare behind the house. I shall go beside the house and sit. I shall be watching you."

This is interesting since a family metaphor is commonly applied to the form of taro propagation referred to here. The seed corm is called *inala,* mother, and the side roots are referred to as *litula,* her children (Malinowski 1965, v.2:105–106). Given the traditional importance of yams in the maintenance of descent group identity in the Trobriands, it is surprising that the mother brought taro rather than yams to feed her daughter. It is possible that the existence of this metaphor for taro propagation, which has no parallel in the cultivation of yams, made taro a more felicitous symbolic choice than yams.

Her mother spoke well. She told her she would sit beside the house and watch, but Baroweni by herself was already going on with her things. She forgot. She boiled her food and ate. Her mother was sitting there watching her. She [Baroweni] picked up that container, a coconut shell bowl, a soup bowl. Like those containers that the Lukwasisiga clan drank from. She just picked it up, drank her fill and threw it out beside the house. She threw it out and it drenched her mother's body. Her mother felt it.
    She said, "Hey! Why did you dump that on me?"
    She said, "Oh my! Mother mine, chieftan's wife. Mother no . . . I just forgot. I forgot about you. [Don't be angry] because it can't be a killing since you are already a *baloma.*

This event is outrageous in the Trobriand view of things. Remember that Baroweni's mother had gone to great effort and borne great pain to meet her responsibilities to her daughter. Trobriand children have a like set of responsibilities to their parents. Meeting these obligations is called *velina,* and failing to meet them has moral as well as jural consequences. When children are young and need support, parents supply what is needed. When parents grow old, the roles are reversed. Children must care for their parents in their old age. This role reversal is sometimes marked by a mother's addressing her grown daughter as *inagu,* "my mother." When parents become infirm and require constant care, this job falls largely on the grown children. It is they who must feed their aged parents, bathe them, and, if necessary, carry them on their backs away from the village so that they can defecate in the privacy of the forest. These responsibilities, burdensome though they may be, are taken very seriously by all. It is understandable, however, that parents sometimes complain about not being well treated by their children, and children sometimes come to resent the imposition of a parent's needs on their lives. Here in the myth, Baroweni has failed to meet her obligations to her mother and she has done so in a particularly offensive way. Her mother brought food, and Baroweni has thrown food on her mother. Worse yet, she has done so, she says, because she has forgotten about her mother.

She said, "You have thrown out my soup. I shall return [to Tuma]. I shall return, I shall go. You will stay here. I will split our [inclusive dual consumable] coconut. The lower half is yours. The half with the eyes is mine. [*Directed to me*] Where is that coconut? [*I produce a coconut and she demonstrates*].

She split the coconut. "This half is yours. The end with eyes we shall drink, and it will be my coconut. I will go. I will go and then I will come back and see you. You shall not see me."

This ritual performance concludes the actual telling of the myth itself. The symbolism of the eyes in the coconut is not as transparent as it seems. The end of the coconut without eyes is called *kwesibuna,* which means literally the "cold" part. So the mother has not only taken the eyes, she has taken the "hot" end of the coconut in a world where hot is potent and powerful.

Commentary on the myth

The remainder of the text is the old woman's commentary on the myth and her attempts to show the connection of the myth to the world of experience.

[*Commentary*] Look, now-a-days people die and go [to Tuma] and their *kosi* come around, but we can't see them. He [Toigisasopa's *kosi*] sees us and wakes us up, but we do not see him, and this is the reason. Our ancestors have changed things. They come and see us. Our fathers and mothers die and go away and then they come back and are watching us. We see them not. But this old woman in times long ago started this. This particular *liliu* here. Some think it is just a fairy tale [*kukwanebu*], but it is real *liliu.*

However, if that woman, Baroweni had not done that, had not thrown out the soup, our mothers would be with us now. We would die. Later we would come back and stay and be seen. But here she made her mistake. She grabbed that soup cup, drank from it and threw it out, hitting her mother who was beside the house. The old woman cast an appropriate spell. She said, "Why did you throw soup on my body?"

Notice the inference here: had Baroweni not made her mistake, our parents would be with us, that is, visible to us, now. This is a direct connection between the myth and the situation of life as it is experienced.

She said, "Oh, mother, I forgot about you."
    She said, "You yourself have banished me. You have injured me. I will go back [to Tuma].

Here, the terms of the mother's interpretation of Baroweni's act has escalated. The mother has no sympathy for Baroweni's excuse. She has equated Baroweni's mistake with a grievous form of social punishment, *yoba,* banishment from one's village.

She got a coconut and told her child, she said, "I will split it in half you see. The lower end is yours. The end with eyes is mine. I will go away. When I come back, I will see you. You will not see me." So she went back and stayed.

You see, the other day when Toigisasopa was going around the village as a spirit. We did not see him. Except those who saw him all blackened. Look, [*makes empty circles around her eyes with index fingers and thumbs*] with his eye sockets empty. His whole body was black and when he went to someone, that's what they would see. This was just sleepers, in *kilisala* of course, who saw him thus. The other day I was listening to them screaming in the village. I thought to myself, "What is the source of this? Oh, this thing from long ago." My mind went to these words [this myth].

This is what the old woman had to say by way of explanation for the perceived invisibility of the spirits of the dead. By her account, she has used her knowledge of a myth to find an interpretation of an important and puzzling aspect of life. That in itself is perhaps interesting, but not entirely surprising. It is a confirmation of Malinowski's claim that "myth is not an idle tale, but a hard worked active force" (1954:101). However, more remains to be said about how the force of myth is brought to bear on life.

The historical connection

In her commentary on the story, the old woman emphasizes the fact that the story of Baroweni is the reason for the invisibility of the spirits of the dead. Baroweni's mother declared that Baroweni would no longer see her. The relevance of this myth to the events surrounding the poltergeist behavior of the *kosi* in the village is based on the perception of the *kosi* as an (usually) invisible spirit of the dead. The connection is purported to be historical and causal, where the causality of the connection is based in the cosmological status of *liliu*, sacred myths. The actions of Baroweni's mother (as a spirit) with respect to Baroweni (as a living person) set a precedent for all subsequent relations between spirits and living persons. This causal connection appears in discourse in the form of a pervasive Trobriand metaphor. The myth is the *uula*, root or cause of the current state of affairs, which is, in turn, the *dogina*, extremity or result of the myth. According to the old woman's account, it was this causal connection that led her from her question about the invisibleness of spirits of the dead to the myth of Baroweni. On this view, the events described in the myth were identified as the cause of the salient aspect of the experience.

This connection is also the one emphasized by Malinowski in his analysis of the role of myth in primitive psychology. In considering several related myths, including another version of myth of Baroweni, which he had collected, he notes that such myths provide mundane precedents for some very unpleasant facts of life.

> What it actually does is to transform an emotionally overwhelming
> foreboding, behind which, even for a native, there lurks the idea of an in-
> evitable and ruthless fatality. Myth presents, first of all, a clear realization
> of this idea. In the second place, it brings down a vague, but great ap-

prehension to the compass of a trivial, domestic reality. . . . The separation from the beloved ones after death is conceived as due to the careless handling of a coconut cup and to a small altercation. (1954:137)

There are two loose ends to be attended to here. First, this tantalizing quote raises the question of the source of the great apprehension experienced in connection with the invisibility of the beloved ones after death. Malinowski is surely right that when Trobrianders consider the invisibility of the spirits of the dead they do so with apprehension. If this myth permits that invisibility to be conceived as due to a small altercation, what might it have been conceived as due to that provokes apprehension? That is, if it provides a substitute conception of the invisibility of the spirits, for what is it a substitute? What was the terrifying conception of the cause of the invisibility of the spirits that it replaces?

Second, there is something paradoxical about this historical relation of myth to the nature of life as it is experienced in the present. Things happen in myths that all Trobrianders agree could not happen in life today. The carrying of the taro by the spirit woman in the myth of Baroweni is an example, and in the telling of the myth, the old woman repeatedly reminds us in that context that this is a *liliu;* that it happened long ago. Even though the events of the myth have direct causal relations to states of affairs in the present, the time of myth is not historical time. As Malinowski puts it, ". . . the distinction between the *liliu* and actual or historical reality is drawn firmly, and there is a definite cleavage between the two" (1922:303). Myth must be closely linked to life so that the events of myth can serve as precedents and causes for the events of life; yet myth must also be kept distant from life to protect it from mundane inferences about what might and what might not be possible by present standards.

A mythic schema

When we look more closely at the myth itself and at how it is applied to the interpretation of the behavior of the spirits of the dead, we find other connections between the myth and experience. These connections have to do with similarities in organization between the concepts encountered in the myth and concepts encountered in life.

The myth of Baroweni contains a structure of relationships among things and actors and actions. If we ignore the specific identities of the things and actors and actions and concentrate instead on the organization of the relationships among them, we see a structure I call a *schema*.[5] When particular instances are plugged into the slots in the schema, we say the schema is instantiated, and the result is a proposition that is an assertion about the world. The schema underlying this myth encodes cultural knowledge about relations between the living and the dead. It is based on a set of implicit cultural theories about human motivation and human psychology. It implicitly attributes abilities, failings, behaviors, and reactions to deceased persons and to their survivors.

The basic points of the myth can be summarized in the following simple three-term propositions.

M1. Baroweni   threw soup on   Baroweni's
                                                      mother

M2. Baroweni's   became invisible to   Baroweni
         mother

These two propositions are related to each other in that the event described in proposition *M1* led to the event described in *M2*. Baroweni's mother's action in *M2* somehow "caused" present-day spirits of the dead to be invisible to the living.

M3. Baloma   are invisible to   the living

Since each event uniquely precipitated its successor, the negations of these propositions also form a plausible sequence. That is, if Baroweni had not thrown soup on her mother, then her mother would not have been angry at her and would not have made herself invisible and, so argues the old woman who told the myth, present-day spirits of the dead would still be visible to the living. It is clear how these propositions are connected to each other and how the old woman can use the connections to make inferences about how things might have been different than they are. It is less clear how this is connected to the world of contemporary experience.

The structural connection

The question really is how one gets from the notion of contemporary spirits of the dead being invisible (proposition *M3*) to the idea of Baroweni's mother becoming invisible to Baroweni (proposition *M2*). No historical mechanism is offered in the telling of the myth or in its commentary, but both of these propositions are instantiations of the same structure, "*x* is invisible to *y*." This suggests that the relation might be analogical rather than historical. Support for the analogical interpretation requires a single schema that, when instantiated in different ways, generates the propositions of the myth as well as the propositions describing the conditions of life. Such a schema would be a structure composed of more general terms than those found in the instances to be accounted for. To discover the underlying schema, we examine the terms in the propositions of the myth and of the description of the relevant bit of life and find for them the most specific category that is general enough to contain the set of terms. For example, Baroweni's mother, the *kosi,* and our dead parents are all instances of deceased persons, whereas the living and Baroweni are instances of survivors.

INTERPRETING ACTIONS

Finding the appropriate general terms for the actions in the schema is more difficult. Baroweni's mother leaves her and becomes invisible, the *baloma* are invisible to the living, yet the *kosi* is occasionally visible while frightening people. Fortunately, there are other instances at hand and other ethnographic evidence that can help determine the more general categories of action of which the throwing of soup and the coconut ritual are instances. Within the myth itself, the throwing of the soup and the splitting of the coconut are given metaphorical interpretations. Baroweni's mother says that her daughter has injured her and has banished her by throwing the soup on her. So Baroweni's act is an instance of injury and one of banishment as well. The mention of banishment here is interesting because in one version of the myth of Baroweni collected by Malinowski (1954:133–134), the same soup-throwing incident and subsequent coconut-splitting ritual were posed as being both the cause of the invisibility of the *baloma* and the origin of the banishment of the *baloma* to the island of Tuma. In that version of the myth, prior to Baroweni's mistake, the spirits of the dead were visible to the living and resided in their natal villages after their deaths. Before Baroweni's mistake, it seems, dying was not really much of an inconvenience. In fact, being dead looks quite a lot like being alive, with the possible exception that one gains considerable magical power by dying. Seen in this light, Baroweni's mistake is an enormously important event. It is as a result of her action that death acquires its most salient and distressing features: exile to Tuma and invisibility. Because of Baroweni's actions, death comes to mean removal of the spirit from the sphere of social intercourse.

Now, in the telling of the myth and in providing commentary on it, my old informant gave several paraphrases of the conversation that took place between Baroweni and her mother. In one of those, she attributes the following words to Baroweni, *"Gala bisimamatila, pela bogwa baloma"* – "It is not a killing because (you are) already a *baloma*." Baroweni protests to her mother that she could not have killed her because she is already a spirit. Where does this talk of killing come from? After all, Baroweni might have harmed her mother by throwing hot soup on her, but killing seems out of proportion to the nature of the mistake. It is, however, in perfect proportion to the consequences of that mistake. In spite of Baroweni's urgent denial, her act is a killing in the sense that before this act, there is no death as Trobrianders now know it. True, her mother had previously died, but her spirit was visible and interacted with her daughter as a living mother would. Death to Baroweni's mother did not mean what death means now. And, in fact, in terms of the Trobrianders' current understanding of death, Baroweni's mother did not "die" until this altercation had taken place. It is as a result of Baroweni's actions that death becomes the horrible state of separation from the living. In this light, the soup-throwing incident can be seen as a metaphor for killing, accidental to be sure, but killing nevertheless. The mother's reactions to this are the ritual splitting of the coconut and the pronouncements about how things will be henceforth. The old woman telling the myth called this a just punishment for Baroweni, but it is also the mother's act of dying. With this act, Baroweni's mother declares she will leave, that is, not help Baroweni with her child soon to be born, and when she returns she will be invisible.

Remember also that Baroweni's action occurs in the context of mother meeting her responsibilities to her daughter, but daughter, Baroweni, reciprocates by negligently failing to meet her obligations to her mother. Thus, while the story is in one sense about a trivial mistake, it is also about a daughter's inadvertently ending her mother's life through negligence. This is a theme that is probably universal. Freud, writing about his European patients says,

> When a wife loses her husband, or a daughter her mother, it not infrequently happens that the survivor is afflicted with tormenting scruples, called "obsessive reproaches" which raise the question whether she herself has not been guilty through carelessness or neglect of the death of the beloved person. (1918:80)

Freud describes the source of these thoughts as follows:

> Not that the mourner has really been guilty of the death or that she has really been careless, as the obsessive reproach asserts; but still there was something in her, a wish of which she herself was not aware, which was not displeased with the fact that death came, and which would have brought it about sooner had it been strong enough. The reproach now reacts against this unconscious wish after the death of the beloved person. Such hostility, hidden in the unconscious behind tender love, exists in almost all cases of intensive emotional allegiance to a particular person, indeed it represents the classic case, the prototype of the ambivalence of human emotions. (1918:80)

This ambivalence resonates perfectly with the Trobrianders' feelings about *velina*. We know that children often feel anxiety about meeting their obligations to their parents, and we know that in the Trobriands (as in our own culture) elderly parents often complain that they are not properly treated by their children. If the historical causal link were indeed the only link between the myth and the experience it is marshaled to explain, then there are many scenarios that could arrange events in which spirits become invisible here ever after. Yet, this mythic structure mirrors the thoughts and fears that are experienced by Trobriand children (whether in childhood or as adults) on the death of a parent. In a world in which there are no natural deaths and in which elderly parents depend on their children for their very existence, a fleeting secret wish that one's burdensome parent were dead or doubts about having met one's filial obligations can easily lead to self-reproach on the death of one's parent. In the earlier discussion of Malinowski's account of the connection of myth to life, we asked, 'What could have been the original terrible conception of the cause of the invisibility of the spirits of the dead that must be replaced?' The answer for the survivors is that the dead are invisible because we killed them. This is the source of the Trobrianders' great apprehension over the separation from the beloved ones to which Malinowski referred.

Reading the throwing of soup as a gloss for wishing death on and inadvertently killing the deceased makes the dynamics of the retaliatory nature of the myth clear. According to Freud, the defence against the hostility that was felt toward the deceased

> ". . . is accomplished by displacement upon the object of hostility, namely, the dead. We call this defence process, projection. The survivor will deny that he has ever entertained hostile impulses toward the beloved dead; but now the soul of the deceased entertains them and will try to give vent to them. . . ." (1918:81)

The anger of the deceased at the survivor, then, is a projection of the survivor's hostility toward the deceased.

TRANSFORMING THE MYTHIC SCHEMA

The parallelism of these schemas is easy to show. The psychodynamic schema described in the paragraphs from Freud is as follows:

> *P1.* survivor   wished death to   deceased
>
> *P2.* deceased   punishes   survivor

Here, *P2* arises from *P1* when the survivor projects to the deceased the hostility that the survivor felt toward the deceased.

The myth mirrors this structure, although it is not a direct instantiation of it. The structure of the myth was:

> *M1.* Baroweni   threw soup on   Baroweni's mother
>
> *M2.* Baroweni's mother   became invisible to   Baroweni

where the mother's act can be seen both as dying and as punishing Baroweni. The myth is reputed to explain the facts of life. The claimed connection is that Baroweni's mother's act somehow "caused" the observable phenomenon that the spirits of the dead are not visible to the living. In particular, it was claimed that dead parents are not visible to their living children. This is experienced by all surviving children. Furthermore, had Baroweni not made her mistake, the dead parents would be visible. Instantiating the psychodynamic schema in the first person (as experienced by the survivor) yields the propositions:

> *T1.* I   wished death to   my dead parent
>
> *T2.* my dead parent   punishes   me

Obsessive scruples turn this active hostility, wishing death, into a passive animosity, negligent killing, and turn the punishment into a passive projected retaliation, becoming invisible and going into self-imposed exile.

> *L1.* I   negligently killed   my dead parent
> *L2.* my dead parent   is invisible to   me
>   and leaves

The first proposition here is one that elderly parents sometimes voice in their complaints about the way their children neglect them. The second is a statement of the phenomenon the myth is supposed to explain. This transformation of the mythic schema, then, provides a simple explanation of the invisibility of the spirits of the deceased, which is, after all, what is in need of explanation here, but it is a very painful explanation indeed.

This is the schema that underlies the myth. It arises in the minds of the survivors following the death of a person with whom they have been involved in life. To this point, we have considered evidence about the myth and its telling as well as psychodynamic theory in order to discover the schema underlying the myth. Suppose this is the schema underlying the myth, how could the myth come to be structured the way it is?

We have already seen that the defence process of projection operates in the composition of the internal structure of the schema. It is the source of the retributive nature of the myth. The defence process of projection and two others, intellectualization and displacement, also operate in the transformation of the propositions that represent the experienced relations between the living and the dead into the myth of Baroweni. Suppes and Warren (1975) propose a scheme for the generation and classification of defence mechanisms that is directly applicable to sets of propositions such as those discussed. In their model, defence mechanisms are created by transforming propositions of the form, "self + action + object." The classification of the defence mechanism is based on the nature of the transformations applied. Among the transformations they describe are putting another in the place of self, projection; changing the nature of the act performed, intellectualization; and changing the identity of the object, displacement. The myth of Baroweni is produced by applying all three of these transformations to the original repressed propositions *L1* and *L2* as follows. Let us begin with the underlying propositions:

> *L1.* I   negligently killed   my dead parent
> *L2.* my dead parent   is invisible to   me
>   and leaves

Projection changes the identity of the self, and displacement changes the identity of the object. In the case of the myth, Baroweni takes the place of self and Baroweni's mother takes the place of one's own dead parent.

1. Baroweni	negligently killed	Baroweni's mother
2. Baroweni's mother	punishes	Baroweni

Intellectualization changes the nature of the act performed. In the case of the myth, negligent killing becomes negligent handling of food, and the punishment is the experienced invisibility of the dead. This brings us back to the propositions that summarize the myth.

M1. Baroweni	threw soup on	Baroweni's mother
M2. Baroweni's mother	became invisible to	Baroweni

Having arrived at the schema underlying the myth, we are ready to return to the phenomenon that brought these issues to light in the first place – the terrifying visits of the *kosi* of Toigisasopa. By placing Toigisasopa in the role of decedent and those villagers who experienced the presence of his *kosi* in the role of survivors, substitution into the psychodynamic schema produces the following set of propositions:

K1. Villagers	wished death to	Toigisasopa
K2. Toigisasopa	punishes	villagers

These propositions, like those involving the parents, are likely to be repressed. Given that this may be an important structure for the organization of ideas about the nature of relations between the living and the dead, it is easy to see the mechanism underlying Trobrianders' assertions that if a person is bad in life, his or her *kosi* will haunt the village for a long time and will be malevolent. Those who are sorcerers, adulterers, or thieves are likely to evoke hostility in their neighbors. Those who are none of these things are less likely to be hated and/or wished dead by their companions in life. Thus, the deaths of powerful and evil persons may evoke many reactions of this sort from the community, whereas the deaths of more sociable people are likely to evoke few such reactions.

I have argued that the way the myth accounts for the invisibility of the spirits of the dead is not through the historical connection claimed by the Trobrianders, but through the fact that the myth is a disguised version of the inadmissible cognitive and affective structure experienced on the death of a loved one. We find also that a different instantiation of the same schema underlies the interpretation of the haunting of the village by the *kosi*. In each case, there is independent sociological evidence concerning the reality of the repressed propositions.

What do they know?

The application of schemas across sets of instances is a ubiquitous cognitive activity. Instantiation in conventional ways is involved in understanding, reasoning, and predicting (Hutchins 1980). Unexpected insights often seem to arise from unconventional instantiations. Metaphors and some types of humor are also based on the assignment of new instances to familiar schemas (cf. Lakoff this volume). This same process is also apparently at work in the creation and use of myths. This myth is both a charter or a precedent for an unpleasant fact of life and a cultural model of relationships between the living and the dead. The schema it embodies is as applicable to contemporary personal relationships as it is to those of the ancestors with each other.

If what I have said is true, then there is an important problem for those of us interested in the role of cultural knowledge and belief in everyday cognition. When we turn to the complexities of cognition in real-life settings, distinctions between the realm of the cognitive and the realm of the affective begin to melt away.[6] It is clear that a great deal of knowledge used in the interpretation of everyday events is never explicitly stated. The sort of knowledge that resides in these unpleasant and unstated instantiations of the mythic schema cannot be ignored. To the extent that they may influence memory, judgments, inferences, and other cognitive processes, they are things that are "known." Yet, in a sense, they are things that are too painful to be known. Trobrianders (or anyone, for that matter) need cultural knowledge to understand the myth, and they use the schema of the myth to understand, perhaps in a more profound sense than they can admit, the events of their everyday lives.

Why sacred myths are sacred

In the telling of the myth, the old woman went to some pains to assert the truth of the myth and to impress on me that the events in myth cannot always be made sense of in terms of what we know about the present-day world. Having examined the use of the *liliu* of Baroweni in the interpretation of these modern events, we can see why it is that the sacred myths are so adamantly defended. They are formulations that from the Trobriander's perspective *must be true*. Were they not true, then experience could be exceedingly threatening. Remembering the myth must be a very rewarding experience since it allows the myth to perform its role as a defence mechanism. It allows the believer to confront the ugly subjective realities of deceased parents who can no longer be seen or a visit from a *kosi* with the sense that these are explicable phenomena. Not only can they be explained explicitly in terms of historical causality, but the process of remembering the mythic schema that explains the events also binds the dangerous, unstated, unconscious propositions to a conscious and innocuous isomorph. The situation is explained, and the disruptive propositions in the unconscious are transformed into acceptable elements of a description of an event that happened to someone else, long, long ago.

Malinowski documented the reasons that the Trobriand people gave for the legitimacy of myth and interpreted their insistence on the truth of myth as deriving from the necessity to maintain the historical connection to the precedents of the past. That is part of the reason the *liliu* are sacred; as we have seen, however there is more to it than that. The myth as a defence mechanism must be both legitimized and protected from challenge. If the myth must be literally true to have its historical/causal effects and if, given what we all accept about how the world works now, the myth cannot be literally true, then what we all accept about how the world works now cannot be applicable to myth. The gulf between the present and the distant past (*omitibogwa*), the larger-than-life quality of the characters and their actions in myth, the unquestioned justice of their decisions, the insistence that in the past things were of a different sort than they are now, the denial that the inferences we would make today are applicable to the events in myth, in short, the whole collection of reasons people give for the legitimacy of myth, are a secondary defence structure erected to protect the primary defence of the myth.[7]

The sacred *liliu* must be true because the putative historical/causal connection of myth to life depends on the myth's being literally true, and that connection is the only connection between myth and life that can be explicitly recognized. If the myth is to be recalled and used as an interpretive resource in understanding some troubling real-world event, there has to be some connection between it and the event other than the inadmissible fact that it shares a common schema with the unconscious propositions evoked by the event. The historico–causal link provides that connection.

Conclusion

We began with a description of an actual encounter between a Trobriand village and the spirit of one of its deceased members. For one villager, at least, this raised the question of why the spirits of the dead are nearly always invisible. We saw how myth was marshaled as an interpretive resource to provide an understanding of this troubling aspect of the experience. The story of Baroweni's clumsiness and her mother's retribution are taken as an historical precedent for all subsequent interactions between the living and the dead. An examination of the myth itself, and of the putative historical–causal connection of the myth to experience, has shown that there is another, more compelling connection. That is that the myth is a disguised representation of repressed thoughts and fears concerning relations between self as survivor and the deceased. We cannot say by which link the myth was retrieved from the old woman's memory. But we can say that the way it accounts for the invisibility of the spirits of the dead is via the structural connection rather than the historical connection.

The schema instantiated by the myth is the same schema unconsciously instantiated by survivors following the death of someone important to them. It embodies the anxiety about possible responsibility for the death and the projection onto the deceased of the repressed hostility of the sur-

vivor toward the deceased. But the mythic version is a safe version. It is
not about self. It is about someone else – a special someone else whose
actions long ago caused all spirits to be invisible. The myth, as a transformed instantiation of this schema, is a culturally constituted defence
mechanism. Furthermore, even though the *kosi* is sometimes visible, the
underlying schema also describes the relationship of living villagers to *kosi.*
We expect the hostility that is projected onto the deceased, and therefore
the severity of the deceased's punishment of survivors, to be all the more
intense when the deceased was hated in life. This appears from the Trobri-
and perspective as the observation that the *kosi* of evil people haunt the
village for a long time. So, the schema that underlies the myth of Baroweni
and explains the invisibility of the spirits also appears to be the schema
that causes villagers to experience the *kosi* as well.

This chapter shows that there is a living connection between myth and
experience in the Trobriand Islands. By its structural connection to life,
the myth provides a way of thinking about things that are too painful or
too threatening to address directly. By way of its historical connection
to life, it is both a causal precedent for the current state of affairs and
a story that exonerates the living from culpability in the disappearance
of the dead.

Notes

1. Earlier versions of this paper were presented at the Conference on Folk Models
   held in 1983 at the Institute for Advanced Study, Princeton, New Jersey, and
   in the symposium organized by Dorothy Holland and Naomi Quinn for the
   80th Annual Meeting of the American Anthropological Association and entitled Folk Theories in Everyday Cognition. Field research during which the
   data reported here were collected was supported by a grant from the Social
   Science Research Council. Text processing facilities were provided by the Navy
   Personnel Research and Development Center, San Diego. I am grateful to
   Roy D'Andrade and Laurie Price for reading and commenting on an earlier
   draft of this chapter. Whatever errors it contains are my own. My greatest
   debt is to Bomtavau, who told me the myth and provided her own rich commentary on it.
2. See Malinowski's paper, "Baloma: Spirits of the Dead in the Trobriand
   Islands," for a more detailed discussion of the nature of *baloma* and *kosi* and
   of their relationships to the living.
3. I also collected a supposedly historical story in which a woman encounters
   a more horrible fate. The woman converted to Christianity and married a native
   pastor. After a few years of marriage, she fatally poisoned her husband, moved
   to a different village, and remarried. When her second husband died, she
   moved back to her own natal village, where she eventually died. Her *kosi*
   plagued the village for months, and it was finally determined that Topileta
   had closed the doors of Tuma to her, and God had closed the doors of heaven
   as well.
4. Unfortunately, I do not know just who (or even how many) among the villagers
   actually claimed to have seen the *kosi,* nor do I know what relationship those
   few I talked to bore to the deceased.

5. Current approaches to implementing cultural knowledge representations include schemas, frames, scripts, and more. For our purposes, it is not important which approach is used so long as it captures the structural relationships of the terms of the propositions.
6. D'Andrade (1981:190–193) argues the importance of cognitive scientists' looking at cognition and affect together as related parts of meaning systems.
7. This device is not unique to technologically primitive societies. Consider, for example, the following testimony given by a creation scientist in a recent court hearing,

> We cannot discover by scientific investigation, anything about the creative process used by the creator because He used processes which are not now operating anywhere in the natural universe. (Lewin 1982:144)

> In order to assert the literal truth of accounts which, by our present criteria of truth and falsehood, cannot be literally true, the claim of the special nature of that time must be made.

References

D'Andrade, R. G.
   1981. The cultural part of cognition. Cognitive Science 5(3):175–195.
Freud, S.
   1918. Totem and Taboo. New York: Vintage Books.
Hutchins, E.
   1980. Culture and Inference: A Trobriand Case Study. Cambridge, Mass.: Harvard University Press.
Lewin, R.
   1982. Where is the science in creation science? Science 215(4529):142–146.
Malinowski, B. K.
   1922. Argonauts of the Western Pacific. London: Routledge and Kegan Paul.
   1954. Magic, Science, and Religion and Other Essays. New York: Doubleday and Company. (First published in 1948; contains Baloma; The spirits of the dead in the Trobriand Islands, first published in 1916; and "Myth in primitive psychology, first published in 1926.)
   1965. Coral Gardens and Their Magic. Bloomington: Indiana University Press. (First published in 1935.)
Suppes, P. and H. Warren
   1975. On the generation and classification of defence mechanisms. International Journal of Psycho-Analysis 56:405–414.

12

Goals, events, and understanding in Ifaluk emotion theory[1]

Catherine Lutz

I have three goals in this paper. The first is to represent formally the knowledge about emotions held by the Ifaluk people of Micronesia. That knowledge can be seen to be structured in two fundamental ways: The first is in terms of salient events in everyday life, and the second is in terms of the culturally constructed goals held by the Ifaluk. The second aim is to address the question of the actual status of ethnotheory in social interaction; I stress the idea that the emotional understanding this ethnotheory allows is, in actual practice, an understanding that is negotiated between individuals. Third, I reject the view that ethnotheoretic models of emotion are aptly characterized as involving "cognition about emotion" or "thinking about feeling."

Introduction

I would like to tell two stories here. To understand each story, it is necessary to present the underlying cultural and cognitive model that structures the understanding of the characters in them. The first story is a simple one because it merely involves narration, an assertion made by one character and left unanswered by others. The complexity of the second story arises because it tells a more fully social tale; the characters not only theorize, they also attempt to convince others that their theory is at least plausible, if not the only possible route to proper understanding of the events at hand.

The first story occurs on the atoll of Ifaluk in the Western Pacific. I am sitting outside the house of a sick person whom I have come to visit. The illness does not appear to be very serious, and I am idly chatting with the woman sitting next to me. We pause for a moment and a girl of about 4 years of age approaches us. As she nears, she does a little dance, makes a silly face, and waits. "She's cute," I think, and smile at her antics. The woman sitting next to me has observed this, and she reprimands me, saying, "Don't smile at her – she'll think that you're not justifiably angry." In that statement, the woman is telling me much more than she explicitly says. Some of the inferences she would have had me draw are presented below in the process of outlining a formal model of Ifaluk theories about emotion.

The study of ethnotheory involves the identification of the knowledge structures that underlie speech, and more generally, understanding. This knowledge is largely below the level of explicit awareness and generally remains unverbalized. One special circumstance that permits the recognition of both one's own and others' tacit knowledge is the crossing of cultural boundaries. The (at least partial) nonsharing of knowledge across those boundaries encourages the identification and verbalization of taken-for-granted realities. Thus, one special methodology that anthropology provides for the study of enthnotheories,[2] is the immersion in environments that maximize the possibilities for *mis*understanding. In the process, the mechanisms of understanding become more apparent.[3]

In their concern with cultural belief systems, anthropologists share the desire of cognitive scientists to make explicit what it is a person needs to know to come to appropriate understandings of people and events. These two perspectives also share a concern with representing the knowledge people have in the most accurate way. The goal has been to construct representations that are both general, or able to describe knowledge in many domains, and efficient, or able to process information quickly, accurately, and with minimal moves (Winograd 1977). The inability of the anthropologist to go beyond a literal understanding of the discourse going on around him or her in the early days of the field experience finds its analogue in the failure of the computer to be able to process information with a program that is flawed or incomplete in particular ways (although there are obvious and important ways in which this analogy is limited).[4] The formal modeling advocated by many cognitive scientists has been used successfully by Hutchins (1980) to represent Trobriand knowledge about land tenure and land transfer. This chapter uses his approach in modeling some aspects of the ethnotheory of emotion among the Ifaluk.

Events and emotions in Ifaluk ethnotheory

Ethnotheories of emotion describe a fundamental and ubiquitous aspect of psychosocial functioning. They are used to explain why, when, and how emotion occurs, and they are embedded in more general theories of the person, internal processes, and social life. As they play a central role in the organization of experience and behavior, an examination of the structure of emotion ethnotheories can contribute to both cultural and psychological models of emotion and social action. In addition, the existence of dense networks of connections between this domain and other knowledge systems among the Ifaluk gives this ethnotheory wide ramifications in their social life.

Although ethnotheory may be an explicit and abstract body of knowledge, it is more often pragmatic, being used as implicit assumptions in daily discourse and understanding. The investigation of Ifaluk theories of emotion reported here thus includes the collection of several thousand instances of the use of emotion words in everyday talk and of natural definitions (Boehm 1980), as well as interviews that elicited more generally stated propositions about emotions.

The most fundamental unit of any theory, implicit or explicit, is the concept. The central elements of Ifaluk emotion theory are the concepts of emotion that are represented in linguistic form by (among other things) words for discrete emotions. There are almost 100 words in at least occasional use that represent these concepts; a core group of 10 to 15 words can be heard in daily conversations, where they are used in the descriptions of striking or salient events.

The Ifaluk define, explain, and understand emotions primarily by reference to the events or situations in which they occur. This aspect of their ethnotheory of emotion contrasts with our own emphasis on the internal and private, rather than the social, nature of emotion. For example, definitions of emotion terms collected on Ifaluk relatively rarely contain reference to the physiological feeling tone associated with a particular emotion; American English emotion concepts, on the other hand, are often defined by reference to the physical and/or private mental state of the person experiencing the emotion (Davitz 1969; also see Averill 1974; Izard 1977).

The kinds of situations that are related in theory to emotions are depicted by informants at several levels of generality. They include the more specific, such as "Someone gets drunk and comes to your house every night," or "Your children are adopted to another village and don't come to visit you for a long time," or "The pig eats your food," as well as the more general – "Something happens that we want to happen," or "There is something we don't know [or understand]," or "Something bad happens that we don't expect to happen." Which level of generality is chosen by informants depends on, among other things, the kinds of contrasts and comparisons being drawn in any particular case.

Thus, although the emotion concept can be considered the primary element in this domain of Ifaluk ethnotheory, it is also evident that the definitions of these or any words are in fact themselves propositions of a particular type (Casagrande & Hale 1967). It is useful to look at the underlying structure of those propositions in terms of the modeling used by Hutchins (1980), who succinctly outlines the relationship between the terms of such formal modeling; using the example of land use rights in the Trobriand Islands, he states that a

> relation always links one instance from the range of concepts that are people to one instance from the range that are economically appropriatable units of land. When a relation is stated in terms of such variable ranges as these, it is a *schema*. When the ranges are replaced by concepts (a process called *instantiation* because it is the assignment of specific instances to the

relation), the schema becomes a *proposition*. A schema is then a form or a template from which an arbitrarily large number of propositions can be constructed. (1980:51)

The definition of each Ifaluk emotion concept is an instantiation of the following general schema:

(1) If Event X, then Emotion Y.

or

Ev [   ] =====> Em [   ]

Here, as in further schema and proposition representations, broken arrows indicate that the causal relationship is a probabalistic one (e.g., If someone violates a rule, it is likely he or she will experience *metagu*, or fear/anxiety); solid arrows indicate a more deterministic relationship, in the sense that the proposition's first condition necessarily leads to the second condition.[5] Although the understandings that Americans have about emotion can also sometimes be found to be organized in the same kind of structure as (1), at least as common would be a schema of the general form, "If Internal Feeling X, then Emotion Y."[6]

Some examples of propositions, evident in everyday Ifaluk discourse, that instantiate this schema include the following:

Ev [Illness]
Ev [Travel from the
  island]
Ev [Lack of food]   =====> Em [*Fago* (compassion/
Ev [Nurturance]   love/sadness)]
Ev [Gentle or calm
  behavior]

Ev [Rule violation by
  self]
Ev [Spirit present]   =====> Em [*Metagu* (fear/
Ev [Call to eat by someone   anxiety)]
  unfamiliar]

Some emotion words in the Ifaluk language share situational definitions, including both those that can be described as general and those that are more specific. Determining which emotion term will appropriately apply in any concrete situation involves a determination of some other characteristics of the individuals involved in the situation. These characteristics include particularly their social status ranking relative to each other, the history of their relationships with each other, and the possible influence of third parties on the actions of those involved.[7] The process whereby these forms of knowledge are applied to a particular case can be examined both as a cognitive and as a social process. In the extended example of emotional negotiation examined later, these other factors in understanding that are secondary to the general event–emotion schema are treated in more detail.

In summary, emotion concepts on Ifaluk are the fundamental units of an ethnotheoretical system that informs the understanding of salient events. These concepts are not conceptual primitives but rather are complex in meaning and schematic in form. To utter an emotion word on Ifaluk is not primarily to evoke an image of internal churnings or of particular ways of hotly thinking; rather, it is to evoke an image of a particular kind of event, a particular relationship between a person and the world. More generally, we can expect culturally variable ethnotheories relating to any topic to be evident in equally variable word meanings. Central concepts or key words, then, are not simple insertions into the schematic relations of an ethnotheory but are themselves ethnotheoretic and schematic.

The Ifaluk use at least three other central schemas in the process of emotional understanding. One schema states:

(2) If we experience Emotion X, then we may perform Act Y.

or

Em [   ] =====> A [   ]

This schema is familiar to us as it is a framework for emotional understanding in American ethnotheories of emotion as well. From both the American and the Ifaluk ethnotheoretical perspectives, emotions and action are closely linked.

It is important to note, however, that the causal link between action and emotion is much more probabalistic in American ethnotheory, where an emphasis on the control of emotions means that a situation of "unexpressed emotion" very commonly occurs. For the Ifaluk, on the other hand, control becomes an issue only in special circumstances (which particularly include cases in which the potential action is physically aggressive). In fact, one action commonly linked to virtually all emotions in instantiations of the above schema is "Telling someone about the emotion." It is expected, as a sign of maturity and intelligence, that a person will declare an emotional stance in appropriate situations (of which there are many).

Notwithstanding the similarity in the general form of this schema in both American and Ifaluk ethnotheories, examining some specific propositional examples reveals several culturally distinctive instantiations of the schema.

Em [*Ker* (happiness/ excitement)]	=====>	A [laugh]
		A [talk a lot]
		A [misbehave]
		A ["walk around," i.e., neglect work, show off]

                                        A [give food]
Em [*Fago* (compassion/ ====⇒ A [cry]
    love/sadness)]   A [talk politely]

                                        A [don't speak]
                                        A [talk impolitely]
Em [*Song* (justifiable   ====⇒ A [reprimand]
    anger)]   A [don't eat]
                                        A [pout]

For example, one culturally standard expectation is that people who are justifiably angry might refuse to eat. Alternately or additionally, they might speak to others without common politeness markers, such as the use of the term "sweetheart" before a request. People thus use particular behaviors as signs of specific types of emotional understandings in others.

All the listed instantiations of schema (2) are not equivalent, however, in terms of either their frequency of occurrence or cultural salience. A frequently occurring proposition is likely to be one that is particularly useful (for reasons that can be ethnographically described). In addition, each proposition evokes ethnotheoretical corollaries and semantic associations of differing degrees of richness; for example, the laughter that accompanies *ker* (happiness/excitement) is a relatively impoverished instantiation of schema (2) when compared with the idea that "happy/excited people walk around." The later notion is frequently evoked in condemnatory gossip about others; its links the emotion to amoral behavior; and it justifies the generally unspoken idea that people ought to stay close to their homes unless an errand calls them elsewhere. A rich and useful model of any cultural knowledge system specifies the density or weight of each proposition enumerated.

Another schema the Ifaluk use in discussing and understanding emotions is of the form,

(3) If we experience Emotion *X,* then another person should or might experience Emotion *Y.*

or

Em 1 [   ] ====⇒ Em 2 [   ]*

Propositional instantiations of this schema include the following:

Em 1 [*Song* (justifiable ====⇒ Em 2 [*Metagu* (fear/
    anger)]   anxiety)]

Em 1 [*Ker* (happiness/   ====⇒ Em 2 [*Song* (justifiable
    excitement)]   anger)]

Em 1 [*Chegas* (romantic ====⇒ Em 2 [*Lugumet*
    pride/self confidence)]   (discomfort/guilt)]

*The numbers are used to distinguish the different actors involved in an emotion event.

Em 1 [*Tang* (frustration/ $=====>$ Em 2 [*Fago* (compassion/
grief)]   love/sadness)]

Schema (3) can be termed a basic level schema on the basis of the frequency of explicit statements and implicit, necessary inferences that would instantiate it in everyday Ifaluk discourse. On the other hand, propositions of this sort may be formed through a chain of inference linking together propositions of types (1) and (2). For example, the statement that *song* (justifiable anger) in one person leads to *metagu* (fear/anxiety) in another person could be formed in the following way (note that one person's actions become an emotion-producing event for another person):

(2) Em 1 [*Song*] $=====>$ A [reprimand]

(1) Ev [reprimand] $======>$ Em 2 (*Metagu* (fear/anxiety)]

Propositions of type (3) probably are formed sometimes in this latter way and in other cases formed directly on the basis of a schematic structure of type (3). The more common and frequent dyadic links between emotions, such as that between *song* (justifiable anger) and *metagu* (fear/anxiety) likely are learned by children in the direct form of schema (3). Knowledge of these dyadic links, in fact, is evident in children at a very early age and in children who seem simultaneously unaware of some of the particular propositions of types (1) and (2) that form part of the chain of inference necessary to link conceptually emotions in two different individuals. In other words, children who do not demonstrate understanding of the link between, for example, *song* (justifiable anger) and rule violation are yet able to predict that *song* (justifiable anger) in one person will produce *metagu* (fear/anxiety) in the other. On the other hand, many statements about the relation between emotions in self and other are created *de novo* on the basis of schemas (1) and (2) alone. Whether a chain of propositions of types (1) and (2) or an instantiation of schema (3) is involved in any particular case is an empirical question; however, it can be assumed that cognitive operations of the latter sort are more likely when the more common emotion pairs are involved.

Other evidence for the schematic nature of the structure underlying propositions of this type is also available. In talking about the emotions, the Ifaluk treat them as fundamentally social phenomena rather than, as in the case of American ethnotheory, as predominantly internal psychophysiological events that are simply correlated with social events. A proposition of type (3), if generated by an American, probably more likely would have been made on the basis of inferences about the likely correlations between environmental triggers of an emotion in the first person and an emotion in the second. Among the Ifaluk, on the other hand, people are conceptualized as more directly influencing one another. This means that emotions in one person can lead in a more immediate way to emotions in another. People on Ifaluk believe that they hold important responsibility for the emotions of others; they may be held responsible for causing an emotion in another (as in the statement "He is needy," which is literally, "He causes me to feel compassion") or for responding with the correct emotion to another's. The expectation of an important degree of emotional symbiosis between individuals is implicitly outlined in Ifaluk emotion theory and lends meaning and schematic form to propositions of type (3).

The dyadic linking of emotions in Ifaluk theory is also informed by the social roles and situational positions of the two individuals involved. The *role structure* that White (unpublished data) has identified as an important aspect of emotion attribution among the A'ara of the Solomon Islands is also involved here; the *speaker, agent,* and *affected* within an event may necessarily have different stances and hence different emotional responses. Although propositions of type (3) do not specify the position of the actors involved, such information is efficiently stored in the definitional propositions that are nested within them.

For example, the pragmatic information encoded in the term *song* (justifiable anger) includes the notion that judgments about whether a particular act constitutes a rule violation are more aptly made by people of higher social status, including the chiefs and older individuals. Someone who claims to be "justifiably angry," therefore, is simultaneously claiming to be in a relatively superior position vis-à-vis the person who has erred. Conversely, the individual who asserts "fear/anxiety" appeals to that term's definitional schema, whose instantiations include a correlation between that emotion and events in which the individual is in a weak (and, hence, often dangerous) position in relation to others or the environment.

A fourth and final schema underlines the Ifaluk view that the situations associated with emotions are not static. This schema represents the recognition that these situations develop in ways that are often predictable, thereby creating expected sequences of emotion in an individual involved in that situation.

> (4) If we experience Emotion X, then we may later experience Emotion Y.
>
> or
>
> Em [   ] $=====>$ Em [   ]

Sequences of events that are of high frequency underlie many instantiations of this schema. Some examples include:

> Em [*Ma* (shame/ $=====>$ Em [*Song* (justifiable
>   embarrassment)]   anger)]
>
> Em [*Rus* (panic/fright/ $=====>$ Em [*Song* (justifiable
>   surprise)]   anger)]

Em [*Pak* (homesickness)] =====> Em [*Nguch* (sick and
tired/bored)]

Em [*Ker* (happiness/   =====> Em [*Metagu* (fear/
excitement)]   anxiety)]

Em [*Filengaw* (incapa-   =====> Em [*Ma* (shame/
bility/discomfort)]   embarrassment)]

As with propositions of type (3), it is not necessary to postulate a single schema that necessarily generates all of the propositions of type (4). Rather, some of the propositions, in fact, can be generated as composites of other schemas. The sequence of *ker* (happiness/excitement) and *metagu* (fear/anxiety), for example, follows from these three propositions:

(2) Em 2 [*Ker* (happiness/ =====> A [misbehavior]
excitement)]

(1) Ev [misbehavior by   ======> Em [*Song* (justifiable
other]   anger)]

(3) Em 1 [*Song* (justifiable ======> Em 2 [*Metagu* (fear/
anger)]   anxiety)]

or, in more expanded form:

(2) Em 2 [*Ker* (happiness/ =====> A [misbehavior]
excitement)]

(1) Ev [misbehavior by   ======> Em [*Song* (justifiable
other]   anger)]

(2) Em 1 [*Song* (justifiable =====> A [reprimand]
anger)]

(1) Ev [reprimand]   ======> Em 2 [*Metagu* (fear/
anxiety)][8]

This returns us to the story of the prancing little girl and the witless anthropologist with which this chapter began. I had interpreted the girl's antics with an ethnotheoretical framework in which happiness is the ultimate good (as well as being "inevitable" in children), but our adult companion viewed the child's behavior in light of the link that, in her view, holds between *ker* (happiness/excitement) and misbehavior. In an effort to head off the disruption that "happiness/excitement" is expected to bring, the woman asked me to stop smiling to open up the possibility of appearing *song* (justifiably angry). This justifiable anger was expected to produce "fear/anxiety" in the young girl. This fear would, in fact, constitute a recognition of the error of her ways; in Ifaluk ethnotheory, the experience would be a positive one that would help her mature into moral awareness.

Goals and schematic range

Schemas are, by definition, very open and abstract knowledge structures. It is clear, however, that in practice only a limited number of instantiations of particular schemas are found and/or acceptable in any culture. Some mechanism must be posited that operates to restrict the range of variables that can be inserted into the terms of schemas. One important factor contributing to the cultural construction of that range as well as to the overall coherence of the ethnotheoretical system is goals.

Goals have a central place in Schank and Abelson's theory of knowledge structures (1977:101–130); in this, goals parallel the traditional position of values in many anthropological theories that attempt to account for the organization and motivation of behavior. According to Schank and Abelson, understanding of events is enabled by the knowledge people have about the goals typically held, both by people in general and by particular types of individuals. Both the prediction and the production of behavior is predicated on detailed knowledge of the plans that can be used for achieving particular goals (1977:70–71).

It is necessary to add that both knowledge about goals and the goals themselves are culturally constructed. Thus, knowledge about the goals of others allows for prediction of behavior, and goals assist in the construction, in the first place, of ethnotheoretical knowledge systems. This relationship between goals and knowledge can be stated more abstractly as a dialectical one between direction (goals or values) and structure (knowledge) in human meaning systems.

Not all goals are created equal. In the first instance, goals exist on several levels from (in Schank and Abelson's example) the most general, such as "Eat," to the more specific, such as "Eat steak at The Steak Pit" (1977:109). At all levels of generality, however, cultural factors work to produce many of the goals held. The question of whether these various types of goals are hierarchically arranged is important. In anthropological discourse, the related question has been raised as to whether or to what degree the general goals entailed in cultural values actually order more specific day-to-day goals and behavior. On the other hand, it may be more apt to characterize things in the converse way (i.e., it may be that the more specific, grounded goals are the dog to the tail of more general goals). Although this issue cannot be dealt with here, it is important to link emerging cognitive science frameworks on the relationships between various types of goal-related knowledge structures with the trail of this traditional anthropological debate.

Each goal also has differential weight or salience. Description of an ethnotheoretical system requires a treatment of the degree of emphasis on a particular goal within a cultural system; thus, although both the Ifaluk and Americans may have the goal of avoiding violence, rates of physical aggression in the two societies and beliefs about those rates are in dramatic contrast, in part due to cultural differences in the importance attached to that goal.

With the notions of goal generality and goal salience in mind, it is possible to discuss the kinds of goals that operate to constrain and construct the Ifaluk ethnotheory of emotion. At the highest level in any system are culturally constituted goals that apply across many or all domains of knowledge. A general goal such as "Be first" can motivate behavior in a supermarket line, in the classroom, or in discussions with one's spouse. In the Ifaluk case, some of the most important higher-order goals include "Avoid confrontation," "Share food with others," "Comply with the demands of those more highly ranked than oneself," and "Avoid aggression."[9] These goals help structure emotion ethnotheory as well as other theoretical domains. Compare these goals with such central middle-class American goals as "Assert yourself," "Control yourself," "Get ahead," "Know thyself," and "Stand on your own two feet."

Are there not goals that are more general than these latter examples in ethnotheoretical systems? It may be only social scientists and philosophers whose theories attempt to model human goals on a level more abstract that those of the sort just mentioned.[10] In social science theorizing, it is frequently the case that one master goal is posited as the structure behind all or most behavior. Thus, all cultural goals, including those found on Ifaluk and in the United States, might be portrayed as examples of the goal of "Being identified by others as a good person" (e.g., Cancian 1975) or as subserving the goal of acquiring protein or maximizing cash inflow.

At another level, there are goals that are specific to, or of much greater importance in, particular domains of knowledge. In the area of emotion, some Ifaluk goals can be stated in the following terms: "Understand the event" (this in contrast to attempting to understand the internal feeling state or the emotion's role in one's own psychohistory), "Avoid illness by communicating one's emotional stance to others," and "Present oneself as a mature and intelligent person by disclosing many of one's emotional perspectives."

Finally, there is the most specific level at which goals exist – the level of the element or emotion word, where the degree of detail expands greatly. What I am claiming here is that emotion words entail goals; that is, when a case of anger or guilt, *fago* (compassion/love/sadness) or *ker* (happiness/ excitement) is identified in a particular person, relationship, or situation, a goal is simultaneously and necessarily identified. Quinn (1982) has argued that goals are also implicated in what she terms *key words,* and that such words "generate" goals. What remains to be done is specifying the process whereby emotion words and key words are linked with goals. A preliminary suggestion is that emotion words do more than just signal the presence of a goal; they may also actively produce goal directionality. By saying that I am angry, I in fact, may produce a motive, or more likely deepen and clarify an existing motive.[11] This additionally suggests that all understanding (including the emotional) is enabled or enhanced by social discourse; in hearing what we ourselves and others say about emotions, we come to understand better (or create) our goals and other perceptions.

Two types of specific goals are encoded in Ifaluk emotion words, including action goals and disclosure goals. An action goal is a motive to act, an inclination, a directional impulse. By many definitions, emotions are intrinsically motivational (e.g., Izard 1977), and hence goal-laden. Action goals for some of the most commonly used emotion terms on Ifaluk include the following.

Song (justifiable anger): "Change the situation by altering the behavior of the offending party."

Fago (compassion/love/sadness): "Change the situation by filling the need of the unfortunate party."

Ker (happiness/excitement): "Make use of the resources in the situation. Maintain situation."

Nguch (sick and tiredness/boredom): "Persevere, or, If no rules would be broken, change the situation by breaking off the pattern of repeated noxious stimuli."

Waires (worry/conflict): "Seek further information. Seek assistance in decision making."

The action goals for these emotions differ in varying degrees from the goals embedded in similar but nonidentical English emotion words. "Anger," for example, might entail more aggressive goals than does *song* (justifiable anger). Compare the goals embedded in any one of the three American English terms needed to translate *fago*.

Disclosure (or attribution) goals are the second type of goal embedded in each emotion word, and they arise by virtue of the degree of social acceptability connoted by each word. The disclosure goals related to Ifaluk emotion words are affected first by the general domain goal of expressing emotion verbally. As noted, statements of one's emotional posture are generally considered a sign of maturity and intelligence, and people frequently make statements of the form "I am (emotion word)" or "We are (emotion word)." The disclosure value of each emotion is somewhat different, however. *Fago* (compassion/love/sadness) and *song* (justifiable anger), for example, follow the general domain goal very closely; that is, it is considered good to attribute these emotions to oneself and to others. Both emotions are considered moral judgments about the world that people should make.

Two emotions in particular entail nondisclosure goals; these are *gasechaula* (hate) and *ker* (happiness/excitement). The action schema (number 2 above) for *gasechaula* (hate) includes intentionally harmful acts; to disclose hate, therefore, is to disclose the intent to harm, which violates the fundamental Ifaluk injunction against aggression. As the logic of the meaning of *ker* (happiness/excitement) outlined earlier indicates, an action schema for this emotion includes misbehavior, another act that by definition incurs negative public reaction. In addition, several emotion words, including *baiu* (romantic love/happiness) and *gas* (happiness/pride/confidence), are taboo in mixed gender conversations, primarily due to the terms' sexual connotations.

These latter examples raise the more general problem of the multiplicity of disclosure goals attached to single emotion words. Although a single predominant or overall disclosure goal can be identified for each emotion word, at least as important is the proliferation of goals based on a large number of pragmatic considerations. Ethnotheories may identify which emotions are acceptably attributed in four different kinds of circumstances – when the attribution is (1) to the self, (2) to others, (3) to particular kinds of others (for example, chiefs vs. commoners), and (4) when it occurs in particular kinds of situations (for example, in "crisis" vs. normal situations or in the presence of diverse audiences, such as "mixed company"). Thus, a particular emotion word may entail the goal of nondisclosure vis-à-vis the self, disclosure vis-à-vis others, attribution to relatives and not to nonrelatives, and nonattribution in "mixed company" but disclosure in single-gender groups.

In sum, it is impossible to talk about ethnotheory without talking about the goals it serves and articulates. This is particularly the case in relation to emotion ethnotheories, as emotions are motivational by definition. To separate cold cognition from hot motivations in delineating ethnotheories is to follow the lines of an American ethnotheory about the dichotomous relationship between the categories of "emotion" and "thought," an issue to which I return in conclusion.

It has been suggested that a relatively limited number of general goals constrain the creativity of ethnotheories. Goals place limits on the number and kinds of concepts that can be inserted into the framework of ethnotheoretic schemas. As knowledge about aspects of the physical and social world is developed in the context of attempts to attain particular culturally constituted goals, it is necessary to examine ethnotheoretical knowledge in the context of those aims it was developed to satisfy.

The negotiation of understanding: an example

Up to this point, Ifaluk ethnotheory has been described as if it were a transparent and exhaustive model used to interpret and respond unambiguously to the statements of others. In actual fact, the model is ambiguous enough to allow for both confusion and negotiation of meaning in actual interactions. The inherent ambiguity of all human messages is due not only to their telegraphic nature but also to the fact that ethnotheories are incomplete, not entirely internally consistent or coherent, in

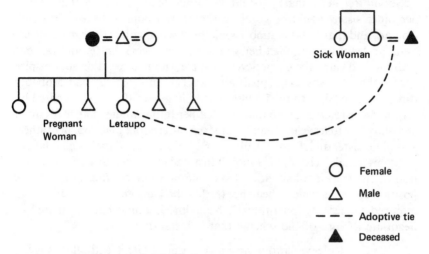

Figure 12.1. Relations among principals involved in the event

process of construction by individuals, and not universally shared in all details among the members of a culture.

This section presents an example of the use of Ifaluk emotion ethnotheory in interaction. The example illustrates that ethnotheories find their meaning in use and in the process of negotiation that occurs each time a situation is linked with an emotion word. This negotiation occurs primarily over whether the case at hand is prototypical of the emotion concept; what is negotiated is the meaning to be assigned to events.

The principal individuals involved in this case are a 32-year-old woman in her 9th month of pregnancy, her father, an older and a younger sister, two younger brothers, and her husband (see Figure 12.1). Word reached this family that a relative, through adoptive lines, of the younger sister Letaupo (a pseudonym) had fallen seriously ill on another island. On hearing this, Letaupo told me and another young woman that she was *waires* (worried/conflicted). She explained that her worry and conflict occurred because she wanted both to be with her pregnant sister and to be with the ill woman, who stood in the relation of "mother" to her.

She did not have to explain that she held the goal that is strongly and universally subscribed to on Ifaluk, which is to be with a relative at the precise moment of death (people have threatened suicide at the prospect of being absent at such a time), nor that she assumed it to be a possibility that her sister might die in childbirth. She also did not have to affirm explicitly her belief that it is very important to be with a female relative during labor and to provide assistance in the seclusion period that follows for mother and child. By asserting her *waires* (worry/conflict), she declared herself to simultaneously hold those two, now conflicting, goals.

Soon after her remark, Letaupo's father came to tell her that he and her older sister would be going to the other island to be with the sick woman, and that she, Letaupo, would be staying with her pregnant sister. Letaupo leapt up, grabbed her young son and work knife, and ran out with them towards the bush. Several people who had seen this all transpire agreed that she was *song* (justifiably angry), and that she had probably run into the bush with the intention of killing herself. She was chased by several other relatives, who told her that her father would change his mind and allow her to leave the island. Later that afternoon, Letaupo, her father, and older sister all left for the distant atoll residence of their sick relative.

By his initial decision, Letaupo's father had attempted to shift the definition of the emotional situation from one of value conflict in Letaupo's position to one in which obedience (rather than any emotional stance) was required of her. By her dramatic behavior, Letaupo had attempted to negotiate the use of the schema that is instantiated as:

$$\text{Ev [Rule violation]} \Longrightarrow \text{Em [\textit{Song} (justifiable anger)]}$$

She did this symbolically by her behavior; running into the bush in that manner was interpreted by other people as an instantiation of schema (2), whereby justifiable anger may lead to suicide.

$$\text{Em [\textit{Song} (justifiable anger)]} \Longrightarrow \text{A [Suicide]}$$

Negotiation continued after Letaupo's departure, however, because not all parties concerned would agree that her father's telling her to stay constituted a rule violation. Negotiation would also continue over the extent to which the father's leaving the island itself constituted a rule violation, thereby justifying *song* (justifiable anger) in others.

After news of the travel plans of their father and sisters reached them, the adult brothers of the pregnant woman arrived at her household to lend support and to express their views of the behavior of the departing family members. Each man stated several times in the prolonged stay at the sister's home that he had come to tell her about his feelings and thoughts so they would "go away" in the process of being verbalized. Each brother's description of his position was different, however; the older brother said he was *nguch* (sick and tired/bored) while the younger (who was very drunk on coconut toddy) declared he was *song* (justifiably angry). At several points during the afternoon and evening, each man said he had cried over the incident earlier in the day. Afterward, several people told me and others of their concern that other men in the village would *gama* (cause shame and embarrassment to) the elder brother in the days to come.

This series of events is only explicable on the basis of some of the goals and ethnotheoretical propositions held by the Ifaluk. Island men should ideally play an active role in problems and decisions affecting their sisters. A woman's husband should in fact defer in matters such as the one at hand to the wishes of her brother(s). Within the group of a woman's brothers, as within most groups on Ifaluk, primary responsibility devolves upon the eldest. In the present case, the brothers should have attempted to force one sister to stay on the island to care for their pregnant sister. Thus, the sisters' leaving constituted a "failure" (rather than a rule violation) for the elder brother. The fear that the brother would be ashamed is based on the definitional schema for shame in which:

$$\text{Ev [being observed in failure]} =====> \text{Em } [Ma \text{ (shame/embarrassment)]}.$$

Given that it is also believed that excessive shame can lead to suicide,

$$\text{Em } [Ma \text{ (shame/embarrassment)]} =====> \text{A [Suicide]}$$

people expressed sensible concern over community reaction to the elder brother.

It is also interesting to note the difference between the two brothers' definitions of the situation. In general, the events and action goals associated with *nguch* (sick and tired/bored) are more appropriate to a relationship among relatives than to one among nonrelated individuals. Although *song* (justifiable anger) occurs among relatives, the goal of maintaining interpersonal harmony and avoiding confrontation is even more important for kin. In comparing the following two series of propositions associated with *nguch* (sick and tired/bored) and *song* (justifiable anger), it should be evident that the goals associated with kin versus nonkin relations determine which action is more condusive to achieving each of those two types of goals. Given the knowledge structures involved in the Ifaluk ethnotheory of emotion, it is often necessary for individuals, like the elder brother, to declare *nguch* (sick and tiredness/boredom), where others would declare *song* (justifiable anger).

(A) Ev [noxious social obligations] =====> Em [*Nguch* sick and tired/bored)]

Em [*Nguch* (sick and tired/bored)] =====> A [tolerate, persevere]

(B) Ev [rule violation] ======> Em [*Song* (justified anger)]

Em [*Song* (justified anger)] =====> A [reprimand]

Finally, the brothers' statements that they had cried entailed implicit ethnotheoretical propositions and constituted an attempted negotiation of the definition of the situation. Of the several emotions whose action shemas may be instantiated by "crying," the most common is *fago* (compassion/love/sadness). Given that several propositions relating to *fago* (compassion/love/sadness) include the following,

Ev [Neediness] =====> Em [*Fago* (compassion/love/sadness)]

Em [*Fago*] =====> A [Nurturance]

and given that the concept also entails the notion of rank, with more highly positioned individuals being able to experience *fago* (compassion/love/ sadness) by virtue of their "nonneediness," it is likely that the brothers were asserting both their compassion for their sister's situation (as well as for their own embarrassing position) and their intention to take care of her needs through the birth, as well as their superordinate status relative to their sister.

The story continues. Let me pass over the long and involved sequence of events in which the principals who remained on the island continued to make creative use of emotion ethnotheory to present themselves and their goals to each other. In particular, discussions about the incident centered around the issue of responsibility and *song* (justifiable anger), with the pregnant woman sometimes expressing the latter, but more often allowing others to declare that emotion in themselves on her behalf. Approximately two months later, the woman had had a healthy baby, and the child's grandfather had subsequently come back to the island.

One evening several weeks after his return, the father arrived unexpectedly at the household of his offended daughter. It was obvious that his purpose was to clear the emotional air. He said he had been thinking about the incident continually and had felt "bad inside." Saying that he had come to ask his daughter to "speak her *nguch* (sick and tiredness)," he proceeded to explain his actions to her; he had gone because he had *fago* (compassion/love/sadness) for Letaupo's adoptive mother, but, he said, "I came right back" (referring to the fact that he had returned to Ifaluk before the death of the ill woman). He told his daughter he had called on the shortwave radio to ascertain her condition, and he had, before he left, asked his sister to take care of her during the birth and postpartum periods. He asked if his sister had in fact done what he asked her to do. If she had, he said, *"Iwe"* (O.K., enough), meaning that there was then no reason for his daughter to be *song* (justifiably angry). If she did not take care of the daughter, *"Ye toar mele i be ser"* ("There is nothing I will say"), meaning he would have no rejoinder to her condemnation of him.

The situation is one that can be defined as creating either *song* (justifiable anger) or *nguch* (sick and tiredness). The father came to his daughter compelled to negotiate a resolution to the emotional impasse at which they had arrived. Even though he might have liked to define the situation as one in which no emotion was even recognizable, his family's general displeasure continued over a long period and required a countermove or response on his part. By asking her to "speak her *nguch*," he placed the event into a category less serious than that of *song* (justifiable anger). He also left the door open for further negotiation by expressing his willingness to listen.

Implicit in his argument is that leaving the island when he did was not a rule violation if the people he instructed to take over his responsibilities had carried out their duties. He also implicitly acknowledged, however, the possibility of a rule violation, and hence *song* (justifiable anger). The father's discourse constituted a "thinking out loud" about the problem of defining the appropriate emotional description of the situation. This discourse occurred within the general constraints of the ethnotheory of emotion he shares with his daughter, but its specific content reveals the goals the father had – goals of maintaining, if possible, the definition of his behavior as moral while reaching a more harmonious state of affairs with his daughter. The evening ended with the father's visit having been taken by his daughter as an apology, and relations between them returned to normal.

In sum, negotiation within and by use of ethnotheory occurs on at least two levels. The first is semantic and involves motivated discussion over the extent to which an event is a prototypical or good example of a particular emotion. The questions people ask of each other here are of the sort, "Is this *song* (justifiable anger) or *nguch* (sick and tiredness/boredom)? Is this a rule violation or simply a noxious but unavoidable situation?" These semantic questions are framed in terms of the underlying schemas that organize knowledge in the particular domain at hand. Thus, whereas negotiation occurs in these Ifaluk examples by use of the event schema, in the American case it would be at least as likely that the physiological or internal feeling state schema would be used; the questions then might be of the form, "Is this anger or am I just tired? Is he sad or is that just a frog in his throat?"

The second level at which negotiation occurs is pragmatic. People discuss whether it is appropriate to use a certain emotion concept with particular other people in particular contexts. Underlying much of the preceding incident, for example, is the question (not explicitly, rigidly, or absolutely answered by Ifaluk ethnotheory) of whether it is appropriate to associate a set of circumstances with *song* (justifiable anger) if relatives (and particularly older ones) are involved.[12]

Conclusion

This short outline of Ifaluk ethnotheories of emotion only suggests the extent and coherence of this knowledge system. It demonstrates, however, that the role of the emotion word is central for the storage and structuring of ethnotheoretical knowledge in this domain. Emotion concepts have embedded in themselves crucial cultural propositions and in turn are nested in larger networks of knowledge about persons, roles, and goals. The various culturally constructed goals that many Ifaluk share are coded in their emotion words. These words frame particular groups of events as similar and meaningful, and they organize action and role taking within that frame. This paper suggests that an understanding of how individuals interpret events and of how they plan their total response to them can be built on an understanding of emotion ethnotheories.

I conclude by rejecting one possible interpretation of the structure of this analysis. It is *not* meant to be a model of how the Ifaluk "really feel," nor is it intended as a model of how the Ifaluk "think about their feelings." I have argued elsewhere that the concern with "true, underlying feeling" is a local cultural preoccupation and that the dichotomous categories of "cognition" and "affect" are themselves Euroamerican cultural constructions, master symbols that participate in the fundamental organization of our ways of looking at ourselves and others (Lutz 1985a; 1986), both in and outside of social science.

These categories and their ramifications are neither universal nor do they appear particularly useful in their current unexamined state for several reasons. Our ethnotheories of the nature of the person, of the social, and of the mind lead us to bifurcate our studies into the cognitive and the affective, to conceptualize ethnotheories as involving primarily or exclusively the former, and then to perplex over how emotion can be "attached" to ethnotheories so dispassionately defined. Thus, the questions that must continually arise (and remain unanswerable) include, "Does any particular ethnotheoretical model have an effect on the way people feel and behave (for we know that thought, being not–affect, is thereby not motivational)?" and, more generally, "How does the structure of ethnotheory acquire direction and force (the latter being, we know, provided by the definitionally excluded emotion and its energy)?" In talking about ethnotheories, we play with the relations between the elements of cognition and affect but maintain the elements themselves as conceptual primitives.

The dichotomy of thought and emotion is all the more powerful and seemingly irresistible as it is integrated into a large number of other basic cultural themes and dichotomies; thus, we talk about the naturalness of emotion and the culturalness of cognition, the uncontrollability of emotion and the controllability of thought (or rather the need for control of emotion and the lack of such need for thought), hidden and dangerous emotion and more overt and safe thought. One of the most powerful cultural distinctions in which the thought–emotion dichotomy is enmeshed is between facts and values. The alienation of emotion from thought in our explicit theories has its parallel in the perceived irreconcilability of facts and values and represents another disadvantage to maintaining the former dichotomy.

The current ideology and practice of science no doubt underline the importance of the distinction between mental activities (thought) and bodily activity (physical labor as well as emotion), between the judgment of matters of fact (primarily executed in the realm of thoughts) and the judgment of good and bad, or matters of value (often associated with the emotional). It would perhaps be surprising if we did *not* tend to model the world on the basis of our own activity and values as social scientists; if we did not find our informants also maintaining a time and a place for rational, cognitive thought and a time and a place for emotional experience, with ethnotheory then clearly representing their efforts in the former field. If the concepts of emotion and thought were more integrated in analyses of ethnotheories, it might be less tenable to maintain the position that social science develops independently of its social and cultural milieu. As an overly rigid distinction between facts and values is predicated on there being an objective distinction between how we think about something and how we feel about it, a breakdown of the latter would undermine the former and, with it, the view that it is possible to do social science independent of one's socially and culturally constructed interests.

This paper, then, represents my motivated representation of how the Ifaluk passionately model a selected aspect of their psychosocial world. In calling this the Ifaluk "ethnotheory of emotion," I do not mean to imply that they, like us, habitually separate cognitive from affective functioning (Lutz 1985b). Their ethnotheory of emotion is, in both their own and my views, a theory of the whole. Rather than an ill-fitting overlay of cognitive understanding on inchoate emotional experience, what is described here is a set of Ifaluk propositions infused with goals and meaning, interest and intentions.

Notes

1. An earlier version of this paper was delivered at the Conference on Folk Models held in May, 1983, at the Institute for Advanced Study, Princeton, New Jersey. A still earlier version was presented at the 80th Annual Meeting of the American Anthropological Association in Los Angeles in 1981, in a symposium organized by Dorothy Holland and Naomi Quinn and entitled Folk Theories in Everyday Cognition. I would like to thank Edwin Hutchins, Bonnie Nardi, and John Kirkpatrick as well as Dorothy Holland and Naomi Quinn for their helpful comments on earlier drafts. The field research on which this paper is based was conducted in 1977 and 1978 with the kind assistance of the people of Ifaluk and with the aid of NIMH Training grant # MH 5-T-2-14088 to Beatrice Whiting.

2. *Folk theory, cultural theory,* and *ethnotheory* are often used synonymously. The latter term is used in this paper to avoid the connotations of the word *folk* (in the American Heritage Dictionary, it is defined by use of the terms *unsophisticated, unrefined,* and *common*), which implicitly and unnecessarily posit a hierarchic relationship between this type of theory and others.

3. It is interesting to compare two of the major directions taken by people pursuing the long-standing anthropological interest in belief systems. Cognitive anthropologists have been interested in examining belief systems as systems of elements or concepts and as a set of relations between those elements (e.g., Casagrande & Hale 1967; Colby 1975; D'Andrade 1976). Another group of individuals has been interested in the simultaneous examination of the belief systems of the anthropological observer and of the observed (e.g., Dumont 1978; Riesman 1977). Despite their interest in the process of understanding and their concern with questions of validity, cognitive anthropologists have

tended to be relatively uninterested in examining the anthropological research act itself as a process of constructed understandings. The positivist tradition within which cognitive anthropology has developed has meant that its methodological task has been construed as one of "eliminating" observer bias rather than illuminating it.

4. The analogue between computer and human subject is one with obvious limits. To maintain a perspective on those limits, it seems useful to conceptualize this particular analogical exercise as a cultural task. As we model the computer in our own image (and as our image of ourselves is affected by the presence of that technology in our midst), and as that image is a culturally constructed and culturally specific one, it follows that the computer's "failure" to process information in the correct manner represents a cultural judgment that we make about the proper or dominant goals, nature, and content of mental activity.

5. This usage follows D'Andrade (1976). In some cases, the indeterminacy noted may be on the part of the ethnographer, but in most cases it represents indeterminacy in observed use of the emotion terms. This indeterminacy of use often reflects the existence of important and specifiable pragmatic considerations; for example, a severe illness in a close relative will definitely call for *fago* (compassion/love/sadness), whereas a minor cold in a stranger would not (the latter marginal case of illness might call for a marginal case of *fago* 'compassion/love/sadness'). Or, frequent requests for tobacco from a beloved friend would not call for being *nguch* (sick and tired), whereas those same requests from a mentally retarded neighbor would. In other cases, the indeterminacy reflects the fact that people can choose from an array of ways of thinking or acting on the basis of their own *tip-* (will/desire/feeling), which may be unpredictable; for example, in a proposition of type (2) described below, a person may choose to "walk around" but not laugh in conjunction with feeling *ker* (happy/excited). Thus, neither of the latter two behaviors has a determinate relationship with the emotion.

Although there are many other potential sources of indeterminacy in this model (e.g., it is an aggregate model, which should reflect the fact that some individuals hold to particular propositions with more certainty than do some other individuals), these three are the major factors leading to the use of the probabalistic broken arrow. It would be important, in a more detailed model that space will not allow, to distinguish among them.

6. Preliminary analysis of transcripts from interviews on emotion with middle-class adults in urban upstate New York reveals that many definitions of emotions are of the latter type. For example, for one man, "[Annoyance is] a sort of a buzz that you have which sort of prevents you from really experiencing things and trying to understand them in some sort of perspective. It's like a narrowing of perspective." And, for another individual, "Boredom to me I guess is having energy and you don't know what to do with it."

7. G. White (unpublished data) presents a framework for examining the emotional discourse of the A'ara people of the Solomon Islands that includes many of these factors. The assessments made by A'ara include (1) moral evaluation of an action, (2) role structure, (3) social relations, (4) responsibility, and (5) intentionality. The notion of "sadness," then, for example, points to a rule violation with a focus on the "lack of intention or on social ties between Perpetrator and Affected." As seen below, when the Ifaluk stress social ties in such a negative situation, they tend to minimize the moral aspects of their emotional judgments and frequently use the term *nguch* (sick and tired/bored) to describe the situation. Comparative contrasts such as these point to the usefulness of an analysis of what White characterizes as "backwards inferenc-

ing" in emotion-word use and to the importance of such understanding for dealing with the problem of translation.

8. Diverse chains of inference may be involved with some of the other propositional examples. For example, *pak* (homesickness) often leads to inactivity (schema 2) brought on by the desire to sit and think about missing loved ones (schema 2). A situation of inactivity often produces *nguch* (sick and tired/bored) (schema 1). Thus, *pak* =====> *nguch*. As another example, *rus* (panic/fright/surprise) is often caused by sudden, unexpected noise, including particularly noises that are thought to be those of a spirit (schema 1). If *rus* (panic/fright/surprise) is found to be caused by an intentional human agent (if, for example, a child has secretly made the noise in order to frighten another), then it is expected that *song* (justifiable anger) might follow, as intentional frightening would be considered misbehavior (schema 1). Thus, *rus* =====> *song*. The Ifaluk have come to expect that one sort of event (e.g., spirit encounters) may sometimes turn out to be an event of another sort (e.g., spirit imitations or misbehavior). In sum, there are a variety of links between and among events, actions, and emotions that may be evoked in understanding sequences of emotion in an individual.

9. For any ethnographic observation, it is almost always possible to object that the description offered could equally well apply to one's own or other contexts and thus cannot be evidence for cultural difference. These objections nearly always arise, it seems, when the question of differential salience or emphasis in goal structures across cultures is ignored.

10. This type of thinking can sometimes be observed in laypersons whose goal it is to characterize, as simply as possible, the behavior of people whose "otherness" is being emphasized. Ethnotheories about women generated by men in many cultures, for example, often appear to describe women as "single-minded," that is, as motivated by a single (and often unworthy) goal. In general, the singleness of the other's supposed purpose is often a sufficient critique in comparison with the more multifaceted goal structure with which the self is theoretically endowed. Thus, it is important to question the social contexts in which goal descriptions, both academic and lay, are generated.

11. See Hochschild (1979), whose notion of emotion work is useful for modeling this creative aspect of emotional response.

12. I am not suggesting here that the Ifaluk are working with an implicit semantic/pragmatic split in their thinking about emotional meanings. In the absence of the referential emphasis that exists in the Euroamerican ethnotheory of language (Good & Good 1982; Rosaldo 1982), the Ifaluk are more likely to recognize implicitly that they are engaged in the process of simultaneously using and constructing their language and their emotional meanings.

References

Averill, J.
   1974. An analysis of psychophysiological symbolism and its influence on theories of emotion. Journal for the Theory of Social Behavior 4:147–190.
Boehm, C.
   1980. Exposing to moral self in Montenegro: The use of natural definitions to keep ethnography descriptive. American Ethnologist 7(1):1–26.
Cancian, F.
   1975. What Are Norms? Cambridge, England: Cambridge University Press.
Casagrande, J. B. and K. L. Hale
   1967. Semantic relationships in Papago folk definitions. *In* Southwestern

Ethnolinguists, D. Hymes and W. Bittle, eds. The Hague: Mouton Publishers. Pp. 165–193.

Colby, B. N.
1975. Cultural grammars. Science 187:913–919.

D'Andrade, R. G.
1976. A propositional analysis of U.S. American beliefs about illness. *In* Meaning in Anthropology, K. Basso and H. Selby, eds. Albuquerque: University of New Mexico Press. Pp. 155–180.

Davitz, J. R.
1969. The Language of Emotion. New York: Academic Press.

Dumont, J.-P.
1978. The Headman and I: Ambiguity and Ambivalence in the Fieldworking Experience. Austin: University of Texas Press.

Good, B. J. and M.-J. D. Good
1982. Toward a meaning-centered analysis of popular illness categories: 'Fright-illness' and 'heart distress' in Iran. *In* Cultural Conceptions of Mental Health and Therapy, A. Marsella and G. White, eds. Dordrecht, Holland: D. Reidel Publishing Company. Pp. 141–166.

Hochschild, A.
1979. Emotion work, feeling rules, and social structure. American Journal of Sociology 85:551–595.

Hutchins, E.
1980. Culture and Inference: A Trobriand Case Study. Cambridge, Mass.: Harvard University Press.

Izard, C. E.
1977. Human Emotions. New York: Plenum Press.

Lutz, C.
(1985a). Depression and the translation of emotional worlds. *In* Culture and Depression: Studies in the Anthropology and Cross-cultural Psychiatry of Affect and Disorder, A. Kleinman and B. Good, eds. Berkeley: University of California Press. Pp. 63–100.
(1985b). Ethnopsychology compared to what?: Explaining behavior and consciousness among the Ifaluk. *In* Person, Self, and Experience: Exploring Pacific Ethnopsychologies, G. White and J. Kirkpatrick, eds. Berkeley: University of California Press. Pp. 328–366.
1986. Emotion, thought, and estrangement: Emotion as a cultural category. Cultural Anthropology 1:287–309.

Quinn, N.
1982. "Commitment" in American marriage: A cultural analysis. American Ethnologist 9(4):775–798.

Riesman, P.
1977. Freedom in Fulani Social Life: An Introspective Ethnography. Chicago: University of Chicago Press. (First published in 1974 as Société et liberté chez les Peul Djelgôbé de Haute-Volta.)

Rosaldo, M. Z.
1982. The things we do with words: Ilongot speech acts and speech act theory in philosophy. Language in Society 11:203–237.

Schank, R. and R. Abelson
1977. Scripts, Plans, Goals, and Understanding: An Inquiry into Human Knowledge Structures. Hillsdale, N.J.: Lawrence Erlbaum Associates.

Winograd, T.
1977. Formalisms for knowledge. *In* Thinking: Readings in Cognitive Science, P. N. Johnson-Laird and P. C. Wason, eds. Cambridge, England: Cambridge University Press. Pp. 62–71.

13

Ecuadorian illness stories
CULTURAL KNOWLEDGE IN NATURAL DISCOURSE[1]

Laurie Price

The theme of illness occurs frequently in conversation the world over. Illness stories, set apart from the conversational flow by certain structural features, encode cultural models of causation, extensive situation knowledge (Holland 1985) about appropriate behavior when someone is sick, and a vast amount of cultural knowledge about types of treatments and health specialists. Because the tasks of coping with illness fall heavily on family members and friends of an afflicted individual, there is a general need for access to cultural knowledge about ways to respond to different illnesses. Through hearing illness stories, individuals expand the cultural models they use to think about and interpret illness.

During the course of conversation in the highland city of Quito, Ecuadorians often tell one another about health problems that they or others have suffered. Many different cultural models can be discerned in this discourse, but it is situation knowledge of social roles that is most dramatically and exhaustively encoded. Ecuadorian illness stories often transcend their topical focus and express general models of the family, of neighbor and friend relationships, and of social hierarchy in Ecuadorian society. Before discussing these models, this paper briefly summarizes the ethnographic context of illness story-telling and the structure of illness stories.

Ethnographic context

This analysis is based on one year's field research in a marginal, largely Mestizo neighborhood of Quito, Ecuador. Residents of the barrio, here called Las Gradas, tell numerous stories that can be broadly labeled *misfortune tales*. In addition to illness narratives, some of these stories concern car accidents, domestic conflicts, and presidential assassination. This discussion refers only to accounts of illness. Data are "extensive stretches of naturally situated talk," to use Michael Agar's phrase (1982:83). Even though I listened to many stories, I cite examples here only from the recorded narratives of 14 individuals discussing 4 cases of illness. As described in Appendix 1, 3 of the afflicted individuals are children; the fourth is a middle-aged woman. The 14 narrators are all people who played an active role in the illness situation they describe. In addition to hearing conversation about these cases, I observed some of the events and relationships pertinent to each case. Such ethnographic observation promotes more valid analysis of narrative material. For instance, observation reveals aspects of a situation that narrators downplay or omit from their accounts; such omissions often suggest underlying assumptions about shared cultural knowledge on the part of the narrator.

A NATURAL FORM OF DISCOURSE

Evidence that illness stories are a natural form of discourse, rather than a task imposed by the investigator, comes from participant observation in the social life of the neighborhood, from the form of the recorded narratives, and from the many references to other stories that informants say they heard from other people. Friends in the barrio told me illness tales before I showed any special interest in them. Once begun, narrators typically continue their stories with little or no prompting. In some of the transcripts, the same information is presented two or three times in the same basic form and even in many of the same phrases. This suggests that certain narrative sections are remembered by the narrator in chunks, perhaps with particular phrasings or key terms attached. Probably, the same chunks had been related before to other listeners. Few of the storytellers refer to being in an *interview frame* in Tannen's sense (1979).

Most compelling of all the evidence for natural occurrence of this discourse is that about half of the 14 recorded narratives refer to *other* illness stories that narrators had previously been told and had remembered. These "stories within stories" demonstrate that not only do people communicate vital information about illness in story form, but they also remember and apply stories they have heard to situations that arise in their own or others' lives at a later date. For instance, in the narratives about Isabel, the child's mother and grandmother retell stories they had heard about two other individuals with similar disabilities and their treatments.

ILLNESS STORIES IN SOCIAL CONTEXT

Illness stories occur most often in conversation among good friends and among barrio residents and relatives living elsewhere. Women tell the most illness stories, and they tell them mainly to other women in settings of semiprivacy. Some individuals are especially adept at telling this type of story, and such "specialists" tell them more often than others.[3] Barrio residents derive a number of cognitive and social benefits from telling and listening to illness stories, although these benefits are generally not consciously sought or recognized.

First, conversation about illness has problem-solving value because it transmits useful technical information about such things as home remedies, disease symptoms, health care specialists.[4] Even if this information is not immediately relevant to the listener's current problems, it enlarges his or her fund of cultural knowledge with which to meet future illnesses.

Second, through exposure to the many causal propositions in illness narratives, listeners expand and refine their own theories about disease. Such propositions constitute the raw material from which people weave "folk systems of interpretation" (Bohannan 1957). In actual illness situations, a viable cultural model helps individuals locate problematic experiences in a framework of meaning and allays some of the anxiety associated with the situations.

Third, many illness stories focus attention on the caretaker role of the narrator. The narrator frequently asserts in an implicit way: "I did the right thing." This public declaration constitutes a way of negotiating the meaning of the illness events and may be an important source of social validation for the narrator. Finally, it may be hypothesized that sharing illness stories reinforces bonds of mutual support among individuals and intensifies friendships, much as sharing life stories appears to deepen social relationships among middle-class North Americans (Linde this volume).

Structure of illness stories

The illness story follows rules for internal coherence and can be regarded as a *speech act* in the sense of a component of a speech genre. It is an unlabeled speech act, though, and Ecuadorians do not as clearly acknowledge it as a distinctive unit in the way that North Americans acknowledge, for example, a therapeutic interview, lesson, or court case as distinctive units (Hymes 1972; Linde this volume).

Several features set the illness narrative apart from the rest of the conversation. The beginning of the narrative is anchored in a particular time and place, the *orientation,* to use Linde's term (this volume). Typically, the orientation describes how the illness started, its earliest symptomology. Sometimes, however, the narrator begins the story further back in time with description of what caused the illness. In a few cases, the narrator's particular role in the events may lead to his or her anchoring the story at the point at which he or she entered the action. Finally, if the narrator has already told the audience at some other time about an on-going illness, he or she may begin subsequent segments of the story at a time and place appropriate to the new installment.

From the beginning time and place, the narrative moves forward chronologically, describing various events along the way that are pertinent to the illness, such as attempts to treat the malady, struggles to get funds to pay for specialist care, and family interactions about the illness. For an illness story to be coherent, the narrator must at some point discuss cause. This usually occurs at or toward the beginning of the story but may recur throughout the narrative, as the unfolding events are associated with changing notions of cause. Like life story segments, many illness narratives contain a *coda* or end phrase. Common ones are: "And, so, that is what happened," or "And now, she is as you can see." Appendix 2 points out the structural features identified in one illness narrative used in this analysis.

Cultural models in illness stories

Stories told among Las Gradans acquaint listeners with entire episodes of illness that they have not personally experienced. As evident in the retelling of such stories, the entire episode often gets stored in listeners' own memories of events, in streamlined form. Such discourse plays a dynamic role in the construction and refinement of shared cognitive models pertaining to illness. Second-hand episodes contribute to development of schemas, particularly schemas for situations that do not occur very often. Furthermore, natural discourse about illness transmits factual information about treatment and specialist alternatives, causal notions, situation knowledge about social roles in illness, and a picture of the narrator's feelings about the events he or she describes – the *affective propositions* expressed in a narrative (Labov & Fanshel 1977:105).

Although notions about the causes of health problems are usually more explicitly stated, situation knowledge (Holland 1985) about appropriate behavior when someone falls ill constitutes the pith of what these narratives communicate and is the primary focus of this analysis. Such situation knowledge is organized within more broadly applied cultural models of the family, of extrafamilial social support, and of social hierarchy and biomedicine in Ecuador.

ANALYSIS OF ILLNESS STORIES

Just as a life story reveals the cultural knowledge by which an urban addict survives (Agar 1980), and interviews with North Americans reveal cultural models of marriage (Quinn 1982), so do Ecuadorian illness stories contain numerous "traces" of cognitive models that bear on interpretation of illness. Because tacit (understood) knowledge shapes natural discourse to such a large degree, important traces are found not only in what is said, but also in what is left unsaid.

In telling illness stories, narrators take for granted that listeners share many of their assumptions about how the world works. The missing "shared knowledge" must be filled in, if outsiders are to understand the logical connections among utterances, and the cultural models that underlie them. For example, Passage A in Appendix 3 forms part of a narrative by Olivia about her little sister Susana's acute illness at the age of 1. Olivia describes the treatment and says: "We did that and it helped her." Her account does not mention the fact that, at the time, Olivia was quite young (12 years of age) to be taking an active role in the treatment and care of her sibling. If a similar story were related in North America, the speaker probably would have included her age as a salient fact. In contrast, among marginal Ecuadorians, young girls are typically expected to carry grave responsibilities in the care of younger sisters and brothers. The Ecuadorian narrator might lose the audience if he or she emphasized this feature of the action. By *not* making a special point about such behavior on the part of a 12-year-old, such a narrative both reflects and reinforces cultural expectations that such behavior is "normal and natural."

What are, from the outsider's standpoint, omissions of information (due to narrators' assumptions about shared cultural knowledge) tell us a great deal about cultural differences between North America and Ecuador. We must also assess parts of the narratives that seem unusual to us as outsiders in the opposite way: that is, why some facets of a story are presented with what seems to us to be overelaborate detail.

Often, elaborations indicate a deviation from the standard expectations for role behavior. For instance, one narrator delivers a lengthy, detailed description of events that prevented her father's presence when her brother died. Clearly, this section of her story constitutes an apology for deviation from the Ecuadorian schema for dying. Narrative passages may also be elaborated not because they represent *deviation* from expectations but because they depict events that are in themselves highly salient to speakers and listeners in highland Ecuador. An example of this is the description of wakes and funerals in Ecuadorian illness stories. The elaborate detail accorded these events no more indicates deviation from the situation schema than does the elaborate detail accorded the dress of the bride and bridal attendants in traditional accounts of weddings in the United States. To understand discourse, we must first determine what the culturally salient actions in a given domain are. Second, we must pay careful attention to narrative context in order to discover how a particular section of highly elaborated discourse relates to the cultural model in question.

Illness stories contain many other traces of cultural knowledge beside the inclusion/exclusion of detail and elaboration patterns. Some other traces explicitly used to analyze discourse include repetitions, key words, generalizations, metaphors, false starts, evaluative statements, and hedges (Bohannan 1957; Labov & Fanshel 1977; Lakoff & Johnson 1980; Quinn 1982; Tannen 1979). Many other discourse analysts undoubtedly base their conclusions on some of these linguistic patterns but are less explicit about doing so. An important question to consider is how each of these traces relates to the underlying knowledge structures that are generating the utterances. E. Hutchins (personal communication) puts the question this way: "By what connections can we claim that generalizations, repetitions, key words, counterexamples, and evaluative statements (and inferences) are traces of knowledge structures in discourse?" A related question concerns the choice of which particular indicators or traces to use in an analysis. With analysis of key words, for example, is it implied that the knowledge structures behind that discourse are primarily organized by way of key words? The following analysis emphasizes patterns of omission and elaboration to show how illness stories transmit cultural information about social roles in illness situations. Evaluative statements and a narrative device I call the *counterexample* are also shown to be important vehicles for ideas about what is inappropriate or unexpected behavior within the Ecuadorian cultural model of illness.

Situation knowledge, organized within particular cultural models, consists of generalizations about the parts people play, the usual activities these entail, and the *role-identities* associated with a particular kind of situation (Holland 1985). Without exception, illness stories encode significant cultural knowledge about the role the narrator played in the events of an illness. Whether husband, neighbor, mother, or sister, the storyteller always focuses considerable attention on action in which he or she took part. The following discussion of cultural models and schemas must necessarily be limited to consideration of these knowledge structures as they relate only to the interpretation of illness. Although it is suggested that the cultural models described here are more broadly applied to other kinds of interpretations and other kinds of tasks, this analysis does not encompass those broader applications.

CULTURAL MODEL OF THE FAMILY

Responsibilities and activities of mothers occupy a distinct and central place in the Ecuadorian model of the family. The mother is the core of the family, as conceived by marginal Ecuadorians. Mother also constitutes an extremely powerful symbolic entity in cultures that, like Ecuador's, are shaped by Hispanic Catholicism. The symbolic power of the mother image derives from associations with the Virgin Mary, "Mother of God," and with numerous miracles attributed to her – miracles that have detailed histories, concrete locations, and tangible commemorative events associated with them. Since motherhood is modeled after Mary, it symbolically entails that peculiar mixture of ravishing but saintly beauty made somehow more beautiful through suffering the pain of love and death. Motherhood as an image embodies the ideal of love that is superhumanly strong but that nevertheless offers practical help and is gentle and approachable.

Motherhood in illness narratives.   A striking example of cultural assumptions about mothers' roles is found in the narrative Sra. Maria tells about her crippled daughter, Susana. The assumptions are revealed not only by what she says but also by what she does not say. In her story of the events, Sra. Maria never mentions that for months she daily carried her 6-year-old daughter (in a cast from waist to ankle) down a 200-step flight of public stairs and 4 blocks to the nearest bus stop so the girl could go to physical therapy. This constitutes an extreme example in that the father of the child drives a bus parked near the house every night. During the many months of this grueling routine, the couple never made arrangements to shift some of the responsibility for Susana's transportation to the father. Also, people talking about the child's condition take for granted this herculean effort on the part of the mother; such efforts are the unmarked case for mothers. General statements about mothers and counterexamples in the stories reveal cultural knowledge about the significance of the mother's role. Narrators say, "Only God knows the mother's heart," and "the pain of a mother is like that." Explicit general propositions about husbands or daughters or other roles or role-identities do not appear in these illness narratives.

Counterexamples, or narrative descriptions of individuals who are not fulfilling their roles adequately or in expected ways, throw into sharp relief the role expectations attached to mothers in illness situations. Passage B of Appendix 3 describes the behavior of mothers who leave their children in the public hospital and do not participate actively in their care during hospitalization. The emotionally charged tone of the passage should be evaluated in light of knowledge about hospitals in Ecuador, with their inadequate nursing attention and risk of death. Both the tone and the repetition of "She didn't come, she didn't come . . ." reveal not only that the narrator is making a statement about a deviation from her cultural schema for the mother's role but also that she has strong feelings about such a deviation. This passage and others like it reveal feeling and thought as "parallel systems of processing" (D'Andrade 1981; Zajonc 1980). The mother is saying, in effect, "Mothers are supposed to be near their children and take part in their physical care, especially if they're in the hospital, because they will probably die otherwise." The emotions attached to this counterexample can be paraphrased as, "I feel bad about these sick, abandoned children and good about myself for not being a mother like that." Affective propositions are so central to most of these illness narratives that it can be said that if cultural models of social roles drive the narratives, emotional propositions are the fuel that empower them.

More counterexamples about motherhood occur in the narrative told by Elsa's neighbor, Mercedes. In fact, Mercedes's account of Elsa's condition is one long counterexample; it thoroughly dramatizes a number of instances in which Elsa failed to meet her responsibilities as mother of a family. Passage C exemplifies counterexample material in Mercedes's illness story. The same facts also appear in accounts of the illness given by other individuals but are not presented to imply personal fault. For instance, Elsa's daughter Rosa mentions the multiple miscarriages as a possible cause of her mother's illness but does not imply that these could have been avoided. The point here is that counterexamples can easily be constructed out of facts pertaining to an illness, but narrators who present counterexamples usually have an affective point to make.

A corollary proposition to the one that the mother is the vital core of family life is that marriages that produce no children are in trouble. In the

Las Gradan model of the family, children not only bring fulfillment to the mother, they are also what "glues" (*pegar*) a man to his wife and conjugal home over the long run. All of this logically fits given the initial premise that a family unit must have a mother to flourish; children are what turn a wife into a "real" mother.

Gender differences, collective responsibility.   The cultural model of family revealed in these illness stories shows clear gender differentiation in expectations about decision making, economic arrangements, nursing, and other role activities associated with health problems. Female family members (e.g., wives, mothers, sisters, daughters) are expected to bear the main burdens of nursing the ill at home and making forays into the specialist health-care system on behalf of their families. Although the prototypic family role for a woman is that of mother, the cultural model prescribes that the burden of caring for the ill be borne collectively by related females within a household compound. (Ethnographic observation confirms this as a general behavioral pattern.) Expectations of collective female responsibility for therapy management and caretaking of children are reflected in narratives about 3-year-old Isabel. The child's mother, grandmother, and aunt reside in the same compound. In talking about attempts to cure the child, each of them uses the plural pronoun "we" rather than "I." Context shows that the "we" refers to the three women. Males make cameo appearances in the accounts but are always clearly identified when they play a part.

Cultural knowledge about male roles.   What do accounts of illnesses convey about Ecuadorian folk theory concerning male roles in such situations? The male head of a household may be described as *padre de la familia* (father of the family) or just as frequently as *jefe de la familia* (chief of the family). This is partly an administrative position but also involves financial support of the family unit. All adult males in the household are expected to earn money and contribute some of their earnings to the family. Apart from this expectation, male roles in family life at home are not as clearly defined as are female roles – there is no single prototypic male role identity nor set of usual activities within the home as there are for females. The model accords males the freedom to come and go, with their primary responsibility being to support the family financially. Even though pain is manifestly and prominently part of cultural expectations about the mother role, male roles within the family are not associated with suffering or pain. It appears that the Ecuadorian cultural model of the family allows, indeed encourages, women to feel fully the anguish of a calamity that befalls a family member but does not prepare men either psychologically or socially to acknowledge that kind of anguish.

Illness narratives indicate that men have, or know where to get, cultural knowledge about seeking therapy and about home treatments. The narratives also indicate, however, that no one expects men to get involved in those activities if women in the family are available to assume the responsibility. In Passage D of Appendix 3, Carmen (the mother of the toddler who fell on the public stairs) recounts events at a moment when the child's condition worsened. She mentions Ramiro's reluctance to wake up and help care for the child but does not evaluate his behavior negatively. Rather, she excuses it by pointing out the hard work that led to the father's fatigue. His refusal to get up does not indicate lack of affection for the child according to his wife's story. She later describes him as desperately wanting to obtain good specialist treatment for Lucia. While at home, however, he sleeps, secure in the knowledge that the mother will do everything she can do to care for the child and in the knowledge that he is not necessarily expected to get actively involved at home.

What happens, given the Ecuadorian model of family life, when the mother of a family becomes chronically ill? Clearly, this kind of situation would be likely to generate different interpretations than the same condition suffered by a child or a male member of the family. Among other things, this type of situation can produce serious role strains within the family, which will be reflected in illness narratives. In Case 4, which is summarized in Appendix 1, Fernando takes an active part in managing his wife's therapy. His 17-year-old daughter is too young to take on full responsibility for this, although she does do all the primary caretaking of her invalid mother at home. (Neither she nor her father point to her full-time devotion to her mother's care as anything worthy of praise; such a role for the eldest daughter at home is the unmarked case.)

Themes of money and treatment costs pervade Fernando's account of his wife's affliction. He talks at length about the expense of various consultations and treatments, giving precise figures, and also about his personal efforts to obtain funds to finance specialist care. Overall, men's narratives show more concern with the economic dimension of illness situations. In addition, female narrators often make a special point of noting the participation of men in the economics of health care. An example of this is found in Passage E, in which Isabel's mother and grandmother give credit to the child's grandfather, her mother's father, for playing a vital role in financial decision-making about treatment. This and other passages reveal that the cultural model of illness situations prescribes an active role for males in matters of money, especially in negotiation with formal financial institutions. (The primary source of commercial loans for marginal Ecuadorians is at their place of employment. Men are more likely than women to hold structured employment. So, men's greater responsibility for this aspect of coping with illness derives from both economic contingencies and cultural ideals.)

Sra. Maria also emphasizes male participation in certain decisions made about surgery for her daughter. She describes her early attempts to get help for the child. The third doctor she consulted told her the child needed an operation immediately. Her story continues, as noted in Passage F, in which she shows that her husband has the final say about treatment. A few years later, Sra. Maria took her daughter to traditional curers, and then, following her mother-in-law's advice, she consulted a physician. First, she says that *she* went to see the doctor. Then she amends this and specifies that she and her *husband* went to see him. Passage G, like many of the narratives, indicates the special recognition given to a man for playing even a minor part in the management of an illness in the family. Narratives reinforce the cultural expectation that women automatically assume major responsibility for caretaking and seeking therapy, while the final authority lies with men to make decisions about treatment that involves more than incidental expense.

Fernando's story about his wife's problems demonstrates abundant knowledge about certain aspects of the specialist health care systems; the majority of this account centers on his efforts to get effective treatment for his wife. The narrative also reveals a cultural bias in favor of including women, even young ones, in efforts to manage the therapy of a sick family member. On most of his forays to seek specialist care, Fernando took along one or more of his older daughters. His grown sons who live at home did not participate actively in the illness situation. Their behavior elicits no special criticism, just as the daughter's caretaking behavior elicits no particular praise; both the sons and the daughters are conforming to the cultural expectations in a case of this sort.

Folk "physics" of health behavior.   Narratives reveal the cultural notion that a special impetus is needed to "get moving" on health problems. A key concept in the "physics" of motivation is embodied in the phrase *hacer empeño*. This phrase means "to get someone (or oneself) moving to accomplish something." Even though people take for granted tremendous ambivalence about acknowledging a health problem as serious and about "moving" into action to seek specialist care, they also expect family members to monitor each other's health and push for specialist consultations. In Passage H, Sra. Maria credits her mother-in-law with pushing her (putting her in motion) to see another surgeon about her child's infirmity. Isabel's mother and aunt discuss their efforts to get a cousin "moving" toward treatment. Illness narratives suggest that the typical "motivator" is a member of one's family network, but not necessarily of one's immediate domestic group. In addition, narratives reveal that pushing for action on a health problem does not necessarily entail expectations of follow-up help with the mechanics of finding or financing specialist care.

MODEL OF EXTRAFAMILIAL SOCIAL SUPPORT
Ecuadorians hold distinctly different notions concerning roles and social support within the family and roles and social support characteristic of extrafamilial relations. Many illness stories implicitly address this ques-

tion: "How do you mobilize other people to help with an illness in the family when they have expertise or access to assistance that you don't have?" A counterbalancing and equally important component of this model consists of propositions to the effect that help available outside the family circle is quite limited and should not be depended on except in certain rare circumstances.

The proposition that only family is expected to help constitutes tacit knowledge and is expressed when illness story narrators simply omit comment on help that is not forthcoming from friends and neighbors. However, when asked about social support, many Las Gradans do not hesitate to state the proposition directly. They say, "neighbors don't help each other here"; "the only ones you can really depend on are family"; and "nobody (neighbors) really knows each others' problems here." This proposition is further embodied in other cultural representations that are part of the Las Gradas verbal tradition, in particular, proverbs. Proverbs such as those cited below reinforce the cultural model of extrafamilial social support by reminding people to keep their distance from others, to think in terms of reciprocity, and to beware of giving or receiving too much kindness, especially outside of a standard reciprocal exchange context.

"Too many visits make you less welcome."
"Give the hand, get grabbed by the elbow."
"Every burro with its own saddle."
"Today for you, tomorrow for me."
"Hands that give, receive."
"If you give bread to a strange dog, you'll lose the bread and lose the
    dog."

Explanations of these proverbs by Las Gradans indicate that people interpret them primarily as advice to use caution in conducting relationships outside the family. Ethnographic observation shows that neighbors and friends do, in fact, help one another considerably in coping with various problems. But this fact in no way detracts from the authenticity of the cultural propositions that they do not, or the admonition that one should not depend on them to do so.

Another counterexample reveals the proposition that only family will help. A neighbor of the toddler's family describes how doctors regard her supportive behavior in that family's crisis as quite unusual. She describes events at two institutions where she accompanies the child's mother to seek treatment. At both locations, staff members ask her: "Who are you? Are you the child's mother? If you aren't, why are you so concerned and involved in this?" Here, the narrator presents her own behavior as a counterexample. By elaborating on the surprise of the medical personnel, the narrative shows that the neighbor interprets her own behavior as an exception to the standard cultural model.

Even while the cultural model of extrafamilial social relations leads marginal Ecuadorians to limit expectations of aid from nonrelatives, it also embodies knowledge about culturally appropriate strategies for developing the kind of extrafamilial relationships that most likely will result in instrumental and other social support. People obtain much of this knowledge from descriptions other people give of how they managed to build these connections. Isabel's family recount how they pursued the ideal strategy for marginal Ecuadorians faced with serious illness. They found benefactors. As described in the narrative, the primary benefactor was located on the advice of a friend and a salesclerk. Isabel's mother and grandmother credit this female doctor (*doctora*) with saving the child's life and curing her infirmity.

CULTURAL MODEL OF SOCIAL HIERARCHY AND BIOMEDICINE

Many different terms exist by which people in highland Ecuador place one another within a distinct social hierarchy. As Stark (1981) demonstrates, how people use these terms in one highland town varies systematically according to the social category in which the speaker fits. However, social classifications are organized in a very clear-cut way on the basis of *palanca* (literally, "lever," or "handle"). Degrees of *palanca* ranging from "no access to goods and services" to "high access to goods and services" are interpreted as the distinctive features that differentiated people from one another within the social hierarchy. As such, they were used as implicit markers, rather than as explicit labels, of social categories (Stark 1981:391).

Las Gradans also conceptualize the social world as a place in which various categories of people have greater or lesser amounts of *palanca*. This term comes up in a number of the illness stories in connection with biomedical institutions. For instance, a friend of Isabel's family talks about their attempts to get assistance with medical expenses: "[The Patronato] is an organization that helps poor children, sick children, and like that. But you know the bureaucracy, no? If we have no 'leverage' (*palancas*), they don't help us." The cultural model of social hierarchy found in Las Gradas conceptualizes people as possessing different amounts of *palanca*. It also divides them in a dichotomous way according to wealth. This division is represented in the terms *pobres* (poor people) and *ricos* (rich people). Residence in certain barrios of Quito almost automatically certifies one as a pobre or a rico. It is tacitly understood that biomedical institutions belong to and are staffed primarily by people belonging to the latter category. Models of wealth and *palanca* together form the cognitive landscape that pervades schemas of biomedical health care.

Physicians in illness stories.   In their illness tales, Isabel's family describes a greedy, unethical doctor who lied to the family during the early stages of their attempts to get treatment for the child. Their descriptions of this physician were constrained and understated, partly because the narrators were uncertain about where I stood with relation to doctors and other professionals, but more because lack of ethics is nothing remarkable in a doctor from their standpoint. A narrative about a different case shows the ramifications of the proposition that physicians are, as a rule, not to be trusted. The mother of the toddler who suffered fatal head injuries says, "I imagine, frankly, that the doctors gave her a poisonous injection so she would die right away." In effect, this narrative proposes that it is not out of the question to suspect doctors of hastening the death of an ill child.

In contrast, narrators from Isabel's family describe the female doctora who befriended them in glowing and elaborate detail. She is transformed into another counterexample. By emphasizing and elaborating the doctora as a character in their stories, the narrators again reveal that expected behavior on the part of physicians does not include real affection for patients, genuine sympathy, "vows of poverty," or being willing to wait for payment. Their effusively grateful language communicates knowledge about how they expect the typical doctor to act.

Because the doctora's behavior constitutes a surprising deviation from the cultural model of social interactions with professionals, Isabel's family attempt to explain this exception to the rule. They do this through references to person theory (Holland 1985). Passage I expresses their proposition that the doctora is kind and compassionate toward poor children because she is pretty and an unmarried woman with no children of her own. Many other passages in the accounts of Isabel's illness also reveal person theory at work, including direct quotes of the doctora's explaining her own unusual behavior as due to "conscience" and other personal factors.

How do counterexamples relate to knowledge structures concerning social roles in illness? First, narrators who present counterexamples are talking about "exceptions to the rule" that are usually highly salient to them. The exception matters because the rule matters. For instance, counterexamples concerning mothers and doctors indicate that these roles are pivotal ones in the domain of illness behavior. Second, this material throws into sharp relief the cultural model of social roles by capturing the essence of what a mother or doctor does not act like, in the usual course of events. By definition, counterexamples pinpoint the "difference that makes a difference" (Bateson 1972; Hutchins, personal communication) from the emic point of view. Thus, from the two counterexamples discussed here, we find that a standard entailment of the mother role is that, "A mother tends her children, whatever happens." A standard entailment of *doctor* can be embodied in this proposition: "A doctor expects his fee immediately, whatever happens."

Nurses in illness stories. The Ecuadorian model of biomedical institutions clearly distinguishes doctors from nurses in terms of their interactional style with pobres. Before specific cultural propositions about nurses are identified, it should be noted that *enfermeras* (nurses) is a category that marginal Ecuadorians use to refer to practically all the nonphysician practitioner roles women play in biomedical treatment systems; in other words, Las Gradans do not generally distinguish between the Ecuadorian equivalents of registered nurses, licensed practical nurses, and nurses' aides. The differences in licensing and education between these practitioner types are not salient to most Las Gradans.

Medical doctors are thought of as typically greedy and not compassionate, but at least they can be approached by pobres. As Sra. Maria says, "Oh the doctors, yeah, they're nice enough. They answer when they are greeted." While you may not get good treatment from a doctor, at least they are 'civil.'" Marginal Ecuadorians put a great deal of emphasis on respectful interaction styles, particularly on greeting and leave-taking rituals. In contrast to physicians, nurses (particularly nurses who work in hospitals) are widely described in natural discourse as *groseras*. This term can be roughly defined as "rude, uncivil, brutal." One narrator says:

> There are children who can't move [in the hospital]. They can't move and the nurses come and throw their food on the bedside table, [saying] "If you can eat, eat; if not, then don't eat." That's how it is. That's how this type of Señorita is – they have no heart, we could say a word. There was one child that couldn't eat, bedridden like this, they had him with a weight attached to his little leg. I fed him when I came. But, the nurse said to him: "There it is. You have to eat it. What do you want me to do, put it in your mouth? If you can eat, go ahead and take it, go on, eat," she said.

Two things should be pointed out about the proposition that nurses are *groseras*. First, not all illness story narrators communicate that proposition, although they would certainly all recognize it as a common idea in their neighborhood. Second, the cognitive model of social hierarchy as applied to biomedical systems in Ecuador dramatically differentiates hospitals (and hospital nurses) from private clinics (and clinic nurses, by extension). Thus, cultural propositions about nurses may not have as much to do with categorizing the type of person who works as a nurse as with categorizing the typical behavior of nurses who work within a certain type of institution.

Clinics versus hospitals. Private clinics in Ecuador are like small-scale hospitals, with their own surgical facilities and patient accommodations. Clinics are expensive and are associated with ricos (rich people). Hospitals, on the other hand, are public and are supposed to charge nothing, by a recent act of national law. Hospitals are associated with pobres and with inadequate, uncaring treatment. Passage J is profoundly shaped by cultural knowledge about how to maneuver as a "marginal" in urban Ecuador. It reveals a proposition that doctors and nurses, with few exceptions, should not be trusted to give adequate or compassionate care if one is poor. A concrete expression of this proposition is found in references to "tipping" hospital personnel. The reference to "tips" in Passage J reveals the assumptions on the part of barrio residents that hospital staff expect to be paid directly for giving good service to patients and that inadequate care will be given to patients who fail to observe this custom.

Schemas of therapy management in getting biomedical treatment are profoundly shaped by the distinction people make between clinics and hospitals and encompass a behavioral routine that guides Las Gradan interpretation of efforts to get biomedical care. It is considered important that therapy managers at least attempt to get private clinic treatment before resorting to hospitalization. Only after inquiring about the expense of clinic treatment and finding it too expensive do they turn to hospitals. Not only is this a behavioral routine, but it also constitutes a highly salient element in illness narrative. Many of the 14 narrators gave attention to the clinic-first, hospital-second pattern. As explained in a later section, when narrators describe their efforts to obtain treatment at private clinics first, they are making a social and affective statement that they "did the right thing."

A cultural model of social hierarchy informs schemas concerning biomedical treatment among marginal Ecuadorians. These 14 illness narratives show that biomedical practitioners are associated with higher social status; a distinction is made between doctors and nurses based on interpersonal interaction styles; private clinic and public hospital treatment facilities and personnel are regarded as dramatically different, partly on the basis of social class factors; and, on the whole, their cultural model of biomedicine guides marginal Ecuadorians to be wary and mistrustful, unless they manage to develop a personal relationship with someone who has palanca in the biomedical system.

As the analysis presented in this section shows, illness tales communicate extensive cultural knowledge about social roles in illness situations, including expectations of male and female kin, neighbors and friends, and physicians and nurses. Communication of such information through conversation and narrative both augments and reinforces shared cognitive models used to interpret illness situations. These models constitute a subset of cultural models of social relations in general, as held by marginal urbanites in the highlands of Ecuador. However, illness narratives do more than encode situation knowledge. The following sections show how narrative communication also acts as a dynamic vehicle for subtle negotiations about illness causation and about feelings associated with illness situations.

Theories of causation in illness stories

Illness narratives reveal much greater fascination with the causes of an affliction than with its symptoms or diagnosis; stories present numerous theories about what caused this or that health problem. A preference for problems of cause has been documented in other cultures as well. For instance, North Americans have been shown to think more about "the consequences and preconditions of illnesses" than the attributes or features that define disease (D'Andrade 1976). Ecuadorians take seriously the task of identifying causes of a sickness, especially in cases of serious or chronic affliction. During informal discussions, people evaluate the truth value of the causal propositions of others. Cultural consensus emerges as participants in a conversation work out the relationships between different beliefs and so refine their explanatory models.

Narratives put forth three kinds of instrumental, or immediate cause. These include physical factors (e.g., temperature), emotional factors (e.g., anger), and behavioral factors (e.g., "She was playing on the stairs.") (Glick 1967). Some narratives also suggest "ultimate" causes, notions that involve some degree of moral judgment of the ill person or family.

MULTIPLE NOTIONS OF CAUSE

It is striking that many narrators put forward a number of different causes for any given illness. Sra. Elsa's daughter, for example, attributes her mother's disease to at least six distinctly different factors: too many miscarriages, anger (*iras*) at children and husband, anger held inside, her son's death, drinking hot medicinal teas prescribed by a curer but not staying in bed afterward, and doing laundry too soon after giving birth to her last child. The daughter's narrative also cites other causes for the disease that have been identified by various health-care specialists and other family members. Sra. Elsa and her husband refer to many of the same causal notions independently of their daughter and each other. The family has obviously discussed the problem of causation, and family members are aware of each others' theories, although no consensus has been reached. Intrafamilial verbal communication about illness is another way in which individuals refine cultural models of illness.

Some narratives demonstrate not only multiple notions of cause, but also an effort to judge the truth of various causal propositions, particularly those promoted by other people. Susana's sister first states that the child's hip malformation was caused by her mother's work as a weaver when pregnant with Susana. Later in her narrative, she returns to the question of cause, presenting a causal notion she has heard from her mother and rejecting it. In Passage K, we see an individual striving for logical consistency between various body notions and propositions about illness causation. Several narrators take such a logical and "constructive" approach to causal theories bearing on illness. In telling illness stories, some individuals are also striving to clarify relationships between different causal notions.

Moral cause and situated social purposes.   Relatively few of the 14 recorded narratives express the proposition that an illness or accident was due to someone's immoral behavior. When these propositions are expressed, it is usually by a speaker who is not related to the sufferer. A neighbor of Carmen and Ramiro's attributes their child's accident and subsequent death to moral shortcomings of family members. The father drinks and abandoned his wife temporarily; the mother does not pray enough. The narrator notes that the child's grandmother had actual caretaking responsibility for the toddler when she fell and yet does not place any blame on this person for negligence. What might seem to us as North Americans to be guilt is not evaluated that way by the neighbor. She is operating with a different set of assumptions about family role responsibilities and about what kinds of actions bring punishment from God and what kinds do not.

A neighbor of Sra. Elsa's traces her illness to many different causes, a number of which consist of irresponsible or immoral behavior. The neighbor, Mercedes, frames her most extreme proposition about moral shortcomings in a way that allows her to get the idea across but dissociate herself from proposing it:

> They say that when an illness can't be cured by doctors, it's a thing caused by the devil. . . .

Dice que, or "they say," is an oft-occurring linguistic device in these stories; it functions to allow the speaker to say something without taking a stand on the truth value of the statement.

When propositions about moral causation are expressed in stories, they reveal a great deal about Ecuadorian models of proper role behavior. The extent to which these notions are openly asserted depends on the narrator's social relationship to the person who is ill and on the narrator's purposes in conversation in a given social context. However, whether narrators openly express such notions, they probably often have these in mind as interpretational possibilities.[5] Thus, social context factors should be taken into account in assessing illness beliefs as a distinctive body of cultural knowledge. How would the system of beliefs about illness that can be distilled from analysis of illness stories compare with the sets of interrelated propositions about illness resulting from a more formal elicitation approach in the same population? This question cannot be answered here since a formal elicitation of illness beliefs was not carried out in Ecuador. However, it seems likely that many illness narratives would reveal more causal propositions of the moral type than would an elicitation study. People tend to think of and talk about moral causes in the context of particular, on-going social relationships. Moral causation probably most often comes to mind in atypical cases of illness – very serious or chronic afflictions. Formal elicitation procedures, on the other hand, may access beliefs only on a general and rather abstract level: Respondents focus on the unmarked case that is largely detached from knowledge of specific people and is irrelevant to the normal social purposes of the respondent in talking about illness.

The point here is that cultural knowledge can best be conceptualized as a system of ideas that people use according to their needs and purposes, rather than as a deterministic grid that directs their thinking. The next, and final, section considers natural discourse from the standpoint of people's social and emotional needs in conversation about illness. Not only do narratives communicate situation knowledge and causal notions, but they also dramatically communicate the narrators' feelings and purposes in the situations they describe.

Communication of feeling in illness narrative

Affect powerfully influences how people apply cultural knowledge to cognitive tasks, as Hutchins shows (this volume). His analysis identifies the affective (in this case, subconscious) connections that lead a Trobriand villager to use a particular myth to explain a seemingly unrelated phenomenon of malevolent spirit visits. It is not surprising that affect also influences the task of formulating interpretations of illness and that many illness narratives make important statements at the affective level.

Most of the recorded narratives analyzed here express feeling in a powerful way, while ostensibly only describing events. The pattern of using narrative to communicate strong feelings indirectly has been documented in other cultures and conversational genres, most dramatically by Labov and Fanshel (1977) in a study of North American psychotherapeutic discourse. In a classic example, they show how a client expresses angry rejection of a therapist's request by telling a story about her aunt. The expanded meaning of the client's story was inferred partly from the authors' knowledge of the client's life (revealed in other therapy sessions) and from such physical factors as the speaker's intonation, pauses, repetitions, and movements. The affective propositions in these Ecuadorian illness narratives have also been inferred partially through contextual information and nonverbal cues.

"I DID THE RIGHT THING."

Many of these illness stories dramatically encode the affective proposition that "I did the right thing" (i.e., "I am a good mother/daughter/ neighbor/husband"). The more caretaking responsibility a narrator has for the afflicted person, the more pronounced this affective message tends to be. The more distant the teller is, socially, from the events and the individuals involved in them, the less pronounced this affective message is. Logically, the "I did the right thing" proposition appears in its most distilled and dramatic form in stories mothers tell about their children's illnesses. The Ecuadorian schema associated with "mother" very clearly incorporates an affective component. Just as the term *hot* fuses together a representation of the "factual external condition" and how we feel about that (D'Andrade 1981), so the term *mother* among marginal Ecuadorians automatically entails a large potential for pain. People are aware of this component of the role and even point it out with general statements. Part of this cultural knowledge is directly experiential. The personal experiences, however, are shaped and reinforced by cultural representations, particularly religious representations.

A mother describes her second round of struggle to get treatment for her child (Case 1). The public hospital to which Sra. Carmen wants the child admitted tries to get her to take the girl to another hospital across town. In Passage L, the woman asserts implicitly that she did all she possibly could to ensure the child's recovery by struggling to keep her in what she thought was the safest hospital available. The same mother presents a second variation of the proposition "I did the right thing" when she describes her resumption of normal life after a long period of incapacitating grief. First, she recounts the events in which a female acquaintance advises her not to cry any more. She describes how friends urge her to moderate her grief, reminding her that the child is in heaven and is watching over and praying for her mother and the rest of the family. Even more central to Sra. Carmen's narrative is description of a dream she had in which her deceased daughter appeared as an angel. In the dream, the child asks her mother not to grieve any more, because the mother's tears are keeping the child from entering a beautiful paradise. Both sections of narrative implicitly assert that the narrator is "doing the right thing" by overcoming depression about her child's death and going on with life.

In his story about his wife's disease (Case 4), Fernando communicates two major affective propositions. The familiar "I'm doing the right thing" assertion is embodied in his repeated and detailed accounts of the many hospitals, clinics, doctors, and religious healing specialists he has taken his wife to see for diagnosis and treatment. The second proposition is the less common, "This illness (ill person) makes me angry and frustrated!" Fernando communicates this proposition through detailed description of how his wife accuses him of being unfaithful, makes unreasonable demands on his time, and does not "really try" to get well (see Passage M).

Another account of Elsa's illness, by her caretaker daughter Rosa, contains the complete and spontaneously included narrative of how Rosa's brother died from cancer. As part of her narrative, she recounts her brother's dying words:

> My aunt told me, "Your brother said this to me. He told me to tell you that he is going to take care of you, to keep watch over you, in order that you go on caring for her." Because I am the only one [of us in the family] that takes care of my mother, that takes care of her, that has the strength to take care of her.

The affective point of this segment of narrative can be paraphrased: "I am struggling, and afraid of this burden, but I am proud of the strength I have shown so far." Of all the illness situations, that of a disabling chronic disease for which many treatments have been tried and failed provokes the most thought and feeling. Just as the situation is complex and emotionally charged, so are the stories told about it.

WHY SAY IT WITH NARRATIVE?

People often express affective propositions implicitly, rather than explicitly, precisely because making these assertions directly in conversations violates rules of social interaction. Because illness experiences that are worth talking about tend to be highly emotionally charged, feelings may be what narrators most want to communicate to their listeners. Affective propositions that are prominent in many Ecuadorian illness stories can be paraphrased as follows: "I did the right thing"; "My part in these events was important"; "I care deeply about this (ill) person and am upset by his or her suffering"; and "This situation makes me very angry and frustrated." One other affective proposition that many illness narratives clearly express concerns specialist health care, particularly biomedical health care. This emotional theme can be paraphrased along the lines of: "We resent being deceived and treated disrespectfully by medical personnel without compassion; we feel bad being so powerless." Since Ecuador offers no recourse to victims of medical malpractice, illness stories constitute one of the few ways to air grievances and warn others of especially hazardous health-care facilities.

Although documentation of this pattern awaits further research, illness stories suggest that Ecuadorians prefer to exchange information about emotions by means other than emotion words. The recorded narratives analyzed here contain very few direct statements about feelings (statements of the sort: "I was very sad about that"; or "They have been very anxious and worried"). We can imagine that in the United States someone telling a story like that of Elsa's daughter Rosa would include direct statements about emotion states, such as "I feel so frustrated, but determined, in this situation." In Ecuador, however, the narrative description of events implies the emotions of the narrator, and native listeners are enculturated to be sensitive to this dimension of the communication. In addition, some social negotiation about the interpretation of events may occur when the story is told. Often, this negotiation is itself implicit rather than explicit, as, for instance, when a listener responds to a narrative about a child's accident with the comment, "those public stairs are certainly a menace to children," or with a personal story about medical mistreatment.

Discussion

As this analysis of 14 recorded narratives shows, Ecuadorian illness stories encode a great deal of cultural knowledge; some of this knowledge is expressed directly, but much of it is expressed implicitly. In the task of interpreting and talking about illness, Las Gradans draw on cultural models of the family and of extrafamilial social support, a cultural model of social hierarchy (with associated schemas of biomedical institutions), and a set of interrelated notions about illness causation. Narratives show that most of the cultural knowledge Las Gradans bring to bear in interpreting illness episodes is situation knowledge. References to person knowledge (e.g., values and attitudes, general character, person "types") are rare. The elaborate personality trait model to which North Americans often resort when interpreting behavior does not appear to be part of the explanatory tool kit Ecuadorians use in talking about illness.[6]

Two kinds of roles are thrown into sharp relief in illness narratives: roles played by close family members and roles played out in interactions between the poor and biomedical personnel. Some family roles, such as that of mother, are seen in these stories to entail many obligatory activities in illness situations; other roles allow for more leeway and personal choice. Illness sets in motion superhuman efforts by mothers that are, typically, taken for granted. It may also set in motion superhuman efforts by men; but, if so, these efforts will be highlighted in the narratives. The cultural model of family also specifies the feelings that are predictably and acceptably attached to each particular role. For instance, it is accepted that male relatives may feel and express resentment about the demands of being a caretaker for someone who is ill, whereas women, typically, may not.

Expectations about family roles in illness situations, as reflected in illness discourse, can be regarded as a subset of a broader model of roles in everyday family interactions. Likewise, much of the cultural knowledge encoded concerning interactions with medical personnel and institutions is also used to understand encounters with other nonmedical professionals and institutions. Much of the social role knowledge discussed here is not restricted to interpretation of only illness situations but should also show up in narratives about other kinds of situations. On the other hand, the same cultural models may be used somewhat differently in accomplishing other "tasks," for instance advice-giving or actual treatment-choice.

Hearing illness stories can influence knowledge structures in several ways. Individuals gain information about entire illness episodes without having personally experienced those events. Such secondhand episodes are integrated with those the person has directly experienced and become part of his or her current scripts concerning illness. Since illness situations are quite variable, no one is likely to experience enough episodes firsthand to develop robust scripts. Verbal transmission of the outlines of other episodes also affects development of general cultural models. Because illness stories occur in the context of conversational exchange, they contribute to "socially generated knowledge" (Clement 1982). Cultural models are carried by individuals, but they are partly constructed and refined through conversation and reflection. Nowhere is this more clearly seen than in the discussions of causation in illness narratives. As demonstrated here, there is a fascination with causal propositions, and narrators not infrequently turn their attention (and that of listeners) to the truth value of various propositions.

Finally, it is argued here that many illness narratives have an important affective dimension that must be taken into account in analysis of this discourse. Propositions such as "I did the right thing" are often what people most emphatically communicate in telling an illness story. Ecuadorians rely on narrative communication more than do North Americans to express feelings they are not allowed to express directly in conversation. Furthermore, feelings as well as thoughts and accounts of particular events are socially negotiated through exchanging stories and assessing responses to them.

To sum up, the illness story as told among this population of marginal urban Ecuadorians may be regarded as a culturally identified (although unlabeled) way of talking about illness, with certain structural features that set it apart from ordinary conversation. This type of discourse encodes multiple cultural models, most importantly, situation knowledge about social roles in illness. The discourse also implicitly encodes affective propositions made by narrators about the events and provides a vehicle for social negotiation about thoughts and feelings. Verbal communication of this type supplies both raw material and a forum for the refinement of cultural knowledge bearing on illness. For all of these reasons, the verbal traditions concerning illness that exist in Las Gradas are important in the transmission and generation of cultural models.

Appendix 1

ECUADORIAN ILLNESS STORIES - CASES AND NARRATORS

1. **Lucia** - toddler who suffered head injuries in falling on the public stairs in front of her house; taken to hospital, released; condition deteriorated; taken back to different hospital, died there.
   Narrators - mother, female neighbor, another female neighbor.

2. **Isabel** - 3-year-old born with foot deformity; treated at private clinic for long period of time with no improvement; ultimately received operation in a different private clinic thanks to intervention of a doctor who befriended the family; considerable community involvement in helping this family.
   Narrators - mother, aunt, grandmother, male neighbor, female community leader.

3. **Susana** - 6-year-old who suffered severe hip malformation, starting at the age of about 1 year (possibly due to polio); many different health care specialists consulted and therapies tried to bring about cure; ultimately received operations on both legs in the public children's hospital, then physical therapy, then spiritual curing after physical therapy proved less than totally effective.
   Narrators - mother, child's older sister.

4. **Sra. Elsa** - middle-aged woman with degenerative nervous system disorder of about 5 years' duration; mother of nine children, youngest age 2; many different health care specialists consulted, diagnoses made, and therapies tried; family under great strain in trying to cope with the illness and the recent death of the oldest son in the family.
   Narrators - husband, caretaker daughter, female neighbor, and Sra. Elsa.

Appendix 2

STRUCTURAL FEATURES OF A TYPICAL ILLNESS NARRATIVE

(Case 1, Mother Speaking)

Initial events of illness
[Orientation]

Susana walked normally at 1 year of age. Then she got an infection. We took her to a clinic.

Causation

At the clinic, they gave her IV and four injections. We believe the injections created little "pellets" or balls in her hips.

Chronology of events
[Some of these segments may be "explanations," in Linde's sense (this volume), but they occur in chronological order within the narrative.]

From then on (after the injections), she began to limp, sway from side to side like a duck. When she was 2, I took her to a doctor in Ambato; he said we had to operate immediately. My husband raised objections and there was no money. Then, I consulted a bone specialist in Latacunga. He said there was no reason to operate, that she would be an invalid all her life. That caused me so much pain, I didn't have her examined by anyone else. Then we came here to Quito to live. My mother-in-law was the one who "got me going" to go consult Dr. G. in the hospital to see if he could operate.

Before going to see him, I took her to Conocoto for treatment from a "bone-setter"; but that took too much time and I couldn't keep doing it; besides she wasn't getting better. At this time, she wasn't in pain.

Then I [correction] we, my husband and I, went to see the doctor; he gave us hope and said "Bring her in."

The doctor operated on the first leg. In physical therapy, the doctor said it wasn't so good. I massaged the bone here at home with a remedy I know, and the bone began to move bit by bit into place.

Then they operated on the other one.

The outcome still isn't known.

After 6 weeks, they will look and see how it is. For the first one, they called me after 4 weeks to see how it was; it was 3 months before they took the cast off.

I believe it will be 3 months for this one, too.

Coda

I am praying to God that it will all come out OK, whatever happens after that.

Coda (*cont.*)

[*Questions by investigator lead to further narrative segments.*]

Interview with social worker at the hospital concerning possibility of reduced charges.

Remedies used and care of Susana in recent past.

Stories of two children in the hospital, the nurses' interactions with them, and her own role.

Final coda   I hope that God's will is to cure her. There is no [other] help, nothing to do but bear the pain of a mother.

Appendix 3

PASSAGES FROM ECUADORIAN ILLNESS STORIES

A. *Narrator:* Olivia, older sister of Susana, child with hip malformation (Case 3).
"The neighbors said she had eaten something, maybe, something that stayed in her intestines and couldn't get out. So they said we had to give her an internal bath with camomile, lemon [and glycerine] in order to clean everything out of there. We did that and it helped her. Then we put grape leaves on her stomach with almond oil, you see, curing her on the outside. We put that on her and she got better. . . ."

B. *Narrator:* Maria, mother of Susana, child with hip malformation (Case 3).
"I have seen mothers go to leave their children in the hospital there. They [the children] are forgotten there and the mothers don't go to see them again. One Señora left a little boy about 2-years-old. He was there, he was there 15 days. They had already operated on his little leg, and his mother didn't come, she didn't come. I don't understand that. She didn't come. I don't know how it turned out, since my daughter was discharged. I don't understand it. [*Pause.*] The poor little thing just stayed right there. I didn't know if she would come get him or not. Another Señora from Santo Domingo did the same thing."

C. *Narrator:* Mercedes, neighbor of Sra. Elsa (Case 4).
"She went to events like soccer games, outside [*al aire*] almost unclothed. To dances, in that air, can you believe it? And, on the second or third day after miscarrying [the same thing]. . . . One should take care of oneself, and the Señora, note that in one month it's said she had three miscarriages, in one month. That is, neither she nor her husband were taking care [of her health] to conceive again right away. . . . [Elsa does not take her medicine] because she doesn't want to. She's irresponsible. Doesn't it seem so to you? If she were a responsible person, she would try to get better, strive to overcome it. The way I see it, overcoming things in order to keep the home together is the essence of the "mother." And she doesn't like any of that, no. So there it is. And that's why her family doesn't love her."

D. *Narrator:* Carmen, mother of toddler who suffered head injuries in a fall (Case 1).
"My daughter started to have convulsions, to shake. I saw it and tried to wake my husband up because he was sleeping. I told him that the child was getting worse. He had gotten up at dawn and worked until late at night. So I told him, 'Look, the child's getting worse.' He didn't answer me. Then he said, 'Let me sleep.'"

E. *Narrators:* mother and grandmother of Isabel, child with foot deformity (Case 4).
Mother: Then we came to our senses about my child, who was crippled in the same way. . . . She wanted to talk and she couldn't and she cried. So in view of that, we took the risk of trying to find someone who would operate.
Grandmother: But, on the other hand, my husband said: 'My dear daughter,' he said, 'and the money, the money? Where are we going to get it? Where

are we going to get it from?' And he applied [for a loan] in order to be able to do it, because he works at the utility company. But, the loan was refused. It looked like everything had gotten messed up and we couldn't obtain the money, we just couldn't. We had no place to get it.

F. *Narrator:* Maria, mother of Susana, child with hip malformation (Case 3). "But, my husband told me that it couldn't be that, all of a sudden, like that, she had to be treated, to be operated on. And, at that time, there was no money. So she stayed like that. . . ."

G. *Narrator:* Maria, mother of Susana, child with hip malformation (Case 3). "I went to the doctor. [correction] *We* went, my husband and I, to his office. He gave us such hope. He said, bring her, we will operate – in the clinic if you want, or in the hospital, if you want. My husband said, 'Doctor, how much would it cost us to do it in the clinic?'"

H. *Narrator:* Maria, mother of Susana, child with hip malformation (Case 3). "My mother-in-law was the one that 'got me going,' the one who gave me the impetus to go and consult Dr. G., there in the hospital, about doing the operation."

I. *Narrators:* mother and aunt of Isabel, child with foot deformity (Case 2).
   Mother: She is so wonderful, the doctora!! She charges so little, and she really got things going to get the operation done fast.
   Aunt: That's why we finally did take the risk enough to do it. And she's really fine, really pretty. She helps the poor more than anything. And, above all, she's attached to children. It's because she's an unmarried woman.

J. *Narrator:* Maria, mother of Susana, child with hip malformation (Case 3). "I don't know what it is with hospitals. There's a lot of favoritism shown toward some people and nothing for others. . . . I think it's because one doesn't have money, that's why they don't take care of you. People who give them their tips get the attention."

K. *Narrator:* Olivia, older sister of Susana, child with hip malformation (Case 3). "We thought the crippling must be due to the injections they gave her in the clinic. But, no. I believe that an injection won't move a bone, no. The injection was right here, but the bone is over there. I think the cause was the dehydration she suffered [during her illness at 1 year of age]. The dehydration affected the bones. That is, she was cured of the illness, but it affected the bones."

L. *Narrator:* Carmen, mother of toddler who suffered head injuries in a fall (Case 1).
   "I wasn't daunted because a woman had told me, she said, '*Don't* take her to Ortiz,' she said. 'You will never be able to take her out of there; she would die there,' the woman said. 'It's much better to take her,' she said, 'to Espejo.' So that's how it is my little child died in Espejo."

M. *Narrator:* husband of Sra. Elsa, woman with nervous system disease (Case 4). "I am currently waiting for some insurance money [from his son's death]. With that money, I *have* to get her diagnosed, whether she wants it or not. I must put her in the hospital. . . . She will for sure get better if we put her in the clinic, keep her in there. We will avoid a lot of frustration and hassle that way, for me and my daughters. And for me, too, in order to be able to get out again. Right now I have no way to go anywhere. I have to be here doing whatever [make-work], just so she can see that I'm here. It irritates her so much if I go out anywhere. . . ."

Notes

1. Thanks go to the National Science Foundation and R. J. Reynolds, for financial support of this research project. Much appreciation also to Dorothy Holland, Ed Hutchins, and Wendy Weiss for their valuable contributions to the development of this paper. Earlier versions of the paper were delivered at the "Conference on Folk Models" and at the 80th Annual Meeting of the American Anthropological Assocation in Los Angeles in 1981, in a symposium organized by Dorothy Holland and Naomi Quinn and entitled "Folk Theories in Everyday Cognition."
2. There are two primary types of natural discourse about illness between non-specialists in Ecuador: illness stories and therapeutic recommendations. Therapeutic recommendations pertain to ongoing health problems and may be solicited from, or offered spontaneously by, family members, friends, or neighbors. Even though the structure of this discourse is conversational, it does not follow the pattern of chronological narrative that characterizes illness stories. Therapeutic recommendations lead rather naturally into narratives, however, if a story exists to be told, if time permits, and if the social context is appropriate.
3. For Ecuadorian women, the genre of illness storytelling constitutes what we might call "shop talk" because one of their special gender role responsibilities is management of family illnesses. Such conversations have immense problem-solving value, and women tend to launch into conversation about illness much more readily than men. One exception occurs when men are known to be carrying out direct therapy-managing roles in an illness situation; these men will be the recipients of therapeutic recommendations from friends and family and will be told pertinent illness stories, just as female caretakers are recipients of such communication.
4. Although illness stories do transmit information about specific remedies and home-treatment principles, there is less of it than might be expected given the widespread use of home therapies in Las Gradas. Why do cognitive heuristics such as home treatment sequences (Mathews 1983) not figure more prominently in this discourse? A plausible explanation is that home treatments are less valued than those prescribed by specialists and so receive less attention. Another probable explanation is that narrators deemphasize or omit these details from their accounts because they assume their audience already possesses that information or will ask for it specifically if they need to know. Just as a storyteller in the United States would assume that listeners know the heuristic of drinking plenty of fluids and taking aspirin for a cold, so do Ecuadorian narrators take for granted that everyone knows the more common herbal remedies and specialist treatment options. This cultural pattern also affects ethnographic data collection. To obtain detailed information about such treatments, the ethnographer must usually ask about them directly.
5. Reasons for not openly acknowledging propositions about moral causes for

a particular illness include family loyalty, self-implication by such an interpretation, and inappropriate audience.
6. Whether North American narrators instantiate propositions about personality traits in telling illness stories is a question that requires further research. Only with documentation of the illness storytelling genre cross-culturally can analysis be made of differences between the models that shape the discourse, and of the social or historical reasons for such differences.

References

Agar, M.
    1980. Stories, background knowledge and themes: Problems in the analysis of life history narrative. American Ethnologist 7(2):223–240.
    1982. Whatever happened to cognitive anthropology: A partial review. Human Organization 41(1):82–86.
Bateson, G.
    1972. Pathologies of epistemology. *In* Steps to an Ecology of Mind. New York: Ballantine Books. Pp. 478–487.
Bohannan, P.
    1957. Justice and Judgement among the Tiv. London: Oxford University Press.
Clement, D.
    1982. Samoan folk knowledge of mental disorders. *In* Cultural Conceptions of Mental Health and Therapy, A. J. Marsella and G. M. White, eds. Dordrecht, Holland: D. Reidel Publishing Company. Pp. 193–215.
D'Andrade, R. G.
    1976. A propositional analysis of U.S. American beliefs about illness. *In* Meanings in Anthropology, K. H. Basso and H. A. Selby, eds. Albuquerque: University of New Mexico Press. Pp. 155–180.
    1981. The cultural part of cognition. Cognitive Science 5(3):179–195.
Glick, L. B.
    1967. Medicine as an ethnographic category: The Gimi of the New Guinea Highlands. Ethnology 6:31–56.
Holland, D.
    1985. From situation to impression: How Americans use cultural knowledge to get to know themselves and one another. *In* Directions in Cognitive Anthropology, J. Dougherty, ed. Urbana: University of Illinois Press. Pp. 389–411.
Hymes, D.
    1972. Models of the interaction of language and social life. *In* Directions in the Ethnography of Communication, J. J. Gumperz and D. Hymes, eds. New York: Holt, Rinehart and Winston. Pp. 35–71.
Labov, W. and D. Fanshel
    1977. Therapeutic Discourse: Psychotherapy as Conversation. New York: Academic Press.
Lakoff, G. and M. Johnson
    1980. Metaphors We Live By. Chicago: University of Chicago Press.
Mathews, H.
    1983. Context-specific variation in humoral classification. American Anthropologist 85(4):826–843.
Quinn, N.
    1982. "Commitment" in American marriage: A cultural analysis. American Ethnologist 9(4):775–798.

Stark, L.
  1981. Folk models of stratification and ethnicity in the highlands of Northern
  Ecuador. *In* Cultural Transformations and Ethnicity in Modern Ecuador,
  N. Whitten, ed. Urbana: University of Illinois Press. Pp. 387–401.
Tannen, D.
  1979. What's in a frame? Surface evidence for underlying expectations. *In* New
  Directions in Discourse Processing, Vol. 2, Advances in Discourse Processes,
  R. O. Freedle, ed. Norwood, N.J.: Ablex Publishing Company. Pp. 137–181.
Zajonc, R. B.
  1980. Feeling and Thinking. American Psychologist 35:151–175.

14
Explanatory systems in oral life stories[1]

Charlotte Linde

This chapter defines the *explanatory system* using oral life stories of middle-class American speakers as a source of data. An explanatory system is a system of beliefs and relations among beliefs that provide the environment in which one statement may or may not be taken as a cause for another statement. More specifically, an explanatory system of the type discussed here is a system of beliefs that occupies a position midway between *common sense,* the beliefs and relations among beliefs that any person in the culture may be assumed to know, if not to share, and *expert systems,* which are beliefs and relations among beliefs held, understood, and used by experts in a particular domain. An explanatory system is a system of beliefs derived from some expert system but used by someone with no corresponding expertise or credentials. Note that the term *common sense* as defined here closely corresponds to the notion of *cultural models* or *cultural theories* as used throughout this volume. The term *expert system* or some close equivalent is similar to the usage of Kempton, and Collins and Gentner (this volume). The term *explanatory system* represents an intermediate level that, to my knowledge, has received relatively little attention.

To clarify the definition of explanatory system, let us turn to two (constructed) example pairs. The first (1) gives a reason that relies on commonsense beliefs to account for professional choice.

(1a) How did you come to be an accountant?
(1b) Well, I guess I have a precise mind, and I enjoy getting all the little details right.

In contrast, in order to understand (2b) as a relevant answer to (2a), the hearer must know if not share the popular Freudian explanatory system which locates the real causes of events in early childhood.

(2a) How did you come to be an accountant?
(2b) Well, my mother started toilet training me when I was six months old.

Using this notion of explanatory system, this paper first discusses the methodological background and data for the study of explanatory systems, then examines in detail the explanatory systems that have been found, and finally discusses the historical relation between common sense, explanatory systems, and expert systems.

The life story

This section first defines *life story* as a technical term and then discusses the types of data and methodology necessary for its study. This discussion is necessarily brief, as the present study forms part of a larger study of the creation of coherence in oral life stories (Linde n.d.).

THE LIFE STORY

The definition of life story used in this study is an attempt to render precise and accesible to analysis a notion in common use by speakers of English. Intuitively, we believe that we "have" a life story and that any normally competent adult has one. This nontechnical sense of life story is something like, "What events have made me what I am"; "What you must know to know me."

Technically, the definition of a life story is: All the individual stories and the relations drawn between them told by an individual during his or her entire lifetime that satisfy the following criteria:

1. The stories contained in the life story make a point about the speaker, not about the way the world is.
2. The stories have extended reportability. That is, they are tellable over the course of a long period of time.

The first point in this definition is that an entire life story is constantly added to and changed in the course of a lifetime, so that to have a record of an entire life story would require all of the talk ever produced by a given speaker. This is in principle possible, in practice impossible. Nonetheless, it is possible to study the life story by using a small sample of the stories that comprise it, since the interest of the present study is not the specific form of the entire story but rather the principles by which it is constructed.

The next point is that not all stories told by a speaker form a part of the life story. One criterion for the inclusion of a story as part of the life story is that its evaluative point is directly about the speaker or some event framed as relevant to the speaker, as opposed to a story that makes some evaluative point about the world in general. That is, I would want to consider as part of my life story a story about what happened to me when I was in the hospital, but not a story about the same events told to show what's wrong with hospitals.

A further criterion for inclusion is that the story have extended reportability. This means that the story can be retold over a long period of time. Thus, the story of a career decision, or a divorce, or a major illness are relevant and reportable over a major portion of one's life. In contrast, a story about the funny thing the guy in the health food store said is reportable for a day or two at most as a story about what happened to me (although it may retain extended reportability as a story about what people in health food stores are like).

A final point is that the life story is not defined simply as a particular subset of stories but as the relations the speaker draws among them as well. Thus, as new stories enter the life story, old ones may have to be dropped or revised to maintain coherence. It is this form of relation among stories that permits the life story to express our entire sense of what our life has been about without ever necessarily forming a single narrative organizing our entire lives.

Note that *life story* defined here is related but not identical to *autobiography* and *life history*. Both the life story and the autobiography are produced by a person presenting his or her own life in a form that will make sense to other people. They differ, first, in their medium – spoken versus written language. The life story also differs from autobiography in being a temporally discontinuous, ongoing account, whereas an autobiography is a crystallization at a given time of what has happened to the author and what it means. Finally, autobiographies are subject to the economic process of publishing, and so published autobiographies tend to be by people either socially defined as important or interesting, or by undistinguished people what can be taken as typical members of a class of interest – cancer victims who survived, or housewives who have found God, for example.

In contrast, every adult is entitled to and indeed required to have a life story. The notion of *life story* also contrasts with *life history*, a term mainly used in anthropology, although also somewhat current in psychology. The life story in anthropology is usually presented as a form of autobiography of someone in another culture, a presentation of his or her experience and sense of self that is the collaborative product of the subject and the anthropologist. The major difference is that the presentation of self in this form may not be at all a natural discourse form for the subject; indeed, the whole notion of *self* present in the subject's culture may be quite different from that of the anthropologist. (For an extended review of the notion of *life history*, see Langness & Frank (1981:ch.4)

THE DATA OF THIS STUDY

The data of this study come from oral interviews on choice of profession. Fourteen people were interviewed; they were chosen because they all had professions that were important to them and that could be expected to form a major part of their life stories. The interview began with the question, "What is your profession" and went on to ask "How did you arrive at that," or "How did you become a _____." When the speaker had apparently finished, I probed for more, either by a further question or by an extended silence.

The interviews focused on the choice of profession since, at least for middle-class professional speakers, it is a necessary part of one's account of oneself. One need only recall how often one is asked, "What do you do?" to verify this. Another demonstration of the centrality of profession is to consider the case in which one is acquainted with someone but does not know that person's occupation; this is anomalous, and after some time, sinister. One's occupation is a publicly available piece of information, from which many inferences may be drawn as to what sort of person one is.

Note that profession is public knowledge in just that social world in which it plays a major role in the definition of the self. This is, of course, not true for all societies, nor even for all classes of our own society. However, with that restriction, we may note that professional choice works excellently as an interview topic because it is so relevant to self-presentation and because it forms a relatively public portion of one's biography.

The data are then analyzed using the methods of discourse analysis. For a full discussion of discourse analysis, see Linde (1981; n.d.). In brief, the component discourse units are identified – in the case of the life story, they are narrative, chronicle, and explanation. The internal structures of these units are then analyzed. Of particular relevance for the study of explanatory systems is the analysis of the evaluative structure of these units, that is, the portions of text that comment on what has been said, informing the addressee of how this is to be understood.

The construction of coherence

An important property of the life story, both linguistically and psychologically, is that it must be coherent. Its coherence is not a property of the life, but rather an achievement of the speaker in constructing the story.

Coherence in this sense is a property of texts; it is one set of relations by which we may understand a text. Specifically, the coherence of a text consists of the relations that the parts of the text bear to one another. A text may be described as coherent if its parts, whether on the word level, phrase level, sentence level, semantic level, or level of larger units, can be seen as being in a proper relation to one another and to the text as a whole. Thus, a narrative will be heard as coherent if it is clear for the hearer what relation its parts bear to one another – that is, given that A and B were said, why B follows A (Becker 1977).

We can recognize at least three different levels of coherence in these texts. The first level is the basic linguistic level of text structuring devices. The devices of this level are widely used across an entire language and are dependent on the obligatory morphological and syntactic categories of that language. An example of a device at this level is this narrative presupposition: the rule of interpretation stating that the order of past-tense main-clause verbs shall be taken as the order of events. The second level of coherence is the level of implicit philosophical categories, such as, in English, causality, accident, continuity, and discontinuity. These categories depend on the coherence established by the previous level and in some sense represent an elaboration of it. The third level of coherence is the level of semiexplicit explanatory systems, the level of interest for this paper. The systems at this level all presuppose the categories of the previous level. That is, they all assume the existence of causality and then give different answers to the question of what a possible cause might be.

We turn now to a more detailed discussion of these levels.

THE LEVEL OF MORPHOLOGY: THE NARRATIVE PRESUPPOSITION

As mentioned in the previous section, the narrative depends on the fact that tense is an obligatory category in English – all sentences have a main verb, and this main verb has some tense. Further, speakers of English take tense to be iconic; that is, we assume there really is such a thing as time, and that it naturally consists of past, present, and future. This belief permits the narrative presupposition: the assumption that the order of a sequence of sentences or main clauses matches the order of events. The following examples illustrate the automatic character of this assumption.

(3)   I got flustered and I backed the car into a tree.

(4)   I backed the car into a tree and I got flustered.

In (3), getting flustered is assumed to precede backing into the tree; in (4) it is assumed to follow backing into the tree.

These examples further illustrate the relation of tense and the beginnings of the assumption of causality. The natural logic of English is *post hoc, ergo propter hoc;* in (3) we assume that getting flustered caused the speaker to back into a tree, in (4) we assume that backing into a tree caused the speaker to get flustered. More complex forms of causality are built on this foundation.

COHERENCE PRINCIPLES: CAUSALITY AND CONTINUITY

We have seen that at the morphological level, the temporal order of clauses, or narrative order, represents the major resource for the creation of the implication of causality, since any temporal order is likely to be understood as a causal order as well. We turn now to the level of the major coherence principles used in organizing life stories, which are primarily causality and continuity, both of which are based on the previous establishment of order.

In telling a life story, one major task for the speaker is to establish that the causal sequence of events is an adequate one. We define *adequate causality* as a chain of causality that the hearers can accept as a good reason for some particular event or sequence of events. For the data of this study, establishing adequate causality for the choice of profession means establishing that there are obvious good reasons for the speaker's choice of profession, or showing that even if the reasons do not seem at first glance to be acceptable, actually there are reasons for accepting these reasons.

Establishing adequate causality for a given professional choice, or for any sequence of events, is both a social and an individual achievement. Part of the social aspect is the fact that there are cultural and subcultural beliefs about proper lives, proper sequences, and proper reasons for professional choice. For example, one socially sanctioned and very strong form of adequate reason for a career choice is ability or character. If a speaker can claim, "I like that sort of thing," or "I'm good at it," a standard form of adequate causality has been established and no further reasons need be given. Similarly, we have beliefs about what would be inadequate or frivolous reasons for choosing a career; for example, "I was in love with a girl who was enrolled in premed, so I decided to become a doctor."[2]

In addition to this store of common-sense beliefs about adequate causes, there is also a strong element of individual creativity in the creation of adequate causality. The individual speaker's adroitness or ineptness in framing his or her story can also determine whether a given sequence will be heard as adequate or inadequate.

To establish adequate causality, not only must the reasons be adequate, but the chain of reasons must also be neither too thin nor too thick. Too thin an account suggests that one's life has proceeded at random, discontinuously. Too thick an account suggests that the speaker implicitly accepts a deterministic or fatalistic theory of causality. Neither of these extremes is generally acceptable, and both are subject to correction. The correction may be made by the speaker, following a deterministic account with an accidental one, or vice versa. That is, the speakers often perform a sort of philosophical wobble around a socially determined equilibrium point, which carefully avoids taking any position to its logical extreme. If the speaker does not maintain this equilibrium, the addressee may correct the story in the direction of equilibrium.

In studying adequate causality in the interview situation, we may recognize an account as adequate by the fact that its speaker treats it as sufficient; that is, the speaker does not follow it with another account and holds to the same account even if challenged by the interviewer. In this set of data, I found two forms of adequate accounts of the reason for a professional choice: those based on character traits and those based on multiple noncontradictory accounts.

One of the most powerful accounts possible for choice of profession is character. Speakers appear to take character traits as a primitive, referring to them as obvious causes for career decisions, with no need to account for these traits. We thus find examples like (5) given as an account for a career as an English professor, and (6) as an account for a career as an editor.

(5) I seemed to be very good in reading and analyzing books and writing so I became an English major and from then on since I knew I would go as far in whatever I chose as I could possibly go, getting a Ph.D. became a necessity.

(6) I always was nitpicky, I was always good at grammar, um I like to correct things rather than create them. And I'm interested enough in reading and I like to spend the time reading, that at least now that I'm on journals that are even vaguely interesting, it can be a lot of fun.

Both of these are given as adequate and final reasons for the choice of profession.

Another very strong form of adequate causality is richness of account. An account may be rich because it covers a long period of time; that is, the reason for the choice of profession is located far back in the speaker's past. Of course, one form of temporally well rooted account is the explanation by character trait. But citing ambition, family interest in some sphere of activity, schooling, or childhood hobbies may equally permit a professional choice to appear well-rooted in time. Another way an account may be rich is by containing many noncontradictory reasons for a choice. In one such example, a speaker who is a professor of English studying science and literature gives the following accounts for her profession: She was at a university that was trying to bring together academic disciplines and medicine; she had good verbal skills because of her family's interests; she had an interest in science but not the aptitude for it; in her undergraduate career, she had encountered one noted scholar with a similar blend of interests; her quarrelsome family led her to be a peacemaker, which led to some attempt to reconcile science and literature. Such multiple noncontradictory accounts provide adequate causality because they show that a choice was not random or insufficiently motivated.

In addition to adequate causality, there are accounts that must handle the fact that the speaker perceives the causality or the ordering of events to be in some way insufficient or problematic. These can be divided into accounts structured in terms of accident and accounts containing a socially recognizable discontinuity. In the context of a life story, accident means the absence of sufficient, socially recognized causality. When an event has been presented as an accident, a common pattern is to narrate that event as an accident and then follow it by a demonstration of how it was not really an accident, since there were multiple routes to the same point in life. Thus, although the particular route was an accident, the goal was not.

In telling a story, the narrator may perceive and present the events as discontinuous. A (constructed) example of such discontinuity is, "I was a banker until I was 35, and then I dropped it all and became a potter." As members of the culture, we recognize that this is a conventionally discontinuous sequence of professions. One of the clearest patterns in these data is that this form of discontinuity must be managed in some way; some evaluation or explanation of the discontinuity must be given. Among the forms of management of discontinuity found in these data are:

1. Discontinuity as Apparent Break. Discontinuity is seen as only apparent, not real. That is, a later state appears to be very different from an earlier one, but they can be seen as having characteristics that make them continuous.
2. Discontinuity as Temporary. An apparent break is shown to be due to a temporary discontinuity; for example, an early interest was abandoned and then resumed.
3. Discontinuity of Actor. The speaker may distance himself or herself from the protagonist of the story. Such distancing focuses the blame of discontinuity, so to speak, on some other person than the present speaker.
4. Discontinuity as Continuity. In this logically more complex strategy, the speaker uses a series of discontinuous events to establish that discontinuity forms a continuity for him or her. An example of this strategy is, "I think I could be a dilettante all my life as long as I could do it with some intensity."

EXPLANATORY SYSTEMS

Moving up from the level of the management of causality, we turn to the level of the explanatory system. We have defined the explanatory system as providing the conceptual environment in which something may or may not a cause of something else. Thus, within a Freudian explanatory system, the course of development of childhood sexuality may be a cause of adult character, whereas in other systems, one would look elsewhere for the cause of character, or might not seek it at all.

In later sections, we see that the explanatory systems present in these data are popular versions of expert systems. However, not all explanatory systems are expert systems. We may view the ordinary system of common sense as the most pervasive explanatory system and the most unnoticed. As defined, common sense is the system of beliefs assumed to be shared by everyone and requiring no special circumstances or standing for its use. Thus, a speaker who said, "I quit banking because I didn't like it" would be invoking an explanatory principle from common sense. In contrast, a speaker who said "I quit banking because my father was a banker, and I've always had a love–hate thing with my father" would be invoking a psychological explanatory principle.

In later sections, we explore some of the explanatory systems present in these data. We do not, however, consider the elements of the system of common sense, as this is a task beyond the scope of the present study.

Definition and function of explanatory systems

This section gives a fuller definition of explanatory system and attempts to sketch its function for speakers.

One view of the explanatory system is that it not only guides the construction of a story but also provides an evaluation of what the story means and what its value is. When a life story is analyzed by an analyst other than the speaker, a number of evaluation principles might be used. The most obvious is factuality: Do the events narrated correspond to reality? If the analyst is a biographer or a district attorney, this is an appropriate criterion. However, since my interest in this entire research program is how speakers construct life stories as coherent, it is possible to work entirely with the internal relations of the text, bracketing the question of relation to some postulated real world. However, there also is a more sophisticated form of evaluation by an analyst. The analyst may subscribe to some system that gives a principled basis for deciding whether the speaker's account is one that could possibly be valid, using the organization of the account, its coherence, and its choice of topics. Such a system may be a political theory, a psychological theory, or a religious theory, and so on. For example, for a Marxist analyst, none of the accounts of career choice given by these speakers could possibly be valid since they are not based on, and indeed give no account of, social class or economic circumstances. Within this explanatory system, real explanation lies within the domain of economics, and so all other forms of explanation represent surface phenomena or false consciousness. Similarly, a Freudian analyst can claim to have resources to determine whether an explanation given by a speaker is a correct product of genuine insight or whether it is the result of one of the deceptive complicating processes the mind uses to hide from itself. (See Frank 1981 for a discussion of the basis of such validation.)

As these examples show, an explanatory system is a system that claims to give a means for understanding, evaluating, and interpreting experience or accounts of experience and usually, as a consequence of that understanding, also gives, either explicitly or implicitly, a guide for future behavior. Presumably, this definition would include such local explanatory systems as theories of the right kind of food to maintain optimal health, or the best way to win at roulette. However, the interesting examples of explanatory systems are those with some reasonable claim to completeness, those purporting to explain most or all realms of experience, not merely local areas of life. The most obvious current examples are Freudian psychology, or more generally, psychoanalytic theory, Marxism, and most religious systems. An understanding of much of experience as the product of a worldwide conspiracy of the Bavarian illuminati or the unrecognized influence of higher plane entities would equally qualify as explanatory systems, albeit less widely held ones.

This definition of explanatory systems is not equivalent to any concept in general use. It is related to the term *belief system* or *cultural system* as used, for example, in Geertz (1973) but differs in that the explanatory system is specifically a semiexpert system, related but not equivalent to either belief systems shared by an entire culture or belief systems exclusive to some class of experts.

We now turn to the question of how these explanatory systems function for their users. If we look at the social conditions under which expert systems are used to evaluate experience, we find that such a system is often used by a person with special status, trained in its terms and argument forms, to criticize some nonexpert account of experience. One obvious example is the use of case history material by a psychologist. The subject produces a life story, or this life story is summarized, and then the psychologist can use expert knowledge to demonstrate what is really going on. Depending on theoretical persuasion, the psychologist may use the array of psychoanalytic techniques and arguments, or the armamentarium of diagnostic psychology, including personality tests, and projective tests. In either case, these implements of expertise have primacy; they confirm or invalidate the correctness of the speaker's own account of his or her life.

It is not experts alone who have theories that offer the "real" reasons for people's behavior and hence can be used to evaluate the correctness of any explanation given. Any adult has a wide variety of theories available that can be used to make sense of his or her life. These theories may be explicit systems requiring formal subscription, such as a particular religion or political philosophy. Or, they may be extremely inexplicit belief systems implicit in the culture, which require no formal recognition or allegiance and which, without careful analysis, pass unnoticed as theories, appearing to be just one further example of how we speak about these things.

When we examine how explanatory systems are used, we find that because they are all popularized versions of expert theories, they permit the speaker an extra level of distance, allowing him or her to be an expert, to step back from the personal account to give a deeper, or apparently more objective, or truer account than can be conveyed in a common-sense narrative. To clarify the nature of the distance created by the use of an explanatory system, note that all first-person narration has an implicit distance between the narrator and the protagonist. This distance permits us to tell a story about some bad or ill-judged or embarrassing action we took, since even though the protagonist acted in this way, the narrator knows better and so is able to tell the story in a way that indicates present allegiance to the norm that was in the past broken. However, the use of an expert explanatory system introduces an additional layer of distance beyond that of narrator and protagonist. Although the narrator may know better than the protagonist, they are still the same order of being, operating by the same rules, with the same type of knowledge. In contrast, the expert is different from the protagonist, possessing different and superior knowledge of why the protagonist acts and how he or she should act.

THE SET OF EXPLANATORY SYSTEMS IN THE DATA

The theories I have found thus far in these data are versions of Freudian psychology, behaviorism, astrology, Zeitgeist theory, and Catholic theory of sin and confession. Each theory has its associated expert – a practicing psychoanalyst, an academic psychologist, an astrologer, a sociologist, or a priest. This paper explicates the first three theories, since they are most clearly represented in my data.

This list of explanatory systems raises a number of questions. Is the list exhaustive? How many more explanatory systems would be discovered by doing more interviews, or interviews on another topic? How many such explanatory systems can be present in a culture at a given time? It would take a different research program and a rather extensive one to answer these questions. However, my estimation is that this list is not at all exhaustive; other interviews and particularly interviews on other topics would undoubtedly produce further examples. However, the number of explanatory systems would not be very great. There is a necessary limit on the number of such explanatory systems that will be present in a given culture at a given time, since one's addressee must at least recognize if not share any explanatory system one choses to use.

Certain absences in the list of explanatory systems in these data are particularly striking. For example, no one cites economic opportunities or class limitations as factors in professional choice; the speakers all appear to assume that professional choice is dictated by personal abilities and by degree of psychological adjustment, which either permits or prevents one from seeing and talking advantage of opportunities. This view of a world without politics and without social class appears to be particularly American (Lasch 1979; Schur 1976; Sennett 1977).[3]

Another striking absence is the lack of invocation of race or ethnicity to explain available opportunity. Since all the speakers are white, it is perhaps understandable that race is not dominant in their understanding of the factors that shaped their professional lives. However, the sample does include people from a variety of ethnic groups and religious backgrounds, only one of whom mentions this as a factor influencing his personal psychology. This is in strong contrast to a previous generation of speakers, for whom ethnic origin, and more specifically, generation of immigration were crucial in understanding anyone's life story.

Explanatory systems in these data

Of the explanatory systems in these data, the most common appears to be that of Freudian psychology. I thus begin with it, give the fullest discussion of it, and use it as a detailed example of the relation between the expert and the popular versions of an explanatory system.

POPULAR FREUDIAN PSYCHOLOGY

To get the flavor of this explanatory system, consider the following example, which comes as the conlusion to a story about how the speaker took a banking job that he did not like and that did not last very long.

(7) . . . so I didn't really make much of a decision there. I think that's one way of looking at it. I made a decision. It was the decision that I didn't like at the time, so that's why I have the sense that I was forced into it, but there are all kinds of psychological things that make you do things at various moments in your life.

From a common-sense point of view, this seems to be a rather weak justification of a bad decision. That is, common sense suggests that one should be in control of one's action, or if one is not, that one should be forced into making decisions by strong external forces. However, further analysis suggests that this text implies an explanatory system that gives a way of making sense of the phenomenon of doing things that one does not like or approve of.

The speaker himself gives the clue to the system he is invoking by the phrase "psychological things." This system is a psychological model, more specifically, as we see, a popular version of Freudian psychology. A number of components to this popular version show up in the present data. These are:

1. The splitting of the self into component parts, which are in disagreement.
2. The notion that real causes are to be found in childhood and childhood experiences.
3. The notion of levels of personality, some of which are deeper than others.

Let us begin with the split of the self into component parts in disagreement. The speaker of (7) feels that he was "forced" into a decision and attributes this to "psychological things that make you do things." This fragmentation of experience and the identification of the speaker with the fragment that is not in control is a strong component in popular Freudian psychology. Another related notion at work in this example is the idea that one can act for reasons of which one is unaware or does not understand. Thus, we hear statements like, "I was in Paris at the time and I thought I was happy, but really I wasn't." A more extended example of this phenomenon is (8).

(8) I married someone who was older than I was, who was a bit of a self-centered tyrant, and for that I got, uh, to whom I was not very, even sexually attracted,

and was very temperamentally different than I am, and uh although I was in a certain way attracted to him sexually I was not, really.

Here, again, we have an example of someone telling about acting because of feelings which she felt, or thought she felt, but which were not real.

Both of these assumptions about the nature of action are based on a complex form of distancing. The first is the distance the speaker maintains from the protagonist of the story. As discussed, this is part of any form of narration. However, in stories containing this additional element of a Freudian explanatory system, the speakers, in achieving this distance, are able to place themselves in the position of an expert, commenting on their own life.

A further form of distancing, buried more deeply within the story, is the distancing between the component parts of the person. The part that feels or believes it feels is not the part that causes action. As the speaker of (7) indicates, this permits a curious paradox in which one is simultaneously active and passive, forced into action by oneself.

Another, perhaps more familiar, tenet of popular Freudian psychology is the notion that real causes are to be found in childhood and childhood experiences. We see a version of this belief in (9), combined with the metaphor of splitting oneself into component parts. The speaker, who is also the speaker of (8), is explaining her combination of literary and scientific interests. She has already told a number of stories about how she arrived at these interests, which have to do with the opportunities were available to her in the course of her education. She then steps back, as it were, from this historical presentation, to give what the language interestingly allows us to call a deeper reason.

(9)   Another idea that, well, in my more – uh I often wonder why I have this need to make, to write, to kind of split myself off in two directions or to try and take on many, to take on what might seem to be warring, I see what I do as, as reconciling things and why do I need to reconcile things? I came from a family that was very conflict-prone. And I was the peacemaker in the family. And I don't like conflict. And I, or rather, I, I am really very upset by it.

The assumption of this explanation, which permits the speaker to offer it as an explanation, is that one's childhood emotions and actions are crucially relevant in providing an explanation of any further developments. It is important to note that I am not claiming that only Freudian psychology admits childhood experience as important and that no other explanatory system admits it. Rather, the claim is that Freudian psychology gives it a primacy, which means that any adequate explanation within this system is likely to include it.

A further theme of this explanatory system, which is related to the splitting of the individual into component parts of the personality, is the metaphor of levels, the notion that some of these parts are deeper, or further down than others. We get an oblique reference to this notion in (10):

(10)   And I think that the source of one's power professionally comes from some deep s-, deep thing. And if you don't tap that, you're sunk.

The idea here seems to be that the components of the personality are ordered vertically, with the higher ones being more accessible to consciousness and the lower ones being out of the reach of ordinary self-inspection. A further part of this metaphor is that the deep components have a certain amount of autonomy and can, in unseen ways, motivate actions, which may or may not be in agreement with the desires and plans of the more conscious surface components.

The foregoing discussion has presented a sketch of a semiexpert theory of the mind, which contrasts both with a common-sense theory of the mind and with the professional Freudian model. D'Andrade (this volume) provides an explication of the common-sense or cultural theory of the mind, which is clearly quite different from the Freudian model in both its expert and semipopular form. The most interesting locus of difference lies in causality – the cultural model treats conscious mental states as having central causal powers, whereas the Freudian model treats unconscious mental states as the causal center.

The popular Freudian explanatory system also differs from a professional or expert Freudian model in a number of ways. These differences are discussed in detail in the section on the synchronic relation between popular and expert systems. In brief, like all cultural models, the popular Freudian system represents a considerable simplification of the original model, reducing both the number of themes and concepts it uses and the complexity of the connections between them.

BEHAVIORIST PSYCHOLOGY

The Freudian psychological explanatory system is quite familiar because of its pervasiveness in the culture. In contrast, let us now turn to behaviorist psychology, a rare system, represented in these data by only one speaker. More specifically, one speaker presents her life in behaviorist terms, taking the role not of the conditioner but of the subject of conditioning, not Skinner but one of Skinner's pigeons.

Three themes in her account of her life lead one to an analysis of her explanatory system as behaviorism. These themes are:

1. The need for reinforcement, and reinforcement as the cause of action.
2. The separation of the self from emotion.
3. Nonagency – the self described in such a way as never to be an active agent in causing events.

Reinforcement is the most obvious component of the behaviorist explanatory system, and it is the factor this speaker uses explicitly in explaining her history. After college, she worked as a social worker and then went back to school to get a master's degree of computer science. At the time of narration, she worked as a computer programmer. The two major focuses in her account of her career history are the change from social work to programming and the fact that she has held a number of programming jobs at different companies. She feels that both of these facts need accounting for, and she accounts for both of them as arising from her need for reinforcement.

(11)   I like concrete results. I, I need to be able to see what I've done. I need that kind of reinforcement. If you get me out of that mode, I'm just, I have little tolerance for it. I, I need the strokes of seeing what I'm doing as I'm doing it.

(12)   So when I was doing social work, and I did that for five years, I need to have, I need results. I'm a result person. OK. I need to, I like to manipulate symbols, I like those kind of machinations in your head. And I like to see what I've done. OK? If I, I can not go extended periods without that, I don't have the tolerance for it and it was, I came to that realization while doing social work, that I had to find something that was, that gave me that kind of concrete kind of [unclear].

(13)   I guess my chief feeling about XYZ Co. [where she formerly worked as a programmer] was that it was very, there was no point in working. Because it didn't matter whether you did or whether you didn't. There were no strokes for working, there were no punishments for not working.

This notion of reinforcement as the motive for behavior is identical to Skinner's views, with the additional specification of her personal need for a reinforcement schedule with a very short time delay. Although the terms *reinforcement* and *strokes* have become part of the common vocabulary, this account of one's life is not coherent within the common-sense explanatory system but only within the expert system of behaviorism.

Another similarity to Skinner's thought lies in this speaker's treatment of her emotions and mental states. In her stories about her professional history, the speaker frequently mentions that she must have had certain emotions, but does not claim them directly. For example:

(14)   And it began to be very demoralizing to me. Uh so I left and whatever I, and I had at that time decided that I really wanted to get to, I guess somehow I had decided I wanted to get serious again about working.

The correction from "I had at that time decided . . ." to "I guess somehow I had decided . . ." is a perfect example. Most psychologists would regard this as a small but pathological form of distancing oneself from one's emotions. However, from a behaviorist point of view, the belief in autonomous mental states that act as determinants of behavior is an error, indeed the fundamental error in understanding human psychology. However, it is an error that nontechnical language almost forces one into. The speaker here denies any actual belief in or sensation of decision as an autonomous mental entity, while indicating some loyalty to the ordinary forms of discourse and understanding, which require them.

Closely related to the nonexistence of mental states is the third theme: nonagency. What this term is intended to convey is that this speaker does not use personal agency in the way most speakers do. Normally, speakers describe their experiences in such a way that they are active agents in their stories: "I did so and so"; "I decided such and such"; "I solved the problem facing me." This speaker does not construct her stories in this way: The active agents are either abstract motivations or other persons, not herself. The following story is an example of both kinds of agency. The situation is that the speaker was working as a social worker, which she did not like, and was investigating the possibility of becoming a computer programmer by speaking to a professor of computer science.

(15) I spoke to Dr. *K* a long time. He decided, oh yeah, I had really gone over there, wasn't asking to go to graduate school. I was asking to take a course in the evening. And I figured I could qualify because I had graduated from *U* and it wouldn't, what big deal would it be for him to let me take a course. I, by the time I was out of there, he had me enrolled in this whole program, and he says, "Oh you have to do it this way." And it must have appealed to me, because I went ahead and did it.

In this story, Dr. *K* is the agent, not the speaker. It is his somewhat surprising actions that move events along. The speaker had intended to take a single course, but as a result of Dr. *K*'s actions, finds herself enrolled in a master's program, and a simultaneous BS in mathematics. Even in the smaller level details of sentential construction, we find that she is not the agent. For example, note the nonagency of the phrase "By the time I was out of there" as compared with the possible "By the time I left there."

The theme of nonagency is extremely strong, so much so that even when it is directly challenged, it is still maintained. As part of the interview procedure, after I had obtained the speakers' own accounts of their professional history, I attempted to reframe the questions, using explanatory systems different from those the speakers had used. I did this in an attempt to see to what extent the speakers were willing to adapt their explanatory systems to my apparent beliefs and to what extent they would maintain them in the face of a proposed alternative conceptualization. Answer (16) represents a response to such a challenge. I had asked the speaker about choice points in her life, a formulation that implies choices as relevant entities. Although the speaker does not explicitly deny the existence of choice points, or the possibility of choice, the story she tells, apparently using this vocabulary, is completely consistent with her previous system of nonagency.

(16) *Speaker:* I chose to flunk out of a masters program in psychology. Uh huh.
        That was a choice point.
      Interviewer: What do you mean, you chose to flunk out?
      Speaker: I got one too many C's.
      Interviewer: Why?
      Speaker: Because I just didn't know that I w-. I wasn't interested. I just
        couldn't bring, I had this big struggle with myself as to why I was doing
        what I was doing and I decided well I, I just have to do this because I'm
        supposed to do this, and it just didn't, it was, well, there wasn't any rewards
        in it for me. And uh it's an interesting choice because I could have picked
        myself up and left, which I didn't do, I just sat there and waited for it
        to all come crashing down on me until "Oh jolly!" So, but that, but
        definitely a choice that I made somewhere in that, in that interim.

To speak of choosing to flunk out of a program by doing nothing until
one is thrown out is clearly a subversion of the ordinary sense of choice.
For a speaker operating within a psychoanalytic belief system, such a formulation might represent a recognition of personal responsibility for events
that might ordinarily be taken as beyond one's control. In this case,
however, I believe the speaker is denying my formulation of life as
motivated by choices that occur at choice points. It would be extremely
difficult, both conceptually and in terms of etiquette, to make explicit and
then deny my presupposition that choices exist and are relevant; rather,
she has implicitly redefined the sense of choice until it can be used in a
story that does not conflict with her system.

Comparing this speaker's explanatory system to the popular writings
of Skinner (1948; 1979), the two are in agreement. The one striking difference is that Skinner's model provides a place for the agent, the force
that arranges the contingencies of reinforcement. In the laboratory, of
course, this is the experimenter. In the ideal community, it is a planner,
or a board of planners, who experiment with various social and physical
arrangements that will produce happy and good people. In the ordinary
state of affairs, the environment rather haphazardly supplies positive and
negative reinforcement, which, in Skinner's view, would be better sup-
plied by a more conscious agent.

In the examples we have seen, and in the entire life story given by this
speaker, there is no sense that reinforcements are provided by a particular
agent. She speaks of the reinforcement process as something sought by
the person to be reinforced, but in a rather passive way, something like
Skinner's notion of shaping a behavior.

(17) . . . and the whole process of finding what it is that gives you your strokes
        OK? is not an easy one.

(18) So that's what you're asking about, the process of finding out what is posi-
        tively reinforcing to you OK? is not an easy thing to do and I don't know
        how people hit upon . . . .

This is related to Skinner's notion of the environment as agent, except that she has not formed any notion of the environment as an entity that acts on her.

A number of questions remain. One concerns the rarity of this explanatory system. Since only 1 speaker out of 14 in the sample uses this behaviorist explanatory system, is it justifiable to posit it as an explanatory system present in the culture, or should it rather be considered an idiosyncracy of this speaker alone? This system is unique in the data of this study, and I believe that even in a considerably larger sample, it would be quite rare. However, although this explanatory system sounds somewhat odd, its relation to a known expert system is recognizable.

Furthermore, it is comprehensible; we may be surprised by the sorts of things the speaker cites as reasons, but we understand why they count as reasons. This is in strong contrast to fully idiosyncratic explanatory systems, whose connections are incomprehensible. We may also ask how this speaker came to use such a rare system. This is a tantalizing question, but if it is answerable at all, it requires psychological and biographical information that lie beyond the scope of this study.

ASTROLOGY

Another explanatory system present in these data is astrology. This system is used only jokingly and only in the relaxed later part of the interview as it modulated into a flirtation. This is not surprising. Since astrology is a less respectable explanatory system than the others we have examined, it is less likely to turn up at all in an interview situation. Therefore, only traces of the system are present; it is impossible to give a listing of all the themes present in the system.

The most striking use of astrology is to give an explanation of character and character differences. It is used, both in the examples below and in casual uses I have heard, to provide an understanding of why an incomprehensible or obnoxious character trait cannot be changed, or why two otherwise reasonable people cannot get along with one another. Unlike psychological explanations of character types, astrological types are not presented as pathological and, therefore, there is no demand or expectation that the person of a particular type could or should change that type by becoming better adjusted or more mature.

The following examples of use of an astrological explanatory system are taken from an interview with a single speaker.

(19)   *Speaker:* Yeah. The one thing that I don't miss from the East Coast are
         the arguments.
       Interviewer: (*Laughs*) Yeah.
       Speaker: OK. (*Laughs*) Talking, yeah, uh but the arguments, and almost
         the creation. It's sort of like, my mother does that too. She's really
         beautiful. She called me up one night and she said "How are things?"

And I said "Fine, you know, kind of beautiful, right in the middle." Which is where I like things, being a Libra. And she says, "Oh, I can't stand them when they're that way." She says, "I gotta have some *excitement* in my life." She says, "I noodge your father a little bit to get." So she creates an argument just to get a little stimulation. Yeah. I, that's not for me. That's for my m–, who's a Scorpio, my mother is a Scorpio, so.

(20) *Speaker:* What's *your* sign?
  Interviewer: Uh, Capricorn.
  Speaker: Perfect. Methodical. They like it to go right. Intelligent. Yeah.
  Interviewer: I'm not methodical.
  Speaker: You're *not?* Your mind works that way.
  Interviewer: Hm. (*Laughs*) You should see my drawers.
  Speaker: The hell with the drawers. (*Laughs*) Your mind works very methodical. I have a very close friend that's a Capricorn. And he uh, you know, he, everything is, he does it *right* the first time. He can't do a half-assed job. It'd bug the shit out of him. He figures, you know, and I agree with him, too, that the easiest way is the right way.
  Interviewer: Capricorn has always struck me as one of the more *boring* signs.
  Speaker: Hmmmm. Not to me. Well, I dig minds, OK. So minds have uh, uh, they turn me on. I dig when I I'm talking to people, somebody intelligent.

These examples represent a popular form or popular use of astrology as an explanatory system. In the more serious use, it presents, as we have seen, an explanation and reconciliation of character types. Its use as a flirtation device functions both by rekeying the talk on a less serious level than that of interview and by providing a legitimate way of talking about the other person's character.

Like the other explanatory systems discussed in this study, astrology has in addition to its popular form an expert version. Like other experts, the astrologer may provide not only an account of character but also advice on how to live.

The relation of popular to expert explanatory systems

Thus far, this study indicates the existence of a number of popular explanatory systems and claims a relation to corresponding expert systems. It is now necessary to consider the nature of this relation. The discussion first examines the synchronic relation between a popular explanatory system and its corresponding expert system and then considers the historical development of popular explanatory systems from expert systems.

The discussion uses popular Freudian psychology as a model, since this is the explanatory system most fully represented in the data and about which there is the most historical evidence. It should be emphasized that I do not claim to have given a full picture of the Freudian explanatory system as it is represented in popular thought. Rather, I am attempting

to demonstrate the existence of popular explanatory systems and to un-
tangle some of the relations between popular and expert systems.

SYNCHRONIC RELATION BETWEEN POPULAR AND EXPERT EXPLANATORY SYSTEMS

Let us begin by considering the current relation between the popular and
expert Freudian systems. The first point is that the popular version uses
a very small number of the concepts present in expert Freudian psychology.
Most notably lacking are any references to theories of sexual development
and sexual functioning. These are, in fact, the concepts that first come
to mind in considering the influence of Freud on popular culture. However,
the topic of the interview – professional history – does not encourage
discussion of sexuality, although a number of speakers do mention it
obliquely, as we have seen. There are also many other Freudian concepts
not present: the Oedipus complex; the tripartite structure of ego, superego,
and id; and the stages of psychosexual development, for example. This
lack appears to be characteristic of all relations between popular and expert explanatory systems. A professional astrologer looking at the popular
use of astrology as an explanatory system would perceive a similar im-
poverishment of the system in including only birth sign and failing to consider rising sign, moon, and so on.

A second point is that isolated concepts have been borrowed, but not
the entire system as system. The concepts of popular Freudian psychology
do not require the dense interconnections of Freud's argumentation.
Similarly, we may say that the difference between a popular use of
astrology and a serious professional use comes in the drawing up of an
astrological chart, which permits the expert to investigate patterns, rather
than relying on isolated facts about individual signs.

Finally, and perhaps most important, those concepts of the expert explanatory system are included that do not contradict other popular theories
of the mind and the reasons for human behavior. That is, Freudian
psychology, as it filters into popular thought, is an expert explanatory
system that supplements other more widespread theories, rather than sup-
planting all of them.

THE HISTORICAL DEVELOPMENT OF EXPLANATORY SYSTEMS

This section considers the process by which an expert explanatory system
can develop, give rise to popular explanatory systems, and finally become
part of common sense. To understand this process for any given explanatory system would require extensive research in intellectual history,
research that has, for the most part, not yet been done. Therefore, the
current discussion is restricted to a schematic model of how such historical
development might occur. Figure 14.1 shows such a model.

The first part of the process is the move from common sense to expert
theory. This is the point at which the originator of some expert model

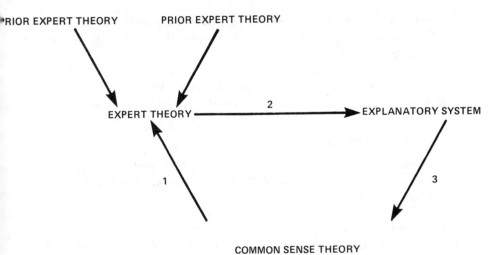

Figure 14.1. Historical development of an explanatory system

of the nature of mind, human behavior, and so on begins the development of the model. The new expert model arises within a context of currently held ideas, both those of common sense and of already existing expert systems. Much of the new expert system will be in opposition to common-sense theories. At the same time, there must be common-sense constraints on the new theory; too entirely radical a theory of mind could not be recognized as a theory of mind at all. Other relevant expert theories extant at the time will also have an effect on the type of models that can be constructed.

We now turn to the second leg of the diagram in Figure 14.1, the move from expert system to explanatory system. This is the process by which this diffusion of ideas takes place from expert into culture. As mentioned, the full expert theory does not become part of this explanatory system; only a limited subset of ideas is chosen. How this selection takes place is a fascinating question. It seems likely that the common sense of the period affects the selection so that the most radical and startling portions of the theory are *not* chosen.

Finally, we turn to the last leg of the diagram, the move from explanatory system to common sense. As a given explanatory system becomes better known and more widely held, it begins to move closer to common sense and may eventually come to form a part of common sense. As an example, we take the notion of the Freudian slip, which seems to be a part of the general, common-sense body of accepted notions and which does not require the support of the Freudian explanatory system to be comprehensible.

To document the historical process suggested in Figure 14.1, extensive research in the history of popular culture would be required. Such research is not currently available for any of the explanatory systems discussed in this paper, although there is some related research on the history of the development of Freud's ideas.[4]

In the absence of such detailed reseach, this section has attempted to indicate a model for such historical studies and the value they would have in understanding both explanatory systems and common sense.

Issues in linguistics and anthropology

This section discusses some of the questions about explanatory systems that may arise in linguistics and anthropology and sketches directions for further research in this area.

LINGUISTIC ISSUES

From the point of view of linguistics, this work attempts to show that one component of oral life stories is the explanatory system, which furnishes a system other than that of common sense by which the actions narrated can be understood and justified. A possible criticism arising from this point of view is whether this analysis makes too much of the available evidence. That is, we have seen speakers using such phrases as "strokes" or "reinforcement" or "deeper reasons" or "Libra." Since these are common in ordinary conversation, what justification is there to use them to assert the existence of as complex and hypothetical an entity as the explanatory system?

One argument for the postulation of the explanatory system is that speakers do not use metaphors from several systems. That is,we do not find a single speaker using both Freudian and behaviorist metaphors. Since the mixing of metaphors is a common phenomenon in speech, when we find metaphors kept separate in this way, it argues that they come from separate systems, which, in some sense, are known to the speakers.

A second argument is that in narratives exhibiting the effects of a particular explanatory system, the details of construction at the level of the sentence and the entire narrative are consistent with the content of the explanatory system claimed for the life story. This effect is particularly evident in the behaviorist life story examined earlier; however, it is present to some extent in all life stories that use an explanatory system.

These two arguments together suggest that however common the metaphors of these explanatory systems may be, they do indicate the existence of a number of systems, rather than an unstructured collection of concepts that can be used promiscuously and without regard to coherence.

CULTURAL ISSUES

From the point of view of anthropology, or of social history, a number of questions are raised that cannot be answered within the scope of this paper. One issue is how many explanatory systems are present in a given culture, and what they are. This question could be answered by an extensive study of a number of types of discourse on a number of different topics, as well as an analysis of the most widely disseminated forms of popular culture. A second issue is the relation between popular and expert forms of an explanatory system. As already discussed, the relation could be investigated using the usual techniques of social history. A third issue is more psychological: How serious are these explanatory systems for their users and how are they related to their behavior? This is a more difficult question, but it could perhaps be approached using a mixture of psychological and participant observation techniques.

These questions, I believe, indicate interesting and valuable directions for research. The present research indicates the existence of a level of conceptual organization that is necessary to understand the structure of life stories. This is already an extremely important finding since it allows us to understand one mechanism by which people make sense of their own lives.

Notes

1. I am grateful to Eleanor Rosch and Dan Slobin for introducing me to autobiography as an area of investigation. My interest in discourse analysis and my understanding of it are due to William Labov. I have also been greatly aided by discussions with Joseph Goguen, A. L. Becker, Veronika Ehrich, Gelya Frank, Nathan Hale, George Lakoff, Willem Levelt, Livia Polanyi, Naomi Quinn, Larry Selinker, Sandra Silberstein, and James Weiner. My primary debt is to the people who told me something of their lives and whose stories are here treated dispassionately as objects for analysis.

   This work was partially supported by Office of Naval Research, Contract Number N00014–82–K–0711.
2. The examples of this paragraph have been constructed by the author.
3. The data discussed were gathered from 1977 through 1979. I have noted that starting in 1980, as economic conditions worsened, stories of professional choice have begun to include at least a mention of economic circumstances, although they still do not mention social class.
4. For example, Ellenberger (1970) discusses the social history of the development and spread of Freud's thought. Sulloway (1979) discusses the relation of Freud's theories to the theories of biology extant at that time. Bakan (1958) discusses Freud's debt to the Jewish mystical tradition of linguistic interpretation. Hale (1971) gives a history of the acceptance and modification of Freud's thought in the American professional psychological circles. All of these works, though, concentrate on Freud's relation to other expert systems and to his acceptance by other experts. There is no systematic history of the effect of Freud's thought on the general public.

References

Bakan, D.
   1958. Sigmund Freud and the Jewish Mystical Tradition. New York: D. Van Nostrand Company.

Becker, A.
　　1977. Text building, epistemology, and aesthetics in Javanese shadow theater.
　　In The Imagination of Reality, A. Becker and A. Yengoyan, eds. Norwood,
　　N.J.: Ablex Publishing Corporation. Pp. 211–243.
Ellenberger, H.
　　1970. The Discovery of the Unconscious: The History and Evolution of Dynamic
　　Psychology. New York: Basic Books.
Frank, G.
　　1981. Venus on wheels: The life history of a congenital amputee. Unpublished
　　Ph.D. Dissertation. University of California, Los Angeles.
Geertz, C.
　　1973. The Interpretation of Cultures. New York: Basic Books.
Hale, N. J.
　　1971. Freud and the Americans, Vol. 1, The Beginnings of Psychoanalysis in
　　the United States. New York: Oxford University Press.
Langness, L. L. and G. Frank
　　1981. Lives: An Anthropological Approach to Biography. Novato, Calif.:
　　Chandler and Sharp Publishers.
Lasch, C.
　　1979. The Culture of Narcissism. New York: W. W. Norton and Company.
Linde, C.
　　1981. The organization of discourse. *In* Style and Variables in English, T. Shopen
　　and J. M. Williams, eds. Cambridge, Mass.: Winthrop Publishers. Pp. 84–114.
　　n.d. The Creation of Coherence in Life Stories. Unpublished manuscript in
　　preparation. Structural Semantics, Palo Alto.
Schur, E. M.
　　1976. The Awareness Trap: Self-Absorption Instead of Social Change. New
　　York: Quadrangle Books.
Sennett, R.
　　1977. The Fall of Public Man. New York: Alfred A. Knopf.
Skinner, B. F.
　　1948. Walden Two. New York: Macmillan Company.
　　1979. The Shaping of a Behaviorist. New York: Alfred A. Knopf.
Sulloway, F. J.
　　1979. Freud: Biologist of the Mind. New York: Basic Books.

PART V
An appraisal

15
Models, "folk" and "cultural"
PARADIGMS REGAINED?[1]

Roger M. Keesing

Some ten years ago, I reflected in a series of papers (1972a; 1972b; 1972c; 1974) on the limitations of cognitive anthropology as then practiced: "ethnoscience," "ethnographic semantics," "the new ethnography." I argued that in its preoccupation with inductive rigor and cultural uniqueness, cognitive anthropology had followed the premises of American descriptive linguistics, even as the Chomskyan revolution had made these premises untenable in the realm of language. Analyzing the semantics of folk classification on the promise that the methods and models so developed could be extended so as eventually to produce a "cultural grammar" was, I thought, naïve. The focus on artificially simple and simplified problems (especially the semantics of kin terms in their genealogical senses) had deflected our attention from the deep complexities of meaning and context and deep questions about the rule-governedness of social behavior. I pointed to the incredible complexity of the organization of mind and brain, as then beginning to emerge in the neurosciences and artificial intelligence research. In this light, anthropologists' attempts to describe cultural knowledge seemed curiously unrealistic:

> Cognitive anthropology has so far been an Alice in Wonderland combination of sweepingly broad aspirations and ludicrously inadequate means. We have been cheerfully and optimistically using high school algebra to explore the most profound mysteries of the natural world. (1972c)

Yet, my message in these critiques was not entirely pessimistic. In "Paradigms Lost," I noted that pioneers of the linguistic frontier such as Charles Fillmore and George and Robin Lakoff had made impressive incursions into the territory claimed by cognitive anthropology, and I suggested that paths connecting the two disciplines were opening up once more. In my 1972 University of Illinois lecture on "Toward a New Cognitive Anthropology," I noted that while proponents of "The new ethnography" were trying to characterize formally the cultural knowledge of native actors, artificial intelligence (AI) researchers were trying to write "cultures" for automata. There and in an assessment of kinship studies (1972b), I pointed toward a potential convergence between AI research and cognitive anthropology: Both were making parallel simplifying assumptions, and both were facing the same intractable problems of pattern and relationship; each had something to learn from the other. I further suggested that a nascent understanding of categorization in terms of prototypes, contexts, and fuzzy edges in anthropology (Berlin & Kay), cognitive psychology (Rosch), linguistics (Lakoff), and AI pattern-recognition research could revolutionize the simplistic models of then-prevailing ethnographic semantics.

That in 1983 a surviving little band of battered pioneers of the early cognitive anthropology could sit around a conference table with George Lakoff, with students of Rosch and Kay pursuing complexities of semantics in terms of prototypes and fuzzy edges; with Jaime Carbonell, who is trying to teach automata to reason analogically as human beings do; and with a new generation of cognitive anthropologists collaborating with AI researchers, suggests that my guarded optimism and glimpses of a new cognitive anthropology were not so far off the mark.

But is all this more than collective optimism, fraught with the same old naïveté? Do we simply have new catchwords for the 80s – "folk models," "prototypes," "schemas," "instantiations," "conventional metaphors" – that disguise the same old difficulties with new labels? Is the interdisciplinary venture genuine, or have we cognitive anthropologists just enticed outsiders into our wild goose chase? Or joined theirs?

A detailed summary and retrospective of the past decade of cognitive anthropology would be tedious. However, some assessment of the new developments in relation to the past, to the future, and to the deep problematic of characterizing what native actors know and how that shapes what they do, may be worthwhile.

An ambiguity in this task needs to be made explicit at the outset. My assigned task, at the conclusion of the Conference on Folk Models, was to assess retrospectively the papers presented in the conference and the theoretical concern with *folk models* that had been their focus. After an initial version of my paper had been circulated – indeed, my critique may have been one of the stimuli to the change – the concept of folk models was recast as *cultural models* by the editors. Moreover, the set of papers initially given and discussed at the conference was considerably reduced, and some key contributors to conference discussion are not represented in this volume. Was I, then, to present a retrospective critique of a conference on folk models? Or, was I to summarize a volume addressed to essentially the same problematic, differently labeled, and with a substantially reduced set of papers? I have chosen a middle course, addressing myself mainly to papers included in the volume, but alluding where worthwhile to other participants in the conference and points raised there. I also look both at folk models and their mutated version, cultural models.

Cultural knowledge and cultural theory

I have argued (1974; 1981) that an ideational theory of culture does not commit us either to a monolithic view of "a culture" as a shared system of symbols or to a deterministic view of culture as directly generating behavior. An ideational theory of culture can look at cultural knowledge as distributed within a social system, can take into account the variation between individuals' knowledge of and vantage points on the cultural heritage of their people. It can also view cultural knowledge as shaping and constraining, but not directly generating, social behavior.

In their pursuit of *cultural grammars,* however, pioneers of the new ethnography had seldom dealt with variation and the distribution of knowledge. The *cultural code* was an idealized set of rules assumed (heuristically) to be shared; and despite the protestations about accounting for appropriate, not actual, behavior, a view of human beings as rule-following and appropriateness-maximizing had pervaded early cognitive anthropology. This orientation left little room for the processes of co-creation, negotiation, and contextual shifting on which ethnomethodologists and other social interactionists have focused. The assumption that behavior is pervasively rule-governed led in many cases to a strategy of inference whereby unconscious rules were posited to account for observed behavior, even where there was no evidence for the "rules" other than the behavior they were assumed to be generating.

Has an emerging new cognitive anthropology transcended the limitations of a view of an idealized native actor mechanically enacting implicit rules? The past decade has seen an increased concern with problems of cognitive variability, which had been foreshadowed by Sankoff (1971), Wexler and Romney (1972), and others. This has been most clear in study of folk classification, as in Gardner's (1976: 464) examination of cognitive variability and sharing and "the model of the omniscient informant."

Have the frontiers been carried still further, toward an understanding of how the distribution of knowledge and perspective articulates with the structure of social systems? I see in the conference papers and volume some grounds for optimism, some for pessimism.

In place of the idealized native actor, we are presented with "folk" and "experts." The folk, in turn, may have different models from one another (e.g., Kempton's alternative models of how thermostats work, the alternative metaphors of marriage explicated by Quinn, and the folk models of electrical current as water or lemmings discussed by Dedre Gentner at the conference). There thus is room here for variable versions of a common culture – and that I take to be an advance. But the folk/expert dichotomy, if we take it seriously, would seem itself to represent a folk model of society: and one which, I argue below, is itself fraught with difficulties. *Cultural models* may steer us clear of some of these traps; but the reconceptualization raises further problems.

The conception of human beings as pervasively rule-following is being transformed into a more sophisticated framework for looking at culture and behavior. The cognitive models explored in these papers constitute paradigms through which one places constructions on everyday experience; conventional metaphors represent simplified, transformed, culturally defined realities. But these are frameworks of interpretation, not sets of rules and routines native actors follow to maximize the appropriateness of behavior. There is room here for choice, for alternative constructions, for creativity. There is also an emerging concern with the creative social processes of co-construction of situationally shared and negotiated realities. Quinn's paper (this volume) and her other recent work vividly show how an understanding of a marriage is negotiated, fashioned together in (as well as from) ongoing interaction by husband and wife; Price (this volume) shows how cultural interpretations of disease are fashioned in the process of interaction. We are even learning that lexical semantic analysis may require reference to the situational context of speech, as Eve Sweetser's elegant analysis of the semantics of *lie* in English (this volume) illustrates.

These developments and continuing advances by students of pragmatics in linguistics and speech act theory in philosophy make it clear that the static and deterministic models of early cognitive anthropology were sterile not because they were (or aspired to be) cognitive. They were sterile because, as preliminary mappings of what human beings know about their world, they were not placed within an adequate, multisided paradigm of how what we know articulates with the social worlds we create together (and which, dialectically, create us and what we know). This is a problem to which I return.

In my review of cultural theory (1974) and more recent assessments of culture (1981; 1982) I have noted that a cognitive view of culture, while potentially allowing us to interpret the distribution and variability of knowledge and the situational co-construction of shared worlds, renders it difficult to capture the publicness and collectiveness of culture as symbol systems (Geertz 1972). As Varenne (1984:291) has perceptively written in critically assessing "individualist" theories of culture, the collective tradition of a people is in an important sense external and transcendant in relation to any individual; such a cultural tradition

> *is always already there.* It is in this sense that ideology, or culture, is an external social fact that is part of the environment of individuals. To the extent that it is part of the environment, it is something to which individuals will adapt and against which they may react. . . .

This sense of externality and transcendance, which is easily lost if we either reduce a culture to the "head" of an idealized omniscient native actor or distribute versions of "it" through the "heads" of a population of native actors, is potentially captured more clearly in the notion of *folk models, cultural models,* or *folk knowledge* (Clement 1982). These models are at once cultural and public, as the historically cumulated knowledge of a people and the embodiments of a language, and cognitive, as paradigms for construing the world.

Models, "folk" and "cultural"

The central concern with folk models at the Princeton conference and its Los Angeles predecessor represents a confluence of several streams of thought. One is the continuing quest in cognitive anthropology to capture the uniqueness of a culturally constructed world, now tempered with realism: If one cannot go from folk taxonomies boldly out to write a cultural grammar, one can usefully seek a partial but systematic model of a single target domain.

Another stream of thought comes from Lakoff and Johnson's (1980) exploration of how conventional metaphors build on paradigmatic, experientially based models. The models embedded in and constitutive of language itself offer hope of systematic methods of inference; we can use as data materials less elusive than evanescent behavior, less directly constituted by ethnographic interviewing, perhaps, than the spuriously "hard" data of early ethnoscience.

Another stream comes from semantic theory, particularly the prototype semantic theory pioneered by Eleanor Rosch (1973; 1975; 1977; 1978) and Brent Berlin and Paul Kay (Berlin & Kay 1969; Coleman & Kay 1981). These models of the cognized world build on prototype relationships in a number of ways that promise to make prototypy, along with conventional metaphor, a pervasive organizing principle. We find in these papers not only prototypic or canonical exemplars of categories (the chairiest chair), but also the prototypic idealized interactional situation (the purely informative speech act) and the prototypic sequence or scenario (an idealized family structure or life history).

Finally, the concern with models of everyday reality in cognitive anthropology parallels, and is closely tied to, an emerging concern with *naïve theory* or *mental models* in cognitive psychology (see, e.g., Gentner & Stevens 1982; Johnson-Laird 1981; McCloskey, Caramazza, & Green 1980), a tradition represented here by Collins and Gentner (this volume).

The focus on folk or cultural models by cognitive anthropologists and fellow cognitivists in kindred disciplines raises a number of theoretical and methodological issues. I look at most of them in the sections to follow; some bear examination at this stage.

A first question, which I raise here and touch on again in the next section but do not attempt to answer systematically, is how we are to define folk or cultural models so they usefully delimit some sectors, but not all, of the cultural knowledge of individuals. What are such models? And what do human beings know that does *not* comprise these models? There are at least two important dimensions here: One concerns their sharedness, as folk or cultural constructions; the other concerns their "model-ness." The original characterization of these models as "folk" did not reflect their adherence among the untutored masses,[2] but their common-sense nature. Such models comprise the realms of (culturally constructed) common sense. They serve pragmatic purposes; they explain the tangible, the experiential (hence perspectivally egocentric), the probable; they assume a superficial geology of causation; they hold sway in a realm in which exceptions prove rules and contradictions live happily together. I return to the experientially based, culturally conventional commonsensicality of such models. What, then, makes them "models"? Presumably, it is their paradigmatic, world-proposing nature. These cultural constructions of the everyday world do not consist of disconnected bits of cultural wisdom, expressed in precepts, parables, proverbs, or pragmatic, probabilistic operating strategies, but of the world-proposing (however simplified and internally or externally contradictory) models embodied or expressed in these bits. Such models, then, are not *presented* to us in what everyday people say and do in their everyday lives, or in the stuff of metaphoric talk; they are *re*presented, in fragmentary surface facets. We must infer the more coherent, if unarticulated, models that lie beneath (as we infer native actors must, in learning them). How such models of everyday reality relate to other modes and realms of cultural knowledge then becomes a central question.

How diverse are such models in different culturally constructed worlds? What constrains their diversity? This second question is raised by D'Andrade (this volume) at the end of his superb paper on American models of the mind. In many realms, folk conceptualizations – of emotions, time, mental processes, and so on – are turning out to be more similar than might have been expected (especially in the light of anthropological dogmas about cultural uniqueness and the relatively arbitrary nature of cultural constructions). Conventions for talking about mental processes are different on Ifaluk and in the United States in ways congruent with differences in cultural precept and practice, but they are not *very* different – more shadings of value and emphasis than unique conceptualizations. If that turned out to be true of Balinese and Tikopia and Eskimo, as well, their varied ways of saying the same thing could not necessarily be taken as expressing deep truths about the cognitive organization of information. It would, I think, tell us more clearly about the experiential nature of consciousness, the way members of our species experience and perceive the operation of mind/brain. Loosely speaking (with apologies to Paul Kay), it tells us not about the nature of human heads, but about how it feels to live inside them.

A third question, implied by D'Andrade (this volume) and raised more squarely by Linde (this volume), is the degree to which scientific discourse builds on and with such common-sense models. The physical sciences have progressively penetrated through and beyond everyday, common-sense models of experienced "reality." Yet the physicist leaves subatomic particles and relativity behind, the mathematician non-Euclidean geometry, as they enter the parking lot and drive home through a world of seemingly solid objects, flat surfaces, and straight lines. Moreover, conventional metaphors and common sense cannot be expunged from the natural languages to which the most precise scientists must have recourse (Kuhn 1979). Disengaging what passes for behavioral science from "folk" models and conventional metaphors is hopeless: Most of psychology (and, we could add, much of sociology and anthropology) reflects common-sense cultural models of the mind and reified metaphors.

Are "folk" or "cultural" models cognitive?

Granted that conventional models of everyday reality are a worthwhile focus for anthropological concern, why should they be analyzed cognitively? Or, put another way, anthropologists have been characterizing such models for decades as (elements of) other peoples' cultures; nowadays, our symbolist colleagues interpret them as public systems of shared meaning. What is gained by interpreting models of everyday reality as cognitive codes rather than as cultural texts?

Let me exemplify with the work of Clifford Geertz, who watched with some wonder at the Princeton conference as cognitive anthropologists explored the realm of culturally constructed common sense as if it had just been discovered. Much of Geertz's work has explored this realm in cultural terms. Consider, for example, his brilliant essay in which the cockfight as cultural text is illumined by Balinese models of society and sociality (1972). Consider the depiction of the Moroccan scenario of Cohen and the sheep (1973) as articulation and negotiation of cultural models. The comparative interpretation of conceptions of self and person in Bali and Morocco (1966; 1974) depicts culturally constructed models of the most fundamental takens-for-granted about human-beings-in-the-world. Finally, Geertz's essay on "Common Sense as a Cultural System" (1975) explores conceptions of personhood, sociality, sexuality, and other realms of the everyday.

There is a double twist to cognitive anthropology's emergent concern with models of everyday cognition – with folk models of the mind, of emotion, of mundane experience. A good deal of Geertz's work, and, of course, much of phenomenology (Husserl, Schutz, Heidegger, Merleau-Ponty), is precisely about models of everyday cognition: about what thinking, remembering, understanding, seeing, communicating, getting angry, the passage of time are, experientially, to human beings; and, more or less explicitly, how they are culturally constructed, how they are shaped by language and metaphor. What, then, is specially to be gained by characterizing models of everyday experience in cognitive terms? Are putatively cognitive accounts of models of the mind more perceptive, systematic, or powerful than, say, a psychoanalytically informed cultural-symbolist account such as Paul's (1976) analysis of the Sherpa temple as a "model of the psyche"? Do we gain from our cognitive assumptions and commitments? Or, do we achieve, perhaps more pretentiously and less gracefully, what is achieved through the word-magic of a Geertz depicting personhood in Bali (1966) or a Schutz (1962; 1967) or Natanson (1967; 1970) depicting the phenomenology of self and role?

The papers in this volume provide ample evidence that there are wide differences, theoretical and methodological, between symbolists and contemporary cognitivists; and that the cognitivists are achieving important new insights. Where symbolists mainly view their task as interpretive, cognitivists mainly view theirs as scientific. For the latter, the primary data – transcribed tapes of interviews or other discourse or other "hard" records of the behavior of individuals – are crucial, and the inferences drawn from them systematic and explicit. The naïve inductivism of much early ethnoscience is tempered now with realism and appreciation for interpretive insight as well as with rigor; however, concern for methodological precision emerges clearly in these papers. It is misleading that Geertz's metaphor of culture as text to be read suggests close convergence: The texts of the cognitivist exploring models of everyday reality mainly comprise what individual subjects and informants said and did.

Inevitably, the perspectives these approaches yield are quite different. Where symbolists find coherence and systematic structures, cognitivists are likely to find in their primary data contradictions, alternative constructions, small and partial coherences, individual variations. This difference in perspective does not rule out our finding global structures or systematic models underlying apparent diversity – witness D'Andrade's model of American models of the mind or Lakoff and Kövecses's model of models of anger embodied in American English (both in this volume). It is perhaps no coincidence that the most coherent and global models of everyday reality described in these chapters are the schemas built into a language. Even here, however, as Kay's paper reminds us, there are alternative if not quite contradictory models expressed in conventional usage. Cognitivists' engagement with such models does take them into domains already extensively explored by symbolists and others; but the insights this exploration is beginning to yield are complementary to, and in some important ways corrective of, those discovered along different paths.

I am concerned that this exploration takes place with adequate appreciation of how extensively mapped this territory already is and of the insights to be gleaned from earlier work. Cognitive anthropology grew up curiously innocent of social theory; it need not remain so in its maturity. Past explorations of everyday cognition and common-sense constructions of reality include not only those of the phenomenological tradition and its offshoots (Husserl, Schutz, Heidegger, Merleau-Ponty, Foucault, Ricoeur) but also those of the Marxist tradition and its offshoots (Marx, Gramsci,

Althusser, Bourdieu). In this Marxist tradition, the realm of common sense is viewed as refracting as well as reflecting, disguising as well as illuminating, shaped by as well as shaping the realities of a social world.

I am also concerned about what I see as a problematic theoretical disjunction between folk models as cognitive structures and as social and cultural patterns. Early cognitive anthropologists radically oversimplified matters by reducing "a culture" to an idealized cognitive system. However, the solution proposed by Clement (1982) – that we see *folk knowledge* as having its locus "in the group" and not in the individual – seems to pose another set of dangers. Clement contrasts her concern with folk knowledge with the earlier assumptions of ethnoscience in these terms:

> In . . . ethnoscience, attention is focused on cultural competence –
> . . . mentally held principles and recipes that the individual has learned
> which allow him or her to behave in a culturally appropriate manner. . . .
> In contrast . . . , *folk* knowledge is viewed as an aspect of the group. Folk
> representations, the means through which folk knowledge is expressed, are
> . . . products of the institutionalized patterns of information processing
> and knowledge distribution within the group. (1982:194)

If what we study is collective, however, if its locus is "in the group" and not in "mentally held principles and recipes," can we usefully regard ourselves as cognitivists and effectively and legitimately borrow models and methods from the cognitive sciences? What we want to study, I think, ultimately is how individuals cognize and use models they (partly) share with others, models that are common coin in the community. That will require that we see folk models *both* as collective and social *and* as "mentally held principles and recipes."

Perhaps, then, we need to distinguish between models (*I*), the pool of common-sense knowledge and understandings of the community, and encoded in its language; and models (*II*), the (alternative, partial) versions of these models cognized and invoked by individuals in everyday perception, thought, and interaction. If early ethnoscience erred in imagining that we could adequately characterize level (*I*) as an idealized version of level (*II*), we equally err, I think, if we try to characterize level (*I*) using theoretical frameworks derived from and appropriate to cognitive science (chunking, instantiations, etc.). It is true that the pools of ideas in communities can include only ideas that are thinkable and knowable by individual humans. As systems, however, these pools are not subject to many other constraints that structure the cognition of individuals, and their dynamics are quite different. We can be wiser cognitive anthropologists if we distinguish these two loci of conceptual models and levels of analysis and engage ourselves with the nature of each and the interplay between them. Replacing *folk* with *cultural* in designating the models we are concerned with avoids some of the problems raised by the term *folk* (and the folk model of society it itself embodies) to which I pointed in earlier versions of this commentary. In locating the models as collective and shared, however, it perhaps renders more problematic than *folk* did attempts to analyze such models as if they represented the cognition of individuals.

Perhaps an example, to which I later return, will serve to clarify. Consider the folk models constructed around the concept of *luck* in American culture as a set of public, largely shared conventions for talking, for explaining outcomes, for characterizing good or bad fortune. Linguistic conventions ("some people have all the luck," "thank my lucky stars") and cultural icons (rabbits' feet) are cultural coin of the community. Yet, at a level of individual cognition, these cultural models of luck (folk models *I*) are drawn on in quite different ways. When I talk about having all the luck on the tennis court on a particular day – the day when all my let-cord shots dropped over and the occasional desperate lunge yielded a winning drop volley off the racket frame – I do not surmise that my "luck" was anything but random chance. Other people, on the tennis court or in poker games or reflecting on the trajectory of life, invoke (I think) *luck* with a conviction that the outcome of events is ultimately determinate, or at least skewed in favor of some, against others. Some people carry rabbits' feet or other amulets, wear "lucky" headbands or use "lucky" putters, convinced that this will affect the outcome of events. Individuals perceiving contradictions between their "rational" and magical beliefs may invoke the folk concept of *superstition* to rationalize their conjunction. In the cognition of individuals, conceptions of luck may be central (e.g., to a gambler) or peripheral, may be invoked with metaphysical implications or without, may be "believed" or not. The same conventional linguistic expressions and metaphors regarding *luck* may be used by different speakers of American English with radically different implications: The folk models (*I*) embodied in language structure our talk whatever our personal folk models (*II*) of luck. In the cognition of individuals, folk models (*II*) articulate with, exist side by side with, evoke and are evoked by other systems of folk models drawn from the pool of the community in diverse ways.

To take another example, my color vision differs from that of the majority in the community in that I am neurophysiologically incapable of making color distinctions (greens vs. reds, in some perceptual environments) made by normal members of the population. I and a substantial minority are constrained to use a conceptual system we lack the perceptual equipment to use properly, or at least conventionally. Like other people in the population, however, we turn green with jealousy, red with anger; we use folk models (*I*) of the community as best we can.

If cognitive anthropologists are to pursue more deeply and more formally the place of folk models *in* the mind, not simply *of* the mind, then some further questions are in order. One characteristic of such models, or of some of them, is their probabilistic and partial nature. They are, as elements of culturally constructed common sense, models that work well enough for everyday use. But human beings, operating in a universe of unique constellations of events, must deal with the atypical, the improbable, the unexpected – not simply with ideal types, canonical circumstances, the probable, and the normal. As Haviland (1977) and Randall (1976) observe, we must have ways of engaging, construing, and acting on circumstances our rules of thumb do not aptly comprehend – despite our high tolerances for living with contradiction, for not only holding mutually incompatible models but also for maintaining models in the face of their demonstrated inadequacy. ("The exception proves the rule," as Geoff White's proverb [the volume] might remind us.)

But do we have, in addition to the models of culturally constructed common sense, deeper grammars to which we have recourse in the face of the atypical and complex? Do common-sense models, enabling us to deal with the world probabilistically on the basis of typical scenarios, "canned" or formulaic routines, and ideal types, operate in conjunction with cognitive processes whereby we decompose situations into their deeper constituents and interpret them with an underlying grammar when we have to? Or, do we simply muddle through by extrapolation, approximation, and ad hoc invention? I raised these questions more than 15 years ago (1970) in looking at what I took to be an underlying grammar on which folk sociological models of roles were constructed; and I reflected again on the adequacy of such an inferred grammar when, five years later, I was assessing my exploration of roles in relation to the state of play in cognitive anthropology:

> One facet of the miraculous and still mysterious process of everyday, mundane social life is the way we act, and perceive others to be acting, in culturally standardized *capacities*. We enact *roles:* or so social science theory, drawing on the theatrical metaphors of folk sociology, would have it. (1975:5)
>
> But since no adequate description of roles had ever, to my knowledge, been formulated – and certainly not in a non-Western culture – I could not *assume* that the metaphor of 'role', derived from our folk sociology, would turn out to fit the way the Kwaio [of the Solomon Islands] organized their knowledge of their social world. 'Social identity' and 'role' might not turn out to reflect the deeper and unconscious levels at which cultural algorithms were coded. (1975:9)

I had provisionally inferred, using the method described in my 1970 paper, that the labeled more-or-less standardized capacities in which Kwaio acted were often composites of underlying elements.

> This conception of social identities as fractionated elements from which we formulate social personae has . . . advantages analytically and theoretically. The elements, if they have any cognitive salience, are ways of organizing knowledge at an unconscious level. . . . In this view, social identities serve as "building blocks" or elements that, by "grammatical" rules of combination, are combined into composite social personae with

predictable role entailments. We are conscious of, and often label, typical
high-probability combinations. They are the 'pre-packaged' units of a
culture. Navigating probabilistically in our social world, we expect physicians or attorneys or gas-station attendants to be male, and expect fathers
to give their daughters away as brides; yet we can deal in culturally appropriate ways with less familiar and less typical combinations. (Keesing
1975:16)

Some are improbable, some rare, and a few probably unique. The point is
that instead of taking a small set of ready-made social identities as the
basic units of a cultural inventory, we would view our actors as continually *creating* 'social personae' . . . out of the elements provided by the
culture. (Keesing 1970:434)

My point is that a cognitive theory of folk models, as culturally constructed common sense, would perhaps in the long run not want to take
these models as representing cognitive organization but as representing
a set of operating strategies for using cultural knowledge in the world;
they comprise sets of shortcuts, idealizations, and simplifying paradigms
that work just well enough yet need not fit together without contradiction into global systems of coherent knowledge. A cognitive theory of such
models of everyday reality would, I think, ultimately want to take them
not as the constituents of cultural knowledge but as their surface manifesta-
tions. (I have similarly argued that, contra the early ethnoscience, an adequate cognitive theory would not assume that lexemes or taxonomies are
the fundamental constituents of cultural knowledge but rather would see
labeling and taxonomic classification as emergent phenomena to be explained in terms of more fundamental constituents and processes [Kees-
ing 1970:444–45; see also Randall 1976].) Against this line of speculation
can be counterposed an argument, articulated by Quinn and Holland in
their introduction, that it is the simplifying power of the models of culturally constructed common sense, in codifying the prototypical, that
allows human beings to cognize such vastly complicated natural and social
worlds.

The problem of how we human beings deal – whether by extrapolation, analytic decomposition, feature-weighting, flexible modes of pattern matching, or whatever – with the atypical, the marginal, the fuzzy,
or categorically liminal – has received little attention in cognitive anthropology to this point. It squarely confronts AI researchers, notably
in pattern recognition; and it faces us in various forms when we work with
prototype analyses, whether in semantics or other realms. (See, for example, Kempton 1981 and Kronenfeld, Armstrong, & Wilmoth 1985.)
Cognitivists in anthropology and kindred fields need to confront these
problems, at once formal and substantive, more directly. It may be, as
Lakoff (1984) has recently argued, that explorations of the logics and patterns of prototype categorization will in the long run not only revolutionize

our understanding of cognition but also demand reformulation of the basic Aristotelian premises of western logics. My point is that if we are going to be cognitivists, in relation to models conceptualizing everyday reality, we need to be good ones, to explore deeply the way cultural knowledge is organized and applied to the world.

If our models of other peoples' models are to fit into the emerging conceptualizations of cognitive science, and at the same time are to fit into the wider anthropological enterprise, we need to be asking strategic questions about the structure of cultural knowledge and the way it is used in ongoing social life.

Culture, memory, and behavior

I noted a decade ago that despite a common boundary beween cognitive anthropology and cognitive psychology, a curious gap had arisen between them. Pioneers of cognitive anthropology such as Frake and Conklin had read and learned cognitive psychologists such as Miller, Galanter, and Pribram (1960). But especially as psychologists probed memory experimentally, *memory* as conceptualized psychologically and *culture* as conceived anthropologically had become strangely separated. Short-term and long-term memory represented "real" cognitive processing capacities; but what was remembered was artificial, an artifact of experimental procedures.

Human beings, of course, remember particularities – people, places, experiences; but they also abstract from particularities to derive general rules, models of meaning, expectations and strategies and routines. These abstractions from experience,

> rules for deciding what is . . . , what can be . . . how one feels about
> it . . . what to do about it . . . and . . . how to go about doing it.
> (Goodenough 1961:552)

comprise cultures, as cognitive systems.

Early attempts in artificial intelligence and cognitive psychology to create models of memory dealt mainly with memory as a psychological construct – that is, with remembered particularities (see Norman & Rumelhart 1975). But as AI models were pushed further, the need to simulate the "internal models of reality" (Gregory 1969) on the basis of which complex organisms perceive and act became clear. Automata had to be programmed with "cultures"; and much progress in AI in the last decade has been in this direction.

I return later to the growing convergence between cognitive anthropology and artificial intelligence. My concern at this stage is to look more closely at the interplay between memory of particularities and generalized "rules" in ongoing behavior.

In 1974, I had raised the question of the degree to which the knowledge human beings use to act in the world is generalized. Could it be that "the cultural code" is as much an artifact of our assumptions and methods as "memory" was for experimental cognitive psychology?

> It remains an open question to what degree human action is guided by a general conceptual code, a theory of the world and the game of social life that can be disentangled from the particularities and immediacies of each individual's unique experience and life space. (Keesing 1974:93)

Do we human beings interpret the unique situations of life by extrapolating from unique past situations as well as by applying generalized models of the possible and appropriate? John Haviland warns that:

> it is difficult to distinguish an "ideational" component, which involves knowledge of the general rules of the culture, from knowledge of a wide set of contingencies which are in no sense common to a cultural tradition. We ordinarily have thought of one's cultural competence as composed of codes: conceptual schemata for, say, plants and animals, kinship systems, political structures, and so on. The conceptual schemata have, we assume, an independent existence prior to any particular configuration of animals, any set of actual kin, any actual political operation. But in gossip the nonparticular is irrelevant before the actual; the contingencies determine the general principles – for they are all there is. In gossip, the world becomes more than ideal schemata and codes; it rests on the Who's Who, much expanded, on history, on reputations, on idiosyncrasies, on exceptions and accidents. Gossip exalts the particular. Much of an actor's cultural competence rests on a vast knowledge of contingent fact, raw unconnected trivia. . . . (Haviland 1977:181)

Similar questions about the relationship between cultural models, individual experience, and situational factors are explored by Brown (1985).

Could it be that the "cultural code" itself is partly an artifact of the elicitation process? Do we and our informants enter into a process of co-creation, with normative statements as our collective work? Noting "the processes of collective creation whereby situations are defined, social identities assigned, and rules and relationships negotiated in everyday life," I have recently suggested that

> normative assertions are very often contextually created to suit the purposes of the moment, not simply *cited*. The 'rules' we ethnographers have decontextualized, in turn, may often be constructions fabricated as collective 'work' by the ethnographer and his or her subjects. The ethnographer fashions, with informants, situations in which the construction of normative statements is their joint 'work', their co-creation. Normative statements that emerge in this process of co-creation are then objectified and decontextualized in the production of ethnographies. (Keesing 1982:43)

Randall (1976:546) has asked whether cultural "rules" are in part situationally created and co-created even in the realm of folk categorization:

... folk taxonomies as we know them from ethnographic tradition [may be] ... constructed by applying normally unexploited principles of native logic to various scraps of knowledge lying around in the mind.

Randall suggests that folk taxonomies are in large measure artifacts of our elicitation procedures and suggests that cognitively stored complexes or associations of characteristics and prototype images are more likely to be the bases of actual categorization than are taxonomic trees. This, he suggests, may be because

> instead of consciously systematizing, most people tackle a different task . . . [i.e.,] to operate adequately in a physically demanding, complex, and often dangerous socioecological environment. Doing this does not involve constructing taxonomic trees, but rather, in a particular situation, selecting a contrast set of characteristics which is both sufficiently specific to achieve a practical and safe result and sufficiently general to accomplish one's purposes efficiently. (1976:552)

Similar concerns about the situational structuring of supposed cultural schemata are expressed by Frake (1977) and Agar and Hobbs (1985).

We must also be wary, in our pursuit of folk models, of doing what we seemingly have done with folk taxonomies: creating more global and coherent models than our subjects in fact cognize. Folk models may by their nature have a partial and situational ad hoc quality, a lack of global systematicity. I am concerned that some of what we take to be folk or cultural models may not exist until our strategies of questioning lead informants to create them; or worse yet, until their responses provide fragments out of which we create them. Perhaps one does not need a generalized model of how thermostats operate, or what electrical current is, until an ethnographer induces us to formulate one, or elicits situational responses suggesting that we are implicitly using one. Perhaps all we need are operating strategies that can be internally contradictory precisely because they are not motivated by any systemic model. That, then, leads to further speculations about the cognitive processes involved.

To what degree do we extrapolate from knowledge of the particular – the canonical case, the prototype example, the closest experience – as well as strategically formulating and choosing abstract models that allow high enough probabilities of adequacy, models that work well enough? Explorers of the cognitive frontier, in anthropology, AI, and other fields, do not yet know. Here, Price's observations of disease diagnosis and interpretation in Ecuador (this volume) are particularly interesting. The "experts" in the process of folk diagnosis she describes have recourse to particular actual case scenarios, from which they derive interpretations of a new case, its possible causes, and best treatments.

It would seem that cognitive interpretation of new situations entails a close interplay between extrapolation from the particular and application of the general, as Haviland (1977) had glimpsed in the gossip of

Zinacantan. Are there then separate cognitive compartments, where memories of the particular and models of the general, rules and codes, are stored and organized? Or, are the general "rules" hung onto, illuminated with, and organized in terms of knowledge of prototypical particularities? The latter intuitively seems more plausible and potentially powerful a system; and I am cheered by Jaime Carbonell's observations (personal communication) that recent research in artificial intelligence is exploring just these possibilities. Here, again, prototype conceptualizations that take as background prototypical contexts (that can then be modeled on or remembered in terms of actually experienced events or exemplars) may provide a crucial link between knowledge of the general and memory of the particular extrapolation from past experience to interpret new experience.

Cognitive anthropology and artificial intelligence

This brings me to the convergence, which I had anticipated a decade ago (see also Colby & Knaus 1974), between cognitive anthropology and artificial intelligence. It had seemed curious to me that AI researchers were beginning to write simple "cultures" for robots with enormous difficulty while the "new ethnographers" were aspiring singlehandedly to write cultural grammars of everything the "natives" knew. Given that the most mathematically sophisticated researchers in the world, working in teams, were hard-pressed to program "knowledge that" allowed automata to recognize and manipulate a few objects in artificially simplified environments, it was hardly surprising that a lone ethnographer in a jungle, virtually illiterate in formal languages, was hard-pressed to write more than token segments of a cultural grammar of Subanun or Kwaio.

Had anthropologists anything to contribute to the development of what I foresaw as an emerging formal science of communications, a general theory of information – "knowledge" – in biological systems and its simulation in automata? Could anthropology's cognitive theories of culture begin to be realized in some more substantial and less evanescent and illusory sense through collaboration with AI researchers and others exploring the formal organization of biological information systems? A decade ago, I had foreseen the prospect of positive collaboration:

> . . . If cognitively oriented anthropology is to survive we will have to add our strengths, our knowledge of cultural variability, to the strengths of interdisciplinary teams working on the frontiers of artificial intelligence research and related fields. The problems of how humans organize their knowledge . . . are too vastly complicated for any single researcher or any single discipline to tackle them alone . . . without the anthropologist's help the cybernetician may well create robots that find their Chinese counterparts inscrutable. (Keesing 1975:20)

[Anthropologists] have, in our studies of other cultural worlds, gained a grasp - mainly intuitive, I think - of how those worlds vary, and how real human beings think, perceive, and choose. . . . The challenge is to make [this knowledge] available to colleagues with the mathematical powers to incorporate our implicit knowledge into their explicit models; and to maintain a continuing dialogue with them that keeps their models anchored in human realities. (Keesing 1972)

I had been concerned that in the early 1970s, AI researchers (especially in pattern recognition) seemed to be making simplifying assumptions parallel to those that were creating a false sense of accomplishment in ethnographic semantics (especially analyses of kin terms). The mysteries whereby human beings recognize patterns across contexts lie at the heart of semantic analysis; cognitive anthropologists studying kinship semantics in narrow genealogical frames were spuriously simplifying the task. AI researchers, by artificially holding frames constant and seeking to capture relational patterns by feature analyses, seemed to be following a similar strategy. I had belatedly realized, as I put it in 1975, that in my own attempts at cognitive analysis, I had been "hunting elephants with a fly swatter." But I suggested that my hunt "posed rather clearly some of the complexities of the phenomena" and hence served "as a corrective against the simplifying assumptions so often made in artificial intelligence and related fields to make dead flies look like elephants" (1975:21).

Both cognitive anthropology and AI still seem prone to celebrate more or less successful fly hunts. At least serious collaboration has begun, however, as witness the work of Ed Hutchins on one side of our conference table and Jaime Carbonell on the other. More formally sophisticated models, both in semantic analysis (prototypes, feature weighting) and pattern recognition, the growing dialogue and common vocabulary emerging from the work of such scholars as Schank (Schank 1980; Schank & Abelson 1977), and engagement with anthropological problems, cognitively framed, by AI researchers such as Klein and his colleagues (Klein 1983; Klein et al., 1981) give cause for measured optimism.

Conventional metaphor

Lakoff and Johnson's provocative 1980 book on conventional metaphor has kindled interest in cognitive anthropology and acquired a central place in the growing concern with folk or cultural models. Lakoff and Johnson (and others less widely read by anthropologists, such as Ortony 1979 and Sacks 1979) have been developing a view of language as pervaded by metaphors that are neither "creative" nor "dead" but conventional and fundamentally constitutive of our ways of everyday talk. Lakoff and Johnson, in particular, have developed a view of metaphor as paradigmatic and experientially based.

A metaphoric schema, establishing a universe of discourse in terms of another universe of discourse (LOVE IS A JOURNEY, TIME IS MONEY), in effect defines the kind of paradigm that has been conceptualized here as a folk or cultural model. The anthropologist can explore the cultural particularity of a particular model-embodied-in-metaphoric-schema and, as brilliantly exemplified in Naomi Quinn's analyses of American marriage (1982; this volume), can go on to show how people live their lives, as well as construe their lives, through such metaphoric schemas.

The focus on metaphor articulates closely with an increasingly generalized understanding of prototypy as an organizing principle. The prototype pattern may be a canonical enactment or expression of the metaphor; as philosopher Mark Johnson, another conference participant, would want to remind us, it may be the quintessential experiential pattern on which the metaphorical relationship is built; it may be a prototypical developmental cycle (the unfolding of an ideal marriage, the course of true love, the cycle of the canonically happy family). A metaphorical schema factors out contingent complexities of real life in proposing homologies of form, pattern, and relationship between the source domain and the metaphorized one. A world thus simplified becomes a world of the prototypical.

A predictable anthropological response to Lakoff and Johnson's provocative book has been to show how distinctive are the conventional metaphoric schemas of other peoples (see, e.g., Salmond's intriguing sketch of Maori metaphor, 1982). In some realms, as in body–part metaphors (J. Haviland, unpublished data), conventional metaphors used in different languages are much less diverse than the anthropological relativist might expect (see also White 1980); and in others (e.g., metaphors of time in terms of space), what appear to be differences probably in fact represent the same metaphor phrased in terms of contrasting perspectival orientations. Yet, there clearly *are* differences in conventional metaphors. Our talk of emotions in terms of *hearts* contrasts markedly with Japanese talk of emotions in terms of *bellies,* or other people's in terms of *livers.* Anger is talked about quite differently in Ifaluk (Lutz this volume) or in Ilongot (Rosaldo 1980) than in English, with its beautifully coherent metaphoric schema of hot liquid in a container (Lakoff & Kövecses this volume).

A crucial question linguistic philosophers have pondered now confronts us. To what extent are conventional metaphors, and the schemas they express, constitutive of our experience? Do varying schemas, whether of emotion, time, causality, social relationships, and so on, reflect contrasting modes of subjective experience, of thought and perception – or of simply different conventions for talking about the world, as creatures with our human brains and sensory equipment and bodies experience it? There is no simple answer. In discussion of his and Lakoff's paper, Kövecses cautioned that the conceptual model of anger they had analyzed could not be assumed to be culturally or experientially salient outside the realm of language. And in my conference paper (Keesing 1985) and discussions, I warned of the danger of imputing to our subjects metaphysical theories that seem to be implied by conventional ways of talk. Out of our conventional ways of talking about *luck,* I suggested, a nonnative observer could be led to infer a metaphysical theory of an invisible substance of which people have more or less. We anthropologists, with our bent for cultural exotica and our propensity for viewing cultures as radically unique and diverse (not to mention our imperfect command of field languages), may often have imputed metaphysical notions to our subjects that in fact represent no more than conventional tropes: "Some people have all the luck."[3]

That leads to a further epistemological concern about conventional metaphors and about the models, folk or cultural, on which conference and volume have been focused. Perhaps, working here on a terrain much more slippery than that of folk classification (though that was more slippery than we realized), we really need to draw on our own intuitions as native speakers, need a deeper command of semantic shadings and hidden connections than we acquire in learning fieldwork languages. At least that could be one implication of the fact that so many of the ethnographic papers of the volume (10 of 13) deal with our native language and culture.

"Folk" or "cultural" models in society

I argue in the second section that early cognitive anthropology was naïvely reductionistic in its tacit premise that cultural rules generate behavior – that social interaction is an epiphenomenal outcome of a shared code, a product of rule-following and maximizing of appropriateness. Early cognitive anthropology was, I think, equally naïve in its tacit assumption that the institutional structures of society are themselves epiphenomenal – that cultural rules generate social systems as well as behavior. Such a view was perhaps intended only as a heuristic corrective to the alternative determinisms – ecological, economic, functionalist – then prevailing in anthropology. However, we nonetheless implied the Subanun, Hanunoo, Trukese, or Kwaio society was a more-or-less direct outcome of the rules of a cultural grammar; cognitive anthropology's task was to uncover these mainly implicit rules.

As heuristic corrective, this view doubtless had some value, especially when applied to a small-scale classless society in the Philippines or Solomon Islands. But cultural "rules" are themselves historically situated, shaped (although not determined) by economic and ecological constraints and social processes. Cultural knowledge does not simply vary from individual to individual. What actors know, what perspectives they take, depend, even in the least complex classless societies, on who they are – whether they are male or female, young or old, leader or led.

Early cognitive anthropology, taking its models from linguistics, grew up curiously innocent of social theory. It was not simply its concern with trivia, its aura of scientistic objectivity, that brought "the new ethnography" into collision with the radical anthropology catalyzed by the blood of Vietnam. An anthropology that reified the cultural status quo into the determinant of institutions as well as behavior, that ignored class and history and economy, that ignored the ideological force of cultural rules, could scarcely be the needed "new" anthropology, revolutionary in both senses.

Both cognitive anthropology and the various modes of radical anthropology have mellowed, become less strident in their critiques, less sweepingly millenarian in their claims and aspirations. Yet cognitive anthropology remains, I think, curiously innocent of social theory.

In the conference focused on folk models, I became something of an ideological gadfly about this issue. The model of society assumed there seemed, from the perspective of Marxist social theory, to be itself a folk model manifesting itself as science. But like other folk models, this one – of society as comprising "experts" who properly understand and properly control knowledge and society and "folk" – has strong ideological force. Like other folk models, it disguises and mystifies real structures of class and power. Models are created for the "folk" as well as by them. As instruments of ideological hegemony, such models – whether we call them "folk" or "cultural" – may legitimate and perpetuate the status quo: whether they be models of Hinduism that reinforce and perpetuate the position of Brahmin priests or the models of illness among the Ecuadorian poor that allow the masses to contend with grim struggles of life and death while the country's oligarchs go to the Mayo Clinic.

Folk models in the form of ideologies of patriotism and empire have led hundreds of thousands of Europeans to "glorious" deaths in service of their rulers. Not all folk models so clearly serve ideological ends. (Such an argument would be hard to make of models of electricity or anger.) But cognitive anthropology's emergent concern with conceptual paradigms of this kind, whether it labels them as *folk* or *cultural* models, needs surely to be tempered by sophistication about the sociology of knowledge and the uses of ideology.

The concept of culture as shared and societal embodies, as social theory, deeply conservative premises (see, e.g., Abercrombie 1980). We need to keep in view (at least in our peripheral vision) the production, control, distribution, and ideological force of cultural knowledge. Anthropologists, like other social scientists, are perforce specialists as well as generalists. Specialized work in cognitive anthropology may leave no room for long excursions into the class structure of society and the production and control of the knowledge we seek to map.[4] But we need to be much more cautious and wise than were the pioneers of "the new ethnography" about embedding the cognitive systems we purport to explore and map within social systems and about our place in the multidisciplinary advances of social/behavioral science.

An emergent social/behavioral theory must bridge between the institutional and abstract and the essentialities of humanness. Social systems are constructed out of, as well as constrained by, what human beings are; and how human beings cognize their worlds constrains and shapes how humans-in-societies reproduce them. Exploration of conceptual models, of metaphors, of the construction and co-construction of meaning, of how what we see is constituted by what we know, can contribute importantly to an emerging composite understanding of humans-in-societies.

We need a specialized concern with cognition. There is challenge enough in trying to keep up with rapidly moving frontiers in AI, psycholinguistics, linguistics, and other subfields of cognitive science. Perhaps it is too much to expect cognitive anthropologists and other explorers of conceptual models of everyday reality to be social theorists as well. At the same time, however, I believe we must also step back regularly to assess how what we are exploring articulates with a wider concern with humans-in-societies. Otherwise, we run the danger that beset "the new ethnography" – of radically misconstruing the place and power of the provisional models. Cognitive anthropology, I think, must be pursued in the long run as part of a multidisciplinary, multisided, and mutually informed exploration.

Notes

1. I was asked by Dorothy Holland and Naomi Quinn to assess the Conference on Folk Models, and developments in cognitive anthropology against the background of my earlier critiques of the field. I have interpreted the invitation as mandate for the self-indulgence reflected in these pages, where I refer to my earlier critiques as if they were divinely inspired. I ask the reader's indulgence for this egocentric perspective on a field in which I have for 20 years been a marginal participant.
2. Clement suggests that cognitive anthropologists are using *folk* "in a broad sense to refer to any group of people participating in a cultural tradition," and that – with no pejorative intent – they "use 'folk' in this broad sense to legitimate the study of indigenous classification systems in their own terms" (1982:211).
3. See Keesing 1985 and Lutz 1985 for discussions of the problem of "false exoticism."
4. For a recent attempt of mine to articulate Marxist perspectives on ideology with recent work on prototype categorization and conventional metaphor, in examining concepts of race and ethnicity, see Keesing (in press).

References

Abercrombie, N.
   1980. Class, Structure and Knowledge: Problems in the Sociology of Knowledge. Oxford: Basil Blackwell.
Agar, M. and J. Hobbs
   1985. How to grow schemas out of interviews. *In* Directions in Cognitive Anthropology, J. Dougherty, ed. Urbana: University of Illinois Press. Pp. 413–431.
Berlin, B. and P. Kay
   1969. Basic Color Terms: Their Universality and Evolution. Berkeley: University of California Press.

Brown, M.
   1985. Individual experience, dreams and the identification of magical stones in an Amazonian society. *In* Directions in Cognitive Anthropology, J. Dougherty, ed. Urbana: University of Illinois Press. Pp. 373–387.
Clement, D. H.
   1982. Samoan folk knowledge of mental disorders. *In* Cultural Conceptions of Mental Health and Therapy, A. J. Marsella and G. M. White, eds. Dordrecht, Holland: D. Reidel Publishing Company. Pp. 193–213.
Colby, B. N. and R. Knaus
   1974. Men, grammars, and machines: A new direction for the study of man. *In* On Language, Culture, and Religion: In Honor of Eugene A. Nida, M. Black and W. A. Smalley, eds. The Hague: Mouton Publishers. Pp. 187–197.
Coleman, L. and P. Kay
   1981. Prototype semantics: The English word 'lie.' Language 57(1):26–44.
Frake, C. O.
   1977. Plying frames can be dangerous: Some reflections on methodology in cultural anthropology. Quarterly Newsletter of the Institute for Comparative Human Development 1(3):1–7.
Gardner, P. M.
   1976. Birds, words, and a requiem for the omniscient informant. American Ethnologist 3(3):446–468.
Geertz, C.
   1966. Person, time and conduct in Bali: An essay in cultural analysis. Yale Southeast Asia Program, Cultural Report Series. (Reprinted in C. Geertz, The Interpretation of Cultures. New York: Basic Books, 1973. Pp. 360–411.)
   1972. Deep play: Notes on the Balinese cockfight. Daedalus 101:1–37. (Reprinted in C. Geertz, The Interpretation of Cultures. New York: Basic Books, 1973. Pp. 412–453.)
   1973. Thick description: Toward an interpretive theory of culture. *In* C. Geertz, The Interpretation of Cultures. New York: Basic Books. Pp. 3–30.
   1974. 'From the natives' point of view': On the nature of anthropological understanding. Bulletin of the American Academy of Arts and Sciences 28, No. 1. (Reprinted in Meaning in Anthropology, K. H. Basso and H. A. Selby, eds. Albuquerque: University of New Mexico Press, 1976. Pp. 221–238.)
   1975. Common sense as a cultural system. Antioch Review 33(1):5–26. (Reprinted in C. Geertz, Local Knowledge: Further Essays in Interpretive Anthropology. New York: Basic Books, 1983. Pp. 73–93.)
Gentner, D. and A. L. Stevens, eds.
   1982. Mental Models. Hillsdale, N.J.: Lawrence Erlbaum Associates.
Goodenough, W. H.
   1961. Comment on cultural evolution. Daedalus 90:521–528.
Gregory. R. L.
   1969. On how so little information controls so much behavior. *In* Towards a Theoretical Biology, Vol. 2, C. H. Waddington, ed. Chicago: Aldine Publishing Company. Pp. 236–246.
Haviland, J.
   1977. Gossip, Reputation and Knowledge in Zinacantan. Chicago: University of Chicago Press.
Johnson-Laird, P. N.
   1981. The form and function of mental models. *In* Proceedings of the Third Annual Conference of the Cognitive Science Society. Berkeley: University of California. Pp. 103–105.

Keesing, R. M.
  1970. Toward a model of role analysis. *In* A Handbook of Method in Cultural
    Anthropology, R. Cohen and R. Narroll, eds. Garden City, N.Y.: Natural
    History Press. Pp. 423–453.
  1972a. Paradigms lost: The new ethnography and the new linguistics.
    Southwestern Journal of Anthropology 28(4):299–332.
  1972b. Simple models of complexity: The lure of kinship. *In* Kinship Studies
    in the Morgan Centennial Year, P. Reining, ed. Washington, D. C.: Anthro-
    pological Society of Washington. Pp. 17–31.
  1972c. Toward a New Cognitive Anthropology. Address presented to Institute
    for Communications Research, May 10, University of Illinois, Urbana.
  1974. Theories of culture. Annual Review of Anthropology 3:73–97.
  1975. Explorations in role analysis. *In* Linguistics and Anthropology: In Honor
    of C. F. Voegelin, M. D. Kinkade, K. L. Hale, and O. Werner, eds. Lisse,
    Netherlands: Peter de Ridder Press. Pp. 385–403.
  1981. Cultural Anthropology: A Contemporary Perspective. 2nd ed. New York:
    Holt, Rinehart and Winston.
  1982. 'Cultural rules': Methodological doubts and epistemological paradoxes.
    Canberra Anthropology 5(1):37–46.
  1985. Conventional metaphors and anthropological metaphysics: The prob-
    lematic of cultural translation. Journal of Anthropological Research
    41(2):201–217.
  (in press). Racial and ethnic categories in colonial and postcolonial States:
    Sociological and linguistic perspectives on ideology. *In* Studies on the Ade-
    quacy of Theories, Paradigms and Assumptions in the Social and Human
    Sciences, M. O'Callaghan, ed. Paris: U.N.E.S.C.O.
Kempton, W.
  1981. The Folk Classification of Ceramics: A Study of Cognitive Prototypes.
    New York: Academic Press.
Klein, S.
  1983. Analogy and mysticism and the structure of culture. Current Anthropology
    24(2):151–180.
Klein, S., D. A. Ross, M. S. Manasse, J. Danos, M. S. Bickford, and K. L. Jenson.
  1981. Surrealistic imagery and the calculation of behavior. *In* Proceedings of
    the Third Annual Meeting of the Cognitive Science Society. Berkeley: Univer-
    sity of California. Pp. 307–309.
Kronenfeld, D. B., J. D. Armstrong, and S. Wilmoth
  1985. Exploring the internal structure of linguistic categories: An extensionist
    semantic view. *In* Directions in Cognitive Anthropology, J. Dougherty, ed.
    Urbana: University of Illinois Press. Pp. 91–110.
Kuhn, T.
  1979. Metaphor in science. *In* Metaphor and Thought, A. Ortony, ed. Cam-
    bridge, England: Cambridge University Press. Pp. 409–419.
Lakoff, G.
  1984. Classifiers as a reflection of mind: A cognitive model approach to pro-
    totype theory. Berkeley Cognitive Science Report No. 19. Berkeley: Univer-
    sity of California Institute of Human Learning.
Lakoff, G. and M. Johnson
  1980. Metaphors We Live By. Chicago: University of Chicago Press.
Lutz, C.
  1985. Depression and the translation of emotional worlds. *In* Culture and Depres-
    sion: Studies in the Anthropology and Cross-cultural Psychiatry of Affect
    and Disorder, A. Kleinman and B. Good, eds. Berkeley: University of Califor-
    nia Press. Pp. 63–100.

McCloskey, M., A. Caramazza, and B. Green
    1980. Curvilinear motion in the absence of external forces: Naive beliefs about the motion of objects. Science 210:1139–1141.
Miller, G. A., E. Galanter, and K. Pribram.
    1960. Plans and the Structure of Behavior. New York: Holt, Rinehart and Winston.
Natanson, M.
    1967. Alienation and social role. In Phenomenology in America, J. M. Edie, ed. Chicago: Quadrangle Books. Pp. 255–268.
    1970. The Journeying Self: A Study in Philosophy and Social Role. Reading, Mass.: Addison-Wesley.
Norman, D. and D. E. Rumelhart
    1975. Memory and knowledge. In Explorations in Cognition, D. Norman and D. E. Rumelhart, eds. San Francisco: W. H. Freeman and Company. Pp. 3–32.
Ortony, A., ed.
    1979. Metaphor and Thought. Cambridge, England: Cambridge University Press.
Paul, R. A.
    1976. The Sherpa temple as a model of the psyche. American Ethnologist 3(1):131–146.
Quinn, N.
    1982. "Commitment" in American marriage: A cultural analysis. American Ethnologist 9(4):775–798.
Randall, R. A.
    1976. How tall is a taxonomic tree? Some evidence for dwarfism. American Ethnologist 3(3):543–553.
Rosaldo, M. Z.
    1980. Knowledge and Passion: Ilongot Notions of Self and Social Life. Cambridge, England: Cambridge University Press.
Rosch, E.
    1973. On the internal structure of perceptual and semantic categories. In Cognitive Development and the Acquisition of Language, T. M. Moore, ed. New York: Academic Press. Pp. 111–144.
    1975. Universals and cultural specifics in human categorization. In Cross-Cultural Perspectives on Learning, R. Breslin, S. Boucher, and W. Lonner, eds. New York: Halsted Press. Pp. 177–206.
    1977. Human categorization. In Studies in Cross-Cultural Psychology, Vol. 1, N. Warren, ed. London: Academic Press. Pp. 1–49.
    1978. Principles of categorization. In Cognition and Categorization, E. Rosch and B. Lloyd, eds. Hillsdale, N.J.: Lawrence Erlbaum Associates. Pp. 27–48.
Sacks, S., ed.
    1979. On Metaphors. Chicago: University of Chicago Press.
Salmond, A.
    1982. Theoretical landscapes: On cross-cultural conceptions of knowledge. In Semantic Anthropology, D. Parkin, ed. New York, London: Academic Press. Pp. 65–87.
Sankoff, G.
    1971. Quantitative analysis of sharing and variability in a cognitive model. Ethnology 10:389–408.
Schank, R.
    1980. Language and memory. Cognitive Science 4:243–284.
Schank, R. and R. Abelson
    1977. Scripts, Plans, Goals and Understanding: An Inquiry into Human Knowledge Structures. Hillsdale, N.J.: Lawrence Erlbaum Associates.

Schutz, A.
   1962. Collected Papers, Vol. 1, The Problem of Social Reality, M. Natanson,
      ed. The Hague: Martinus Nijhoff.
   1967. The Phenomenology of the Social World. G. Walsh and F. Lehnert, trans.
      Evanston, Ill.: Northwestern University Press.
Varenne, H.
   1984. Collective representation in American anthropological conversations about
      culture: Individual and culture. Current Anthropology 25(3):281–299.
Wexler, K. N. and A. K. Romney
   1972. Individual variations in cognitive structures. *In* Multidimensional Scal-
      ing: Theory and Applications in the Behavioral Sciences, Vol. 2, Applica-
      tions, A. K. Romney, R.N. Shepard, and S. B. Nerlove, eds. New York:
      Seminar Press. Pp. 73–92.
White, G.
   1980. Conceptual universals in interpersonal language. American Anthropologist
      83(4):759–781.

Index

Topics marked with an asterick (*) are the focus of one or more whole chapters; see table of contents.